AP® SPANISH LANGUAGE & CULTURE

PREP

11th Edition

The Staff of The Princeton Review

PrincetonReview.com

Penguin
Random
House

The Princeton Review
110 East 42nd St, 7th Floor
New York, NY 10017

ISBN: 978-0-593-51684-3
ISSN: 2690-6716

AP is a trademark registered and owned by the College Board, which is not affiliated with, and does not endorse, this product.

The Princeton Review is not affiliated with Princeton University.

The material in this book is up-to-date at the time of publication. However, changes may have been instituted by the testing body in the test after this book was published.

If there are any important late-breaking developments, changes, or corrections to the materials in this book, we will post that information online in the Student Tools. Register your book and check your Student Tools to see whether there are any updates posted there.

Special thanks to VeinteMundos.com for permission to use their articles in this book. Thanks also to Drake Turrentino for use of the name *Special Olympics*.

Excerpt(s) from COMO AGUA PARA CHOCOLATE by Laura Esquivel, copyright © 1989 by Laura Esquivel. Used by permission of Doubleday, an imprint of the Knopf Doubleday Publishing Group, a division of Penguin Random House LLC. All rights reserved.

Excerpt from *Ecuador Guia de Carreteras Turismo y Ecoturismo 2006* by Dr. Xavier Silva and Falvia Albán. Published December 2005 by Imprenta Mariscal. All rights reserved.

Excerpt from *Juliana Rueda: The Voice Still Distinguishes Us As Humans* published July 2019 in TELOS Magazine. All rights reserved.

Every effort has been made to trace and acknowledge copyright material. The author and publisher would welcome any information from the people who believe they own copyrights to material in this book.

Editor: Patricia Murphy
Production Editors: Ali Landreau and Sarah Litt
Production Artist: Lisa Barham
Content Contributor: Alexis Rivera Valentin

Printed in the United States of America.

10 9 8 7 6 5 4 3 2 1

11th Edition

The Princeton Review Publishing Team

Rob Franek, Editor-in-Chief
David Soto, Senior Director, Data Operations
Stephen Koch, Senior Manager, Data Operations
Deborah Weber, Director of Production
Jason Ullmeyer, Production Design Manager
Jennifer Chapman, Senior Production Artist
Selena Coppock, Director of Editorial
Orion McBean, Senior Editor
Aaron Riccio, Senior Editor
Meave Shelton, Senior Editor
Chris Chimera, Editor
Patricia Murphy, Editor
Laura Rose, Editor
Isabelle Appleton, Editorial Assistant

Penguin Random House Publishing Team

Tom Russell, VP, Publisher
Alison Stoltzfus, Senior Director, Publishing
Brett Wright, Senior Editor
Emily Hoffman, Assistant Managing Editor
Ellen Reed, Production Manager
Suzanne Lee, Designer
Eugenia Lo, Publishing Assistant

For customer service, please contact **editorialsupport@review.com**, and be sure to include:

- full title of the book
- ISBN
- page number

Acknowledgments

The Princeton Review would like to thank Lisa Barham, Ali Landreau, Sarah Litt, and Alexis Rivera Valentin for their invaluable contributions to the 11th edition of this book.

Audio Track List

To access your audio tracks, log on to your online Student Tools to stream and/or download them! Check out the instructions on pages vi–vii.

Contents

(Free) Content
at **PrincetonReview.com/prep**

As easy as **1·2·3**

1 Go to PrincetonReview.com/prep
or scan the **QR code**
and enter the following
ISBN for your book:
9780593516843

2 Answer a few simple questions
to set up an exclusive
Princeton Review account.
*(If you already have one,
you can just log in.)*

3 Enjoy access to
your **FREE** content!

Once you've registered, you can...

- Access your third AP Spanish Language & Culture practice test (there are 2 right here in your book and 1 online), plus an answer key and complete answers and explanations

- Stream and/or download the audio tracks for your listening and speaking practice

- Find additional grammar drills

- Take a full-length practice SAT and/or ACT

- Get our take on any recent or pending updates to the Spanish Language & Culture Exam

- Use our searchable rankings of *The Best 389 Colleges* to find out more information about your dream school

- Access comprehensive study guides and a variety of printable resources

- Check to see whether there have been any corrections or updates to this edition

LET'S GO MOBILE! Access all of these free, additional resources by downloading the new Princeton Review app at www.princetonreview.com/mobile/apps/highschool or scan the QR Code to the right.

Need to report a potential **content** issue?

Contact **EditorialSupport@review.com** and include:
- full title of the book
- ISBN
- page number

Need to report a **technical** issue?

Contact **TPRStudentTech@review.com** and provide:
- your full name
- email address used to register the book
- full book title and ISBN
- Operating system (Mac/PC) and browser (Chrome, Firefox, Safari, etc.)

Look For These Icons Throughout The Book

 ONLINE ARTICLES

 ONLINE AUDIO

 PROVEN TECHNIQUES

 APPLIED STRATEGIES

 MORE GREAT BOOKS

 STUDY BREAK

Part I
Using This
Book to Improve
Your AP Score

- Preview: Your Knowledge, Your Expectations
- Your Guide to Using This Book
- How to Begin

PREVIEW: YOUR KNOWLEDGE, YOUR EXPECTATIONS

Welcome to your *AP Spanish Language & Culture Prep*. Your route to a high score on the AP Spanish Language and Culture Exam depends a lot on how you plan to use this book. Respond to the following questions.

1. Rate your level of confidence about your knowledge of the content tested by the AP Spanish Language and Culture Exam:

    A. Very confident—I know it all.
    B. I'm pretty confident, but there are topics for which I could use help.
    C. Not confident—I need quite a bit of support.
    D. I'm not sure.

2. Circle your goal score for the Exam:

    5   4   3   2   1   I'm not sure yet

3. What do you expect to learn from this book? Circle all that apply to you.

    A. A general overview of the test and what to expect
    B. Strategies for how to approach the test
    C. The content tested by this exam
    D. I'm not sure yet

YOUR GUIDE TO USING THIS BOOK

AP Spanish Language & Culture Prep is organized to provide as much—or as little—support as you need, so you can use this book in whatever way will be most helpful to improving your score on the AP Spanish Language and Culture Exam.

Online Audio

When you register your book online, you can download and/or stream all audio tracks that accompany the listening and speaking sections.

-   The remainder of **Part I** will provide guidance on how to use this book and help you determine your strengths and weaknesses.

-   **Part II** of this book contains Practice Test 1, the Diagnostic Answer Key, answers and explanations for each question, and a scoring guide. (Bubble sheets can be found in the very back of the book for easy tear-out.) We strongly recommend that you take this test before going any further in order to realistically determine:
    o   your starting point right now
    o   which question types you're ready for and which you might need to practice
    o   which content topics you are familiar with and which you will want to carefully review

    Once you have nailed down your strengths and weaknesses with regard to this exam, you can focus your test preparation, build a study plan, and be efficient with your time. Our Diagnostic Answer Key will assist you with this process.

- **Part III** of this book will
    - provide information about the structure, scoring, and content of the AP Spanish Language and Culture Exam
    - help you to make a study plan
    - point you toward additional resources

- **Part IV** of this book will explore various strategies, such as
    - how to tackle multiple-choice questions
    - how to manage your time to maximize the number of points available to you
    - how to write effective essays and responses
    - how to synthesize and interpret integrative listening and reading tasks
    - how to answer effectively in the speaking portions of the exam

- **Part V** of this book is a review of the grammar topics you should understand to do well on the test.

- **Part VI** of this book contains Practice Test 2, its answers and explanations, and a scoring guide. If you skipped Practice Test 1, we recommend that you do both (with at least a day or two between them) so that you can compare your progress between the two. Additionally, this will help to identify any external issues: if you answer a certain type of question wrong both times, you probably need to review it. If you answered it incorrectly only once, you may have run out of time or been distracted by something. In either case, comparing the two exams will allow you to focus on the factors that caused the discrepancy in scores and to be as prepared as possible on the day of the test.

- **Online Resources** contain one additional practice test. Follow the study guide based on the amount of time you have to study for the exam. Use the online drills for additional practice with verb and grammar forms.

You may choose to use some parts of this book over others, or you may work through the entire book. This will depend on your needs and how much time you have. Let's now look at how to make this distinction.

HOW TO BEGIN

1. **Take a Test**

    Before you can decide how to use this book, you need to take a practice test. Doing so will give you insight into your strengths and weaknesses, and the test will also help you make an effective study plan. If you're feeling test-phobic, remind yourself that a practice test is a tool for diagnosing yourself—it's not how well you do that matters, but how you use the information gleaned from your performance to guide your preparation.

    So, before you read further, take Practice Test 1, which is found in Part II of this book. Be sure to do so in one sitting, following the instructions that appear before the test.

2. **Check Your Answers and Reflect on the Test**
   Using the Diagnostic Answer Key on page 40, follow our three-step process to determine how you did on each section of the test. Tally your correct answers to calculate your performance and reflect on the sections where you may have struggled.

3. **Read Part III of this Book and Complete the Self-Evaluation**
   Part III will provide information on how the test is structured and scored.

   At the end of Part III, you will answer questions based on your performance on Practice Test 1 and how much time you have available to prepare for the exam. You will then be able to make a study plan appropriate to your needs and time commitment that will allow you to use this book most effectively.

4. **Engage with Parts IV and V**
   Notice the word *engage*. You'll get more out of this book if you use it intentionally than if you read it passively and hope for an improved score through osmosis.

   Strategy chapters will help you think about your approach to the question types on this exam. Part IV will open with a reminder to think about how you approach questions now and then close with a reflection section asking you to think about how/whether you will change your approach in the future.

   The Part V grammar review is designed to provide an overview of the verbs and grammar forms you should be proficient in by test day. You will have the opportunity to assess your knowledge of this content through several drills and a reflection section.

5. **Take More Practice Tests and Assess Your Performance**
   Once you feel you have developed the strategies you need and gained the knowledge you lacked, take Practice Test 2. You should do so in one sitting, following the instructions at the beginning of the test.

   When you are done, check your answers to the multiple-choice sections. See whether a teacher will read your responses to the free-response questions and provide feedback.

   Once you have taken the test, reflect on what areas you still need to work on, and revisit the chapters in this book that address them. Through this type of reflection and engagement, you will continue to improve. Then, take Practice Test 3 online.

6. **Keep Working**
   As we will discuss in Part III, there are other resources available to you, including a wealth of information on the AP Students website. You can continue to explore areas in which you can stand to improve and engage in those areas right up to the day of the test.

Part II
Practice Test 1

Practice Test 1

Following are the audio track numbers for **Practice Test 1.** You can find them in your online Student Tools to stream or download.

- Track 1: Selección 1 (Fuente 2)

- Track 2: Selección 2 (Fuente 2)

- Track 3: Selección 3

- Track 4: Selección 4

- Track 5: Selección 5

- Track 6: Question 2: Argumentative Essay (Fuente 3)

- Track 7: Question 3: Conversation

It's a good idea to have a device handy with which to record and time yourself for the speaking sections.

Good luck!

AP® Spanish Language and Culture

SECTION I: Multiple-Choice Questions

DO NOT OPEN THIS BOOKLET UNTIL YOU ARE TOLD TO DO SO.

Instructions

Section I of this examination contains 65 multiple-choice questions. Fill in only the ovals for numbers 1 through 65 on your answer sheet.

Indicate all of your answers to the multiple-choice questions on the answer sheet. No credit will be given for anything written in this exam booklet, but you may use the booklet for notes or scratch work. After you have decided which of the suggested answers is best, completely fill in the corresponding oval on the answer sheet. Give only one answer to each question. If you change an answer, be sure that the previous mark is erased completely. Here is a sample question and answer.

At a Glance

Total Time
1 hour and 35 minutes
Number of Questions
65
Percent of Total Grade
50%
Writing Instrument
Pencil required

Sample Question

Sample Answer

Chicago is a
(A) state
(B) city
(C) country
(D) continent

Use your time effectively, working as quickly as you can without losing accuracy. Do not spend too much time on any one question. Go on to other questions and come back to the ones you have not answered if you have time. It is not expected that everyone will know the answers to all the multiple-choice questions.

About Guessing

Many candidates wonder whether or not to guess the answers to questions about which they are not certain. Multiple-choice scores are based on the number of questions answered correctly. Points are not deducted for incorrect answers, and no points are awarded for unanswered questions. Because points are not deducted for incorrect answers, you are encouraged to answer all multiple-choice questions. On any questions you do not know the answer to, you should eliminate as many choices as you can, and then select the best answer among the remaining choices.

GO ON TO THE NEXT PAGE.

Part A

Interpretive Communication: Print Texts

You will read several selections. Each selection is accompanied by a number of questions. For each question, choose the response that is best according to the selection and mark your answer on your answer sheet.	Vas a leer varios textos. Cada texto va acompañado de varias preguntas. Para cada pregunta, elige la mejor respuesta según el texto e indícala en la hoja de respuestas.

Selección número 1

Introducción

La siguiente entrevista apareció en una revista latinoamericana en junio 2014.

Este profesor de Educación Física, de 35 años y oriundo de Santiago de Chile, hizo realidad un sueño que muchos bailarines caribeños anhelan: ser bicampeón mundial de rumba. ¡Y en Europa! Hace ya casi diez años, Cristian Vera dejó su país y se trasladó a España para ejercer su profesión y también su gran pasión: la danza. En dicho continente ha viajado por múltiples países enseñando este baile tropical y participando también en diferentes competencias. Anécdotas y experiencias tiene muchas. Aquí podemos conocer algunas.

¿Cómo llega un chileno a convertirse en bicampeón mundial de rumba?

En Barcelona se realiza cada año el festival cubano más importante de Europa; y en ese evento se lleva a cabo una competencia de carácter mundial denominada "Buscando al rumbero". Es un concurso individual donde cada competidor, proveniente de distintos lugares del mundo, muestra su talento en el baile. En mi primera participación, en 2011, salí segundo y luego logré dos años seguidos el primer lugar. Después de eso, me convertí en el primer profesor no cubano en enseñar folclore en ese festival.

¿Cómo llegaste a la rumba? ¿Qué fue lo que te motivó a practicar esta disciplina?

Lo que me inspiró fue una película: "Dance With Me"; ahí vi a los protagonistas bailando salsa en Cuba. La verdad es que siempre tuve el baile en la sangre porque toda mi familia se dedica a esto. Cada día, cuando me levanto tengo deseos de bailar; y sigo teniendo las mismas ganas y energía que al inicio. Por eso, además, me he ido perfeccionando en la danza. Cada día voy aprendiendo algo nuevo de distintos tipos de bailes.

¿Por qué has desarrollado tu carrera en Europa?

En el año 2007 me fui becado a la Universidad ITK de Leipzig para realizar un postgrado en Ciencias Aplicadas al fútbol. Luego de eso, estuve tres meses en España realizando una pasantía en el club Villareal, que era dirigido en ese momento por Manuel Pellegrini. Ahí el preparador físico del equipo me habló de un máster que él había hecho en Barcelona. Por eso luego de volver a Chile y trabajar un tiempo, junté dinero y emprendí rumbo nuevamente a la Madre Patria para inscribirme en ese curso de especialización.

¿Crees tú que este tipo de baile es hoy más popular en Europa que en Latinoamérica?

En el Viejo Continente tienen una ventaja: los países están cerca y los vuelos no son costosos. De esta forma, los bailarines y aficionados a danzas como la salsa pueden viajar a diferentes competencias y festivales. Los concursos tienen gran éxito porque a la gente no solo le apasiona el baile sino que además tienen la posibilidad de acudir en masa. Hay mucha demanda.

Los bailes latinos son alegres y sensuales. ¿Es eso lo que le gusta al europeo de estos ritmos?

Los europeos, en general, son disciplinados y en el caso de la danza se enfocan bastante en tratar de conocer a fondo la cultura del baile. Muchos, incluso, aprenden español para entender las canciones; no solo quieren bailar y hacer una mímica. Yo creo que todos los europeos que aprenden a bailar danzas cubanas quieren ir a conocer Cuba.

¿Y qué impresión se lleva la gente cuando ve a un bailarín chileno enseñando salsa cubana?

Yo nunca he estado en Cuba. Pero mucha gente me pregunta cómo es posible que baile con ritmo y estilo tan marcadamente tropical. Me confunden con cubano, y no precisamente por mi acento, sino por mi forma de bailar. Te puede jugar en contra, por supuesto, porque hay un tema de tradición y referencia con los cubanos, pero creo que aquel que se la juega por esto y lo siente en la piel, va a tener éxito.

GO ON TO THE NEXT PAGE.

¿Te ves o te sientes como un embajador en Europa de la salsa?

El cubano es muy celoso de su cultura. Cuando saben que yo bailo salsa, pueden tener una especie de prejuicio al principio. Pero una vez que me ven en la pista de baile, todo cambia. Yo espero que me juzguen siempre por lo que hago. Y en ese sentido, he logrado ganar el respeto de los grandes maestros cubanos de la salsa. Me parece que más que un embajador propiamente tal, me gusta verme como una persona que ha podido dar el ejemplo de que sí se puede bailar salsa o rumba sin ser cubano. Me gusta poder representar a toda esa gente.

1. ¿Quién es Christian Vera?

    (A) Un maestro cubano de la salsa

    (B) Un profesor chileno de rumba y salsa que vive en España

    (C) Un profesor español de rumba y salsa que vive en Cuba

    (D) Un maestro chileno de la salsa

2. ¿Por qué les gustan a los europeos los ritmos latinos?

    (A) Porque son alegres y sensuales

    (B) Porque es más fácil conquistar las mujeres con el baile

    (C) Porque pueden conocer la cultura de Cuba

    (D) Porque ofrecen contrasto a la disciplina que existe en Europa

3. ¿Cómo llegó Vera a la rumba?

    (A) Era una parte fundamental de su cultura.

    (B) Era una parte integral de su familia, y entonces su padre le enseñó.

    (C) Pasó un rato en Cuba para aprender la rumba.

    (D) Vio una película de baile latino y fue inspirado por el.

4. ¿Por qué ha desarrollado su carrera en España?

    (A) Había estudiado en Europa con una beca cuando aprendió de una maestría en Barcelona.

    (B) Pasó parte de su infancia en Europa y quería regresar.

    (C) Aprendió el baile en Latinoamérica primero y decidió a moverse a España.

    (D) Es el primer enseñador no cubano en enseñar el folclore cubano.

5. ¿Cómo aceptan los otros bailarines al chileno cuando baila la salsa?

    (A) Los europeos lo aceptan como cubano.

    (B) Al principio hay un poco de prejuicio, pero todo cambia cuando Vera está bailando.

    (C) Nunca puede bailar tan bien como los cubanos.

    (D) Siempre le aceptan como un cubano sin preguntas.

6. ¿Qué responde Vera al entrevistador a la última pregunta?

    (A) Responde que sí, es el embajador oficial a Cuba.

    (B) Responde que no, es demasiado presión para él.

    (C) Responde que sí, desea ser el embajador de baile para todos.

    (D) Responde que no, los cubanos no lo aceptan cuando está en la pista de baile.

GO ON TO THE NEXT PAGE.

Selección número 2

Introducción

El siguiente artículo apareció en un libro del arte contemporáneo en 2008.

Pablo Picasso, el revolucionario

Hay pintores que transforman el sol en una mancha amarilla, pero hay otros que, gracias a su arte y a su inteligencia, transforman una mancha amarilla en sol. —Pablo Picasso

Pocos artistas han generado tanta controversia, discusión y admiración como Pablo Picasso (1881–1973). Una obra monumental, en cantidad y calidad; una vida exuberante y prolongada; escándalos de alcoba y magníficos desplantes hacen de Picasso un verdadero personaje. Pero sin duda la mayor justicia está en descubrirlo y reconocerlo como el mayor artista del siglo XX.

Durante más de ochenta años de vida artística y más de veinte mil trabajos, el pintor andaluz sorprendió y descolocó una y otra vez al mundo del arte con una obra no sólo anticonvencional, potente y original, sino absolutamente revolucionaria.

Así como la historia de la cultura reconoce al Renacimiento y luego al Impresionismo como los grandes hitos de la pintura occidental, el siglo XX se rinde ante el cubismo; y al decir cubismo surge, indeleble, el nombre de Pablo Picasso.

Polifacético y gruñón, desconsiderado y pasional, extrovertido y oculto a la vez, Picasso es todo eso y mucho más. Es, fundamentalmente, un ser desnudo y vulnerable vestido de invencible minotauro, en cuya piel sensible el mundo deja su rastro de llagas y cicatrices y él las devuelve hechas pinturas.

Varias esposas, unos cuantos hijos, una multitud de libros y películas que lo ensalzan o condenan, son apenas un síntoma de la personalidad de este hombre nacido para destacarse.

En su siglo, que asoma como la aurora del progreso y la profecía cumplida, el arte intuye la fragmentación y el desvelo, la desarmonía y el caos. La guerra, la muerte, el genocidio, las promesas quebrantadas de una ciencia arrebatadoramente seductora y atrozmente desequilibrante quedan plasmadas en una obra revulsiva y desestructurante que viene a cuestionar los propios cánones de la belleza y erige al feísmo como categoría artística.

Picasso seguramente no habría sido quien fue, de no ser por la magnifica cofradía de contemporáneos en la que desfilaron de Rousseau a Matisse, de Braque a Juan Gris, de Gertrude Stein a Alfred Jarry, de Bretón a Cocteau, de Paul Eluard a…Pero sin duda, el siglo tampoco habría sido lo que fue, sin la presencia grandilocuente, transgresora y especular de un pintor, escultor, grabador, dibujante y hasta poeta que hacía de las manchas amarillas soles nuevos con la intuición de un niño y la impronta de un hombre que aun desguarnecido resiste desde la creativa trinchera de la imaginación.

GO ON TO THE NEXT PAGE.

7. ¿Cuál es el propósito del artículo?

    (A) Sostiene que Picasso fue el mejor pintor del siglo XX.

    (B) Presenta información sobre la personalidad y la vida personal de Picasso.

    (C) Describe unas obras de arte que hizo Picasso.

    (D) Da algo de información sobre la vida y la producción artística de Picasso.

8. El artículo incluye la cita al principio para

    (A) demostrar el genio de Pablo Picasso

    (B) ilustrar que el sol tiene una mancha que no se puede ver

    (C) explicar que muchas artistas sólo pueden pintar de una manera abstracta

    (D) dibujar como muchos artistas no tienen talento

9. Podemos inferir que

    (A) Picasso estaba gruñón y desconsiderado todos los días

    (B) el Renacimiento y el Impresionismo fueron épocas menos importantes que la de Picasso

    (C) había otros artistas importantes durante el siglo XX

    (D) Picasso hizo más obras de arte que sus contemporáneos

10. ¿Por qué se menciona sus esposas e hijos?

    (A) Muestra unos atributos de la personalidad de Picasso.

    (B) Nombra algo de inspiración detrás del arte de Picasso.

    (C) Revela algo de la vida personal de Picasso.

    (D) Demuestra que Picasso era un esposo malo.

11. Se mencionan a Rousseau, Matisse, Braque, Juan Gris y otros nombres para

    (A) comparar Picasso con los otros artistas

    (B) nombrar algunos artistas de diferentes épocas

    (C) sugerir que Picasso era el artista mejor que todos en el siglo XX

    (D) enumerar los artistas iluminarias que fueron contemporáneos de Picasso

12. La influencia de Picasso es una de

    (A) confusión

    (B) intuición

    (C) ofensa

    (D) belleza

GO ON TO THE NEXT PAGE.

Selección número 3

Introducción

El siguiente artículo apareció en un periódico hispánico en diciembre 2016.

Cuba es hoy el país de moda. Personalidades como El Papa Francisco, Beyoncé, Rihanna y Pelé han llegado en avalancha hasta esta hermosa isla del Caribe. Sin embargo, fue la visita del presidente norteamericano Barack Obama una de las más trascendentes, quizás porque hacía 88 años un mandatario estadounidense no venía al país caribeño. Pero no es solo la estadía en sí, sino también su significado: Obama en Cuba representó el posible fin de la "Guerra Fría".

Para David Soler, Subdirector de la Oficina de Patrimonio Cultural de Cienfuegos, una ciudad con amplias ofertas de turismo cultural, el país ha aumentado los números de turistas extranjeros paulatinamente, y "con la reanudación de las relaciones diplomáticas y comerciales con EE.UU., se espera que aumente drásticamente la presencia de empresarios y turistas norteamericanos. Somos la nación más cercana que tienen después de México y Canadá", explica.

Como argumenta este investigador de la cultura cubana, todos los estadounidenses que vendrán a Cuba a invertir o a hacer turismo, traen su cultura y sus formas de comerciar, de proyectarse y hasta de comer, y los cubanos poco a poco tratarán de adecuar los servicios y negocios a este nuevo tipo de turista/empresario.

"Fíjate cómo puede verse influenciada la cultura cubana, podría pasar nuevamente lo ocurrido con la llegada del primer crucero norteamericano a La Habana a inicios de mayo de este año; los visitantes fueron recibidos por mulatas voluptuosas vestidas con los símbolos patrios cubanos. Así contribuyeron a asentar los estereotipos sobre nuestro pueblo: que esta es solo una tierra de mulatas bailarinas, de ron y de tabaco, cuando la realidad es mucho más rica que eso", se queja Soler.

Según afirma el subdirector, todos estos cambios conducen a un intercambio cultural muy peligroso, donde el que viene de fuera trata de implantar sus formas y su cultura. "El cubano, interesado en que los norteamericanos inviertan aquí, puede cometer el error de responder solamente a los intereses del norteño y olvidarse de su identidad y cultura", señala.

Aunque todavía no ha llegado la oleada grande, el investigador asegura que se espera pronto. "La gente aquí se está preparando para ello, estudiando más inglés, alistando sus negocios para el turista estadounidense y estudiando las costumbres norteñas, a veces menospreciando las propias", nos confiesa con pesar este amante del patrimonio cultural cubano.

Todos los cambios ocurridos desde el 17 de diciembre de 2014, cuando ambos presidentes anunciaron el restablecimiento de relaciones diplomáticas, apuntan a un futuro inmediato muy relacionado con el turismo y los servicios, obviamente enfocados en el mercado norteamericano. Los cubanos, lógicamente, ven la "reconciliación" como una fuente de ingresos directa.

El cambio puede traer transformaciones más allá de lo político e influir grandemente en los negocios entre ciudadanos de ambas naciones. Jenny Lleonart Cruz, joven emprendedora cubana y dueña de un lujoso hostal privado en Cienfuegos, asegura que "una cosa tan sencilla como tener una cuenta de PayPal o aceptar pagos con tarjetas de crédito es algo que se avecina. Eso beneficiaría mucho el cobrar o pagar bienes y servicios. También posibilitaría el comercio electrónico en Cuba. Hasta cosas tan sencillas como ir a Miami a comprar suministros para mi hostal sería factible".

Pedro Gómez, residente de La Habana, es más cauteloso y señala que los cubanos no pueden dar el brazo a torcer y caer de nuevo en el sistema capitalista. "Es lo que quieren los americanos. Para ahí no podemos volver porque en esa época se sufría mucho por la economía tan desigual que había. Por eso hay que tener mucho cuidado con lo que se avecina, los cambios pueden ser peligrosos también".

Definitivamente los vientos de cambios que soplan en Cuba con el restablecimiento de las relaciones con EE.UU. modificarán la vida de los cubanos, pero también de algunos países de América Latina. Algunos de estos se beneficiarán o perjudicarán, como los polos turísticos de Punta Cana y la Riviera Maya, que ven una gran competencia en una Cuba abierta al mercado norteamericano.

En tanto, los cubanos caminan en su día a día por las calles de este país y sueñan con cambios milagrosos. Tienen la esperanza de que de una forma u otra, este puente político que se tendió entre las dos naciones no se rompa de nuevo, y funja como vía al desarrollo económico de los habitantes de esta hermosa isla, que emerge del centro del Caribe.

GO ON TO THE NEXT PAGE.

13. ¿Cuál es el propósito del artículo?

(A) El puente político entre Cuba y los Estados Unidos todavía está débil.

(B) Los cambios económicos pueden ser difíciles para Cuba en este punto de transición.

(C) El restablecimiento de las relaciones con EE.UU. modificarán la vida de los cubanos.

(D) El fin del embargo y mandatorio significa unos cambios económicos para la isla.

14. ¿Por qué se mencionan a El Papa Francisco, Beyoncé, Rihanna y Pelé en el primer párrafo?

(A) Son embajadores a Cuba para sus países respectivas.

(B) Quieren viajar a Cuba, pero no es posible hasta el fin de la "Guerra Fría".

(C) Fueron unas de las primeras personas que viajaron a Cuba después del fin del mandatorio estadounidense.

(D) Son algunos artistas que han dado conciertos en Cuba.

15. En el segundo párrafo, David Soler espera que

(A) la economía cubana sufra a causa de recursos desiguales

(B) el cambio sea el fin de la "Guerra Fría"

(C) el cambio aumente la presencia del comercio y turismo

(D) la influencia cubana cambie el mundo

16. ¿Por qué se menciona Paypal y tarjetas de crédito en el párrafo 8?

(A) Son elementos de la economía norteño que pueda beneficiar los negocios cubanos.

(B) Son indicadores del comercio electrónico en Cuba.

(C) Son métodos de pagar en los negocios cubanos.

(D) Son peligros para los negocios de Cuba porque tienen intereses norteños.

17. ¿Qué piensa Pedro Gómez del cambio económico en Cuba?

(A) Piensa que el capitalismo va a destruir el país.

(B) Piensa que hay que tener cuidado porque hay una desigualdad de recursos.

(C) Piensa que es invaluable para que los cubanos aprendan inglés.

(D) Piensa que el futuro de la economía cubana es el turismo.

18. Según el último párrafo, ¿qué esperan los cubanos?

(A) Esperan que el cambio en la relación entre los dos paises sea beneficial.

(B) Esperan que los presidentes de los dos países sean amigos.

(C) Esperan que el puente político que se tendió entre las dos naciones se rompa de nuevo.

(D) Esperan que Cuba adapte a la cultura norteña.

GO ON TO THE NEXT PAGE.

Selección número 4

Introducción

El siguiente panfleto apareció en 2005 por el Acción Global de Salud.

Reduciendo las Inequidades de Salud en el Mundo

La crisis contemporánea de la salud mundial es un reflejo de las crecientes inequidades que existen entre los países y dentro de ellos. Los avances científicos y tecnológicos han aportado a un mejoramiento de la salud de algunos. Sin embargo, cada vez más gente vive en la pobreza y 30.000 niños mueren cada día.

El Observatorio Global de Salud 2005–2006 presenta las disparidades en salud y llama la atención hacia los mecanismos mediante los cuales los gobiernos, instituciones internacionales y la sociedad civil pueden aplicar para combatirlas.

Los trabajadores de la salud en particular pueden jugar un papel vital en transformar la retórica sobre derechos universales de la salud y ciudadanía global en una realidad. Aquellos que viven en las zonas más ricas del mundo tienen la particular responsabilidad de presionar hacia un cambio.

La interdependencia generada bajo la globalización incrementa estas responsabilidades éticas.

Los temas cubiertos por el *Observatorio* son diversos, pero todos ellos destacan las inequidades económicas, sociales y políticas que destruyen la salud.

Este documento de campaña enfoca áreas claves donde las presiones colectivas deben ejercerse.

■ Construyendo un mundo justo

La conquista de un mundo justo donde se elimine la pobreza y desarrolle la salud implica cambiar la manera en que la economía global es manejada, e incrementar sustancialmente la transferencia de recursos de los países centrales hacia los países periféricos.

■ Defendiendo y extendiendo el sector público

La reparación y desarrollo de los sistemas de atención en salud pública son cruciales para detener las amenazas de la mercantilización y reducir los crecientes abismos sociales y de salud. Este reporte propone una agenda de diez puntos para la acción.

■ Migración, farmacéuticas y grandes corporaciones

La migración de trabajadores de la salud, las normas globales de propiedad intelectual que incrementan los precios de las medicinas y el impacto de las multinacionales en salud destacan como tres ejemplos de la manera en que la globalización y la subordinación de los derechos de la salud a objetivos comerciales afectan directamente la salud y los sistemas de salud a través del mundo.

■ Tomando acciones frente a los cambios climáticos y al militarismo

El cambio climático global y el militarismo son dos de las más importantes causas presentes y futuras de deterioro de la salud a través del mundo. La incapacidad actual de enfrentar dicha problemática de modo significativo señala la urgente necesidad de mayor movilización de la sociedad civil, de las organizaciones populares y de los trabajadores de la salud para arrancar soluciones más efectivas y justas.

■ Afirmando el liderazgo por la salud global en la Organización Mundial de la Salud

El mundo necesita una agencia de salud multilateral que sea capaz de proteger y promover la salud, reducir las desigualdades y asegurar la vigencia plena de los derechos universales frente a las necesidades básicas y de salud. Para que esto suceda, la OMS requiere más recursos y ser más sensible a las necesidades de los pueblos, alcanzando estándares de administración mejores.

Acción Global de la Salud ("Global Health Action") demanda al *Observatorio* en recomendar una agenda que oriente la lucha de los trabajadores de la salud y los gestores de la campaña.

GO ON TO THE NEXT PAGE.

19. ¿Cuál es el propósito del panfleto?

    (A) El panfleto quiere diseminar información sobre la salud global y unas razones para los cambios mundiales.

    (B) El panfleto quiere demostrar que Acción Global de la Salud quiere mostrar los problemas que no se pueden resolver.

    (C) El panfleto quiere demostrar que Acción Global de la Salud es la organización más equipado a solucionar los conflictos mencionados.

    (D) El panfleto quiere mostrar que el mundo necesita una agencia de salud multilateral que sea capaz de proteger y promover la salud.

20. Según el autor en el primer párrafo, ¿por qué hay una crisis contemporánea de salud mundial?

    (A) Las agencias hoy en día son incapaces de ayudar y promover la salud con sus pocos recursos.

    (B) El militarismo ha destruido la salud pública.

    (C) Los avances científicos y tecnológicos destruyeron el orden del mundo.

    (D) Hay un crecimiento de inequidades que existen entre los países y dentro de ellos.

21. En el primer párrafo, ¿por qué se incluyó "Sin embargo, cada vez más gente vive en la pobreza y 30.000 niños mueren cada día"?

    (A) Es increíble que tantos niños mueren cada día.

    (B) Hay una yuxtaposición entre la gente con buena salud pública y la gente que no la tiene.

    (C) Se necesita más recursos y ser más sensible a las necesidades de los pueblos para salvar a los niños.

    (D) Los niños sufren a causa de la globalización y la subordinación de los derechos de la salud.

22. ¿Como se refiere a un "mundo justo" en el panfleto?

    (A) Un mundo justo puede cambiar la manera en que la economía global es manejada.

    (B) Un mundo justo salva vidas porque puede proteger la gente y promover la salud.

    (C) Es un mundo en que todos pueden vivir en armonía.

    (D) Es un mundo que tiene precios bajos para las medicinas para los ricos.

23. ¿Qué tiene que ver el sector público con la salud pública?

    (A) Puede obtener recursos importantes para los niños.

    (B) Es una de las causas presentes y futuras del deterioro de la salud a través del mundo.

    (C) Mantiene y crece el militarismo.

    (D) Puede detener las amenazas de la mercantilización.

24. ¿Por qué se menciona el militarismo en el panfleto?

    (A) Se menciona para reducir las desigualdades entre países.

    (B) Es una de las más importantes causas de deterioro de la salud global.

    (C) Se menciona los militares como las organizaciones populares de salud.

    (D) El militarismo proporciona empleo a muchos trabajadores.

25. Todas son metas de la Acción Global de la Salud SALVO:

    (A) reparar y desarrollar los sistemas de salud pública

    (B) reducir desigualdades económicas

    (C) asegurar la vigencia plena de los derechos universales

    (D) aumentar los precios de las medicinas

GO ON TO THE NEXT PAGE.

Selección número 5

Introducción

El siguiente prólogo apareció en la autobiografía de Frida Kahlo, una artista mexicana durante el siglo XX.

Mi cuerpo es un marasmo.* Y ya no puedo escapar de él. Como el animal siente su muerte, yo siento la mía instalarse en mi vida, y tan fuerte que me quita toda posibilidad de luchar. No me creen, ¡me han visto luchar tanto! Y ya no me atrevo a creer que podría equivocarme, esos relámpagos se van haciendo raros.

Mi cuerpo va a dejarme, a mí, que he sido siempre su presa. Presa rebelde, pero presa. Sé que nos vamos a aniquilar mutuamente, y así la lucha no habría dejado ningún vencedor. Vana y permanente ilusión de creer que el pensamiento, como sigue intacto, puede separarse de esa otra materia hecha de carne.

Ironía de la suerte: quisiera tener aún la capacidad de debatirme, de tirar puntapiés a ese olor a éter, a mi olor a alcohol, a todas esas medicinas, inertes partículas que se amontonan en sus cajitas—¡ah! Son asépticas hasta en su grafismos ¿y para qué?—, a mis pensamientos en desorden, al orden que se esfuerzan por poner en esta habitación. A los ceniceros. A las estrellas.

Las noches son largas. Cada minuto me asusta, y todo me duele, todo. Y los demás tienen una preocupación que yo quisiera ahorrarles. Pero ¿qué puede una ahorrarle a los demás cuando no ha podido evitarse nada a sí misma? El alba está siempre demasiado lejos. Ya no sé si la deseo o si lo que quiero es hundirme más profundamente en la noche. Sí, quizás sea mejor acabar.

La vida fue cruel al encarnizarse tanto conmigo. Hubiera debido repartir mejor sus naipes. Tuve un juego demasiado malo. Un tarot negro en el cuerpo.

La vida es cruel por haber inventado la memoria. Como los viejos que recuperan los matices de sus más antiguos recuerdos, al borde de la muerte mi memoria gravita alrededor del sol, y él la ilumina. Todo está presente, nada se ha perdido. Como una fuerza oculta que te impulsa para estimularte todavía: ante la evidencia de que no hay más futuro, el pasado se amplifica, sus raíces se fortalecen, todo en mí es rizosfera, los colores cristalizan sobre cada estrato, la más mínima imagen tiende a su absoluto, el corazón late en crescendo.

Pero pintar, pintar todo eso está hoy fuera de mi alcance.

¡Oh! ¡Doña Magdalena Carmen Frida Kahlo de Rivera, Su Majestad la Cotija, cuarenta y siete años de este pleno verano mexicano, gastado hasta la urdimbre, el dolor abrumador como nunca, ahora estás en lo irreparable!

¡Viejo Mictlantecuhtli, dios, libérame!

---

* **marasmo:** marasmus (n.): severe undernourishment, causing a child's weight to be significantly below a normal percentile

GO ON TO THE NEXT PAGE.

26. ¿Cuál es el propósito del pasaje?

    (A) Kahlo lamenta de los fracasos en su vida.

    (B) Kahlo comprende más profundamente el dolor que pinta en sus obras.

    (C) Kahlo describe unas obras de su arte.

    (D) Kahlo describe su estado emocional y físico hacia el final de su vida.

27. ¿Qué significa la frase *presa rebelde, pero presa* en el segundo párrafo?

    (A) Que Kahlo había luchado por su vida, pero no puede más

    (B) Que Kahlo está organizando una rebelión en México

    (C) Que algo está cazando a Kahlo para comérsela

    (D) Que Kahlo está alejado de la realidad

28. Se menciona los detalles en el cuarto párrafo para

    (A) ilustrar que Kahlo tiene miedo de la oscuridad

    (B) mostrar el dolor físico y emocional que siente Kahlo

    (C) describir una de las obras más profundas de Kahlo

    (D) demostrar que Kahlo no puede escapar de sus fantasías

29. ¿Por qué dice "Pero pintar, pintar todo eso está hoy fuera de mi alcance"?

    (A) No sabe donde están sus lápices ni cepillos.

    (B) Ahora no le gusta pintar.

    (C) No tiene la habilidad física para pintar más.

    (D) Tiene que cambiar su profesión.

30. ¿Qué significa la última frase?

    (A) Que Frida quiere estar fuera de su situación

    (B) Que Frida está encarcelada

    (C) Que Frida quiere morirse

    (D) Que Frida no sabe donde está

GO ON TO THE NEXT PAGE.

Part B

Interpretive Communication: Print and Audio Texts (combined)

You will listen to several audio selections. The first two audio selections are accompanied by reading selections. When there is a reading selection, you will have a designated amount of time to read it.

For each audio selection, first you will have a designated amount of time to read a preview of the selection as well as to skim the questions that you will be asked. Each selection will be played twice. As you listen to each selection, you may take notes. Your notes will not be scored.

After listening to each selection the first time, you will have 1 minute to begin answering the questions; after listening to each selection the second time, you will have 15 seconds per question to finish answering the questions. For each question, choose the response that is best according to the audio and/or reading selection and mark your answer on your answer sheet.

Vas a escuchar varias grabaciones. Las dos primeras grabaciones van acompañadas de lecturas. Cuando haya una lectura, vas a tener un tiempo determinado para leerla.

Para cada grabación, primero vas a tener un tiempo determinado para leer la introducción y prever las preguntas. Vas a escuchar cada grabación dos veces. Mientras escuchas, puedes tomar apuntes. Tus apuntes no van a ser calificados.

Después de escuchar cada selección por primera vez, vas a tener un minuto para empezar a contestar las preguntas; después de escuchar por segunda vez, vas a tener 15 segundos por pregunta para terminarlas. Para cada pregunta, elige la mejor respuesta según la grabación o el texto e indícala en la hoja de respuestas.

GO ON TO THE NEXT PAGE.

Selección número 1

Fuente número 1

Primero tienes 4 minutos para leer la fuente número 1.

Introducción

En Panamá, y muchos países de América Latina, muchas personas llevan uniformes al trabajo o a la escuela. Pero hoy en día, con la globalización de la economía, diferentes generaciones se preguntan si los uniformes son necesarios. Este artículo apareció en la prensa panameña en febrero de 2012.

Uso De Uniformes: Un Hábito Muy Latino

Aquí en Panamá, los uniformes son muy comunes. Lo utilizan desde las microempresas hasta el propio gabinete presidencial de la República. ¿Pero de dónde viene este éxito de los uniformes en Panamá? Dos hechos importantes de la historia del siglo XX contribuyeron a cambiar la percepción de los uniformes. El primero de ellos fue la integración masiva de mujeres en la fuerza laboral. El segundo hecho, y el más decisivo, fue el comienzo de la Era Espacial.

Unas personas creen que estas nuevas tendencias inspiradas en la tecnología y en la ciencia-ficción influenciaron el espíritu de la gente y su forma de vestir. En todos lados las personas querían uniformarse y ser parte de esta gran "revolución futurista".

Las aerolíneas fueron las primeras en usar este nuevo estilo. Cambiaron las sencillas vestimentas de tipo naval por uniformes de diseñador. Pronto fueron adaptados por compañías alrededor del mundo para sus empleados. En muchas partes fue una moda pasajera, pero no en Panamá. El negocio de los uniformes se convirtió en un trabajo muy rentable.

Pero el hecho de entregar uniformes no significa que los empleados sean personas mal vestidas o de mal gusto. En Panamá, si la gente no tiene un "código de vestuario", automáticamente escogerá prendas frescas y ligeras, ideales para soportar el calor tropical. Pero no son adecuadas para un ambiente serio y profesional. Muchas personas que utilizan uniformes piensan que es práctico y realmente les simplifica el proceso de prepararse para ir a trabajar. Pero a otras no les gusta la idea de tener que usar uniformes.

En la actualidad, camisetas sencillas con logos son la forma más popular de uniformes en Panamá. Representan el estado más simple y casual del uniforme. Muchas empresas, especialmente bancos e instituciones estatales, utilizan aún uniformes formales de varias piezas. Sin embargo, es una tendencia que va en disminución, ya que el negocio de la costura, que en su tiempo fue un próspero sector, también va decayendo.

Adapted from "Uso De Uniformes: Un Hábito Muy Latino," by María Carolina Crespo. Used by permission of VeinteMundos.com.

GO ON TO THE NEXT PAGE.

Fuente número 2

Tienes 2 minutos para leer la introducción y prever las preguntas.

Introducción

Esta grabación trata de los uniformes en el trabajo o la escuela. Los siguientes entrevistados comparten sus opiniones sobre los uniformes. La grabación dura aproximadamente tres minutos.

Ahora escucha la fuente número dos.

PLAY AUDIO: Track 1

Ahora tienes un minuto para empezar a responder a las preguntas para esta selección. Después de un minuto, vas a escuchar la grabación de nuevo.

(1 minute)

Ahora escucha de nuevo.

PLAY AUDIO: Track 1

Ahora termina de responder a las preguntas para esta selección.

31. ¿Qué evento contribuyó a cambiar la percepción de los uniformes del siglo XX?

    (A) Los ambientes serios y profesionales demandaron los uniformes.

    (B) A la gente le gustaba la ciencia-ficción y fue inspirada por las historias del género.

    (C) Había una integración de las mujeres en la fuerza laboral.

    (D) Muchas empresas, especialmente bancos e instituciones estatales, utilizaban uniformes de varias piezas.

32. ¿Generalmente, quiénes usan los uniformes en los "EE.UU."?

    (A) Los productores de televisión

    (B) Los profesores en la universidad

    (C) Los bomberos y militares

    (D) Los asistentes jurídicos

33. Se menciona la frase la "revolución futurista" para

    (A) referirse a la revolución social inspirada por la ciencia-ficción

    (B) hablar del "código de vestuario" que existe en todos los modos de trabajo

    (C) ilustrar la creencia de que unas personas que llevaban uniformes al trabajo querían uniformarse

    (D) describir la integración de mujeres en la fuerza laboral

34. ¿Por qué se menciona el clima en la discusión de los uniformes?

    (A) Muestra que el clima tropical se presta para usar prendas ligeras, pero no son suficientemente profesionales para los ambientes serios.

    (B) Muestra que las prendas frescas son ideales para el ambiente profesional.

    (C) Muestra que el código de vestuario depende del clima.

    (D) Muestra que en Panamá, toda la gente quiere vestirse de ropa ligera para soportar el calor.

35. ¿Cuál es el tono de Eduardo?

    (A) Perplejo

    (B) Negativo

    (C) Odioso

    (D) Estático

36. Según la fuente auditiva, ¿cuál es la opinión de los entrevistados jóvenes?

    (A) Ellos odian la idea de los uniformes.

    (B) Depende de la profesión del individuo.

    (C) Sólo a las personas más conservadoras les gusta.

    (D) Ellos son indiferentes porque es parte de la cultura.

GO ON TO THE NEXT PAGE.

37. Todas son razones que dan los entrevistados para llevar los uniformes SALVO:

    (A) crean un sentido de pertenencia

    (B) cubren cosas como tatuajes

    (C) el salario se puede invertir en cosas más importantes que ropa de trabajo

    (D) no permiten expresar la individualidad

38. ¿A cuáles de los entrevistados les gustan los uniformes?

    (A) Eduardo y Roberto Sánchez

    (B) Liz y Eduardo

    (C) Liz y Roberto Sánchez

    (D) Roberto Sánchez y María Carolina

39. ¿Cuál de las afirmaciones mejor resume este artículo?

    (A) Muchos de los uniformes para el trabajo son de mal gusto.

    (B) El futuro de los uniformes está condenado porque los negocios de costura están decayendo.

    (C) Muchas personas tienen distintas opiniones sobre el uso de los uniformes en el trabajo.

    (D) Hubo muchos cambios en la economía del siglo XX que contribuyeron al uso de los uniformes.

GO ON TO THE NEXT PAGE.

Selección número 2

Fuente número 1

Primero tienes 3 minutos para leer la fuente número 1.

Introducción

Esta información apareció en el sitio de Web globalchange.org, sobre la deserción escolar de los jóvenes en América Latina. Las estadísticas son de agosto de 2013.

¿Por qué abandonan la escuela secundaria los jóvenes latinoamericanos?

Con uno de cada dos estudiantes que no termina secundaria, la deserción escolar afecta a jóvenes de todos los sectores de la sociedad. Sin embargo, los siguientes grupos registran tasas elevadas de abandono escolar de forma desproporcionada.

Son muchos los factores que influyen en la deserción escolar. Históricamente, problemas de acceso han propiciado altas tasas de deserción escolar en América Latina. En las últimas décadas, los países latinoamericanos han logrado avances notables en el acceso a la educación secundaria.

Si bien los problemas económicos y de acceso siguen suponiendo obstáculos para la educación en ciertas zonas, no ilustran la historia completa de la situación actual. Varios factores influyen en el abandono escolar y las razones por las que los jóvenes dejan los estudios pueden sorprender. Según datos de encuestas de hogares de 8 países, la mayoría de los estudiantes entre 13 y 15 años que no van a la escuela identifican la falta de interés —por encima de los problemas económicos, de acceso o familiares— como la razón principal de abandono escolar.

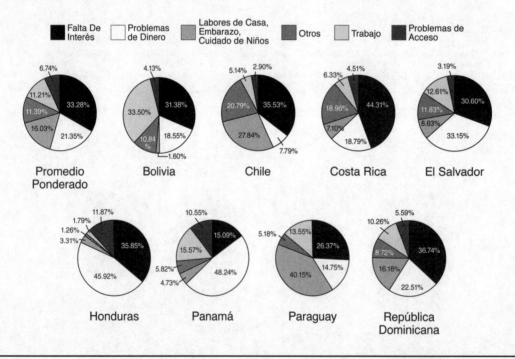

Fuente número 2

Tienes 2 minutos para leer la introducción y prever las preguntas.

Introducción

Esta grabación trata de la deserción escolar. La grabación es una conversación entre dos amigos, Miguel y Loren, que viven en Zacapa, Guatemala. La grabación dura aproximadamente tres minutos.

Ahora escucha la fuente número dos.

> **PLAY AUDIO: Track 2**

Ahora tienes un minuto para empezar a responder a las preguntas para esta selección. Después de un minuto, vas a escuchar la grabación de nuevo.

(1 minute)

Ahora escucha de nuevo.

> **PLAY AUDIO: Track 2**

Ahora termina de responder a las preguntas para esta selección.

40. ¿Cuál es el propósito del artículo y de las estadísticas?

   (A) Los estudiantes entre 13 y 15 años necesitan trabajar y ayudar a sus familias.

   (B) Hay muchas razones por la deserción escolar y la razón más grande identificada es la falta de interés.

   (C) No se sabe por qué hay una falta de interés en los estudiantes entre 13 y 15 años de edad.

   (D) Todavía los problemas económicos y de acceso siguen suponiendo obstáculos para los jóvenes.

41. Históricamente, ¿cuáles son los problemas citados por falta de asistencia?

   (A) Problemas de acceso

   (B) Trabajo

   (C) Falta de interés

   (D) Problemas de dinero

42. Todas las siguientes son razones de abandonar la escuela secundaria SALVO:

   (A) problemas de acceso

   (B) falta de interés

   (C) embarazo y cuidado de niños

   (D) presión de los padres

43. Las razones mayores para la falta de asistencia en Bolivia son

   (A) falta de interés y labores de casa

   (B) falta de interés y problemas de dinero

   (C) falta de interés y trabajo

   (D) falta de interés y problemas de acceso

GO ON TO THE NEXT PAGE.

44. Se puede inferir que

    (A) todos los jóvenes en Latinoamérica tienen una falta de interés en los estudios escolares

    (B) las razones de la deserción escolar varían dependiendo del país

    (C) los problemas de acceso son del pasado

    (D) los problemas económicos y de acceso siguen suponiendo obstáculos grandes en todas partes

45. ¿Cuál es el problema principal de Miguel?

    (A) A Miguel le falta interés en sus estudios secundarios.

    (B) Necesita ayudar a sus padres.

    (C) Necesita solicitar una beca para asistir a la universidad.

    (D) Necesita encontrar empleo.

46. ¿Quiénes son María, Joaquín y Carolina?

    (A) Son los amigos de Miguel y Loren.

    (B) Son los hermanos menores de Loren.

    (C) Son los hermanos mayores de Miguel.

    (D) Son los hermanos menores de Miguel.

47. ¿Qué va a hacer Miguel durante su año sabático?

    (A) Va a cuidar a sus niños y trabajar para su padre.

    (B) Va a asistir a la Universidad de Guatemala y después la Facultad de Medicina.

    (C) Va a trabajar con su padre mientras cuida de sus hermanos con su madre.

    (D) Va a pasar un rato trabajando y viajando con su padre.

GO ON TO THE NEXT PAGE.

Interpretive Communication: Audio Texts

Selección número 3

Introducción

Primero tienes un minuto para leer la introducción y prever las preguntas.

La siguiente grabación fue parte de un broadcast del "Mundo de deportes," un programa de radio dedicado a los deportes de todas partes.

Ahora escucha la selección.

PLAY AUDIO: Track 3

Ahora tienes un minuto para empezar a responder a las preguntas para esta selección. Después de un minuto, vas a escuchar la grabación de nuevo.

(1 minute)

Ahora escucha de nuevo.

PLAY AUDIO: Track 3

Ahora termina de responder a las preguntas para esta selección.

48. ¿Cómo es el campo de golf de Saint Andrew's en Escocia?
    - (A) Nuevo y moderno
    - (B) Pintoresco
    - (C) Histórico y prestigioso
    - (D) Innovador

49. ¿Qué tiempo hacía durante el torneo?
    - (A) Hacía un tiempo agradable.
    - (B) Hacía calor.
    - (C) Nevaba.
    - (D) Hacía un tiempo tempestuoso.

50. ¿Al principio, cómo reaccionó Alfonso García frente al tiempo variable en Escocia?
    - (A) Se sintió frustrado.
    - (B) Se sintió muy a gusto.
    - (C) Se sintió nostálgico.
    - (D) Se sintió triste.

51. ¿Cómo se interesó Alfonso García en el golf?
    - (A) Jugaba golf con su padre.
    - (B) Acompañaba a su abuelo en el campo de golf.
    - (C) Jugaba golf con su hermana.
    - (D) Jugaba golf con su abuela.

52. ¿Cómo pasa Alfonso la mayoría de su tiempo?
    - (A) Descansando con sus padres en Buenos Aires
    - (B) Viajando en el Tour de la PGA
    - (C) Jugando tenis con su hermana menor, Patricia
    - (D) Pasando tiempo con su abuelo maternal

GO ON TO THE NEXT PAGE.

Selección número 4

Introducción

Primero tienes un minuto para leer la introducción y prever las preguntas.

Esta grabación trata del feminismo en España. La grabación es parte de una conferencia sobre el feminismo en España.

Ahora escucha la selección.

PLAY AUDIO: Track 4

Ahora tienes un minuto para empezar a responder a las preguntas para esta selección. Después de un minuto, vas a escuchar la grabación de nuevo.

(1 minute)

Ahora escucha de nuevo.

PLAY AUDIO: Track 4

Ahora termina de responder a las preguntas para esta selección.

53. ¿Cómo interpretan algunos el movimiento feminista en España?

    (A) Una lucha política

    (B) Una cuestión artística

    (C) Una competencia entre iguales

    (D) Un concurso de belleza

54. ¿Cuál característica de la cultura española se puede considerar como el opuesto del movimiento feminista?

    (A) El marianismo

    (B) La honra

    (C) La dignidad

    (D) El machismo

55. Según la conferencia, ¿cuál es el objetivo ideológico del movimiento feminista?

    (A) El triunfo de la mujer sobre el hombre

    (B) La aceptación del marianismo en todo el mundo

    (C) Una identidad individual para la mujer

    (D) La apreciación de la cultura tradicional

56. Según la conferencia, ¿qué pensamiento surgió en la época de Franco?

    (A) Un pensamiento radical

    (B) Un pensamiento tradicional

    (C) Un pensamiento progresivo

    (D) Un pensamiento feminista

57. Según la conferencia, ¿qué debemos guardar de la sociedad tradicional machista?

    (A) El papel de la mujer como madre

    (B) El marianismo

    (C) El papel de la mujer subordinada al hombre

    (D) El machismo

GO ON TO THE NEXT PAGE.

Selección número 5

Introducción

Primero tienes un minuto para leer la introducción y prever las preguntas.

La siguiente grabación trata de los juegos olímpicos especiales convocado el pasado agosto. La grabación es una entrevista con Alejandro Martínez, entrenador triunfante del torneo de los juegos olímpicos especiales.

Ahora escucha la selección.

PLAY AUDIO: Track 5

Ahora tienes un minuto para empezar a responder a las preguntas para esta selección. Después de un minuto, vas a escuchar la grabación de nuevo.

(1 minute)

Ahora escucha de nuevo.

PLAY AUDIO: Track 5

Ahora termina de responder a las preguntas para esta selección.

58. ¿Cómo se interesó Alejandro Martínez en los juegos olímpicos especiales?
    (A) Siempre había participado en los juegos especiales.
    (B) Su hermano participaba en los juegos especiales.
    (C) Su hijo respondió favorablemente a los deportes.
    (D) Su esposa está muy metida en los juegos especiales.

59. ¿Cuándo se dedica Alejandro completamente a los juegos especiales?
    (A) Los fines de semana
    (B) Durante las vacaciones escolares
    (C) En invierno
    (D) En verano

60. Según la entrevista, ¿por qué no trabaja exclusivamente con los juegos especiales?
    (A) Porque no gana suficiente dinero
    (B) Porque es maestro de matemáticas
    (C) Porque su hija le ocupa mucho tiempo
    (D) Porque no podría soportarlo

61. ¿Por qué le gusta a Alejandro trabajar con los niños?
    (A) Porque son jóvenes
    (B) Porque son honestos
    (C) Porque tienen mucho interés
    (D) Porque tienen más habilidad

GO ON TO THE NEXT PAGE.

62. Según la entrevista, ¿por qué es terapéutico el ejercicio físico?

    (A) Porque practican ejercicios especiales

    (B) Porque los entrenadores tienen educación en terapia física

    (C) Porque es divertido

    (D) Porque les hace sentir mejor a los niños mental y físicamente

63. ¿Cómo se caracteriza el espíritu colectivo de los niños?

    (A) No saben colaborar con el grupo.

    (B) Entienden instintivamente cómo colaborar.

    (C) No saben funcionar físicamente.

    (D) Hay mucha competencia entre los grupos.

64. Según la entrevista, ¿cuál característica describe mejor a los niños que participan en los juegos olímpicos especiales?

    (A) Son muy delgados.

    (B) Son muy delicados.

    (C) Son muy dedicados.

    (D) Son delegados a los juegos especiales.

65. ¿Qué recomienda Alejandro a las familias que no quieren participar en los juegos?

    (A) Que se enteren de los eventos planeados

    (B) Que sigan su corazón

    (C) Que organicen sus propios juegos con los juegos especiales

    (D) Que no participen

END OF SECTION I

IF YOU FINISH BEFORE TIME IS CALLED, YOU MAY CHECK YOUR WORK ON THIS SECTION

SPANISH LANGUAGE AND CULTURE

SECTION II

Time—88 minutes

50% of total grade

Question 1: Email Reply

You will write a reply to an email message. You will have 15 minutes to read the message and write your reply. Your reply should include a greeting and a closing, and should respond to all the questions and requests in the message. In your reply, you should also ask for more details about something mentioned in the message. Also, you should use a formal form of address.	Vas a escribir una respuesta a un mensaje electrónico. Vas a tener 15 minutos para leer el mensaje y escribir tu respuesta. Tu respuesta debe incluir un saludo y una despedida, y debe responder a todas las preguntas y peticiones del mensaje. En tu respuesta, debes pedir más información sobre algo mencionado en el mensaje. También debes responder de una manera formal.

Introducción

Este mensaje es de su profesor del colegio. Ha recibido este mensaje porque recientemente le había pedido que le escribiera una carta de recomendación para su solicitud de ingreso a la universidad. Tendrá 15 minutos para leer la carta y escribir su respuesta.

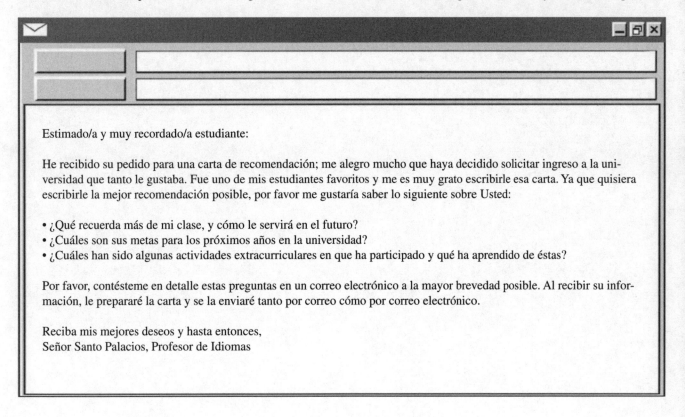

Estimado/a y muy recordado/a estudiante:

He recibido su pedido para una carta de recomendación; me alegro mucho que haya decidido solicitar ingreso a la universidad que tanto le gustaba. Fue uno de mis estudiantes favoritos y me es muy grato escribirle esa carta. Ya que quisiera escribirle la mejor recomendación posible, por favor me gustaría saber lo siguiente sobre Usted:

• ¿Qué recuerda más de mi clase, y cómo le servirá en el futuro?
• ¿Cuáles son sus metas para los próximos años en la universidad?
• ¿Cuáles han sido algunas actividades extracurriculares en que ha participado y qué ha aprendido de éstas?

Por favor, contésteme en detalle estas preguntas en un correo electrónico a la mayor brevedad posible. Al recibir su información, le prepararé la carta y se la enviaré tanto por correo cómo por correo electrónico.

Reciba mis mejores deseos y hasta entonces,
Señor Santo Palacios, Profesor de Idiomas

GO ON TO THE NEXT PAGE.

Question 2: Argumentative Essay

You will write an argumentative essay to submit to a Spanish writing contest. The essay topic is based on three accompanying sources, which present different viewpoints on the topic and include both print and audio material. First, you will have 6 minutes to read the essay topic and the printed material. Afterward, you will hear the audio material twice; you should take notes while you listen. Then, you will have 40 minutes to prepare and write your essay.	Vas a escribir un ensayo persuasivo para un concurso de redacción en español. El tema del ensayo se basa en las tres fuentes adjuntas, que presentan diferentes puntos de vista sobre el tema e incluyen material escrito y grabado. Primero, vas a tener 6 minutos para leer el tema del ensayo y los textos. Después, vas a escuchar la grabación dos veces; debes tomar apuntes mientras escuchas. Luego vas a tener 40 minutos para preparar y escribir tu ensayo.
In an argumentative essay, you should present the sources' different viewpoints on the topic, and also clearly indicate your own viewpoint and defend it thoroughly. Use information from all of the sources to support your essay. As you refer to the sources, identify them appropriately. Also, organize your essay into clear paragraphs.	En un ensayo persuasivo, debes presentar los diferentes puntos de vista de las fuentes sobre el tema, expresar tu propio punto de vista y apoyarlo. Usa información de todas las fuentes para apoyar tu punto de vista. Al referirte a las fuentes, identifícalas apropiadamente. Organiza también el ensayo en distintos párrafos bien desarrollados.

Tema del ensayo:

¿Cómo nos afecta la vida el calentamiento global?

GO ON TO THE NEXT PAGE.

Fuente número 1

Introducción

Este artículo apareció en un sitio de Internet de España en mayo de 2008.

Las consecuencias del calentamiento global asociadas con un aumento en el nivel de mar

Con la destrucción de la capa de ozono, observamos una mayor penetración de rayos solares al planeta. Estos, a su vez, contribuyen a una expansión térmica de los océanos y el derretimiento de grandes números de montañas glaciares y de los casquetes de hielo ubicados en las partes orientales de las Tierras Antárticas y Groenlandia. Ya con estos niveles elevados del mar, se pronosticarán graves cambios para el porvenir del planeta.

El nivel del mar ya aumentó en entre 4 y 8 pulgadas en el siglo pasado. Se predice que los niveles del mar podrían aumentar en desde 10 hasta 23 pulgadas para el año 2100. Lamentablemente los niveles vienen creciendo más de lo previsto—la capa de hielo de Groenlandia ha disminuido en la última década. Este declive contribuye aproximadamente una centésima de pulgada anualmente al aumento del nivel del mar. La cifra parece ser mínima a primera vista, pero hay que tener en cuenta que Groenlandia cuenta con alrededor de 10% de la masa total del hielo mundial. Si el hielo de Groenlandia fuera a derretirse, los niveles de los mares mundiales podrían aumentar en hasta 21 pies. Este año, por primera vez, los barcos pudieron pasar por las aguas árticas sin la ayuda de un barco rompehielos. O sea, que las predicciones de los científicos que el hielo empezaría a derretirse han acontecido 25 años por adelantado. Esto también significará graves consecuencias para el planeta. Ya se pronostica que el oso polar, los lobos marinos y ciertas especies de pingüinos estarán al borde de la extinción en pocos años.

Con la destrucción de los glaciares y casquetes del hielo, más agua dulce entra al mar, y así aumentando los niveles actuales. Estos derretimientos provocarán inundaciones severas en áreas costeñas. Si el nivel de mar subiera apenas 6 metros, arrasaría con lugares como Miami, Florida y San Francisco, California en los Estados Unidos; en China dejaría hundidas a ciudades como Shangai y Beijing, y en India, la ciudad de Calcuta estaría bajo agua. Estos últimos tres centros urbanos figuran entre las ciudades más pobladas del mundo.

GO ON TO THE NEXT PAGE.

Fuente número 2

Introducción

Este artículo apareció en la prensa argentina en julio de 2008.

Advertencia: El calentamiento global traerá consigo graves consecuencias sobre la vida y la salud humana

"No es ninguna especulación —es una realidad. Los días del planeta están contados. Ya es la hora de actuar y poner en marcha programas de planificación y contingencia", comentó Francisco García, director general de la Organización de Preservación Mundial, en rueda de prensa durante la undécima convocatoria general de La Semana del Planeta celebrada en Buenos Aires, Argentina. Representantes de más de 35 países se reunieron en la capital argentina para discutir, analizar data y formular planes de acción para que las organizaciones internacionales y nacionales entendieran con mayor profundidad las consecuencias del calentamiento global. Es su esperanza, que una vez armados con esta información los países adopten programas para evitar un desastre que, según García, "está al acecho".

Una de las charlas más alarmantes dio a conocer las cifras actuales sobre enfermedades y desastres por el mundo. El doctor alemán Martin Teuscher, profesor de la Universidad de Tübingen, explicó que el ser humano ya ha sido expuesto a varias enfermedades causadas por cambios o exageraciones del clima. "Es una realidad que hemos estado viviendo durante este siglo. Pero fíjense que con el cambio climático, las bajas serán aún mayores. Intensificarán el balance delicado entre el desastre y la prosperidad, entre tener hogar y ser desamparado, y finalmente, entre la vida y la muerte". Señaló, en concreto, que mundialmente mueren más de 4 millones de personas por la malnutrición, más de 2 millones por enfermedades diarreicas, y 1,2 millones por enfermedades como la malaria. Indudablemente, estas cifras aumentarán con el cambio del clima mundial. Dijo Teuscher que no estaría fuera de lo posible que esas cifras triplicaran en apenas 5 o 10 años.

Los descensos no pararán ahí. Con las temperaturas más cálidas, los insectos y otros organismos maléficos tendrán más oportunidad de desarrollarse y contagiar a los seres humanos como resultado. Se espera que ocurrirán más brotes de dengue y epidemias de malaria. Ambas enfermedades se trasmiten por la picadura de mosquitos. El calentamiento global favorece a estos insectos portadores de enfermedades. Otro resultado del calentamiento global son las inundaciones, las cuales proveen el ambiente ideal para la cría de mosquitos y las temidas pandémicas de cólera. Los recientes estudios realizados por los científicos ilustran la gravedad del problema del calentamiento global. En apenas 15 años, el número de personas en el continente de África expuesta a la malaria podrá llegar a las 100 millones. Globalmente, el dengue podrá amenazar a casi unos 2.000 millones de personas.

El calentamiento global ha traído trastornos en los climas mundiales, y cada año se manifiestan cambios y matices climáticos jamás vistos anteriormente. Por ejemplo, las olas de calor en Europa y los Estados Unidos significan miles de muertos cada año y los huracanes cada vez se vuelvan más devastadores y potentes. "El huracán Katrina de 2005 y el Huracán Mitch de 1998 destrozaron grandes partes del territorio americano", puntualizó Felipe Fonseca, meteorólogo mexicano que habló sobre los cambios sufridos en el Golfo de México por el calentamiento global. "Estos efectos sociales, económicos y políticos, aún se sienten. En 50 años podríamos encontrar partes del América del Norte bajo agua".

Las emisiones ocasionadas por los automóviles, camiones y aviones envenenan el aire que respiramos. Esa contaminación del aire causa casi un millón de muertes al año. Según los estimados citados por los expertos, por cada grado centígrado que aumente la temperatura global, habrá casi 30.000 muertos anuales adicionales por enfermedades cardiorrespiratorias. Con los recientes aumentos de precio de los combustibles, la demanda no ha disminuido lo suficiente para reducir la contaminación del aire. Muchos temen que con el crecimiento de las economías emergentes de Asia, más el gran número de chóferes que tendrán acceso a automóviles, el daño ambiental continúe perjudicando cualquier intento de conservar el medioambiente.

"El individuo sí tiene el poder para hacer una diferencia", explica Rachel Johnson, estudiante alemana y miembro de GreenWatch, un movimiento estudiantil que educa a jóvenes sobre la conservación y el reciclaje. "Esa bolsa plástica que arrojas a la basura sin pensarlo tardará un centenar en descomponerse. La gasolina y el petróleo influencian casi todos los aspectos de nuestra vida, y al mismo tiempo perjudican al nuestro bienestar y el del planeta. Tenemos que cambiar nuestra manera de pensar y actuar ahora. En mi país hay un dicho que dice: *Macht es jetzt! Warte nicht auf bessere Zeiten.* (¡Hazlo ahora! No esperes mejores momentos.) Si no hacemos el esfuerzo ahora, nuestras futuras generaciones se condenarán a una vida sin vida".

GO ON TO THE NEXT PAGE.

Fuente número 3

Tienes 30 segundos para leer la introducción.

Introducción

Este informe, que se titula "Los expertos señalan mayores riesgos de salud por el calentamiento global" se emitió por la emisora hispanoamericana Enteramérica en julio de 2005.

Ahora escucha la fuente número tres.

PLAY AUDIO: Track 6

Ahora escucha de nuevo.

PLAY AUDIO: Track 6

Ahora tienes cuarenta minutos para preparar y escribir un ensayo persuasivo.

(40 minutes)

GO ON TO THE NEXT PAGE.

Question 3: Conversation

<table>
<tr><td>You will participate in a conversation. First, you will have 1 minute to read a preview of the conversation, including an outline of each turn in the conversation. Afterward, the conversation will begin, following the outline. Each time it is your turn to speak, you will have 20 seconds to record your response.

You should participate in the conversation as fully and appropriately as possible.</td><td>Vas a participar en una conversación. Primero, vas a tener un minuto para leer la introducción y el esquema de la conversación. Después, comenzará la conversación, siguiendo el esquema. Cada vez que te corresponda participar en la conversación, vas a tener 20 segundos para grabar tu respuesta.

Debes participar de la manera más completa y apropiada posible.</td></tr>
</table>

Tienes un minuto para leer la introducción.

Introducción

Has solicitado una posición de aprendiz en una empresa multinacional latinoamericana. Imagina que recibes una llamada telefónica del director del Departamento de Recursos Humanos para hablar sobre la posición que has solicitado.

PLAY AUDIO: Track 7

Entrevistador	Te saluda
Tú	Contesta la pregunta
Entrevistador	Te hace una pregunta
Tú	Responde a la pregunta
Entrevistador	Continúa la conversación
Tú	Responde a la pregunta
Entrevistador	Continúa la conversación
Tú	Responde a la pregunta
Entrevistador	Continúa la conversación
Tú	Contesta que no es posible y ofrece una alternativa
Entrevistador	Continúa la conversación
Tú	Despídete

GO ON TO THE NEXT PAGE.

Question 4: Cultural Comparison

You will make an oral presentation on a specific topic to your class. You will have 4 minutes to read the presentation topic and prepare your presentation. Then you will have 2 minutes to record your presentation. In your presentation, compare your own community to an area of the Spanish-speaking world with which you are familiar. You should demonstrate your understanding of cultural features of the Spanish-speaking world. You should also organize your presentation clearly.	Vas a dar una presentación oral a tu clase sobre un tema cultural. Vas a tener 4 minutos para leer el tema de la presentación y prepararla. Después vas a tener 2 minutos para grabar tu presentación. En tu presentación, compara tu propia comunidad con una región del mundo hispanohablante que te sea familiar. Debes demostrar tu comprensión de aspectos culturales en el mundo hispanohablante y organizar tu presentación de una manera clara.

Tienes cuatro minutos para leer el tema de la presentación y prepararla.

(4 minutes)

Tema de la presentación:

Se sabe que los idiomas enriquecen la vida de uno. Explica de qué manera los idiomas han influenciado la sociedad en que tú vives y en otra ciudad hispanohablante que tú hayas observado, estudiado o visitado.

Compara tus observaciones acerca de las comunidades en las que has vivido con tus observaciones de una región del mundo hispanohablante que te sea familiar. En tu presentación, puedes referirte a lo que has estudiado, vivido, observado, etc.

Tienes dos minutos para grabar tu presentación.

STOP

END OF EXAM

Practice Test 1: Diagnostic Answer Key and Explanations

PRACTICE TEST 1: DIAGNOSTIC ANSWER KEY

Let's take a look at how you did on Practice Test 1. Follow the three-step process in the Diagnostic Answer Key and go read the explanations for any questions you got wrong, or you struggled with but got correct. Once you finish working through the answer key and the explanations, go to the next chapter to make your study plan.

STEP 1 ››› **Check your answers and mark any correct answers with a ✔ in the appropriate column.**

Section I: Multiple Choice—Interpretive Communication: Print Texts									
Q #	**Ans.**	**✔**	**Passage type**	**Chapter One Practice Passage**	**Q #**	**Ans.**	**✔**	**Passage type**	**Chapter One Practice Passage**
1	B		Interview	Practice Passage 7	16	A		Article	Practice Passages 1 & 2
2	C		Interview	Practice Passage 7	17	B		Article	Practice Passages 1 & 2
3	D		Interview	Practice Passage 7	18	A		Article	Practice Passages 1 & 2
4	A		Interview	Practice Passage 7	19	A		Promotional Material	Practice Passage 5
5	B		Interview	Practice Passage 7	20	D		Promotional Material	Practice Passage 5
6	C		Interview	Practice Passage 7	21	B		Promotional Material	Practice Passage 5
7	D		Article	Practice Passages 3 & 4	22	A		Promotional Material	Practice Passage 5
8	A		Article	Practice Passages 3 & 4	23	D		Promotional Material	Practice Passage 5
9	C		Article	Practice Passages 3 & 4	24	B		Promotional Material	Practice Passage 5
10	C		Article	Practice Passages 3 & 4	25	D		Promotional Material	Practice Passage 5
11	D		Article	Practice Passages 3 & 4	26	D		Literary Text	Practice Passage 6
12	B		Article	Practice Passages 3 & 4	27	A		Literary Text	Practice Passage 6
13	D		Article	Practice Passages 1 & 2	28	B		Literary Text	Practice Passage 6
14	C		Article	Practice Passages 1 & 2	29	C		Literary Text	Practice Passage 6
15	C		Article	Practice Passages 1 & 2	30	A		Literary Text	Practice Passage 6

Section I: Multiple Choice—Interpretive Communication: Print and Audio Texts (Combined)

Q #	Ans.	✔	Passage type	Chapter One Practice Passage	Q #	Ans.	✔	Passage type	Chapter One Practice Passage
31	C				40	B			
32	C				41	A			
33	C				42	D			
34	A		Print and Audio Texts (Combined)	Sample Print and Audio Texts (Combined) Selection	43	C		Print and Audio Texts (Combined)	Sample Print and Audio Texts (Combined) Selection
35	B				44	B			
36	B				45	B			
37	D				46	D			
38	C				47	C			
39	C								

Section I: Multiple Choice—Interpretive Communication: Audio Texts

Q #	Ans.	✔	Passage type	Chapter One Practice Passage	Q #	Ans.	✔	Passage type	Chapter One Practice Passage
48	C		Audio Broadcast	Audio Selection 1	57	A		Audio Speech	Audio Selection 2
49	D		Audio Broadcast	Audio Selection 1	58	C		Audio Interview	Audio Selection 3
50	A		Audio Broadcast	Audio Selection 1	59	D		Audio Interview	Audio Selection 3
51	B		Audio Broadcast	Audio Selection 1	60	B		Audio Interview	Audio Selection 3
52	B		Audio Broadcast	Audio Selection 1	61	B		Audio Interview	Audio Selection 3
53	A		Audio Speech	Audio Selection 2	62	D		Audio Interview	Audio Selection 3
54	D		Audio Speech	Audio Selection 2	63	B		Audio Interview	Audio Selection 3
55	C		Audio Speech	Audio Selection 2	64	C		Audio Interview	Audio Selection 3
56	B		Audio Speech	Audio Selection 2	65	A		Audio Interview	Audio Selection 3

Section II: Free Response

Q #	Ans.	✔	Passage Type	Chapter Two Practice Passage
1	See Explanation		Email Reply	Question 1: Email Reply
2	See Explanation		Argumentative Essay	Question 2: Argumentative Essay
3	See Explanation		Conversation	Question 3: Conversation
4	See Explanation		Cultural Comparison	Question 4: Cultural Comparison

Tally your correct answers from Step 1 by passage type. For each passage type, write the number of correct answers in the appropriate box. Then, divide your correct answers by the total number of questions (which we've provided) to get your percent correct.

PRINT

CORRECT ANSWERS

$$\frac{}{30} = \boxed{} \%$$

TOTAL QUESTIONS   PERCENT CORRECT

AUDIO

CORRECT ANSWERS

$$\frac{}{18} = \boxed{} \%$$

TOTAL QUESTIONS   PERCENT CORRECT

PRINT & AUDIO COMBINED

CORRECT ANSWERS

$$\frac{}{17} = \boxed{} \%$$

TOTAL QUESTIONS   PERCENT CORRECT

Use the results above to customize your study plan. You may want to start with, or give more attention to, the chapters with the lowest percents correct.

SECTION I

Note: These explanations make use of some of the strategies introduced in Part IV. Please refer to pages 95–167 to make the most of this section!

Interpretive Communication: Print Texts (Page 10)

Selection 1: Translated Text and Questions, with Explanations

Introduction

The following interview appeared in a Latin American magazine in June 2014.

This Physical Education teacher, 35 years old and a native of Santiago, Chile, realized a dream that many Caribbean dancers yearn for: to be two-time world champion of rumba. And in Europe! Almost 10 years ago, Christian Vera left his country and moved to Spain to practice his profession and great passion: dance. On said continent, he has traveled many countries teaching this tropical dance and also participating in different competitions. He has many anecdotes and experiences. Here we will come to know a few.

How does a Chilean come to be the two-time world champion of rumba?

The most important Cuban festival in Europe is held in Barcelona every year; and during that event there is a world competition called "Searching for the Rumba Dancer." It is an individual competition in which all the competitors, coming from different parts of the world, show their dance talent. The first time I entered, in 2011, I came second and then I managed first place two years in a row. After that, I became the first non-Cuban teacher to teach folklore at that festival.

How did you arrive at rumba? What was it that motivated you to practice this discipline?

What inspired me was a movie: *Dance With Me;* in it I saw the protagonists dancing salsa in Cuba. The truth is that I always had dance in my blood because my whole family is dedicated to it. Every day when I wake, I want to dance; and I still have the same enthusiasm and energy as in the beginning. That is also why I have been perfecting my dance. Every day I am learning something new from different types of dance.

Why has your career developed in Europe?

In the year 2007, I had a scholarship to the ITK University in Leipzig to obtain a postgrad in Applied Sciences toward soccer. After that, I was in Spain for three months doing an internship with Villareal club, which was directed at the time by Manuel Pellegrini. There, the team's physical trainer told me about a master's that he had done in Barcelona. That's why after returning to Chile and working for a time, I gathered money and again headed to the Mother Country to enroll myself in that specialized course.

Do you believe that this type of dance is today more popular in Europe than in Latin America?

In the old continent there is an advantage: the countries are very close and flights are not expensive. Thus, the dancers and aficionados of dances like salsa can travel to different competitions and festivals. The competitions have lots of success because the people are not only impassioned about dance, but also have the possibility of attending en masse. There is a lot of demand.

Latin dances are lively and sensual. Is that what Europeans like about these rhythms?

Europeans, in general, are disciplined, and in the case of dance, they focus a lot on trying to get to know in-depth the culture of the dance. Many even learn Spanish in order to understand the songs; they don't just want to dance and mimic. I believe that all the Europeans who learn to dance the Cuban dances want to get to know Cuba.

And what impression do people get when they see a Chilean dancer teaching Cuban salsa?

I have never been to Cuba. But many people ask me how it is possible that I dance with rhythm and style so markedly tropical. They mistake me for a Cuban, and not exactly because of my accent, but rather because of the way I dance. It can work against you, of course, because there is a theme of tradition and reference among Cubans, but I believe that whoever goes with that and feels it in their skin will have success.

Do you see yourself as or feel like an ambassador of salsa in Europe?

Cubans are very protective of their culture. When they find out that I dance salsa, they can have a type of prejudice at first. But once they see me on the dance floor, everything changes. I expect that they will always judge me for what I do. And in that sense, I have come to earn the respect of the great Cuban salsa masters. It seems to me that more than an ambassador proper, I like to see myself as a person who has the power to be an example that yes, one can dance salsa or rumba without being Cuban. I enjoy being able to represent all of those people.

1. Who is Christian Vera?
    (A) A Cuban salsa master
    (B) A Chilean rumba and salsa teacher who lives in Spain
    (C) A Spanish rumba and salsa teacher who lives in Cuba
    (D) A Chilean salsa master

The question asks who Christian Vera is. The first sentence states that he is an *oriundo de Santiago de Chile,* so eliminate (A) and (C). Now evaluate the difference between (B) and (D). The first paragraph also states that he is a *bicampeón mundial de rumba,* so the answer must include rumba in addition to salsa; eliminate (D). The correct answer is (B).

2. Why do Europeans enjoy Latin rhythms?
    (A) Because they are lively and sensual
    (B) Because it is easier to seduce women with dance
    (C) Because they can get to know Cuban culture
    (D) Because they offer contrast to the discipline that exists in Europe

The question asks why Europeans enjoy Latin rhythms. The passage states in the sixth paragraph that Vera believes *todos los europeos que aprenden a bailar danzas cubanas quieren ir a conocer Cuba.* Therefore, the answer should contain a reference to Europeans wanting to get to know Cuban culture. Eliminate (A) because this is a Words Out of Context answer. While the passage does mention the lively and sensual nature of the dances, this does not answer the question. Eliminate (B) because nowhere in the passage does it mention seducing women (and besides, this answer is offensive). Keep (C) since it matches the prediction. Eliminate (D) because the passage does not mention a contrast between disciplines. The correct answer is (C).

3. How did Vera arrive at rumba?
    (A) It was a fundamental part of his culture.
    (B) It was an integral part of his family, and therefore his father taught him.
    (C) He spent some time in Cuba to learn rumba.
    (D) He saw a movie about Latin dance and was inspired by it.

The question asks how Vera arrived at the rumba. In the third paragraph, Vera states that *Lo que me inspiró fue una película:* Dance with Me. Eliminate answers that don't match the prediction. Eliminate (A) since rumba was not part of his Chilean culture. Eliminate (B) because his father did not teach him. Eliminate (C) because he did not go to Cuba: he learned the rumba after having watched the film. Keep (D), which matches the prediction. The correct answer is (D).

4. Why has his career developed in Spain?
   (A) He had studied in Europe with a scholarship when he heard about a master's in Barcelona.
   (B) He spent part of his childhood in Europe and wanted to return.
   (C) He learned to dance in Latin America first and decided to move to Spain.
   (D) He is the first non-Cuban to teach Cuban folklore.

The question asks why his career developed in Spain. In the fourth paragraph, Vera states that *En el año 2007 me fui becado a la Universidad ITK de Leipzig.* He continues, stating that he heard about *un máster… en Barcelona,* so he *junté dinero… para inscribirme en ese curso de especialización.* Eliminate answers that don't match the prediction. Keep (A) since this matches the text. Eliminate (B) since the passage never mentions his childhood in Europe. Eliminate (C) because there is no evidence in the passage that he studied dance in Latin America. Eliminate (D) since it is a Right Information, Wrong Question trap, which does not answer the question. The correct answer is (A).

5. How do other dancers accept the Chilean when he dances salsa?
   (A) The Europeans accept him as a Cuban.
   (B) At first there is a bit of prejudice, but everything changes when Vera is dancing.
   (C) He can never dance as well as the Cubans.
   (D) They always accept him as Cuban without question.

The question asks how other dancers accept the Chilean when he dances salsa. Vera states in the last paragraph that other dancers *pueden tener una especie de prejuicio al principio. Pero una vez que me ven en la pista de baile, todo cambia.* Eliminate answers that don't match the prediction. Eliminate (A) because he is not trying to be accepted as a *Cuban.* Keep (B), which matches the prediction. Eliminate (C), which contains extreme language, saying that he could *never* dance as well as the Cubans. Eliminate (D) because they do initially have some prejudice. The correct answer is (B).

6. How does Vera respond to the interviewer's last question?
   (A) He responds that yes, he is the official ambassador to Cuba.
   (B) He responds that no, that is too much pressure for him.
   (C) He responds that yes, he wants to be the dance ambassador for everyone.
   (D) He responds that no, the Cubans do not accept him on the dance floor.

The question asks how Vera responds to the interviewer's last question, which is about whether Vera sees himself as an ambassador of salsa to Europe. Vera states in the last sentence *me gusta poder representar a toda esa gente,* referring to his example that *sí se puede bailar salsa o rumba sin ser cubano.* Eliminate answers that don't match the prediction. Eliminate (A) because he is not an *official* ambassador. Eliminate (B) because he never talks about *too much pressure.* Keep (C) because it matches the prediction. Eliminate (D) because the passage does say the Cubans accept him on the dance floor. The correct answer is (C).

Selection 2: Translated Text and Questions, with Explanations

Introduction

The following article appeared in a book of contemporary art in 2008.

Pablo Picasso, The Revolutionary

There are painters who transform the sun into a yellow spot, but there are others who, thanks to their art and intelligence, transform a yellow stain into the sun. —Pablo Picasso

Few artists have generated as much controversy, discussion, and admiration as Pablo Picasso (1881–1973). A monumental body of work, in quantity and quality; an exuberant and prolonged life; bedroom scandals and magnificent upsets make Picasso a true character. But without a doubt, the greatest justice lies in discovering him and recognizing him as the greatest artist of the 20th century.

Through more than eighty years of artistic life and more than twenty thousand works, the Andalusian painter surprised and outmaneuvered the art world again and again with a body of work not only unconventional, powerful, and original, but also absolutely revolutionary.

Just as the history of culture recognizes the Renaissance and then Impressionism as the great landmarks of Western painting, the 20th century surrenders to Cubism; and when talk of Cubism arises, so too does the name Pablo Picasso.

Multifaceted and grumpy, inconsiderate and passionate, extroverted and secretive at the same time, Picasso is all that and much more. He is, fundamentally, a naked and vulnerable being dressed as an invincible minotaur, on whose sensitive skin the world leaves its trail of sores and scars and he turns them into painted works.

Several wives, a few children, a multitude of books and movies that exalt or condemn him, are only a symptom of the personality of this man born to stand out.

In his century, which appears as the dawn of progress and fulfilled prophecy, his art intuits fragmentation and development, disharmony and chaos. War, death, genocide, and the broken promises of an overwhelmingly seductive and atrociously unbalanced science are embodied in a revulsive and destructured body of work that questions the canons of beauty and erects ugliness as an artistic category.

Picasso surely would not have been who he was if it were not for the magnificent brotherhood of contemporaries, among whom parade from Rousseau to Matisse, from Braque to Juan Gris, from Gertrude Stein to Alfred Jarry, from Breton to Cocteau, from Paul Eluard to ... But without a doubt, the century would not have been what it was, without the grandiloquent, transgressive, and specular presence of a painter, sculptor, engraver, draftsman, and even poet who made yellow spots into new suns with the intuition of a child and the mark of a man who, even though unguarded, resists the creative entrenchment of the imagination.

7. What is the purpose of the article?

    (A) It maintains that Picasso was the best painter of the 20th century.

    (B) It presents information about the personality and personal life of Picasso.

    (C) It describes some artworks that Picasso made.

    (D) It gives some information about the life and artistic output of Picasso.

The question asks about the main idea of the passage. The passage talks about Picasso's life and artistic output, which matches (D). Eliminate (A) because the passage states *el mayor artista del siglo XX* but never maintains that Picasso was the *best* artist. Eliminate (B) because his personality and personal life are only part of what the article includes. Eliminate (C) as well because his artwork is, again, only part of what the article talks about. The correct answer is (D).

8. The article includes the quote at the beginning in order to

(A) **show the genius of Pablo Picasso**

(B) illustrate that the sun has a spot that can't be seen

(C) explain that many artists only can paint abstractly

(D) illustrate how many artists do not have talent

The quote in the beginning is by Picasso: in it, he describes finding and transforming material into inspired works. The quote shows how Picasso sees and transforms seemingly ordinary things into works of genius, so keep (A). It does not literally mean that the sun has a spot on it, so eliminate (B). While many painters do paint abstractly, that is not Picasso's point; eliminate (C). Eliminate (D) because while he says *Hay pintores que transforman el sol en una mancha amarilla,* his emphasis is on those that can make transformative art. The correct answer is (A).

9. We can infer that

(A) Picasso was grumpy and inconsiderate every day

(B) the Renaissance and Impressionism were less important periods than Picasso's

(C) **there were other important artists during the 20th century**

(D) Picasso made more works of art than did his contemporaries

This question asks what the reader can infer, and this must always be something that can be supported by the passage. Eliminate (A) because while the passage does say that Picasso was *gruñón y desconsiderado*, it does not say that Picasso was like this every day. Eliminate (B) as well, because the passage never places the Renaissance and Impressionism in comparison with Picasso's era. Keep (C) because there is a whole list of other important artists mentioned in the final paragraph, such as Rosseau and Matisse. Eliminate (D) because while Picasso has made *más de veinte mil trabajos*, there is no evidence that he in fact created *more* than his contemporaries. The correct answer is (C).

10. Why are his wives and children mentioned?

(A) It shows some attributes of Picasso's personality.

(B) It shows something of the inspiration behind Picasso's art.

(C) **It reveals something about Picasso's personal life.**

(D) It demonstrates that Picasso was a bad spouse.

The question asks why Picasso's *esposas e hijos* are mentioned. They do not have anything to do with Picasso's personality, so eliminate (A), nor does the passage say that they influenced his art; eliminate (B). They do have something to do with his personal life, so keep (C). The fact that Picasso had more than one wife does not make him a bad spouse; eliminate (D). The correct answer is (C).

11. Rousseau, Matisse, Braque, Juan Gris, and other names are mentioned in order to

    (A) compare Picasso with other artists

    (B) name some artists from different epochs

    (C) suggest that Picasso was the best artist of all in the 20th century

    (D) enumerate the luminary artists who were contemporaries of Picasso

The question asks why the other names are mentioned. It never compares them with Picasso, but rather shows how strong the time period was for art; eliminate (A) and (C). They are *la magnífica cofradía de contemporáneos* of Picasso, so eliminate (B) and keep (D). The correct answer is (D).

12. The influence of Picasso is one of

    (A) confusion

    (B) intuition

    (C) offense

    (D) beauty

This is a general question which should be done after the specific questions. The influence of Picasso is strong, but not confusing or offensive. Eliminate (A) and (C). The quote in the beginning supports Picasso's intuition and ability to take simple things and turn them into extraordinary works. While some of his works are considered beautiful, the author writes that Picasso is able to take ugliness and turn it into art: the last sentence of the sixth paragraph states that Picasso's work *erige al feísmo como categoría artística,* which eliminates (D). The correct answer is (B).

Selection 3: Translated Text and Questions, with Explanations

Introduction

The following article appeared in a Hispanic newspaper in December 2016.

Cuba is a hot spot today. Personalities such as Pope Francis, Beyoncé, Rihanna, and Pelé have flocked to this lovely Caribbean island. Nevertheless, the visit of the U.S. president Barack Obama was one of the most momentous, perhaps because it had been 88 years since a United States Head of State traveled to the Caribbean country. But it is not just the visit itself, but also its significance: Obama in Cuba represented the possible end of the "Cold War."

For David Soler, deputy director of the Office of Cultural Heritage of Cienfuegos, a city with ample cultural tourism on offer, the country has increased the numbers of foreign tourists gradually, and "with the resumed diplomatic relations and commerce with the United States, we hope this will dramatically increase the presence of North American businesses and tourists. We are the closest nation they have after Mexico and Canada," he explains.

As this researcher of Cuban culture argues, all the United States citizens who will come to Cuba to invest or as tourists bring their culture and their forms of trade, their ways of portraying themselves, and even of eating; little by little the Cubans will try to adapt their services and businesses to this type of tourist/businessperson.

"Notice how Cuban culture can be influenced, how what happened with the arrival of the first North American cruise to Havana in early May this year might repeat: the visitors were received by voluptuous mixed-race women dressed in patriotic Cuban symbols. In this way they contributed to reinforcing stereotypes of our people: that this is just a land of mixed-race dancers, of rum and tobacco, when in reality it is much richer than that," grumbles Soler.

According to the deputy director, all these changes lead to a very dangerous cultural interchange, where those who arrive from abroad try to put in place their own ways and culture. "Cubans, interested in North American investment here, may make the mistake of responding only to northern interests and forgetting their own identity and culture," he notes.

Even though the larger wave has not yet arrived, the deputy director assures that it is expected soon. "The people here are preparing for it, studying more English, preparing their businesses for U.S. tourists, and studying northern customs, at times looking down on their own," this lover of Cuban culture confesses to us with a heavy heart.

All the changes that have occurred since December 17, 2014, when both presidents announced the reestablishment of diplomatic relations, point to an immediate future closely linked with tourism and services, obviously focused on the North American market. The Cubans, logically, see the "reconciliation" as a source of direct revenue.

The change can bring transformations beyond the political and greatly influence business between citizens in both nations. Jenny Lleonart Cruz, a young Cuban businesswoman and owner of a luxurious private inn in Cienfuegos, says that "something as simple as having PayPal or accepting credit card payments is something that is just around the corner. This would help a lot with receipt of and payment for goods and services. It would also make electronic commerce in Cuba possible. Even something as simple as going to Miami to buy supplies for my inn would be feasible."

Pedro Gómez, Havana resident, is more cautious and notes that Cubans cannot allow themselves to give in and fall again into a capitalist system. "That is what the Americans want. We cannot return to that because in that time there was much suffering because of economic inequality. So Cuba must be very careful with what approaches; the changes can be dangerous as well."

Definitely, the winds of change that blow in Cuba with the reestablishment of relations with the United States will change the lives of Cubans, but also of some other Latin American countries. Some of these will benefit or be harmed, such as the tourist attractions of Punta Cana and the Mayan Riviera, which see great competition with Cuba open to the North American market.

Meanwhile, Cubans go on with their day-to-day through the streets of the country and dream about miraculous changes. They have hope that in one form or another, this political bridge extending between both nations will not break again, and will function as a pathway to economic development for the inhabitants of this beautiful island which rises from the center of the Caribbean.

13. What is the point of the article?

   (A) The political bridge between Cuba and the United States is still fragile.

   (B) The economic changes may be difficult for Cuba during this transition.

   (C) The reestablishment of relations with the United States will change the lives of Cubans.

   (D) The end of the embargo and mandate signifies some economic changes for the island.

The question asks for the main point of the article. The first paragraph mentions President Barack Obama visiting Cuba and its significance: *Obama en Cuba representó el posible fin de la "Guerra Fría"*. Eliminate answers that don't match the prediction. Eliminate (A) because the passage does not state that politics between Cuba and the United States are still fragile. Eliminate (B) because the passage is mainly about the significance of these changes, and both positive and negative aspects are mentioned. Eliminate (C) because it contains extreme language (the lives of Cubans *will change)*. Keep (D) because the changes are likely to occur, but not definite. The correct answer is (D).

14. Why are Pope Francis, Beyoncé, Rihanna, and Pelé mentioned in the first paragraph?

   (A) They are ambassadors to Cuba for their respective countries.

   (B) They want to travel to Cuba, but it is not possible until the end of the "Cold War."

   (C) They were some of the first people to visit Cuba after the end of the United States mandate.

   (D) They are some of the artists who have given concerts in Cuba.

The question asks why Pope Francis, Beyoncé, Rihanna, and Pelé are mentioned in the first paragraph. They are examples of famous people who have visited Cuba since the embargo was lifted, as *Cuba es hoy el país de moda*.

Eliminate answers that do not match the prediction. Eliminate (A) since they are not ambassadors. Eliminate (B) since it is possible to travel to Cuba, hence their travel there. Keep (C), which matches the prediction. Eliminate (D) because the passage does not mention concerts in Cuba. The correct answer is (C).

15. In the second paragraph, David Soler hopes that
    (A) the Cuban economy suffers because of unequal resources
    (B) the change will be the end of the "Cold War"
    (C) the change will increase the presence of commerce and tourism
    (D) Cuban influence will change the world

The question asks what David Soler hopes in the second paragraph. In the second paragraph, Soler states that *con la reanudación de las relaciones diplomáticas y comerciales con EE.UU., se espera que aumente drásticamente la presencia de empresarios y turistas norteamericanos.* Eliminate answers that don't match the prediction. Eliminate (A) because the economy suffering is not Soler's hope. Eliminate (B) because the Cold War is not part of Soler's response. Keep (C), which matches the prediction. Eliminate (D) because he is not talking about Cuban influence. The correct answer is (C).

16. Why are PayPal and credit cards mentioned in paragraph 8?
    (A) They are elements of the northern economy that could benefit Cuban businesses.
    (B) They are indicators of electronic commerce in Cuba.
    (C) They are methods of payment in Cuban businesses.
    (D) They are dangers for Cuban businesses because they contain northern interests.

The question asks why PayPal and credit cards are mentioned in paragraph 8. Go to the eighth paragraph and re-read it. The passage states that PayPal and credit cards *beneficiaría mucho el cobrar o pagar bienes y servicios. También posibilitaría el comercio electrónico en Cuba.* Eliminate answer choices that don't match the prediction. Keep (A) since the text states this could benefit Cuban businesses. Eliminate (B) since this is a Words Out of Context trap answer. Eliminate (C) because they do not already exist for Cuban businesses, but rather are possibilities. Eliminate (D) because the passage never states that they are dangerous. The correct answer is (A).

17. What does Pedro Gómez think of the economic change in Cuba?
    (A) He thinks that capitalism will destroy the country.
    (B) He thinks that Cuba should be cautious because there is an inequality of resources.
    (C) He thinks it is invaluable in order for Cubans to learn English.
    (D) He thinks the future of the Cuban economy is tourism.

The question asks what Pedro Gómez thinks of the economic change in Cuba. Use the key words *Pedro Gómez* to locate the window for the answer. In the ninth paragraph, Gómez states *"Es lo que quieren los americanos. Para ahí no podemos volver porque en esa época se sufría mucho por la economía tan desigual que había…los cambios pueden ser peligrosos también."* Eliminate answers that don't match the prediction. Eliminate (A) because it contains extreme language (the change *will destroy* the country). Keep (B) because Gómez does believe that Cubans should be cautious and that there are dangers. Eliminate (C) since he never mentions Cubans learning English. Eliminate (D) because he never mentions tourism as the *future* of the economy. The correct answer is (B).

18. According the last paragraph, what do Cubans hope?

   (A) **They hope that the change in the relationship between the two counties may be beneficial.**

   (B) They hope that the presidents of the two countries can be friends.

   (C) They hope that the political bridge that was made between the two nations breaks again.

   (D) They hope that Cuba adapts to northern culture.

The question asks what Cubans hope for in the last paragraph. Go to the last paragraph and reread it. The last paragraph states that *los cubanos…sueñan con cambios milagrosos. Tienen la esperanza de que de una forma u otra, este puente político…no se rompa de nuevo.* Therefore, the answer must contain something to do with Cubans being hopeful about the future, but knowing this hope is fragile. Eliminate answers that don't match the prediction. Keep (A) because they do hope the change in the relationship between the countries will be beneficial. Eliminate (B) because the last paragraph never mentions the presidents. Eliminate (C) because they do not hope that the relationship will break down again. Eliminate (D) because the last paragraph never mentions northern culture. The correct answer is (A).

Selection 4: Translated Text and Questions, with Explanations

Introduction

The following pamphlet appeared in 2005 from Global Health Action.

Reducing the Inequalities of World Health

The contemporary world health crisis is a reflection of the growing inequalities that exist between countries and within them. Scientific and technological advances have contributed to an improvement in the health of some people. Nevertheless, there are ever more people living in poverty, and 30,000 children dying every day.

The Observatory of World Health 2005–2006 presents disparities in health and calls attention to the mechanisms that governments, international institutions, and civil society can apply to combat them.

Health workers, in particular, can play a vital role in transforming the rhetoric about universal health rights and global citizenship into a reality. Those who live in more prosperous areas of the world have a particular responsibility to push toward change.

The interdependence generated under globalization increases these ethical responsibilities.

The topics covered by the *Observatory* are diverse, but all of them highlight the economic, social, and political inequalities that destroy health.

This campaign document focuses on key areas where collective pressure should be exercised.

■ **Constructing a just world**
   The achievement of a just world in which poverty is eliminated and health is developed entails changing the way the global economy is run, and substantially increasing the transfer of resources from central countries to peripheral ones.

■ **Defending and extending the public sector**
   The repair and development of public health care systems are crucial to stop the threats of commercialization and to reduce widening social and health chasms. This report proposes a ten-point agenda of action.

■ **Migration, pharmaceuticals, and large corporations**
   The migration of health workers, the global norms of intellectual property that increase the prices of medicine, and the impact of multinational corporations on health stand out as three examples of the manner in which globalization and subordination of health rights to commercial objectives directly affect health and systems of health throughout the world.

- **Taking action in the face of climate change and militarization**
  The change in global climate and militarism are two of the most important causes, present and future, of the deterioration of health throughout the world. The current inability to confront said predicament in any significant way indicates an urgent need for better mobilization of civil society, popular organizations, and health workers to pull off more effective and just solutions.

- **Affirming leadership for global health in the World Health Organization**
  The world needs a multilateral health agency that is capable of protecting and promoting health, reducing inequalities, and securing full protection of universal rights with regard to basic needs and health. In order for this to succeed, the WHO requires more resources and to be more sensitive to the needs of the people, achieving higher administration standards.

Global Health Action demands that the *Observatory* recommend an agenda that is oriented toward the fight of health workers and campaign administrators.

19. What is the purpose of the pamphlet?

(A) **The pamphlet seeks to disseminate information about global health and some reasons for world changes.**

(B) The pamphlet seeks to demonstrate that Global Health Action wants to show the problems that cannot be solved.

(C) The pamphlet seeks to demonstrate that Global Health Action is the best-equipped organization to solve the mentioned conflicts.

(D) The pamphlet seeks to show that the world needs a multilateral health agency capable of protecting and promoting health.

The question asks for the purpose of the pamphlet. Since this is a general question, it should be done after all the specific questions. The passage states in the first paragraph that *La crisis contemporánea de la salud mundial es un reflejo de las crecientes inequidades que existen entre los países y dentro de ellos.* Therefore, the answer must contain something about inequality. Eliminate choices that don't match the prediction. Keep (A) since it matches the prediction. Eliminate (B) since the pamphlet never says the problems *cannot* be solved. Eliminate (C) because the pamphlet never says that Global Health Action is the *best-equipped* organization to handle problems. Eliminate (D) because, while the pamphlet does state that the world needs an agency like the one described in this choice, that is not its primary purpose. The correct answer is (A).

20. According to the author in the first paragraph, why is there a contemporary world health crisis?

(A) Agencies today are incapable of helping and promoting health with the few resources they have.

(B) Militarism has destroyed public health.

(C) Scientific and technological advances destroyed the order of the world.

(D) **There has been a growth of inequalities that exist between countries and within them.**

The question asks why there is a contemporary world health crisis. Find the first paragraph and reread it. The passage states that *La crisis contemporánea de la salud mundial es un reflejo de las crecientes inequidades que existen entre los países y dentro de ellos.* Eliminate choices that don't match the prediction. Eliminate (A) since it is insulting to the agencies that exist today. Eliminate (B) and (C), which are both Words Out of Context trap answers. Keep (D) because it is true that there has been growing inequality, and this is why the authors of the pamphlet are calling the situation a *crisis.* The correct answer is (D).

21. In the first paragraph, why did the author include "Nevertheless, there are ever more people living in poverty, and 30,000 children dying every day"?

(A) It is unbelievable that so many children die every day.

(B) There is a juxtaposition between those who have good public health and those who do not.

(C) It is necessary to have more resources and to be more sensitive to the needs of the people to save the children.

(D) The children suffer due to globalization and subordination of global health rights.

The question asks why the author includes the phrase *Sin embargo, cada vez más gente vive en la pobreza y 30.000 niños mueren cada día*. Reread the paragraph. It states *Los avances científicos y tecnológicos han aportado a un mejoramiento de la salud de algunos* and continues with the statement in the question. This creates a contrast between those who are served by the scientific advances and those who need help still. Eliminate choices that don't match the prediction. Eliminate (A) because while the statement is a sad reality, this does not answer the question. Keep (B) because *yuxtaposición* is a synonym for *contrast*, which matches the prediction. Eliminate (C) and (D), which are both Words Out of Context trap answers. The correct answer is (B).

22. How does the pamphlet refer to a "just world"?

(A) A just world can change the manner in which the global economy is run.

(B) A just world saves lives because it can protect people and promote health.

(C) It is a world in which everyone can live in harmony.

(D) It is a world that has low medicine prices for the rich.

The question asks how the pamphlet refers to a "just world." Use the key phrase *mundo justo* and read a window around the phrase. The passage states in the first bullet point that *La conquista de un mundo justo donde se elimine la pobreza y desarrolle la salud implica cambiar la manera en que la economía global es manejada, e incrementar sustancialmente la transferencia de recursos de los países centrales hacia los países periféricos*. Eliminate choices that don't match the prediction. Keep (A), which is a paraphrase of the words in the first part of the sentence. Eliminate (B) because the passage never says it saves lives. Eliminate (C) since it does not match the text. Eliminate (D) since the window never mentions *low medicine prices*. The correct answer is (A).

23. What does the public sector have to do with public health?

(A) It can obtain important resources for children.

(B) It is one of the present and future causes of the deterioration of health throughout the world.

(C) It maintains and grows militarism.

(D) It can stop the threats of commercialization.

The question asks what the public sector has to do with public health. Look for the key phrase *sector público* to find the window within the passage. The passage states in the second bullet point that *La reparación y desarrollo de los sistemas de atención en salud pública son cruciales para detener las amenazas de la mercantilización y reducir los crecientes abismos sociales y de salud*. Eliminate choices that don't match the prediction. Eliminate (A) since the window never mentions *children*. Eliminate (B), which is a Words Out of Context trap answer. Eliminate (C) because *militarism* is outside the window. Keep (D), which matches the text. The correct answer is (D).

24. Why does the pamphlet mention militarism?

(A) It is mentioned to reduce inequalities between countries.

(B) It is one of the most important causes of global health deterioration.

(C) Militaries are mentioned as popular health organizations.

(D) Militarism provides employment to many workers.

The question asks why the pamphlet mentions militarism. Use the key word *militarismo* to find the window within the passage. In the fourth bullet point, the passage states that *El cambio climático global y el militarismo son dos de las más importantes causas presentes y futuras de deterioro de la salud a través del mundo*. Eliminate choices that don't match the prediction. Eliminate (A), which focuses on the wrong window of the passage. Keep (B), which is a paraphrase of the text. Eliminate (C) because militarism is a problem, not a health organization. Eliminate (D) because the passage never mentions *employment*. The correct answer is (B).

25. All of the following are goals of Global Health Action EXCEPT:

(A) repairing and developing systems of public health

(B) reducing economic inequalities

(C) securing full protection of universal rights

(D) raising the prices of medicines

The question asks which are goals of Global Health Action: the word SALVO means the correct answer will be the choice that is NOT a goal. Look for the goals that are mentioned in the passage. Eliminate (A), (B), and (C) because Global Health Action is committed to these goals: *proteger y promover la salud, reducir las desigualdades y asegurar la vigencia plena de los derechos universales frente a las necesidades básicas y de salud*. It does not want to raise prices of medicine, so the correct answer is (D).

Selection 5: Translated Text and Questions, with Explanations

Introduction

The following prologue appeared in the autobiography of Frida Kahlo, a Mexican artist of the 20th century.

My body is a marasmus. And I can't escape it anymore. As the animal feels its death, I feel mine settling in my life, and so strong that it takes away all possibility of fighting. They don't believe me; they've seen me fight so much! And I no longer dare to believe that I could be wrong; those lightning bolts are becoming uncommon.

My body is going to leave me, I, who have always been its prey. Rebellious prey, but prey. I know that we are going to mutually annihilate each other, and so the fight will not have left any victor. A vain and permanent illusion to believe that thought, remaining intact, can be separated from that other material made of flesh.

Irony of luck: I would like to still have the ability to debate myself, to kick that smell of ether, my smell of alcohol, all those medicines, inert particles that pile up in their boxes—oh! They are aseptic even in their graphics and for what?—to my thoughts in disorder, to the order that they strive to impose on this room. On ashtrays. On the stars.

The nights are long. Every minute scares me, and everything hurts, everything. And the others are concerned and I would have liked to save them. But what can one do to save others when she has been able to do nothing to save herself? Dawn is always too far. I do not know anymore whether I desire it or whether what I want is to sink deeper into the night. Yes, it may be better to be done.

Life was cruel in becoming so fierce with me. It should have dealt its cards better. I had a terrible game. A black tarot on the body.

Life is cruel for having invented memory. Like the old people who recover the nuances of their oldest memories, on the verge of death my memory gravitates around the sun, and is illuminated. Everything is present, nothing has been lost. As if a hidden force that drives you to keep stirring yourself up: before the evidence that there is no more future, the past is amplified, its roots are strengthened; everything in me is rhizosphere; the colors crystallize on each stratum; the slightest image tends to its absolute; the heart beats in crescendo.

But to paint, to paint all that is today out of my reach.

¡Oh! ¡Doña Magdalena Carmen Frida Kahlo de Rivera, Your Majesty La Cotija, forty-seven years of this Mexican midsummer, spent down to the fabric, overwhelming pain like never before, now you are in the irreparable!

¡Old Mictlantecuhtli, god, free me!

26. What is the main purpose of the passage?
    (A) Kahlo laments the failures in her life.
    (B) Kahlo understands more profoundly the pain that she paints in her works.
    (C) Kahlo describes some of her works of art.
    (D) Kahlo describes her emotional and physical states toward the end of her life.

The question asks for the main purpose of the passage. Kahlo describes the pain she feels physically, her exhaustion, and her fears as death becomes more real through sentences such as *Mi cuerpo es un marasmo, Mi cuerpo va a dejarme,* and *La vida fue cruel al encarnizarse tanto conmigo.* She does not lament the failures in her life, so eliminate (A). While she does understand pain, she does not state that she has a new understanding of it, so eliminate (B) as well. She never describes works of art, so eliminate (C). Keep (D) because it matches the prediction. The correct answer is (D).

27. What does the phrase *rebellious prey, but prey* mean in the second paragraph?
    (A) That Kahlo has fought for her life, but no longer can
    (B) That Kahlo is organizing a rebellion in Mexico
    (C) That something is hunting Kahlo in order to eat her
    (D) That Kahlo is removed from reality

The question asks what the phrase *rebellious prey, but prey* means. Use the context to understand the quotation fully. Kahlo uses the analogy of being prey to describe how she cannot fight any longer against the inevitable death that she feels is looming, as shown by the sentence *Sé que nos vamos a aniquilar mutuamente, y así la lucha no habría dejado ningún vencedor.* This matches (A), so keep it. Eliminate (B) because the passage never states she is organizing a rebellion in Mexico. Eliminate (C) because it is too literal. Eliminate (D) because there is no evidence that she is out of touch with reality. The correct answer is (A).

28. The details in the fourth paragraph are mentioned in order to
    (A) illustrate that Kahlo is afraid of the dark
    (B) show the physical and emotional pain that Kahlo feels
    (C) describe one of Kahlo's most profound works
    (D) demonstrate that Kahlo cannot escape her fantasies

The question asks why the details in the fourth paragraph are mentioned. The fourth paragraph contains details of how she copes with her own thoughts and insecurities in the night, when she has seemingly endless time to reflect. Eliminate (A), that she is afraid of the dark, since while it can be inferred that she is afraid by looking at this section of the passage: *Las noches son largas. Cada minuto me asusta, y todo me duele, todo,* it does not actually say she is afraid of the dark. Keep (B) because it is consistent with the multiple ways in which Kahlo describes her pain and her thoughts. Eliminate (C) because it never mentions her artwork. Eliminate (D) because she does not mention her fantasies here. The correct answer is (B).

29. Why does she say, "But to paint, to paint all that is today out of my reach"?
    (A) She doesn't know where her pencils or brushes are.
    (B) Now she does not like to paint.
    (C) She does not have the physical ability to paint anymore.
    (D) She has to change her profession.

The question asks why painting seems out of reach to Kahlo. The passage has just given more detail about her physical pain and inability to function as she once did, shown by sentences such as *ante la evidencia de que no hay más futuro* and, in the paragraph that follows, *cuarenta y siete años de este pleno verano mexicano, gastado hasta la urdimbre, el dolor abrumador como nunca, ahora estás en lo irreparable,* so an answer consistent with this will be correct. Eliminate (A) because she has not lost her art utensils. Eliminate (B) because it never says she has lost interest in painting. Keep (C) because it matches the prediction. Eliminate (D) because there is no mention of her wanting or having to change professions. The correct answer is (C).

30. What does the last sentence mean?
    (A) That Frida would like to be free from her situation
    (B) That Frida is incarcerated
    (C) That Frida would like to die
    (D) That Frida does not know where she is

The question asks for the meaning of the last sentence. The last sentence invokes the god *Viejo Mictlantecuhtli* to free her. While it is unclear what she wants to be freed of, eliminate (B) since she is not in prison. Eliminate (C) because it is not clear that she wants to die to escape her situation, but rather that she feels death nearing, as mentioned with the sentence *Como el animal siente su muerte, yo siento la mía instalarse en mi vida* in the beginning of the passage. Eliminate (D) because she knows where she is. The correct answer is (A).

Interpretive Communication: Print and Audio Texts (Combined) (Page 20)

Selection 1: Translated Texts and Questions, with Explanations

Source 1

Introduction: In Panama, and in many Latin American countries, many people wear uniforms to work or to school. Today, however, with economic globalization, there is a dialogue among generations about whether uniforms are necessary. This article appeared in the Panamanian press in February 2012.

The Use of Uniforms: A Very Latino Habit

Here in Panama, uniforms are very common. They are used from the smallest businesses to the presidential cabinet of the Republic. But where did this success of uniforms in Panama come from? Two important movements in 20th-century history contributed to the change in the perception of uniforms. The first of these was the massive integration of women in the workforce. The second cause, and the more crucial, was the start of the Space Age.

Some people may believe that these new tendencies were inspired by technology and science fiction, and thus influenced people's spirits and way of dressing. Everywhere people wanted to make themselves uniform and part of this "futuristic revolution."

The airlines were the first to use this new style. They changed from the simple, naval-type vestments to designer uniforms. Soon, they were adapted by companies around the world for their employees. In many places, this was a passing style, but not in Panama. The business of uniforms became a very lucrative trade.

Giving up uniforms does not mean that employees will be badly dressed or in poor taste. In Panama, if the people do not have a "dress code," they will automatically choose fresh and light garments, ideal for bearing the tropical heat. However, these are not adequate for serious or professional environments. Many people who use uniforms think it is practical and it actually simplifies their process of preparing for work. However, others do not like the idea of having to use uniforms.

Nowadays, simple shirts with logos are the most popular form of uniforms in Panama. They represent the simplest and most casual state of the uniform. Many businesses, especially banks and state institutions, still use multi-piece formal uniforms. Nevertheless, it is a tendency that is decreasing now that the sewing business, which in its time was a prosperous sector, is also declining.

Source 2

Introduction: This recording is about uniforms in the workplace or at school. The following interviewees share their opinions about uniforms. The recording lasts approximately three minutes.

(NARRATOR) Source: the opinions of people of various ages on the subject of uniforms for work or school.

María Carolina, Panamanian, upon arrival in the United States to pursue higher education.

(PERSON 1) Here, the entire world can wear what they want to work! Almost no one, with the exception of police, firefighters, and military officials, has to wear uniforms to go to work or school. I love their freedom of expression!

(NARRATOR) Roberto Sánchez, 62 years old, owner and designer at a uniform factory in Panama.

(PERSON 2) For me it was the most natural thing, the world of suits, ties, fabrics, buttons, zippers, threads, and insignias. Uniforms create a sense of belonging. They improve work conditions, given that there is no time lost in choosing what to wear. Furthermore, people can invest their salaries in more important things than buying clothes for work.

(NARRATOR)   Eduardo is 35 years old, and a producer for a TV channel.

(PERSON 3)   I have never understood the reason for a person with a creative job to have to wear a uniform. It pigeonholes you in a style and doesn't permit you to express your true individuality.

(NARRATOR)   Rebecca de Suiza, from the United States, is an English professor at the National University of Panama.

(PERSON 4)   In my country, uniforms are situation-specific to some professions, such as doctors, nurses, or military members. They also have some ceremonial uses. It is interesting to see that, here in Panama, they are for everyone. To me it seems professional.

(NARRATOR)   Liz, a legal assistant, who works in a legal firm.

(PERSON 5)   For many people, the use of uniforms is difficult. For those with specific physical conditions such as being overweight, it is difficult to wear uniforms. However, even with a normal physique, there are other reasons for wearing uniforms: tattoos.

Many people do not feel comfortable addressing people with tattoos or have prejudices, especially in Latin America. The sleeves of my work blouses are a bit short, so I try to adjust their fit a bit so that my tattoos are not seen.

31. What event contributed to the change in the perception of uniforms in the 20th century?

   (A) Serious and professional atmospheres demanded uniforms.
   (B) People liked science fiction and were inspired by the genre's stories.
   (C) **There has been an integration of women into the workforce.**
   (D) Many businesses, especially banks and state institutions, used multi-piece uniforms.

The question asks which event contributed to the change in the perception of uniforms in the 20th century. Use the key word *percepción* to find the window in the passage. In the first paragraph, the passage states *Dos hechos importantes de la historia del siglo XX contribuyeron a cambiar la percepción de los uniformes. El primero de ellos fue la integración masiva de mujeres en la fuerza laboral. El segundo hecho, y el más decisivo, fue el comienzo de la Era Espacial.* Eliminate choices that don't match the prediction. Eliminate (A) and (B), which do not match the prediction. Keep (C), which does match the prediction. Eliminate (D), which utilizes the wrong window. The correct answer is (C).

32. Generally, who uses uniforms in the United States?

   (A) TV producers
   (B) University professors
   (C) **Firefighters and members of the military**
   (D) Legal assistants

The question asks who generally uses uniforms in the United States. Use the key word *EE.UU.* to find the window in the passage and to listen for in the recording. Rebecca de Suiza, from the United States, answers this question when she says that uniforms are for situation-specific professions such as doctors, nurses, or military members. María Carolina, from Panama, remarks upon arriving in the United States that *almost no one, with the exception of police, firefighters, and military officials, has to wear uniforms.* Eliminate the choices that don't match these predictions: (A), (B), and (D) don't match. Since María Carolina mentions firefighters and the military, and Rebecca de Suiza mentions military members as well, (C) is correct.

33. The phrase "futurist revolution" is used to

    (A) refer to the social revolution inspired by science fiction

    (B) talk about the "dress code" that exists in all modes of work

    (C) illustrate the belief that some people wore uniforms to conform

    (D) describe the integration of women into the workforce

The question asks why the phrase "futurist revolution" is used. Use the key phrase *"revolución futurista"* to find the window in the passage. In the second paragraph, the passage states *En todos lados las personas querían uniformarse y ser parte de esta gran "revolución futurista"*. Eliminate choices that don't match the prediction. Eliminate (A), which is a Words Out of Context trap answer; there is no actual revolution. Eliminate (B), which is an Out of the Window trap answer. Keep (C), which matches the passage. Eliminate (D), which is an Out of the Window trap answer. The correct answer is (C).

34. Why is the climate mentioned in the discussion of uniforms?

    (A) It shows that the tropical climate lends itself to light fabrics, but these are not sufficiently professional for serious environments.

    (B) It shows that light fabrics are ideal for the professional environment.

    (C) It shows that the dress code depends on the environment.

    (D) It shows that in Panama, everyone wants to dress in light fabrics to tolerate the heat.

The question asks why the climate is mentioned in the discussion of uniforms. Use the key words *el clima* to find the window in the passage. The fourth paragraph mentions *la gente… automáticamente escogerá prendas frescas y ligeras, ideales para soportar el calor tropical,* which means that light fabrics lend themselves to the tropical climate in Panama, so keep (A). Eliminate (B), which is a Words Out of Context trap answer. Eliminate (C) because it is not mentioned in the passage. Eliminate (D) since it is too extreme in its language. The correct answer is (A).

35. What is Eduardo's tone?

    (A) Perplexed

    (B) Negative

    (C) Hateful

    (D) Ecstatic

The question asks about Eduardo's tone. Remember, this is a question that should be previewed for the key phrase *el tono de Eduardo* before the audio comes on. Eduardo is not in favor of uniforms for his work as a television director, as he believes it stifles creativity. Eliminate (A) and (D) since they are not negative words. Eliminate (C) since it is extreme. The correct answer is (B).

36. According to the audio source, what is the opinion of the younger interviewees?

    (A) They hate the idea of uniforms.

    (B) It depends on the individual's profession.

    (C) Only the most conservative people like it.

    (D) They are indifferent because it is part of the culture.

The question asks about the opinion of the younger interviewees, according to the audio source. Remember, this is a question that should be previewed for key words before the audio comes on. The different answers depend on each person's profession. Eliminate (A) since only one or two of the interviewees dislike uniforms. Keep (B) since it matches the prediction. Eliminate (C) since neither the passage nor the interview ever mentions conservative viewpoints. Eliminate (D) because the interviewees do have opinions about the topic. The correct answer is (B).

37. All are reasons that the interviewees give for wearing uniforms EXCEPT:

    (A) they create a sense of belonging

    (B) they cover things such as tattoos

    (C) one's salary can be used on more important things than on work clothes

    (D) they do not allow one to express one's individuality

The question asks for reasons for wearing uniforms and ends in the word EXCEPT. Since the question asks for an exception, find reasons that do exist in the recording and in the passage. Eliminate (A) because Roberto states that uniforms can create a sense of belonging. Eliminate (B) because Liz appreciates that she can cover up tattoos at her workplace with a uniform. Eliminate (C) because Roberto also states that he can use his salary on more important things than work clothes. Keep (D) because while Eduardo does mention that uniforms do not allow him to express his creativity, this is not a reason to wear uniforms but an argument against them. The correct answer is (D).

38. Which of the people interviewed are in favor of uniforms?

    (A) Eduardo and Roberto Sánchez

    (B) Liz and Eduardo

    (C) Liz and Roberto Sánchez

    (D) Roberto Sánchez and María Carolina

The question asks which of the people are in favor of uniforms. Remember, this is a question that should be previewed for key words before the audio comes on. Use process of elimination on this question. Eliminate (A) and (B) because Eduardo is not in favor of uniforms. Notice that Roberto Sánchez is in both (C) and (D). Keep (C) and eliminate (D) because Liz is in favor of uniforms, despite having pointed out some difficulties with them initially, while María Carolina neither supports nor rejects them. The correct answer is (C).

39. Which of the following statements best summarizes this article?

    (A) Many work uniforms are in bad taste.

    (B) The future of uniforms is doomed because sewing businesses are dwindling.

    (C) Many people have differing opinions about the use of uniforms at work.

    (D) There were many changes in the economy during the 20th century that contributed to the use of uniforms.

The question asks which of the choices best summarizes the article. Since this is a general question, it should be done after all the specific questions. From both the text and audio sources, there are many varying opinions surrounding uniforms for work or school, so make sure you focus on the opinions in the text. Eliminate (A), which is a Words Out of Context trap answer, as the sentence *Pero a otras no les gusta la idea de tener que usar uniformes* only states that some do NOT like uniforms. Eliminate (B), which predicts the future and uses extreme language when stating that uniforms are *doomed*. Keep (C), which matches the prediction. Eliminate (D) since it is a detail and not the main point. The correct answer is (C).

Selection 2: Translated Texts and Questions, with Explanations

Source 1

Introduction

This information appeared on the website GlobalChange.org, about school dropout amongst youths in Latin America. The statistics are from August 2013.

Why do young Latin Americans abandon secondary school?

With one out of every two students not finishing secondary school, school dropout affects young people in all sectors of society. Nevertheless, the following groups demonstrate disproportionately elevated dropout rates.

There are many factors that influence dropping out of school. Historically, access problems have contributed to high dropout rates in Latin America. In the last decades, however, Latin American countries have achieved notable advances in access to secondary education.

Although problems related to the economy and access continue to pose obstacles for education in certain places, they do not illustrate the complete story of the present situation. Various factors influence school dropout rates, and the reasons for which young people leave their studies can be surprising. According to the data from home surveys in 8 countries, the majority of students between 13 and 15 years old who do not go to school identify a lack of interest—above economic, access, or familial problems—as the principal reason for dropping out of school.

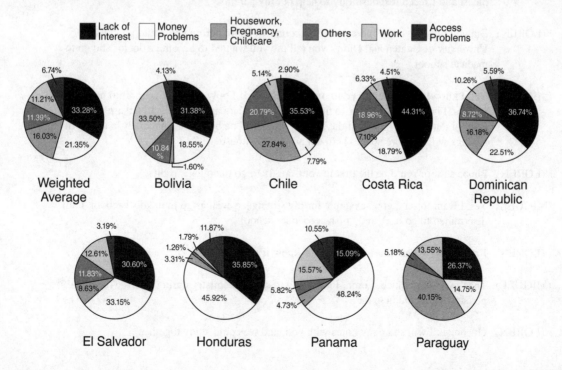

Source 2

Introduction: This recording is about dropping out of school. It is a conversation between two friends, Miguel and Loren, who live in Zacapa, Guatemala. The recording lasts approximately three minutes.

(MIGUEL)   Hi Loren!

(LOREN)   Hi Miguel! How are you?

(MIGUEL)   Well, I've been all right, though a bit preoccupied. And you?

(LOREN)   I'm well, thanks. What's wrong?

(MIGUEL)   I'm thinking about dropping out of school, at least for a bit. I'm not sure what to do.

(LOREN)   Oh, no! But you're such a good student!

(MIGUEL)   Thank you. I don't really want to.

(LOREN)   Why are you thinking of abandoning your studies, Miguel?

(MIGUEL)   Well, my mother needs help caring for my little brother and two sisters, and my father needs help in his grocery store. I'm thinking about taking a year off to work for him and help out my mom at home to take care of my siblings.

(LOREN)   How old are your siblings?

(MIGUEL)   María is 8 years old and Joaquín is 12. Carolina, my youngest sister, is 6 years old.

(LOREN)   And they are still in school?

(MIGUEL)   Yes…and I don't want them to drop out of school. It's difficult for me because I am the oldest and I feel a responsibility to help out my parents.

(LOREN)   But you only have one more year of secondary school before you could go to the University of Guatemala! Didn't you tell me you wanted to become a doctor and go to medical school?

(MIGUEL)   Yes, I know! I still want to go to medical school. If I only take one year off to help my parents, I hope I can go back to finish high school and apply for a scholarship next year. In that time, I hope that the grocery store will be better off financially, and that my siblings will be more able to help out around the house.

(LOREN)   I hope so too. You'd be the first in your family to go to college, right?

(MIGUEL)   Yes. I want to set a good example for my siblings as well as go to medical school. I am determined to go back and finish secondary school.

(LOREN)   I'm so glad to hear that! Please let me know if I can help.

(MIGUEL)   Thank you very much, Loren. I am going to study chemistry during my free time, and perhaps you could help me.

(LOREN)   Of course. I will share my notes with you, and we could study together.

(MIGUEL)   That sounds great.

(LOREN)   Sounds good to me too. You are going to complete your studies!

(MIGUEL)   Well, we should go to class. See you later!

(LOREN)   Goodbye!

40. What is the purpose of the article and statistics?

(A) Students between 13 and 15 years of age need to work and help out their families.

(B) There are many reasons for dropping out of school, and the greatest reason reported is lack of interest.

(C) It is not known why there is a lack of interest in students between 13 and 15 years of age.

(D) Economic and access problems still continue to pose obstacles for young people.

The question asks about the purpose of the article and statistics. Since this is a general question, it should be done after all the specific questions. At the end of the passage it states *Varios factores influyen en el abandono escolar y las razones por las que los jóvenes dejan los estudios pueden sorprender. Según datos de encuestas de hogares de 8 países, la mayoría de los estudiantes entre 13 y 15 años que no van a la escuela identifican la falta de interés—por encima de los problemas económicos, de acceso o familiares—como la razón principal de abandono escolar.* Eliminate (A) and (D) because while true, they are details, not the main point. Keep (B), as it matches the text. Eliminate (C) because neither the text nor the audio source focus on *why* the study found what it found. The correct answer is (B).

41. Historically, what are the problems cited for lack of attendance?

(A) Access problems

(B) Work

(C) Lack of interest

(D) Money problems

The question asks *historically* which problems are cited for lack of attendance. Go back to the text and look for the key word *históricamente*. In the second paragraph, the passage states that *Históricamente, problemas de acceso han propiciado altas tasas de deserción escolar en América Latina.* This supports (A). Eliminate (B), (C), and (D) because these are current problems that are cited in the last paragraph and do not answer the question asked. The correct answer is (A).

42. All the following are reasons for abandoning secondary school EXCEPT:

(A) access problems

(B) lack of interest

(C) pregnancy and caring for children

(D) pressure from parents

The question asks which of the choices are reasons for abandoning secondary school and then uses the word EXCEPT. Since the question asks for an exception, find all the reasons that do exist. Eliminate (A), (B), and (C) since these are categories in the statistics as shown by the labels *Falta De Interés, Problemas de Accesso,* and *Labores de Casa, Embarazo, Cuidado de Niños. Pressure from parents* is never mentioned. The correct answer is (D).

43. The greatest reasons for lack of attendance in Bolivia are
    (A) lack of interest and household chores
    (B) lack of interest and money problems
    (C) lack of interest and work
    (D) lack of interest and access problems

The question asks for the greatest reasons for lack of attendance in Bolivia. The greatest reasons for leaving school in Bolivia are lack of interest and the need to find work, so keep (C). Eliminate (A), which describes Chile instead of Bolivia. Eliminate (B), which describes the weighted average across all countries. Eliminate (D) since *access problems* is a less commonly reported reason for leaving school in Bolivia. The correct answer is (C).

44. It can be inferred that
    (A) all young people in Latin America lack interest in their studies
    (B) the reasons for leaving school vary by country
    (C) access problems belong to the past
    (D) economic and access problems continue to be major obstacles in all places

The question asks what can be inferred from the passage. Since this is a general question, it should be done after all the specific questions. Eliminate (A) since it is extreme and offensive to say that *todos los jóvenes* lack interest in school. Keep (B) since it is consistent with the statistics shown. Eliminate (C) because *los problemas de acceso* are still a present problem. Eliminate (D) since it is also extreme to say *en todas partes*. The correct answer is (B).

45. What is Miguel's main dilemma?
    (A) Miguel lacks interest in his secondary school studies.
    (B) He needs to help his parents.
    (C) He needs to apply for a scholarship to attend the university.
    (D) He needs to find work.

The question asks about Miguel's main dilemma. Since this is a general question, it should be done after all the specific questions. Miguel needs to help his parents by working in his father's grocery store and helping out at home. He is going to help his mother take care of his younger sisters and brother. He does say that he will apply for a scholarship to attend the university, but that is not Miguel's main concern, nor will he do so during his year off, so eliminate (C). Eliminate (A) since he does not lack interest in his studies. Keep (B) since it is consistent with the audio source. Eliminate (D) since he will be working for his father at the grocery store, so he doesn't need to find work. The correct answer is (B).

46. Who are María, Joaquín, and Carolina?
    (A) They are friends of Miguel and Loren.
    (B) They are Loren's younger siblings.
    (C) They are Miguel's older siblings.
    (D) They are Miguel's younger siblings.

The question asks who María, Joaquín, and Carolina are. Use the key words *María, Joaquín,* and *Carolina* to know which part of the dialogue to listen for. María, Joaquín, and Carolina are Miguel's younger siblings. The correct answer is (D).

47. What is Miguel going to do during his year off?
    (A) He is going to take care of his children and work for his father.
    (B) He is going to attend the University of Guatemala and medical school after that.
    (C) **He is going to work with his father while caring for his siblings with his mother.**
    (D) He is going to spend some time working and traveling with his father.

The question asks what Miguel is going to do during his year off. Miguel is going to help his father in the grocery store and care for his younger siblings with his mother. His younger siblings are not his children, so eliminate (A). He needs to finish secondary school before he can attend the University of Guatemala, so eliminate (B). Keep (C) since it matches the audio. Eliminate (D) because Miguel never mentions traveling with his father. The correct answer is (C).

Interpretive Communication: Audio Texts (Page 27)

Selection 3: Translated Text and Questions, with Explanations

Introduction

The following recording was part of a broadcast of "World of Sports," a radio program dedicated to sports from all parts of the world.

(NARRATOR) The Argentine Alfonso García wins the golf championship in Scotland.

(WOMAN) The tumultuous and cold weather here in St. Andrew's, Scotland, yesterday was the catalyst for some extraordinarily high scores in the international golf championship, which was won by the young Argentinian Alfonso García. García, who is only twenty-two years old, is the first Argentinian to win this championship at St. Andrew's, the most historic and perhaps the most prestigious golf course in the world. The efforts of the golfers were complicated throughout the three-day tournament by an implacable wind and intermittent rain squalls.

"I have never experienced such a violent and tempestuous wind," the excited golfer said yesterday. And when he was asked how the weather affected his game, the young Argentinian replied, "At the beginning, I didn't know how to adapt well to the wind and calculate it into each shot. Later, the rain squalls bothered me quite a bit. The first day when I scored a 75, I was feeling very frustrated. But during the second day, when I realized that the other players were also struggling, it was much easier for me to concentrate. I began to think I might actually be able to win this tournament."

García, who comes from a family of athletes, is the first of his family to play golf at the professional level. His father was a tennis champion in the seventies, and his younger sister, Patricia, is also a tennis player. Alfonso spends the majority of his time traveling on the PGA tour, but when he is not traveling, he lives with his parents in Buenos Aires. They say that he acquired his passion for golf from his maternal grandfather, who used to take him out on the golf course regularly.

Certainly, Alfonso García is a new star in the sport of golf.

48. What is the golf course like in St. Andrews, Scotland?
    (A) New and modern
    (B) Picturesque
    (C) Historic and prestigious
    (D) Innovative

The question asks what the golf course in St. Andrews, Scotland, is like. The audio states that the golf course is said to be historic and prestigious, so keep (C). Eliminate (A) because new and modern is the opposite of historic. Eliminate (B) because it does not mean the same as historic and prestigious. Eliminate (D) since the audio never mentions *innovative*. The correct answer is (C).

49. What was the weather like during the tournament?
    (A) The weather was nice.
    (B) The weather was hot.
    (C) It was snowing.
    (D) The weather was tempestuous.

The question asks what the weather was like during the tournament. The audio states that the weather was tempestuous, with wind and rain squalls. Eliminate (A) since the weather was not nice the whole time. Eliminate (B) and (C) since it never states that the weather was hot or that it snowed. Keep (D) since there was a big storm during the beginning of the tournament. The correct answer is (D).

50. How did Alfonso García initially react to the variable weather in Scotland?
    (A) He felt frustrated.
    (B) He felt at ease.
    (C) He felt nostalgic.
    (D) He felt sad.

The question asks how Alfonso García reacted to the variable weather in Scotland. Alfonso felt frustrated initially, but then he realized that other players were experiencing similar challenges and was able to regain his focus. The correct answer is (A).

51. How did Alfonso García become interested in golf?
    (A) He played golf with his father.
    (B) He accompanied his grandfather to the golf course.
    (C) He played golf with his sister.
    (D) He played golf with his grandmother.

The question asks how Alfonso García became interested in golf. The audio states that Alfonso accompanied his maternal grandfather to the golf course frequently. Eliminate (A) and (C) since his father and sister are mentioned, but not in the context of golf. Keep (B), which matches the prediction. Eliminate (D) because the audio never mentions his grandmother. The correct answer is (B).

52. How does Alfonso spend the majority of his time?

(A) Relaxing with his parents in Buenos Aires

(B) Traveling on the PGA Tour

(C) Playing tennis with his little sister, Patricia

(D) Spending time with his maternal grandfather

The question asks how Alfonso spends the majority of his time. The audio states that Alfonso spends the majority of his time touring with the PGA. Eliminate (A) since he spends his downtime with his parents in Buenos Aires, but the recording specifically states that the majority of his time goes to touring. Keep (B) since it is consistent with the audio. Eliminate (C) because the recording never mentions playing tennis with his sister. Eliminate (D) because the recording mentions his grandfather who taught him the love of golf, but not in this context. The correct answer is (B).

Selection 4: Translated Text and Questions, with Explanations

Introduction

This recording is about feminism in Spain. The recording is part of a conference about feminism in Spain.

Feminism in Spain is a strong force. For some it is a political battle. For others it is an economic matter. Yet others search for a theoretical liberation, including a sexual liberation. One thing is certain: it is a movement that continues growing with increasing force. What interests us here is the situation in Spain today. We will examine how the peninsular movement sprang out of Spanish culture and what directions it is likely to take. It is very important that we look at this brand of feminism as a product of Spanish culture. Of course, there is a universal movement going on outside of Spain. However, there are some specific characteristics of the movement in Spain that play a key role in its development there. It will help us to examine a few facets of Spanish culture and later turn our attention to the current state of feminism in Spain today.

One characteristic well-rooted in Spanish culture, and perhaps the most opposed to feminism, is "machismo." Historically, in Spanish society, it is the man who makes decisions. It seems that the informal social laws are written by men to favor men. The concepts of honor and dignity are also very important. What comes out of all of this, then, is the idea of the strong and dignified man, who protects and assures the future of the woman. Similarly, the concept of "marianismo" establishes the desired qualities in the ideal Spanish woman. Also influenced by the ideas of honor and dignity, "marianismo" defines the domain of the woman in the home. Subordinated by the man, the woman personifies the qualities of obedience and self-sacrifice. Almost as if she were to exist through her association with the man, the woman is seen as fulfilled by her union in marriage to the man. After leaving the home of her father, the woman moves on to the home of her husband. Historically, in this culture there was no room for feminist independence.

The reverberations of these basic concepts from Spanish culture provide the foundation for the feminist movement today. According to its own ideology, the feminist movement looks for an individual identity for the woman. Feminists want to reject the traditional concepts of "machismo" and "marianismo." The difficult part, however, is penetrating deeply into a culture that has a long history with these cultural values. The more rooted a culture is in "machismo," the more difficult the struggle for feminism will be.

Now, let us turn our attention to the contemporary situation in Spain today. The reign of Franco marked a period of rigid censorship. This oppressive regime reinforced the traditional values of Spanish culture. It was almost as if it had resuscitated the concepts of "machismo" and "marianismo" in the society of the forties. Or perhaps they never died. In any case, there is most decidedly an important cultural foundation. What comes out of the Franco period are the reverberations of thought that have carried over from the Middle Ages. For that reason, the feminist movement was faced with a monumental obstacle. The feminists in Spain were looking for a way to express and communicate their protest. There are, among the feminist movement in Spain, those who want greater social or political freedom, while others seek the complete elimination of traditional roles for women. There are militant groups and intellectual groups. Thus, the feminist movement in Spain is diverse and growing.

How can we evaluate such a movement? Surely, the extremes and excesses of a "machista" society should be eliminated. It is also essential that the independent identity of the woman be recognized. But with a radical approach, are we also prepared to lose all of the characteristics of femininity? It would seem that there are some traditional feminine roles worth maintaining, such as the nurturing mother figure, the sensible figure, etc. A search for complete equality, without limits or distinctions, surely would be the beginning of a great loss: the loss of the distinct feminine. The role of women in the family, for example, shouldn't be compromised. Furthermore, the characteristics typically considered feminine, such as sensitivity and capacity for emotion, have value in and of themselves. It is important, of course, that in this search for feminine recognition, we don't lose the meaning of femininity. What we need now is to bring about knowledge of feminine reality in a society previously steeped in masculine reality.

53. How do some interpret the feminist movement in Spain?

   (A) As a political battle

   (B) As an artistic issue

   (C) As a competition between equals

   (D) As a beauty pageant

The question asks how some interpret the feminist movement in Spain. It is most closely related to politics, so keep (A). Eliminate (B), (C), and (D) since the audio never mentions artistic issues, competition between equals, or beauty pageants regarding feminine identity, respectively. The correct answer is (A).

54. Which characteristic of Spanish culture can be considered opposite to the ideals of the feminist movement?

   (A) *Marianismo*

   (B) Honor

   (C) Dignity

   (D) *Machismo*

The question asks which characteristic of Spanish culture can be considered opposite to the ideals of the feminist movement. Honor and dignity would not go against feminist ideals, so (B) and (C) should be eliminated immediately. That leaves *marianismo* and *machismo*. If you understood what was said about *marianismo*, you know that *marianismo* defines the role of women in the home and idealizes the qualities of obedience and sacrifice. While these ideals do not seem to support the feminist movement, they are minor in comparison with the ideals that go along with *machismo*. In reality, both terms refer to cultural attitudes that clash with the modern feminist movement. However, the more obvious choice is *machismo*, which the selection, in fact, describes as *perhaps the most opposed to feminism*. The correct answer is (D).

55. According to the selection, what is the ideological objective of the feminist movement?

   (A) The victory of woman over man

   (B) The acceptance of *marianismo* in all parts of the world

   (C) An individual identity for woman

   (D) The appreciation of the traditional culture

The question asks for the ideological objective of the feminist movement according to the selection. Evaluate the answer choices using process of elimination. Eliminate (A) since it contains the extreme language *victory...over man*. Eliminate (B) since *marianismo* is not the ideal of feminism, and this choice also contains the extreme language *all parts of the world*. Keep (C) since the *individual identity* of a woman is consistent with the selection: it states that *according to its own ideology, the feminist movement looks for an individual identity for the woman*. Eliminate (D) because *traditional culture* would be the opposite of feminism as mentioned in the audio. The correct answer is (C).

56. According to the selection, what type of thinking surfaced during the Franco era?
    (A) Radical thinking
    (B) Traditional thinking
    (C) Progressive thinking
    (D) Feminist thinking

The question asks what type of thinking surfaced during the Franco era. Be sure to preview the questions for key words such as *Franco*. The narrative states that Franco was *traditional and conservative*. This supports (B). Evaluate the answer choices using process of elimination. Eliminate (A) and (C), which are opposites of traditional or conservative. Eliminate (D) since *feminist* does not mean *traditional*. The correct answer is (B).

57. According to the selection, what should we keep from the traditional *machista* society?
    (A) The role of the woman as mother
    (B) *Marianismo*
    (C) The role of the woman as subordinated to the man
    (D) *Machismo*

The question asks what we should keep from the traditional *machista* society. Be sure to preview the questions for key words such as *machista*. Evaluate the answer choices using process of elimination. Keep (A) since *the role of woman as mother* is a positive attribute mentioned within the context of *machismo*. Both *marianismo* and *machismo* need to be overcome to move on to a greater state of gender equality, so eliminate both (B) and (D). Choice (C) is clearly one of the reasons to create a feminist movement, so eliminate it as well. The correct answer is (A).

Selection 5: Translated Text and Questions, with Explanations

Introduction

The following recording is about the Special Olympics Games, which convened last August. The recording is an interview with Alejandro Martinez, a trainer who was triumphant at the recent tournament of the Special Olympics Games.

(NARRATOR)   Now you are going to hear an interview with Alejandro Martínez, victorious coach from the recent competition of the Special Olympics Games held in Vermont last August. Alejandro is a coach of many sports, including soccer, tennis, swimming, and field hockey.

(NARRATOR)   Alejandro, first of all, how did you get involved with the world of the Special Olympics Games?

(MARTÍNEZ)   Well, I have always been interested in sports. When I was in college, I played four sports during all four years, so sports have been a fundamental part of my life. The other fundamental part of my life, in chronological order, not order of importance, is my son, Carlos. Carlos was born eight years ago with a mild form of cerebral palsy. I noticed that with increased movement and physical activity, he felt better. For that reason, I have devoted myself to the Special Olympics. We have met other children like Carlos and other families like ourselves. It has been a very positive experience.

(NARRATOR)   Do you work with the Special Olympics all year long?

(MARTÍNEZ)   I wish I could devote myself to the Special Olympics 100 percent, but I also have a job. I am a high school mathematics teacher. So I work with the Special Olympics during the summers, which is the busiest time.

(NARRATOR)   It seems that you are drawn to professions that deal with children. Do you have any other children?

(MARTÍNEZ)   Yes, I have a daughter who just turned four last month. It is true that I enjoy working with children. They are more innocent and honest than adults.

(NARRATOR)   What would you say is the most difficult part of your work with the Special Olympics?

(MARTÍNEZ)   Well, we are faced with new obstacles every day. Perhaps the most difficult part for me is recognizing my own limitations. Frequently, I try to do much more than is reasonable in a day. And the worst thing is that the kids are the same way. Once they have become enthused by an idea or a training exercise, for example, they want to practice for hours without resting. They are very dedicated.

(NARRATOR)   It seems that you too are very dedicated. How do you explain the phenomenal success of your teams?

(MARTÍNEZ)   Well, I think there are two important factors. The first factor is that physical exercise has a very positive effect on the mind and body. It is incredibly therapeutic. It makes the kids feel better physically. And mentally, they are more alert. Of course, they also enjoy the benefits that we all gain when we participate in a physical sport. Our kids feel the pride and dignity that medicine or medical treatment cannot give them. The second factor that contributes to our success is the dedication of our kids. The kids are completely dedicated to their team. They understand instinctively the importance of the group and of working together. Each one of them is completely dedicated to the program. Without them, it would never work. Without our kids, the Special Olympics would not exist.

(NARRATOR)   What is Carlos's favorite sport?

(MARTÍNEZ)   Without a doubt, his favorite sport is American football, perhaps because he knows that I played in college.

(NARRATOR)   What would you recommend to other families with children who at the moment do not participate in the Special Olympics games? Maybe they think these games are silly or too juvenile.

(MARTÍNEZ)   I recommend that they call as soon as possible to find out about the upcoming events that are planned. One only has to go to one competition to see the advantages of this program. It's a great organization. The volunteers are very generous and dedicated. It's a very important experience for the children and for the families.

(NARRATOR)   Well, Alejandro Martínez, many thanks for being here with us.

58. How did Alejandro Martínez become interested in the Special Olympics Games?
    (A) He had always participated in the Special Olympics.
    (B) His brother participated in the Special Olympics.
    (C) His son responded favorably to sports.
    (D) His wife is very involved in the Special Olympics.

The question asks how Alejandro Martínez became interested in the Special Olympics Games. Be sure to preview the questions for key words such as *interesó* and *los juegos olímpicos especiales*. Martínez states that he had been involved in sports all of his life, that his son was born with cerebral palsy, and that exercise helped his son. Evaluate the answer choices using process of elimination. Eliminate (A) since Martínez had not always participated in the Special Olympics Games. Eliminate (B) and (D) since there is no mention of Martínez's brother or wife. Keep (C) since this matches the narrative. The correct answer is (C).

59. When does Alejandro devote himself entirely to the Special Olympics?
    (A) On weekends
    (B) During school vacations
    (C) In the winter
    (D) In the summer

The question asks when Alejandro devotes himself entirely to the Special Olympics. Be sure to preview the questions for the key phase *se dedica…completamente*. Evaluate the answer choices using process of elimination. Martinez states that he works for the Special Olympics during the summers when he is not working as a math teacher, which matches (D). Eliminate (A), (B), and (C) since there is no mention of weekends, school vacations, or winter. The correct answer is (D).

60. According to the interview, why does he not work full time for the Special Olympics?

    (A) Because he doesn't earn enough money

    (B) Because he is a math teacher

    (C) Because he spends a lot of time on his daughter

    (D) Because he couldn't take it

The question asks why he does not work for the Special Olympics full time. Be sure to preview the questions for key words such as *no trabaja* and *exclusivamente*. Evaluate the answer choices using process of elimination. Martínez states that he also has a job as a high school mathematics teacher, which matches (B). Eliminate (A) because he never mentions not earning enough money. Eliminate (C) because his daughter is not mentioned as a reason. Eliminate (D) since Martínez never mentions this reason. The correct answer is (B).

61. Why does Alejandro enjoy working with children?

    (A) Because they are young

    (B) Because they are honest

    (C) Because they are very interested

    (D) Because they are gifted

The question asks why Alejandro enjoys working with children. Be sure to preview the questions for key words such as *los niños*. Martínez states that he enjoys working with children because they are more innocent and honest than adults. Evaluate the answer choices using process of elimination. Eliminate (A) because *innocent* and *young* are not the same. Keep (B), which matches Martínez's description. Eliminate (C) and (D) because neither *interested* nor *gifted* matches the description *innocent and honest*. The correct answer is (B).

62. According to the interview, why is physical exercise therapeutic?

    (A) Because they practice special exercises

    (B) Because the coaches have studied physical therapy

    (C) Because it's fun

    (D) Because it makes the kids feel better mentally and physically

The question asks why physical exercise is therapeutic. Be sure to preview the questions for key words such as *terapéutico* and *ejercicio físico*. Martínez states that it makes kids feel better physically and that they are more alert mentally. Evaluate the answer choices using process of elimination. Eliminate (A) since there is no mention of special exercises. Eliminate (B) because the coaches have not necessarily studied physical therapy. Eliminate (C) because, while tempting, it does not match the prediction of making kids feel better mentally and physically. Keep (D), which does match the prediction. The correct answer is (D).

63. How is the collective spirit of the kids characterized?

    (A) They don't know how to collaborate in a group.

    (B) They understand instinctively how to collaborate.

    (C) They don't know how to function physically.

    (D) There is a lot of competition among the groups.

The question asks how the collective spirit of the kids is characterized. Be sure to preview the questions for the key phrase *espíritu colectivo*. Martínez states that the kids instinctively understand the importance of the group and working together. Evaluate the answer choices using process of elimination. Eliminate (A) since it is a reversal of the prediction. Keep (B), which matches the prediction. Eliminate (C), which is both false and offensive. Eliminate (D), which is not mentioned in the interview. The correct answer is (B).

64. According to the interview, which characteristic best describes the children who participate in the Special Olympics Games?

    (A) They are very thin.

    (B) They are very delicate.

    (C) They are very dedicated.

    (D) They are delegates.

The question asks which characteristic best describes the children who participate in the Special Olympics Games. Be sure to preview the questions for key words such as *característica* and *participan*. Martínez states that the children feel pride and dignity that medicine cannot give them and that they are dedicated to their team. Evaluate the answer choices using process of elimination. Eliminate (A) and (B) because the passage never mentions what the children look like. Keep (C) since *dedicated* matches the interview. Eliminate (D) since Martínez never mentions *delegates*. The correct answer is (C).

65. What does Alejandro recommend to the families who don't participate in the Special Olympics Games?

    (A) That they find out about the planned events

    (B) That they follow their hearts

    (C) That they organize their own games

    (D) That they don't participate

The question asks what Alejandro recommends to the families who don't participate in the Special Olympics Games. Be sure to preview the questions for key words such as *recomienda* and *no quieren participar*. Martínez recommends that they inquire about upcoming events that are planned and attend a competition. Evaluate the answer choices using process of elimination. Keep (A) since it matches the prediction. Eliminate (B), since it is not mentioned in the interview. Eliminate (C) and (D) since they are reversals of what Martínez recommended (that they attend an event of the Special Olympics). The correct answer is (A).

SECTION II
Question 1: Email Reply (Page 31)

Translation of the Question

Introduction: This message is from your high school teacher. You have received this message because recently you had asked him to write a letter of recommendation for your college application.

Dear and very remembered student:

I have received your request for a letter of recommendation; I am happy you have decided to apply to the university that you liked so much. You were one of my favorite students, and it is a pleasure for me to write that letter. Since I would like to write the best recommendation letter possible for you, I would like to know the following about you:

- What do you remember most from my class and how will it serve you in the future?
- What are your goals for the upcoming years at the university?
- What are some of the extracurricular activities in which you have participated and what have you learned from them?

Please answer these questions in detail as soon as possible in an email reply. Upon receiving your information, I will prepare the letter and I will send it to you both by mail and by email.

My best wishes and until soon,
Señor Santo Palacios, Language Teacher

Sample Student Response

Estimado Profesor Palacios:

Es un verdadero placer saludarlo nuevamente. Aunque han pasado un par de años desde que estuve en su clase, recuerdo con mucha nostalgia los buenos momentos que pasamos en el curso. Sobre todo recordaré las lecciones no sólo académicas, sino también las aplicaciones que tuvieron a la vida real. Aprendí a siempre dar mi mejor esfuerzo en todo lo que lleva mi nombre, y que nunca debo darme por vencido ante las situaciones difíciles en la vida.

Me dirijo a usted ya que pienso que usted es el profesor que mejor me conoce y mejor me describirá a la universidad. Puesto que el español será mi concentración en la universidad, mi meta es ser traductor o interprete y trabajar con una empresa multinacional en América Latina. Durante mis años universitarios, me gustaría retarme con cursos en otros idiomas. Otra meta que tengo, y ojalá se haga realidad, es estudiar por un año en una universidad extranjera.

Las actividades extracurriculares que más me impresionaron en el colegio fueron el equipo de tenis, el club de español y el club de servicio comunitario. En el Club de tenis aprendí la importancia de trabajar en equipo y la importancia de la práctica para mejorar las destrezas de uno. En el club de español, tuve la oportunidad de viajar a España y experimentar la cultura directamente. Viajé solo por primera vez en la vida y creo que representé bien a mi escuela y a mi país. Aprendí también que los estereotipos que mucha gente tiene son falsas, y una meta mía en el futuro es ayudar a combatirlos. Y en el club de servicio comunitario, vi que ayudar a los demás es ayudar a uno mismo.

Le doy las gracias por ser un ejemplo positivo en mi vida académica, y por haberme brindado su conocimiento y sabiduría tras los años.

Un saludo cordial,

Josh Messinger

Translation of the Sample Student Response

Dear Professor Palacios:

It is indeed a pleasure to greet you once again. Although a few years have passed since I was last in your class, I remember with great nostalgia the good times we students had in the course. Above all I will remember the lessons: not only academic, but also the applications that they had to real life. I learned to always give my best effort in everything that reflects upon me, and to never give up when facing difficult situations in life.

I am contacting you because I believe you are the teacher who knows me best and can best describe me to the university. Given that Spanish will be my college major, my goal is to be a translator or interpreter and work with a multinational company in Latin America. During my university studies, I would like to challenge myself with classes in other languages. Another goal I have, which I hope is realized, is to study for a year in an overseas university.

The extracurricular activities that most impacted me in high school were the tennis team, the Spanish Club, and the Community Service Club. On the tennis team I learned the importance of working with others and the importance of refining one's skills. In the Spanish Club, I had the opportunity to travel to Spain and experience the culture directly. I traveled alone for the first time in my life, and I think I represented both my school and my country well. I also learned that stereotypes that many people have are untrue, and my future goal is to help combat them. And, in the Community Service club, I saw that helping others really is helping oneself.

I thank you for being a positive role model in my academic career and for having bestowed your knowledge and wisdom throughout the years.

Cordial greetings,

Josh Messinger

Evaluation

Sometimes the AP exam picks topics from "out of left field," which can sometimes catch a student off guard. This essay really forced the writer to reflect on his goals and plans. Perhaps you don't have those defined yet. That doesn't matter. It is okay to make up things to fulfill the answers. The readers are not concerned whether you played tennis in high school or not; they are more concerned with how you answered the question. The exam will in some way ask you to talk about yourself or your academic experience, so make sure you have those details clear in your head so you can access them quickly.

Overall, this essay fulfilled all requirements and maintained good grammar throughout. It also was logically organized and had a clear beginning and showed cultural appropriateness in the opening and closing and in the register used. There was a lack of transition between some of the sentences and a few awkward translations (*retarme con cursos, mi concentración*), but it would most likely receive a 4.

Question 2: Argumentative Essay (Page 32)

Essay topic:

How does global warming affect our lives?

Translation for Source 1

Introduction

This article appeared on an Internet site in Spain in May of 2008.

The Consequences of Global Warming Associated with a Rise in Sea Level

With the destruction of the ozone layer we are observing more solar radiation penetrating to the planet's surface. This, in turn, contributes to thermal expansion of the oceans and the melting of great numbers of glacial mountains and of the icecaps found in the eastern parts of Antarctica and Greenland. With these elevated sea levels, serious changes for the future of the planet are already being forecasted.

Sea level already rose by between 4 and 8 inches during the last century. It's predicted that sea levels could rise by 10 to 23 inches by the year 2100. Unfortunately, levels are rising more than predicted—the Greenland icecap has shrunk in the last decade. This shrinking contributes approximately a hundredth of an inch annually to the sea level rise. This figure might seem minimal at first glance, but one has to keep in mind that Greenland makes up around 10% of the world's total ice mass. If all Greenland's ice were to melt, world sea levels could rise up to 21 feet. This year, for the first time, ships were able to pass through Arctic waters without the help of icebreaker boats. That is to say, the predictions of scientists that the ice would begin to melt have come true 25 years ahead of schedule. This also will mean grave consequences for the planet. Already it is predicted that polar bears, sea lions, and certain species of penguins are facing extinction in only a few years.

With the destruction of glaciers and icecaps, more fresh water enters the ocean, adding to current levels. These melts cause severe flooding in coastal areas. If the sea level were to rise even 6 meters, places such as Miami, Florida and San Francisco, California in the United States would be devastated; in China cities such as Shanghai and Beijing would be left sunken; and in India the city of Calcutta would be underwater. These last three urban centers figure among the most populous cities in the world.

Translation for Source 2

Introduction

This article appeared in the Argentinian press in July of 2008.

Warning: Global Warming Will Bring Grave Consequences for Human Life and Health

"It's not speculation at all—it's a reality. The planet's days are numbered. Now is the time to act and put in place planning and contingency programs," commented Francisco García, general director of the World Preservation Organization, at a press conference during the eleventh general convocation of the Week of the Planet, celebrated in Buenos Aires, Argentina. Representatives from more than 35 countries met in the Argentinian capital to discuss, analyze data, and formulate action plans so that international and national organizations might understand the consequences of global warming at a deeper level. It is their hope that once armed with this information, countries may introduce programs to avoid a disaster that, according to García, "is lying in wait."

One of the most alarming talks gave information about the current figures on illnesses and disasters around the world. German doctor Martin Teuscher, professor at the University of Tübingen, explained that human beings have already been exposed to various illnesses caused by changes or exaggerations of the climate. "The reality is that we've been living during this century. But notice that with the change in climate, the lows will be even lower. It will intensify the delicate balance between disaster and prosperity, between having a home and being helpless, and finally between life and death." He specifically stressed that more than 4 million people die, worldwide, of malnutrition; more than 2 million of diarrheal sicknesses; and 1.2 million of diseases such as malaria. Undoubtedly, these figures will grow with the global change in climate. Teuscher said it would not be impossible for these figures to triple within a mere 5 or 10 years.

The forewarnings do not stop there. With warmer temperatures, insects and other pests will have the opportunity to spread and infect more humans as a result. It is expected that more outbreaks of dengue fever and malaria epidemics will occur. Both sicknesses are transmitted by mosquito bites. Global warming favors these disease-transmitting insects. Another result of global warming is flooding, which produces the ideal environment for mosquitoes to breed and for the feared cholera pandemics. Recent studies carried out by scientists illustrate the gravity of the global warming problem: in barely 15 years, the number of people exposed to malaria on the African continent could reach the hundred millions. Globally, dengue fever could threaten almost 2 billion people.

Global warming has brought upheavals in worldwide climates, and each year previously unknown changes and nuances of climate become evident. For example, heat waves in Europe and the United States mean thousands of deaths each year, and hurricanes are becoming more and more devastating and powerful. "Hurricane Katrina in 2005 and Hurricane Mitch in 1998 destroyed large swaths of American territory," pointed out Felipe Fonseca, a Mexican meteorologist who spoke about the changes the Gulf of Mexico has suffered due to global warming. "Their social, economic, and political effects are still being felt. In 50 years we could find parts of North America underwater."

Automobile, truck, and plane emissions poison the air we breathe. That air pollution causes almost a million deaths per year. According to the estimates cited by the experts, for each degree Celsius the global temperature increases, there will be almost 30,000 additional deaths per year due to heart and lung diseases. With the recent rise in gas prices demand has not diminished enough to reduce air pollution. Many also fear that with the growth of the emerging Asian economies, plus the huge number of drivers that will have access to automobiles, the environmental damage will continue to stymie any attempt at environmental conservation.

"Individuals do have the power to make a difference," explains Rachel Johnson, German student and member of GreenWatch, a student movement that educates youth about conservation and recycling. "That plastic bag you throw in the trash without thinking about it will take a century to break down. Gasoline and petroleum influence almost every aspect of our lives, and at the same time put our wellbeing, and that of the planet, in danger. We must change our way of thinking, and act now. In my country we have a saying: *Macht es jetzt! Warte nicht auf bessere Zeiten.* (Do it now! Don't wait for a better moment.) If we don't make the effort now, our future generations will be condemned to a life without life."

Translation for Source 3 (Audio Track 6)

Introduction

This report, titled "Experts Point to Greater Health Risks Because of Global Warming," was broadcast on the Latin American radio station Enteramérica in July of 2005.

LH: Good afternoon, listening friends. This is Laura Heredia speaking, and I have the pleasure of presenting to you the very esteemed scientist Dr. Michelet Zamor, of the University of Miami. Besides being a university professor, Dr. Zamor is a contributing author of the report on the health risks caused by global warming presented by the Environmental Protection Agency at the recent meeting of experts during the commemoration of International Health Day celebrated at the United Nations in New York. Doctor, thank you for being with us. Please, tell us: which of the discoveries in your report stood out the most?

MZ: Well, upon analyzing data submitted by many sources worldwide, scientists around the world detailed an elevated rate of deaths due to heat waves, will-o'-the-wisps, and the sicknesses and smog caused by global warming. It's the first time in the history of the world that scientists have recognized the grave risks presented by global warming, not just to human beings, but also to foods, energy, and water, upon which human survival depends.

LH: I hadn't thought about it that way. Many people think that global warming is just a question of hotter summers and less snow in the winter.

MZ: If only it were so simple. The risks to human health, to society in general, and to the environment increase as much with the rate as with the magnitude of climate changes. The fault for global warming undoubtedly belongs with human beings. The documents put out by the EPA suggest that climate extremes and illnesses transmitted by fleas and other organisms can kill more people as temperatures rise. Likewise, allergies may worsen because the climatic changes will produce more pollen. Smog, a principal cause of respiratory and pulmonary ailments, also counts among the threats to the world's population. At the same time, however, global warming may mean fewer sicknesses and deaths due to the cold.

LH: What has been the biggest obstacle to adopting legislation to prevent the dangers of global warming?

MZ: While scientists point to the connection between health and climate change, the government, for its part, has not done so—has not even recognized it. This recognition, many believe, would obligate the government to regulate greenhouse gases. This certainly would open a Pandora's box in the search for the governmental effort and support necessary to lend weight and importance to the necessity of embarking on the task of understanding and preventing the devastating consequences of global warming.

Sample Student Response

El calentamiento global trae consigo graves riesgos al bienestar del planeta. El ritmo al cual han crecido tanto la población mundial como la expansión industrial ha puesto en peligro las defensas naturales del planeta. Como resultado, en la Tierra hay una mayor tendencia a ocurrir acontecimientos perjudiciales como desastres naturales, escasez de comida, brotes de enfermedades y una disminución de recursos vitales para sobrevivir. Por consiguiente, nuestras vidas han cambiado también.

Yo diría que los cambios más drásticos se han presenciado en nuestra vida diaria. Los precios de gasolina, comida, y transportación han aumentado muchísimo recientemente. Por ello, nuestra vida económica cotidiana es más difícil. Muchas personas han sufrido ya que sus sueldos no rinden como antes y les es difícil que su presupuesto les alcance para todo lo necesario. Y como recientemente ha surgido conciencia para preservar el planeta, estamos viendo programas de reciclar, ahorrar energía, compartir viajes, explotar recursos locales, descubrir fuentes de energía, y hasta salvar los animales que están en peligro de extinción, particularmente en las zonas antárticas. La calidad de nuestras vidas ha bajado también por el calentamiento global. Por ejemplo, en muchos países subdesarrollados, las cifras de muertes causadas por el calentamiento global han crecido. Las enfermedades como la malaria tendrán más víctimas como nunca ya que el calentamiento global permite que los insectos proliferen y sobrevivan con más facilidad. El derretimiento del hielo de Antártica traerá más inundaciones y consigo más casos de cólera y otras enfermedades. Yo mismo he observado el crecimiento de alergias y problemas cardiorrespiratorios entre la gente de mi familia. Y tal como predijeron los expertos, estos problemas están manifestándose ahora. Si hubiéramos hecho caso a las advertencias de los expertos hace años, tal vez no nos habríamos encontrado en esta situación tan desconsolada.

Finalmente, el calentamiento global ha cambiado nuestra forma de pensar. Se han despertado nuevas maneras de planificar el futuro. Los expertos están educando al público para que varíe su forma de pensar y su percepción en el mundo. El individuo se ha dado cuenta de que sí se puede hacer una diferencia al preservar el planeta y consumir más prudentemente. La gente está tratando de hacer lo posible para preservar el medio ambiente. Cada día se ve más programas para ayudar a preservar los recursos naturales, minerales y humanos del planeta. Solo esperamos que no sea demasiado tarde.

En resumen, se reconoce que el planeta en sí es la base de nuestra existencia y supervivencia. El calentamiento global, fenómeno creado por el ser humano, ha llegado a tal punto que por fin el mundo ha reconocido su importancia, y como resultado, ha tratado de modificar su forma de pensar y actuar. Sin embargo, el daño es extenso, y requiere que también los gobiernos apoyen toda opción necesaria para salvar al mundo. Solo el tiempo dirá si este esfuerzo es suficiente.

Translation of the Sample Student Response

Global warming brings with it severe risks to the wellbeing of the planet. The rhythm at which both the world population and industrial expansion has grown has endangered the natural defenses of the planet. As a result, on Earth there is an increased tendency toward detrimental events such as natural disasters, food shortages, sickness outbreaks, and a decrease in the vital resources necessary for survival. As a result, our lives have changed as well.

I would say that the most drastic changes have been evident in our daily lives. The prices of gas, food, and transportation have gone up tremendously recently. For that reason, our daily economic life is even more difficult. Many people have suffered since their salaries don't go as far as before and it is difficult for their budgets to cover all of their needs. And given that recently there has been an increase in consciousness toward preserving the planet, we are seeing programs for recycling, saving energy, ride sharing, using local resources, discovering alternative energy sources, and even saving endangered animals, particularly in the Antarctic zones. Our quality of life has also gone down as a result of global warming. For example, in many underdeveloped countries, the number of deaths caused by global warming has grown. Sicknesses like malaria will have more victims than ever because global warming allows insects to thrive and to survive more easily. The melting of Antarctic ice will bring more floods and with that more cases of cholera and other sicknesses. I myself have observed an increase in allergies and cardiorespiratory problems among my own family members. And just as the experts predicted, these problems are becoming evident now. If we had paid attention to the experts' warnings years ago, perhaps we wouldn't have found ourselves in this sad situation.

Finally, global warming has changed our way of thinking. New ways of planning the future have been formed. Experts are educating the public to change its way of thinking and its perception of the world. The individual has realized that one can indeed make a difference by preserving the planet and consuming more wisely. People are taking the necessary steps to save the environment. Each day we see more programs to help preserve the planet's natural, mineral, and human resources. We only hope that it is not too late.

In summary, it is known that the planet itself is the key to our existence and survival. Global warming, a phenomenon created by human beings, has come to the point where the world has finally recognized its importance, and as a result, has tried to modify its way of thinking and acting. However, the damage is extensive and requires that governments also support all the necessary options in order to save the planet. Only time will tell whether this effort is enough.

Evaluation

This essay expresses ideas clearly and in an organized manner. It has a good flow and transitions, and it displays excellent grammatical control and breadth of vocabulary. At the end of the introduction, there should be some reference to the topics of the following paragraphs to ease transitions. Another improvement would be to tie the articles in a little bit more, as it referenced them in mostly general terms. Some specifics from the articles could have strengthened the essay. The writer didn't specifically identify the sources mentioned. Perhaps a few lines where they could have said "According to Source #1…" However, given the strong style, grammar, and organization, this essay would have still scored extremely well.

This essay has some very good grammatical points that you should try to use in your essay. Use of good transitions: *Por ello, en resumen, Finalmente, Tal como.* Advanced vocabulary: *ya que, consigo, se reconoce que.* Good use of subjunctive: *Esperamos que, Requiere que, para que.* Good use of verbs: *surgir, rendir, predecir, manifestarse, proliferar, sobrevivir, modificar.* Advanced/Native structures: *tanto…como; les es difícil.*

A good way to write a high-scoring essay is to find vocabulary and expressions that you can use or modify to fit most essays. Choose a few expressions in each of the above categories from essays and readings and try to start inserting them in your essays each time you write in class. For example, "Por ello" is a more sophisticated way to say "por eso," and this is exactly the type of thing the readers are looking for in the essays. Keep a checklist and always try to incorporate some of them into your essay. It will definitely make a good impression with the readers. In addition, try to use a variety of tenses: the above essay used present tense, present progressive, present subjunctive, future, preterite, and conditional. Readers especially like to see the advanced tenses and past subjunctive as well. Don't be afraid to go over the minimum word requirement either; generally you do better by writing more as opposed to less.

Question 3: Conversation (Page 36)

Script with Sample Student Response and Translation

Narrador: Has solicitado una posición de aprendiz en una empresa multinacional latinoamericana. Imagina que recibes una llamada telefónica del director del Departamento de Recursos Humanos para hablar sobre la posición que has solicitado.

You have applied for an internship in a Latin American multinational company. Imagine that you receive a phone message from the director of Human Resources to speak about the position that you have applied for.

Ahora tienes un minuto para leer el esquema de la conversación.

Now you have one minute to read the conversation outline.

Ahora imagina que recibas una llamada del señor Rivero para realizar una entrevista.

Now imagine that you receive a phone call from Mr. Rivero to speak about the position.

MA: Buenos días, le habla el señor Luis Rivero, director de Recursos Humanos de la Empresa Mundiales. Me gustaría hacerle algunas preguntas por teléfono sobre su solicitud. Primero, cuénteme por favor. ¿Qué le motivó a solicitar una posición de aprendiz en nuestra compañía?

Good morning, this is Mr. Luis Rivero from the Human Resources Department of the Mundiales Company. I would like to ask you a few questions by phone about your application. First, please tell me, what prompted you to apply for a position in our company?

Tú: Pues, como su compañía cuenta entre los líderes de su industria, me pareció buena idea solicitar una posición con ustedes para poder aprender más sobre la industria.

Well, since your company is among the leaders of its industry, it seemed like a good idea for me to apply for a position to learn more about the industry.

MA: Muy bien. ¿Qué destrezas y habilidades podrá aportar a nuestro lugar de trabajo?

Very good. What skills and abilities could you contribute to our workplace?

Tú: Hablo tres idiomas: el español, el inglés y el francés. Además, domino varios programas de computadora y soy muy bueno resolviendo problemas.

I speak three languages: Spanish, English, and French. In addition, I am proficient in many computer programs and I am very good at resolving problems.

MA: ¿Qué dirían sus patrones o jefes anteriores sobre personalidad y calidad de trabajo?

What might your previous employers say about your personality and the quality of your work?

Tú: Dirían que soy puntual, leal y que trabajo bien en grupos. En cuanto a mi calidad de trabajo, dirían que soy trabajador, organizado y diligente.

They would say I am punctual, loyal, and that I work well in group situations. In terms of my work quality, they would say I am hard-working, organized, and diligent.

MA: Quisiera saber, ¿cuándo está disponible para trabajar y cuándo podrá empezar?

I would like to know: when are you available to work and when could you start?

Tú: Como las clases terminan a finales de junio, puedo trabajar los meses de julio y agosto. Puedo comenzar el 5 de julio.

As school finishes at the end of June, I can work in July and August. I can start July 5.

MA: Me gustaría que pasara por nuestra oficina para que conociera a algunos de mis compañeros de trabajo. ¿Podrá pasar por la oficina mañana a las 10 de la mañana?

I would like for you to come by our office in order to meet some of my work colleagues. Could you stop by tomorrow at 10 in the morning?

Tú: Desafortunadamente, asisto a la escuela hasta las tres de la tarde. ¿Sería posible que le visitara a las 4?

Unfortunately, I have school until 3 P.M. Would it be possible for me to visit at 4 P.M.?

MA: No hay ningún inconveniente. Nos vemos entonces en esa fecha y hora.

No problem. We'll see you then at that date and time.

Tú: Espero con ganas poderle conocer mañana. Que pase buen día. Adiós.

I look forward to seeing you tomorrow. Have a nice day. Goodbye.

Evaluation

The answers were clear, appropriate, and had some complex structures like conditional and past subjunctive *(sería posible que le visitara)*, and subjunctive *(que pase buen día)*. The rest of the responses advanced the conversation and more than fulfilled the requirements. It would receive at least a 4 due to the quality of its grammar and topic development.

Question 4: Cultural Comparison (Page 37)

Translation of the Question

It is known that languages enrich us. Explain in what way languages have influenced the society in which you live and in another Spanish-speaking city that you have observed, studied, or visited.

Compare your observations about the communities in which you have lived with those of a region of the Spanish-speaking world that you have studied. In your presentation you can refer to what you have studied, experienced, observed, etc.

Sample Student Response

Los idiomas no sólo facilitan la comunicación entre otros, sino que también aportan la oportunidad de que las culturas se asimilen. En los Estados Unidos vemos cada día más que estamos desarrollando una sociedad bilingüe. Hay más de 40 millones de hispanos viviendo en los Estados Unidos. Este grupo reserva poder económico, social y político, e influencian los acontecimientos en muchas de las comunidades donde viven. Pero al nivel humano, como cualquier inmigrante, el hispanohablante trae consigo una larga y rica cultura también. Como resultado de este tremendo oleaje de inmigrantes, la música, comida, vocabulario y lenguaje de la sociedad reflejan una mayor influencia hispana. En mi comunidad, hay letreros bilingües, servicios bilingües y mayores oportunidades de empleo para los bilingües. Casi cada solicitud de empleo hoy en día busca candidatos bilingües.

Paraguay es un país que disfruta una rica cultura gracias a los idiomas. Cuando los españoles asentaron el país, no erradicaron la cultura indígena. Es más, los pioneros españoles aprendieron el idioma de los indígenas—el guaraní. A la vez, los guaranís aprendieron el español. Ambos idiomas son lenguas oficiales de Paraguay, y casi todos los paraguayos dominan los dos. El guaraní es el idioma del amor, de la música, de la poesía y de la vida cotidiana, mientras que el español se usa en los periódicos, la televisión y los negocios. Cada uno ocupa un lugar en la sociedad, y el país, como resultado, ha beneficiado.

Hoy en día en muchos lugares del mundo hay movimientos que están a favor de adoptar un solo idioma oficial. Pero realmente vemos que la sociedad beneficia y hasta se vuelve más tolerante al tener varios idiomas presentes en la sociedad.

Translation of the Sample Student Response

Languages not only facilitate our communication with others, but they also allow cultures to assimilate with each other. In the United States we see each day more and more that we are developing a bilingual society. There are more than 40 million Hispanics living in the United States. This group holds economic, political, and social power, and influences the events in many of the communities in which they live. But at the same time, like any immigrant, the Hispanics also bring with them a rich and long cultural tradition. As a result of this tremendous wave of immigration, the music, food, vocabulary, and language of society reflect a growing Hispanic influence. In my community there are bilingual signs, bilingual services, and greater work opportunities for bilinguals. Almost every job application today seeks bilingual candidates.

Paraguay is a country that enjoys a rich culture thanks to its languages. When the Spanish settled in the country, they did not eradicate the native culture. They actually learned the language of the natives—Guaraní. The Guaraní in turn learned Spanish. Both languages are official languages of Paraguay, and almost all Paraguayans speak both fluently. Guaraní is the language of love, music, poetry, and daily life, while Spanish is used in newspapers, television, and business. Each one occupies a place in society, and the country, as a result, has benefited.

Nowadays, in many parts of the world, there are movements to adopt one official language. However, we truly see that society benefits from multiple languages and even becomes more tolerant when different languages are present in daily life.

Evaluation

The response got better as it went along. The question really wanted to hear more about the personal experience of the writer, which to some extent was absent in the first paragraph. The second paragraph was much stronger because it demonstrated a familiarity with another culture, and most importantly, specific facts. This is what you will need to make the grade on this section. You could have chosen other options: Puerto Rico, Andean languages, Panamá. Notice how you will need to know information about the various regions of the Spanish-speaking world. This response fulfilled the requirements, was well-composed, and showed knowledge of the culture. It would have scored 4 on the AP exam.

HOW TO SCORE PRACTICE TEST 1

Section I: Multiple Choice

Note: this score conversion chart should only be used as an estimate.

Part A: _____ × 1.154 = _____
Number Correct
(out of 30)

Part B: _____ × 1.154 = _____
Number Correct
(out of 35)

Sum = _____
Weighted
Section I Score
(Do not round)

Section II: Free Response

Question 1: _____ × 3.750 = _____
(out of 5)   (Do not round)

Question 2: _____ × 3.750 = _____
(out of 5)   (Do not round)

Question 3: _____ × 3.750 = _____
(out of 5)   (Do not round)

Question 4: _____ × 3.750 = _____
(out of 5)   (Do not round)

_____
Weighted
Section II Score
(Do not round)

AP Score Conversion Chart Spanish Language & Culture	
Composite Score Range	AP Score
107–150	5
90–106	4
73–89	3
56–72	2
0–55	1

Composite Score

_____ + _____ = _____
Weighted   Weighted   Composite Score
Section I Score Section II Score (Round to nearest whole number)

Part III
About the AP Spanish Language and Culture Exam

- The Structure of the AP Spanish Language and Culture Exam
- How the AP Spanish Language and Culture Exam Is Scored
- Overview of Skills Tested
- How AP Exams Are Used
- Other Resources
- Designing Your Study Plan

THE STRUCTURE OF THE AP SPANISH LANGUAGE AND CULTURE EXAM

The AP Spanish Language and Culture Exam consists of the following two sections:

- **Section I** is the multiple-choice section, which tests *reading* and *listening* skills.

- **Section II** is the free-response section, which tests *writing, listening,* and *speaking* skills.

The College Board provides a breakdown of the types of questions covered on the exam. This breakdown will *not* appear in your test booklet: it comes from the preparatory material the College Board publishes. The chart below summarizes exactly what you need to know for the exam.

Section		Number of Questions	Percent of Final Score	Time
Section I: Multiple Choice				95 minutes
Part A	Interpretive Communication: Print Texts	30 questions	50%	40 minutes
Part B	Interpretive Communication: Print and Audio Texts (combined)	35 questions		55 minutes
	Interpretive Communication: Audio Texts			
Section II: Free Response				88 minutes
Question 1: Email Reply		1 prompt	12.5%	15 minutes
Question 2: Argumentative Essay		1 prompt	12.5%	55 minutes (15 minutes to read; 40 minutes to write)
Question 3: Conversation		5 prompts	12.5%	18 minutes
Question 4: Cultural Comparison		1 prompt	12.5%	

The exam is a little over 3 hours long and has two parts—multiple choice and free response. Each section of the exam is worth 50 percent of the final exam grade.

Section I: Multiple Choice—65 questions; 1 hour and 35 minutes (50% of total score)

Part A—30 questions; 40 minutes

- Interpretive Communication: Print Texts. Reading comprehension questions are based on a variety of authentic print materials, including prose fiction, journalistic articles, advertisements, letters, maps, and tables. Some of the written texts may include a visual component or a web page. Questions will ask you to identify the main points and significant details, and make inferences and predictions from the written texts. Some questions may require making cultural inferences or inserting an additional sentence in the appropriate place in the reading passage.

Part B—35 questions; 55 minutes

- Interpretive Communication: Print and Audio Texts (combined). The first of the two listening subsections pairs print texts with audio selections representing a variety of sources (interviews, podcasts, conversations, public service announcements, etc.).
- Interpretive Communication: Audio Texts. The second of the two subsections consists solely of audio selections representing the same types of sources described above. All audio selections will be played twice, and you will have time to preview the questions before answering them.

You are encouraged to take notes during this part of the exam and are given writing space for that purpose. Your notes will not affect your scores. Total scores on the multiple-choice section are based on the number of questions answered correctly. Points are not deducted for incorrect answers, and no points are awarded for unanswered questions.

Section II: Free Response—4 tasks; 1 hour and 28 minutes (50% of total score)

Writing

- Question 1: Email Reply. You'll be asked to read and then write a formal response to an email message. For example, you may be prompted to reply to a job or scholarship offer. (15 minutes; 12.5% of final exam score)
- Question 2: Argumentative Essay. This prompt requires you to synthesize information from a variety of print and audio sources, present the different viewpoints, indicate your own viewpoint, and defend it thoroughly. You'll be given an essay prompt and several minutes to read and listen to the materials before you start writing. (15 minutes to review materials plus 40 minutes to write; 12.5% of final exam score)

> **A Note on Directions**
>
> All directions in the examination booklet will be printed in English and in Spanish. Familiarize yourself with the directions in this book so that you will not have to spend more time on them than necessary. On test day, choose the language you are more comfortable with and skim only that set of the directions. Don't waste time reading both sets of directions, or worse yet, comparing the translations for accuracy. Use that time to jot down notes and organize your responses if possible.

Speaking

- Question 3: Conversation. This section requires you to verbally respond to a series of recorded cues. Your responses will be guided by an outline of a short conversation, which will be provided. You will be assigned one side of the conversation, and the recording will supply the other. Your responses will be recorded. (20 seconds per response; 12.5% of final exam score)
- Question 4: Cultural Comparison. You'll be asked to make a 2-minute presentation on a given cultural topic. Your assignment is to compare cultural features of your own community with those found in an area of the Spanish-speaking world with which you are familiar. You're encouraged to cite examples from materials you've read, viewed, or listened to, as well as from personal experiences and observations. (4 minutes to prepare plus 2 minutes to present; 12.5% of final exam score)

HOW THE AP SPANISH LANGUAGE AND CULTURE EXAM IS SCORED

Your Multiple-Choice Score

In the multiple-choice section of the test, you are awarded one point for each question that you answer correctly, and you receive no points for each question that you leave blank or answer incorrectly. That is, there is no dreaded "guessing penalty." So, even if you are completely unsure, guess. In Part IV, we'll show you how to narrow down your choices and make educated guesses.

Your Free-Response Score

Each AP essay and spoken response question is scored on a scale from 0 to 5, with 5 being the best score. Essay readers (who are high school or university Spanish instructors) will grade your essays and spoken responses, and the score for each section will be worth 12.5% of your total score.

In general, an essay that receives a 5 answers all facets of the question completely, making good use of specific examples to support its points, and is "well-written," which is a catch-all phrase that means its sentences are complete, properly punctuated, clear in meaning, and varied (that is, they exhibit a variety of structure and use a large academic vocabulary). Graders are looking for you to have an ease of expression in the Spanish language, utilizing idiomatic phrases where appropriate and correct vocabulary and grammar. Can you accurately convey your point and go into detail on the essays? on the spoken responses? This knowledge of vocabulary, grammar, and idioms will garner you a high score on Part B of the test. Lower-scoring essays are considered to be deficient in these qualities to a greater or lesser degree, and students who receive a 0 have basically written gibberish or "I don't know." If you write an essay that is not on the topic, you will receive a blank ("—"). This is equivalent to a zero.

Detailed scoring guidelines for each of the four free-response prompts are available for download at the College Board's AP Spanish Language and Culture Exam Information page (see page 91 for a link).

Your Final Score

Your final score of 1 to 5 is a combination of your scores from the two sections. Remember that the multiple-choice section counts for 50 percent of the total and the essay/spoken response section counts for 50 percent. This makes them equal, so you must concentrate on doing your best on both parts. If you can get a score of 44 (number correct) on a multiple-choice section with 65 questions, you have about a 99 percent chance of getting at least a score of 3 on the exam.

What Your Final Score Will Mean

After taking the test in early May, you will receive your scores sometime around the first week of July, which is probably when you'll have just started to forget about the entire harrowing experience. Your score will be, simply enough, a single number that will either be a 1, 2, 3, 4, or 5. Here is what those numbers mean.

Score	2022 Percentage	Credit Recommendation	College Grade Equivalent
5	15.5	Extremely Well Qualified	A
4	27.5	Well Qualified	A–, B+, B
3	35.4	Qualified	B–, C+, C
2	18.1	Possibly Qualified	—
1	3.5	No Recommendation	—

Scores from May 2022 AP administration. Data taken from the College Board website.

OVERVIEW OF SKILLS TESTED

The AP Spanish Language and Culture Exam tests the following skills and knowledge:

Reading and Listening Comprehension. Section I will mostly test that you can:

- Interpret text.
- Determine the meanings of passages and quantitative data.
- Draw connections between sources.

Writing and Speaking. In Section II, you will:

- Integrate text and audio sources, identifying similarities and differences.
- Form opinions and support those opinions with evidence and examples.
- Use a variety of relevant vocabulary.

- Self-monitor and adjust responses to the prompts. If needed, circumlocution and paraphrasing can be helpful to keep yourself on track for answering questions. This may help you, in a pinch, to familiarize yourself with new terms or still convey your point if that vocabulary word you need escapes you.
- Focus on building vocabulary related to the following categories: current events, family, the arts, politics, history, and social issues.

HOW AP EXAMS ARE USED

More Great Books
Check out The Princeton Review's college guidebooks, including *The Best 389 Colleges, The Complete Book of Colleges, Paying for College,* and many more!

Different colleges use AP exam scores in different ways, so it is important that you go to a particular college's website to determine how it uses AP exam scores. The three items below represent the main ways in which AP exam scores can be used.

- **College Credit.** Some colleges will give you college credit if you score well on an AP exam. These credits count toward your graduation requirements, meaning that you can take fewer courses while in college. Given the cost of college, this could be quite a benefit, indeed.
- **Satisfy Requirements.** Some colleges will allow you to "place out" of certain requirements if you do well on an AP exam, even if they do not give you actual college credits. For example, you might not need to take an introductory-level course, or perhaps you might not need to take a class in a certain discipline at all.
- **Admissions Plus.** Even if your AP exam will not result in college credit or even allow you to place out of certain courses, most colleges will respect your decision to push yourself by taking an AP course or even an AP exam outside of a course. A high score on an AP exam shows comprehension of more difficult content than is taught in many high school courses, and colleges may take that into account during the admissions process.

OTHER RESOURCES

There are many resources available to help you improve your score on the AP Spanish Language and Culture Exam, not the least of which are your teachers. If you are taking an AP class, you may be able to get extra attention from your teacher, such as obtaining feedback on your essays. If you are not in an AP course, reach out to a teacher who teaches AP Spanish Language and Culture, and ask whether the teacher will review your essays or otherwise help you with content.

AP Students

Another wonderful resource is AP Students, the official site of the AP exams. The scope of the information at this site is quite broad and includes

- The *AP Spanish Language and Culture Exam Course and Exam Description* (Effective Fall 2020), which includes details on what content is covered and sample questions
- Released free-response questions from the most recent exam, including audio prompts
- Exam practice tips
- Full rubrics for the written and spoken portions of the test
- Sample activities to help you improve your Spanish and prepare for the exam
- Up-to-date information about changes to the format of the AP Spanish Language and Culture Exam

The AP Students home page address is: apcentral.collegeboard.org

The AP Spanish Language and Culture Course home page address is: apcentral.collegeboard.org/courses/ap-spanish-language-and-culture/course

The AP Spanish Language and Culture Exam Information page (where you can find those scoring guidelines mentioned earlier) is: apcentral.collegeboard.org/courses/ap-spanish-language-and-culture/exam

Finally, The Princeton Review offers in-person and online tutoring for the AP Spanish Language and Culture Exam. Our expert instructors can help you refine your strategic approach and add to your content knowledge. For more information, call 1-800-2REVIEW.

DESIGNING YOUR STUDY PLAN

In Part II, you used the Diagnostic Answer Key to identify some areas of potential improvement. Let's now delve further into your performance on Practice Test 1, with the goal of developing a study plan appropriate to your needs and time commitment.

Read the answers and explanations associated with the multiple-choice questions (starting at page 43). After you have done so, respond to the following questions:

Break up your review into manageable portions. Download our helpful study guide for this book once you register online.

- Review the Overview of Skills Tested on pages 89–90 and, next to each one, indicate your rank of the topic as follows: 1 means "I need a lot of work on this," 2 means "I need to beef up my knowledge," and 3 means "I know this topic well."
- How many days/weeks/months away is your AP Spanish Language and Culture Exam?
- What time of day is your best, most focused study time?
- How much time per day/week/month will you devote to preparing for your AP Spanish Language and Culture Exam?
- When will you do this preparation? (Be as specific as possible: Mondays and Wednesdays from 3:00 to 4:00 P.M., for example.)
- What are your overall goals in using this book?

Part IV
Test-Taking Strategies for the AP Spanish Language and Culture Exam

PREVIEW

Take a moment to respond to the following questions about your performance on Practice Test 1:

- How many multiple-choice questions did you miss even though you knew the answers?
- On how many multiple-choice questions did you guess randomly?
- How many multiple-choice questions did you miss after eliminating some answers and guessing based on the remaining answers?
- Did you create an outline before you wrote each essay?
- Did you find either of the essays easier/harder than the other—and, if so, why?
- What was your action plan with the spoken portions of the exam?
- Did you have phrases at the ready as templates to answer the questions?
- Was the spoken portion difficult? If so, which part? How so?

HOW TO USE THE CHAPTERS IN THIS PART

Before you read the following Strategy chapters, take a moment to think about how you approach each question type. As you read and engage in the directed practice, be sure to appreciate the ways in which you can improve. At the end of Part IV, you will have the opportunity to reflect on how you will change your approach.

Chapter 1
How to
Approach the
Multiple-Choice
Section

THE STRUCTURE OF THE MULTIPLE-CHOICE SECTION

The multiple-choice section on the exam breaks down into reading and listening selections. Part A consists entirely of reading comprehension passages, while Part B contains integrated reading and listening passages and listening-only passages. These different combinations of reading and listening require varying ways of interfacing with the material, which we will break down below.

INTERPRETIVE COMMUNICATION: PRINT TEXTS

Reading Passages

Since the test-makers design the test with a serious time crunch, it is important to have a strategy to tackle the passages, and this might not include reading each entire passage. Remember that this is an open-book test, so there is no reason to read and remember an entire passage. Usually, this sort of approach leads to rereading, which wastes valuable time on the test. Instead, know what the questions ask for; this will direct and guide your reading to help you find the answers as opposed to retaining information that you may or may not need.

Basic approach:

1. Read the Introduction
2. Work the Questions
3. Work the Passage and Answers

Step 1: Read the Introduction

Always read the short introduction that gives a little bit of information about the subject *(tema)*, when the piece was written, who is speaking or writing, and where the passage appeared. While this information might seem like a waste of time when there is so much to read in the passages, it gives a bit of context that will make the rest of the passage more digestible. By knowing some context right away, you may be able to enter into the text more easily, which will lead to less rereading and therefore save time on the text. Besides, it actually might help lead you to the answers to the general questions!

If it seems like a difficult passage, find an easier passage to tackle first and then come back to it.

Step 2: Work the Questions

The key to being efficient on this test is to know what the questions are asking ahead of time. That way, you are primed to know what to read or listen for. Many test-takers waste valuable time on the test by reading the entire passage or listening through the entire conversation, and then going back to reread what they partially remember. There is no need to retain the entire passage, so why try? Instead, work the questions.

There are a couple of things to note when working the questions: one is whether questions are general or specific. Take a look at the questions below:

¿Quién narra este pasaje?
Who is narrating this passage?

¿De qué se trata este pasaje?
What is this passage about?

¿Cuál es el propósito del artículo?
What is the purpose of the article?

¿Cuál de las siguientes afirmaciones resume mejor el artículo?
Which of the following statements best summarizes the article?

¿Cuál es una conclusión lógica que se puede hacer sobre este contenido?
What is a logical conclusion based on the content?

Note that none of these questions contains specific information from any particular passage, nor are there any line references to point you in the right direction. Therefore, they must be general questions. Mark them as general questions with a "G" or any other mark of your choice and save them for last. Oftentimes, the test-makers place these types of questions at the beginning of the question bank, but there is no rule saying you have to do these questions in order. Instead, work some questions that do have line references or key words easily found in the text first, and then you will have more information with which to answer those general questions afterward.

Take a look at these specific questions and notice what they contain in contrast to the general questions:

Según el autor en el primer párrafo, ¿por qué hay una crisis contemporánea de salud mundial?
According to the author in the first paragraph, why is there a contemporary world health crisis?

En el segundo párrafo, David Soler espera que
According to the second paragraph, David Soler hopes that

Se menciona Un chien andalou *para*
Un chien andalou is mentioned in order to

¿Cómo llegó Vera a la rumba?
How did Vera come to know rumba?

¿A que se refiere "no aborda la dimensión política" (línea 54)?
What does "he does not address the political dimension" refer to (line 54)?

Notice a few things here: line references, such as *línea 54*, are always wonderful ways to know where to look in a passage for the answers. While line references are not always available, other indicators such as *el segundo párrafo* can lead to the correct window of the text. Other useful tools are key words that are specific to the passage or listening track. Capitalized names and places are great key words to locate in a passage because they are often easier to spot. Titles, words in italics, quotations, and other easily recognizable words or symbols are also great key words to scan the text or listen for.

Finally, know what the question is asking. Most questions are *what* or *why* questions, and knowing which one a question is will frame how you work to answer them. The *what* questions generally begin with *Cuál, De qué,* or other similar phrases that are simply asking what the passage says, and the answer will be a paraphrase of information found directly in the passage or introduction. Questions that contain language such as *por qué* or *se menciona...para* require a bit more analysis of not only what the author says, but also why the author says it. The *why* the question is asking for, however, is always something that can be found in the passage. Unlike more speculative, creative responses you might dream up in English or Spanish literature class, there is always an objectively right response based on the text here.

> Is it a *what* question or a *why* question?

Step 3: Work the Passage and Answers

Now that you know what you are looking for, go to the passage and read what is necessary to answer the questions. Use the questions to look for key words and phrases that are specific to the passage. For listening comprehension, listen for the key words to appear in the context of the lecture or conversation and jot down quick notes about what the characters say. Remember, the answers are always written explicitly in the text or said explicitly in the audio. From there, compare what you know the answer to be with what is given in the answer choices.

> Find the key words before you listen or read!

The Power of POE

Proven Techniques
Use POE to help
boost your score.

The wonderful thing about multiple-choice questions is that the wrong answers are there for you to identify and eliminate. The test-makers write answer choices with common types of wrong answers that, with a bit of practice, will become easily recognizable. Here are some common traps that you might come across:

- **Out of the Window:** It is always tempting to see something you know to be true about the passage. However, use those key words to get to the correct portion of the passage for the answer. If the text in the answer choice is not from the same section, you may run into trouble!
- **Extreme answers:** The College Board never wants to be offensive or get into trouble. Avoid words like *todos, siempre, nunca,* etc., which often turn the statement into something beyond what the passage stated. In addition, if there is anything remotely offensive in the answer choice, it will not be a correct response.
- **Words Out of Context:** This is one of the test-makers' favorite tactics on this exam. Have you ever seen a word that you recognize from the passage or listening and gotten excited? Beware. Sometimes you will see or hear words from the sources that show up in the answer choices, but if they are used differently, outside the window, or taken out of context, it will make the choice too literal or just plain wrong.
- **Right Information, Wrong Question:** Often the test-makers will insert a true statement that does not answer the question. While it may be true, if it doesn't answer what the question is asking, it is a wrong answer.
- **Outside knowledge:** Limit yourself to only things you can point to within the passage or quote from listening. Without proof, any outside knowledge, even if true, will never be a correct response.

Pacing

Pacing is how much time you spend on each passage and even each question. Thinking about pacing requires thinking about ordering your approach in terms of level of difficulty. Remember, questions have varying levels of difficulty, and you don't get extra credit for harder questions. So, take the easy test first! Find the passages that will be easier to answer and complete them before you move on to the more difficult ones. That way, you guarantee yourself points before you tackle the harder questions, and you can take the time you'll need to work on those without worrying about sacrificing any easy points.

Final Advice on the Reading Passages

There are a variety of approaches to tackling the passages, depending on comfort level and reading speed. For some, a general skim is comfortable. For others, reading the first line of each paragraph to see the structure of the passage is helpful. Others search for a key word by reading until they find it. Still others search for the key word and only read the window around the key word or line reference, about 5 lines before and after. Again, this depends on individual comfort, so try a couple of different ways of engaging with the passage to find what works best for you. Consider how much time you have left in the test as well: if you are running out of time, perhaps finding those key words and getting those last couple of points is more efficient than trying to read for the main idea or analysis questions. Let's try a sample passage and apply these strategies.

Sample Passage

SOURCE: https://www.veintemundos.com/magazines/207-en/

(Translation on pages 104–105)

El siguiente artículo sobre una mujer quien descubrió una manera de crear materiales sostenibles para joyería apareció en una revista latinoamericana en 2018.

Celina Brizuela es doctora en química y farmacia, emprendedora y luchadora. Después de trabajar 18 años en una firma de investigación, decidió comprar un taller de joyería. En 2010 empezó a crear materiales con la apariencia de oro y plata tomando como base desechos sólidos (llaves, tuberías, latas) para dar vida a la denominada "ecojoyería". En 2017, Celina ganó el premio a la mejor diseñadora de joyas de Honduras. Sus creaciones llegan hoy a Guatemala, Nicaragua y EE.UU.; a futuro piensa exportarlas a Europa.

Honduras es un país que refleja un fuerte ascenso en las oportunidades laborales femeninas. El Instituto Nacional de Estadísticas confirma que más de 900 000 madres aportan a la economía del país. Los sectores donde hay mayor participación de mujeres son comercio, salud, educación, industria manufactura y microempresas. En la economía informal está todo el aporte femenino de las emprendedoras. A su vez, el núcleo de gran parte de los pequeños emprendimientos es de carácter familiar.

No obstante, la informalidad, la falta de historia crediticia y los altos costos son los principales obstáculos que enfrentan estas empresas. Cabe mencionar que ahora las mujeres están incursionando en otros espacios que tradicionalmente habían sido dominados por los hombres, como el cuidado de los recursos naturales, el medio ambiente y la participación política. Sin embargo, las féminas ganan menos en comparación con los varones.

Una mujer emprendedora enfocada al medio ambiente y el arte es Celina Brizuela. Madre de dos hijas y originaria de Tegucigalpa. Su interés por hacer cosas nuevas surgió en la compañía de investigación norteamericana donde trabajó. Siempre le ha gustado salirse de lo que todo el mundo está haciendo, así que un día decidió seguir su sueño: alquiló un taller de joyería para crear sus propias piezas en base a desechos sólidos metálicos disponibles a nivel local.

Por si fuera poco, por medio de una aleación, Celina logró transformar esos metales de modo que tuvieran las mismas características del oro y la plata. En 2017 fue premiada como la mejor diseñadora de joyas de Honduras por el "Consejo Hondureño de la Empresa Privada y la Cámara de Comercio e Industrias de Tegucigalpa".

"Me gusta observar las tendencias, actualizarme y ver qué es lo que está pasando y qué hacen otros grandes diseñadores de joyas". En 2014 Piso Diez Diseño invitó a Celina a ser parte de su grupo de diseñadores y fue ahí cuando tuvo su primera pasarela con ellos. En 2017 participó en Fashion Week Honduras donde mostró una línea única, romántica, que llevaba por nombre Celeste, su color predilecto y el nombre de su empresa, puesto en honor a su madre, una mujer artista. "Me sentí muy honrada por participar y fue mi primera vez".

Actualmente son nueve personas que trabajan directamente en el taller de Celina. "Somos los únicos que estamos haciendo esa aleación en Honduras. Hay algunas empresas que se dedican a hacer cosas con metales, pero Corporación Celeste es la única firma que saca una aleación para hacer oro y plata", resalta la diseñadora.

Hay mucha gente que la invitó a ir a las universidades para contar su historia. "Mi sueño para el futuro es que la ecojoyería se posicione como una marca hondureña, que podamos mostrar a la gente que en Honduras no solamente hay violencia y corrupción; que vean y aprecien la creatividad y el talento de los emprendedores así como la belleza de nuestro país. Deseo que trascienda lo que estamos haciendo. Hay tantas cosas interesantes en Honduras", concluye Celina.

1. ¿Cuál es el propósito del pasaje?

   (A) Mostrar el poder del oro y de la plata en la economía

   (B) Contar la historia de una emprendedora que ha cambiado la manera en que hace joyería

   (C) Ilustrar como hay un crecimiento de empresarias feministas en Honduras

   (D) Advertir de que la falta de crédito destruye los emprendimientos familiares

2. ¿Cuál de las conclusiones sobre la "ecojoyería" es verdad?

   (A) La aleación transforma los materiales sostenibles al oro y a la plata.

   (B) La manera de hacer joyería con materiales reciclados es la invención de Celina.

   (C) Los materiales reciclados son más duros que el oro y la plata.

   (D) Celeste es el único color que se puede crear con el proceso de aleación.

3. Se menciona la falta de historia crediticia en el tercer párrafo para

   (A) comparar algunos tipos de interés para los emprendedores

   (B) notar que Celina tiene mal crédito

   (C) mostrar que las féminas reciben préstamos más pequeños que los varones

   (D) demostrar algunas dificultades que enfrentan a los emprendedores Hondureños

4. ¿Por qué Celina nombra su negocio Celeste?

   (A) Es en honor de los artistas femeninas.

   (B) Es el color natural que resulta por el proceso de aleación.

   (C) Es el color favorito de su mamá.

   (D) Es su color favorito y en honor de su madre.

5. Podemos inferir que

   (A) Fashion Week Honduras fue el primer pasarela para Celina

   (B) el proceso de aleación convierte los metales sostenibles al oro y a la plata

   (C) Honduras es un país afligido por la corrupción y la violencia

   (D) se puede encontrar la joyería de Celina en los Estados Unidos

6. Un título apropiado para este artículo sería

   (A) "Emprendedoras feministas"

   (B) "Obstáculos financieros para los emprendedores"

   (C) "Joyería recién descubierta: aleación sostenible"

   (D) "Fashion Week y la 'ecojoyería'"

Here's How to Crack It

First, look at the introduction: the magazine article is about a woman who discovered new ways of making jewelry with sustainable materials instead of traditional gold and silver. Next, before diving into the passage, look at which questions are easiest to tackle first.

Questions 1, 5, and 6 are general questions, so save them for later: there is no need to read the whole passage from start to finish to try to answer these first. Rather, find more specific questions to work on first, and then you will most likely have enough information to answer the other questions. Remember also that the introduction can sometimes provide information on the general questions.

2. ¿Cuál de las conclusiones sobre la "ecojoyería" es verdad?

   (A) La aleación transforma los materiales sostenibles al oro y a la plata.

   (B) La manera de hacer joyería con materiales reciclados es la invención de Celina.

   (C) Los materiales reciclados son más duros que el oro y la plata.

   (D) Celeste es el único color que se puede crear con el proceso de aleación.

Okay, this question has a clear key word, *ecojoyería,* so find it in the passage to find the answer. The passage states, *En 2010 empezó a crear materiales con la apariencia de oro y plata tomando como base desechos sólidos (llaves, tuberías, latas) para dar vida a la denominada "ecojoyería".* The sentence refers to Celina, who started to create materials with the appearance of gold and silver. Eliminate (A) because the alloy does not transform the materials *into* gold and silver, but rather to have the *appearance of* gold and silver. Keep (B) because this is a paraphrase of what the passage says: that she started to create materials. While this may not be enough to prove invention, keep it. Eliminate (C) because it does not say that the materials are stronger than gold or silver. Eliminate (D) as well, because the passage does not say the only color that can be created is pale blue. There is further proof in the passage: *Corporación Celeste es la única firma que saca una aleación para hacer oro y plata",* meaning that the only company to do so is Celina's company. The correct answer is (B).

3. Se menciona la falta de historia crediticia en el tercer párrafo para

   (A) comparar algunos tipos de interés para los emprendedores

   (B) notar que Celina tiene mal crédito

   (C) mostrar que las féminas reciben préstamos más pequeños que los varones

   (D) demostrar algunas dificultades que enfrenten a los emprendedores Hondureños

This question has the key phrase *la falta de historia crediticia* as well as a paragraph reference, making this information doubly easy to find in the passage. *Se menciona…para* is essentially a *why* question, so read for why the author mentions the lack of credit history in the passage. The passage states that *la falta de historia crediticia y los altos costos son los principales obstáculos que enfrentan estas empresas.* Therefore, this is an obstacle that entrepreneurs may encounter. The passage does not compare interest rates, so eliminate (A). The passage does not explicitly say that Celina is one of the entrepreneurs who has a lack of credit, so eliminate (B) as well. While the passage mentions women making less money than men, it does not mention them receiving smaller loans as well. Eliminate (C). The information found in the passage does show proof of some difficulties that Honduran entrepreneurs encounter. The correct answer is (D).

4. ¿Por qué Celina nombra su negocio Celeste?

(A) Es en honor de los artistas femeninas.

(B) Es el color natural que resulta por el proceso de aleación.

(C) Es el color favorito de su mamá.

(D) Es su color favorito y en honor de su madre.

This question contains the key words *Celina* and *Celeste*. It is usually easy to locate capital letters in the passage, and *Celeste* specifically appears in the sixth and seventh paragraphs. The passage states that her clothing line *llevaba por nombre Celeste, su color predilecto y el nombre de su empresa, puesto en honor a su madre, una mujer artista.* This quote tells you it's Celina's favorite color and that she also chose the name in honor of her mother, a female artist. Choice (A) is too broad, referring to female artists in general, so eliminate it. Choice (B) is not stated in the passage, and does not match the proof that pertains to *Celeste*, so eliminate this choice as well. While (C) may seem tempting, it does not say that pale blue is her mother's favorite color, but rather Celina's favorite color; eliminate (C). Finally, (D) matches the quote from the passage, so it must be the answer.

Now, go back and tackle the questions that asked about the passage as a whole or that do not have clear line references or key words:

1. ¿Cuál es el propósito del pasaje?

(A) Mostrar el poder del oro y de la plata en la economía

(B) Contar la historia de una emprendedora que ha cambiado la manera en que hace joyería

(C) Ilustrar como hay un crecimiento de empresarias feministas en Honduras

(D) Advertir de que la falta de crédito destruye los emprendimientos familiares

Since you have worked the other questions first, you have now read enough to be able to tackle this one. Remember that the introduction talks about a woman who discovered a way of creating jewelry with sustainable materials. Use POE to eliminate answer choices that do not match. Eliminate (A) because, while gold and silver are mentioned in the passage, they don't represent the main idea. Choice (B) is a paraphrase of the introduction as well as the main idea introduced in the first paragraph, so keep this choice. While (C) may seem tempting, it is a bit too broad and does not mention Celina, the "who" the article is about. Eliminate (D) as well because the passage is not a warning about bad credit, but rather mentions it as a challenge faced by some family businesses. Notice also how the word *destruye* is a bit too strong. The test-makers generally do not use harsh or extreme language in correct answers. The correct answer is (B).

5. Podemos inferir que

(A) Fashion Week Honduras fue el primer pasarela para Celina

(B) el proceso de aleación convierte los metales sostenibles al oro y a la plata

(C) Honduras es un país afligido por la corrupción y la violencia

(D) se puede encontrar la joyería de Celina en los Estados Unidos

With an inference question like this one, let the answer choices help. Unlike in English or Spanish classes, on this test inferences are merely true statements that can be found in the passage. Use the answer choices to find the right windows within the passage. Use *Fashion Week* to locate the right window for (A), reading a few lines before and a few lines after the words,

POE tip:
Avoid extreme language in the answer choices.

POE tip:
Only choose answers that are explicitly in the passage.

Only a detail? Not the main point? Eliminate it!

which appear in paragraph 6. The passage states in the sentence before the mention of Fashion Week, *En 2014 Piso Diez Diseño invitó a Celina a ser parte de su grupo de diseñadores y fue ahí cuando tuvo su primera pasarela con ellos.* This quote is not enough to prove (A), so eliminate it. For (B), look for key words such as *oro* and *plata* or *metales sostenibles* in the passage. The passage states that *En 2010 empezó a crear materiales con la apariencia de oro y plata tomando como base desechos sólidos.* This means the materials she creates have the appearance of silver and gold, but they are not actually silver and gold. Eliminate this choice. Now look for *Honduras* in the passage: it appears in the 2nd and 8th paragraphs. While the second paragraph does not mention violence and corruption, there is mention in the 8th paragraph: *que podamos mostrar a la gente que en Honduras no solamente hay violencia y corrupción; que vean y aprecien la creatividad y el talento de los emprendedores así como la belleza de nuestro país.* Choice (C) is too strong, so eliminate it as well. Now evaluate (D). The passage mentions the United States in the form of *los EE.UU.* in the first paragraph: *Sus creaciones llegan hoy a Guatemala, Nicaragua y EE.UU.* Since they can be found today in the United States, it's definitely possible to find them in the United States! The correct answer is (D).

6. Un título apropiado para este artículo sería

   (A) "Emprendedoras feministas"
   (B) "Obstáculos financieros para los emprendedores"
   (C) "Joyería recién descubierta: aleación sostenible"
   (D) "Fashion Week y la 'ecojoyería'"

With a question that asks you to choose a title for the passage, it is best to save it for last, since you will have a better sense of the passage as a whole after tackling the others first. Use POE heavily on questions like this, comparing the main idea of the passage with the offerings in the answer choices. Consider the first choice, *"Emprendedoras feministas"*: this title is too broad and goes beyond the scope of the text, since the passage talks about female entrepreneurs, not necessarily feminists. Eliminate (A). Evaluate (B): *obstáculos financieros* is certainly something the passage talks about for entrepreneurs, but is it the main point of the passage? The main point is Celina's creation of sustainable jewelry, so eliminate (B). Choice (C), *"Joyería recién descubierta: aleación sostenible,"* talks about a recently discovered way of creating a sustainable alloy for jewelry, so keep this choice, since this is what Celina has done. Choice (D) mentions only details of the passage, not the main point, when it combines Fashion Week with ecojewelry. The correct answer is (C).

Translation:

The following article about a woman who discovered a way of creating sustainable materials for jewelry appeared in a Latin American magazine in 2018.

Celina Brizuela is a doctor of chemistry and pharmacy, entrepreneur, and fighter. After working for 18 years in an investigative firm, she decided to buy a jewelry shop. In 2010 she started to create materials with the appearance of gold or silver taken from solid waste (keys, pipes, cans) in order to give life to the so-called "ecojewelry." In 2017, Celina won the prize for best jewelry designer in Honduras. Her creations can be found today in Guatemala, Nicaragua, and the United States; in the future she is thinking about exporting them to Europe.

Honduras is a country that reflects a strong increase in work opportunities for women. The National Institute of Statistics confirms that more than 900,000 mothers contribute to the country's economy. The sectors where there is the greatest participation from women are commerce, health, education, industry manufacturing, and microbusinesses. In the informal economy, there is a very high degree of feminine support for entrepreneurs. At the same time, the nucleus of most of the small enterprises is a family one.

However, informality, lack of credit history, and high costs are the principal obstacles that confront these businesses. It is fitting to mention that now women are dabbling in other spaces that have traditionally been dominated by men, such as the preservation of natural resources, the environment, and political participation. Nevertheless, women earn less in comparison to men.

A female entrepreneur focused on the environment and art is Celina Brizuela, mother of two daughters and originally from Tegucigalpa. Her interest in creating new things surfaced while she was working at a North American investigative company. She always had enjoyed escaping what everyone else was doing, so one day she decided to follow her dream: she rented a jewelry shop to create her own pieces from discarded solid metals available on a local level.

As if that were not enough, by means of creating an alloy, Celina was able to transform those metals in such a way that they had the same characteristics as gold and silver. In 2017 she was recognized as the best jewelry designer in Honduras by the Honduran Counsel of Private Business and the Chamber of Commerce and Industry of Tegucigalpa.

"I like to observe the trends, update myself, and see what is happening and what other great jewelry designers are doing." In 2014, Tenth Floor Designs invited Celina to be part of a group of designers and it was there that she had her first runway fashion show with them. In 2017, she participated in Honduras Fashion Week where she showed her unique, romantic line called Celeste, her favorite color and the name of her business—named in honor of her mother, a female artist. "I felt very honored to participate and it was my first time."

Nowadays there are nine people who work directly for Celina in her shop. "We are the only ones who are making this alloy in Honduras. There are some businesses that are dedicated to doing things with metals, but Celeste Corporation is the only firm that extracts an alloy to make gold and silver," notes the designer.

There are a lot of people who invited her to go to universities to tell her story. "My dream for the future is that ecojewelry is positioned as a Honduran brand, that we can show people that in Honduras there is not only violence and corruption; I hope that they can see and appreciate the creativity and talent of entrepreneurs as well as the beauty of our country. I want it to transcend what we are doing. There are so many interesting things in Honduras," concludes Celina.

1. What is the purpose of the passage?

   (A) To show the power of gold and silver in the economy

   (B) To tell the story of an entrepreneur who has changed the way in which jewelry is made

   (C) To illustrate that there are a growing number of feminist entrepreneurs in Honduras

   (D) To warn that lack of credit destroys family enterprises

2. Which of the following conclusions about "ecojewelry" is true?

   (A) The alloy process transforms sustainable materials into gold and silver.

   (B) The method of making jewelry with recycled materials is Celina's invention.

   (C) The recycled materials are harder than gold and silver.

   (D) Pale blue is the only color that can be made with the alloy process.

3. Lack of credit history is mentioned in the third paragraph in order to

   (A) compare some interest rates for entrepreneurs

   (B) note that Celina has bad credit

   (C) show that women receive smaller loans than do men

   (D) demonstrate some difficulties that Honduran entrepreneurs may face

4. Why does Celina call her business Celeste?

   (A) It is in honor of female artists.

   (B) It is the natural color that results from the alloy process.

   (C) It is the favorite color of her mom.

   (D) It is her favorite color and is in honor of her mother.

5. We can infer that

   (A) Fashion Week Honduras was Celina's first runway show

   (B) the alloy process converts sustainable metals into gold and silver

   (C) Honduras is a country afflicted by corruption and violence

   (D) it is possible to find Celina's jewelry in the United States

6. An appropriate title for this article would be

   (A) "Feminist Entrepreneurs"

   (B) "Financial Obstacles for Entrepreneurs"

   (C) "Recently Discovered Jewelry: Sustainable Alloy Practices"

   (D) "Fashion Week and 'Ecojewelry'"

PRACTICE PASSAGE 1

Sample Print Texts Selection

You will read several selections. Each selection is accompanied by a number of questions. For each question, choose the response that is best according to the selection and mark your answer on your answer sheet.	Vas a leer varios textos. Cada texto va acompañado de varias preguntas. Para cada pregunta, elige la mejor respuesta según el texto e indícala en la hoja de respuestas.

Introducción

El siguiente artículo apareció en 1996 en el periódico *La Jornada de Lima*.

LIMA, PERÚ: "No hubo ningún otro remedio", explicó el presidente peruano Alberto Fujimori al hablar con Eduardo Taboada, corresponsal extranjero de la emisora
Línea Univisión, durante una entrevista realizada en la capital
5 peruana. Fujimori habló pocos minutos después del ataque militar contra el grupo terrorista Tupac Amaru, que se había apoderado de la embajada japonesa hacía 4 meses. El grupo, integrado por 22 guerrilleros y sus cuatro líderes, secuestró a 72 rehenes, la mayoría de ellos diplomáticos extranjeros,
10 quienes habían sido cautivos dentro del recinto japonés por 130 días.

Los soldados peruanos iniciaron el ataque a las tres de la tarde, según el periodista Taboada, quien presenció el evento tan inesperado. A pesar de que el ataque empleara mu-
15 chas estrategias, apenas duró cuarenta minutos. Un grupo de soldados se dirigió por la parte delantera de la embajada y otro grupo se abalanzó a la parte posterior. Utilizaron armas con láser y rifles que hasta pudieron ubicar a los terroristas adentro, gracias a la ayuda de una computadora especial.
20 Ninguno de los terroristas salió con vida de la residencia, de acuerdo con los informes del noticiero Univisión de Miami. La emisora nacional de Perú, NotiUno, interrumpió su programación para transmitir en vivo escenas de la crisis. Pocos detalles fueron divulgados por la censura de la prensa
25 para proteger a los rehenes.

Fujimori proclamó orgullosamente que habían acabado de una vez con el terrorismo y nunca negociaría con terror- istas, lo cual sigue siendo la política oficial del Perú. Sin embargo, Fujimori se vio obligado a iniciar conversaciones
30 con los rebeldes fuertemente armados después de que varios gobiernos extranjeros, cuyos ciudadanos se encontraban dentro de la embajada, presionaron para evitar un ataque militar. Fujimori sí dialogó con los rebeldes, pero al mismo tiempo iba planeando clandestinamente un asalto militar.
35 Mucha gente de la comunidad mundial opinó que las acciones del gobierno peruano eran innecesarias. Un

sacerdote conocido en el Perú, el Padre Xavier Venancio, reiterando la opinión de la iglesia peruana, pensó que la situación podría haberse resuelto a través de una manera
40 pacífica. El presidente Fujimori reafirmó que no había otra manera de resolver la crisis, ya que "se nos acababa el tiempo y nuestro compromiso principal fue garantizar la seguridad y bienestar de los rehenes. Esperar más no nos convenía". El presidente japonés Hashimoto dijo pocos
45 minutos después de la exitosa liberación de los rehenes que "no debe haber nadie que pueda criticar al presidente". La prensa peruana confirmó esto, a través de unas encuestas realizadas en todo el territorio nacional en las cuales el noventa por ciento (90%) de la población peruana estuvo
50 a favor de la acción militar de Fujimori. Con esta nueva derrota de otro grupo subversivo, Fujimori ya marca su segunda victoria militar contra el terrorismo. En 1992, Fujimori arrasó con el grupo terrorista más temido del pais, El Sendero Luminoso, tras el arresto de su enigmático líder,
55 Abimael Guzmán. Sendero Luminoso fue el grupo terrorista de mayor involucramiento y hegemonía al nivel nacional, habiendo aterrorizado el país por más de 25 años; un peri- odo sumamente violento que ocasionó la muerte de más de 35.000 peruanos. En su auge el grupo se apoderó de casi el
60 40% del territorio peruano. Ese grupo maoísta inspiró a su vez a otros grupos tales como Tupac Amaru que se desa- fiaran del gobierno peruano a través del conflicto armado. Con estos gloriosos éxitos, el gobierno peruano pretende restaurar, según Fujimori, "el progreso, la paz y la prosperi-
65 dad" en la nación andina.

Por ahora reinará la estabilidad en el Perú, pero como nos ha narrado la historia, la tranquilidad es un deleite que se saborea por unos cortos momentos, y sabremos cuándo surgirá otro movimiento subversivo que busque desalojar la
70 tan deseada paz que tanto anhela el pueblo peruano.

La Jornada de Lima, 1996

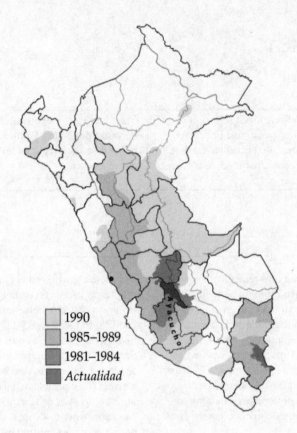

1990
1985–1989
1981–1984
Actualidad

Víctimas de Ataques Terroristas en el Perú

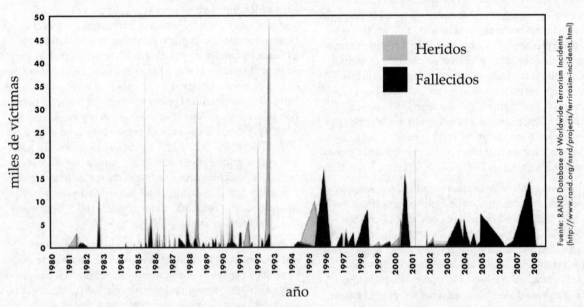

Heridos

Fallecidos

Fuente: RAND Database of Worldwide Terrorism Incidents
(http://www.rand.org/nsrd/projects/terrirosim-incidents.html)

1. ¿Por qué negoció Fujimori con los rebeldes?

   (A) Porque era su política oficial

   (B) Porque había sentido presión de otros países

   (C) Porque le daba tiempo para organizar un ataque militar simultáneamente

   (D) Todas estas respuestas son correctas.

2. ¿Cuál de estas conclusiones sobre el asalto militar a la embajada es falsa?

   (A) El ataque había sido planeado detalladamente.

   (B) El ataque ocasionó el fallecimiento de muchos terroristas.

   (C) El ataque marcó la segunda vez que Fujimori había derrotado a un enemigo del Estado.

   (D) Si se hubiera utilizado la tecnología, la crisis habría podido resolverse de una forma más eficaz y pacífica.

3. Podemos inferir que

   (A) después de la intervención militar de 1996, no se irrumpió más actividad terrorista semejante

   (B) el gobierno peruano siguió las pautas de Fujimori y continuó su política de no negociar con los rebeldes

   (C) al partir de 1996, terrorismo volvió a surgir después de un declive de 5 años

   (D) la tecnología fue el factor clave en reducir la amenaza terrorista después de 1996

4. Un titular apropiado para este artículo sería

   (A) "Fujimori en un jaque mate con los terroristas"

   (B) "Salvajes invaden embajada, perecen muchos"

   (C) "Fujimori deja que los terroristas lo pisoteen"

   (D) "Negociaciones logran defraudar a los terroristas, militares triunfan"

5. La siguiente oración se puede añadir al texto: "Se sabe que la violencia no resuelve nada, y a su vez, perpetúa aún más violencia". ¿Dónde serviría mejor la oración?

   (A) Línea 34

   (B) Línea 36

   (C) Línea 40

   (D) Línea 50

6. Podemos inferir que 1992 fue un año de mucha actividad terrorista en el Perú ya que

   (A) quedó cautivo el líder del grupo subversivo

   (B) otros grupos habían cometido actos violentos como respuesta a la captura del líder terrorista

   (C) hubo elecciones presidenciales en el Perú ese año

   (D) los terroristas aumentaron el territorio bajo su control

Translated Text and Questions, with Explanations

The following article appeared in 1996 in the newspaper *La Jornada de Lima*.

LIMA, PERU: "There was no other solution," explained Peruvian president Alberto Fujimori while speaking with Eduardo Taboada, foreign correspondent for the broadcast station Univisión, during an interview in the Peruvian capital. Fujimori spoke several minutes after the military attack against the terrorist group Tupac Amaru, who had taken control of the Japanese embassy four months earlier. The group, comprised of 22 guerrillas and their four leaders, had kidnapped 72 hostages—the majority of whom were foreign diplomats—and who were held captive inside the Japanese residence for 130 days.

The Peruvian soldiers began the attack at 3 P.M., according to the journalist Taboada, who witnessed the unexpected event. Yesterday's attack lasted only 40 minutes despite the fact that it involved many strategies. One group of soldiers rushed through the front part of the embassy, while the other group rushed the back. They utilized weapons with lasers and rifles that were even able to locate the terrorists inside, thanks to the use of a special computer. None of the terrorists left the residence alive, according to reports from the news station Univisión in Miami. The national broadcast station of Peru, NotiUno, interrupted its programming to transmit live scenes of the crisis. Few details were divulged by the press in order to protect the hostages.

Fujimori proudly proclaimed that he had eliminated terrorism once and for all, and would never negotiate with terrorists, which continues to be the official policy of Peru. However, Fujimori was obliged to begin conversations with the heavily armed rebels, after various foreign governments, whose citizens were inside the embassy, pressured him to avoid a military assault. Fujimori did indeed speak with the rebels, but at the same time was secretly planning a military attack.

Many people of the global community felt that the actions of the Peruvian government were unnecessary. A well-known priest in Peru, Father Xavier Venancio, reiterating the opinion of the Peruvian church, felt that the situation could have been resolved through peaceful means. President Fujimori reaffirmed that there wasn't any other way to resolve the crisis, given that "time was running out for us, and our main goal was to guarantee the safety and well-being of the hostages. To wait any longer wouldn't have been beneficial." The Japanese president Hashimoto said a few minutes after the successful liberation of the hostages that "no one should be criticizing the president." The Peruvian press confirmed this, through interviews carried out throughout the nation in which ninety percent (90%) of Peruvians were in favor of Fujimori's military action. With this recent defeat of yet another subversive group, Fujimori marks his second victory against terrorism. In 1992, Fujimori obliterated the most feared terrorist group in the country, The Shining Path, with the arrest of its enigmatic leader, Abimael Guzman. The Shining Path was the most active and dangerous terrorist group in the nation, having terrorized the country for more than 25 years, an extremely violent period that saw the deaths of more than 35,000 Peruvians. At its peak, the group controlled almost 40% of the country. This Maoist group inspired other groups like Tupac Amaru to challenge the Peruvian government through armed conflict. With these glorious successes, the Peruvian government intends to restore, according to Fujimori, "progress, peace, and prosperity" to the Andean nation.

For now, all is calm in Peru, but as history has shown us, peace is a delicacy that can be savored for only a few short moments, and who knows when another subversive group will appear and attempt to destroy the much desired peace the Peruvian people hope for.

Here's How to Crack It

1. Why did Fujimori negotiate with the rebels?

   (A) Because it was his official policy

   (B) Because he received pressure from other countries

   (C) Because it gave him time to organize a military attack at the same time

   (D) All of these answers are correct.

Choice (B) is the correct answer because the article states that he began dialogue with the rebels because the foreign governments wanted him to avoid a military attack. While (C) may be correct, the article doesn't state that Fujimori used the negotiations to buy time. Choice (A) is incorrect, because Fujimori is quoted as saying he would never negotiate with terrorists. As a result, (D) is also incorrect.

2. Which of the following conclusions concerning the military assault on the embassy is false?

   (A) The attack was planned with great detail.

   (B) The attack caused the deaths of many terrorists.

   (C) The attack marked the second time that Fujimori had defeated an enemy of the state.

   (D) If technology had been used, the crisis could have been solved in a more efficient and peaceful manner.

This type of question is sometimes included to trip up the fast reader. Be sure to focus on the qualifying word *false* in the question. Thus, this question is looking for a false statement. The article states that the attack employed many strategies, which would suggest that (A) is a true statement. Likewise, (B) is also true, as the article stated that there were 26 terrorists and none escaped. Choice (C) is a true statement, as the end of the article discusses Fujimori's past successes. Choice (D) is a false statement, as technology (lasers and computers) was indeed used to end the crisis quickly. Thus, (D) is the correct answer.

3. We can infer that

   (A) after the military intervention of 1996, there wasn't any more similar terrorist activity

   (B) the Peruvian government followed Fujimori's lead and continued its policy of not negotiating with rebels

   (C) after 1996, terrorism resurged after a decline over 5 years

   (D) technology was the key factor in reducing the terrorist threat after 1996

Choice (C) is the correct answer, as the graph shows that terrorism declined for five years after 1996, but then had a sharp increase in 2001. This is a direct contradiction of (A). Choices (B) and (D) may be true, but there isn't any data to support those inferences.

4. An appropriate headline for this article would be

(A) "Fujimori in a checkmate with the terrorists"

(B) "Savages invade embassy, many perish"

(C) "Fujimori lets terrorists step all over him"

(D) "Negotiations manage to mislead terrorists, military triumphs"

The best answer is (D), as it captures the overall main idea of the article. While (A) does show that Fujimori has the upper hand, it doesn't give the detail of (D). Choice (B) refers to *savages*, which would not be used to describe the military in this article. Choice (C) is also incorrect, as it clearly is the opposite of the outcome of the standoff between the president and the terrorists.

5. The following sentence can be added to the text: "It is known that violence doesn't resolve anything, and in turn, perpetuates even more violence." Where would this fit best?

(A) Line 34

(B) Line 36

(C) Line 40

(D) Line 50

The correct answer is (C), as it would be a logical quote by the nonviolent priest mentioned in the article. In this position it advances the flow and meaning of the paragraph. Choice (A), line 34, does follow some text that reinforces the idea of a nonviolent solution, but as our inserted sentence is an opinion, it wouldn't fit here since the previous sentence is about planning a military intervention. Choice (D) is incorrect, as the previous sentence in the article speaks of the nation's overwhelming approval of the attack. While (B) could also accommodate the sentence, a clearly better fit would be (C), given the preceding and subsequent sentences. These types of questions test your ability to accommodate sentences in a paragraph where they would have the best flow and impact; be sure to read the surrounding sentences to get a better idea of where to put them.

6. We can infer that 1992 was a year of much terrorist activity in Peru since

(A) the leader of a subversive group was captured

(B) there were violent acts by other groups as a response to the capture of the terrorist leader

(C) there were presidential elections in Peru that year

(D) the terrorists increased the territory under their control

Choice (D) is the correct answer, as shown by the map. There are no references to (C) anywhere, so it can be eliminated. Choices (A) and (B) are too similar for one of them to be the right answer, and the graph does not show which groups are responsible for the terrorist acts, so it isn't possible to determine this information. In addition, the terrorist leader was captured in December, so the year had already ended: another reason (B) is incorrect.

PRACTICE PASSAGE 2

Introducción

El siguiente artículo apareció en 2015 en una revista electrónica de cultura latinoamericana.

Cuba ¿País de Emprendedores?

Hombres y mujeres cubanos que crean nuevos negocios poco o nada tienen que ver con los emprendedores a nivel mundial. En esta isla del Caribe la economía es muy
Linea diferente al resto cuando se habla de iniciativas, startup y
5 emprendimiento.

En Cuba, cuando se va a comenzar un negocio innovador, en lo primero que se piensa es en la familia: "Mi tío me prestará una parte del dinero; mi hermano trabajará conmigo; mi primo buscará la materia prima, y mi esposa
10 y yo seremos los vendedores. Después repartimos toda la ganancia según los aportes de cada cual". Así piensan los cubanos cuando van a crear un nuevo negocio, desde una simple guarapera hasta un hostal. Orelvys Bormey Torres, un joven ingeniero industrial, altamente especializado en
15 su área, que crea un negocio junto a su familia, asumen los riesgos económicos y tiene éxito.

Por supuesto que este emprendedor de Villa Clara no tiene un pelo de tonto: lo primero que hizo fue inscribir su marca en el Registro Cubano de la Propiedad Industrial.
20 Además, organizó el negocio de tal forma que toda familia pudiese participar. El objetivo es que el negocio fuese más fácil de administrar al tener que pagar menos por empleados externos contratados, entre otras ventajas de trabajar con la parentela.

25 ¿Y por qué el maní? Sencillamente encontraron que había poca diversidad de productos hechos con base en este alimento y los que existían eran muy caros. Así crearon una gama de productos que pueden competir con los del mercado "oficial", pero a menores precios.

30 Un detalle interesante en este negocio es que partieron con materias primas y prácticas tecno productivas que estaban en la familia desde hacía varias generaciones: sus abuelos y sus padres siempre cosecharon el maní en esas tierras. O sea, tenían herramientas, conocimientos y materia prima garan-
35 tizados. Orelvys solo requirió de un pequeño crédito bancario y de sus ahorros, pues en Cuba nadie opta por el crowdfunding, ya que son opciones alejadas por la poca penetración digital que tiene el país.

Sus resultados fueron tan exitosos que fue la primera, y
40 hasta ahora única iniciativa particular cubana que ha obtenido el Premio 2014 de la Oficina Cubana de la Propiedad Industrial a la "Creatividad y la Innovación Tecnológica en la categoría de Signos Distintivos".

Uno de los más rentables es la recarga doble del saldo
45 de telefonía móvil desde el extranjero. ¿Y qué es esto? Un sistema que representa una gran entrada de dinero a la empresa en poco tiempo y a la que solo acceden aquellos que tienen familiares y amigos en el extranjero.

Ese es uno de los nichos interesantes que han descubierto
50 los emprendedores cubanos, creado sitios en Internet desde donde hacer estas recargas y servicios físicos en Cuba. ¿Cómo opera? A nivel local se paga 23 o 25 CUC y desde el extranjero te recargan 20 dólares, que aquí en Cuba se te convierten en 40 CUC.

55 Como en Cuba todo es diferente al resto del mundo, aquí ningún emprendedor usa KickStarter o Indiegogo. En Cuba la financiación de proyectos emprendedores muchas veces cuenta con ayuda de familiares y en otras ocasiones con "inversiones extranjeras" de parientes y amigos que residen
60 en otros países. Eso sí, los encargados del negocio en Cuba nunca reconocen que recibieron ayuda económica desde el extranjero, ya que es algo todavía "gris" en la legislación cubana.

Otra de las opciones que tienen los aventureros y em-
65 prendedores cubanos es pedir un crédito bancario. Pero al parecer no es una oferta muy masificada entre los cubanos, pues recientes informes del Banco Central de Cuba dan a conocer que durante el año 2014 solo 658 de los llamados "cuentapropistas" pidieron créditos a las entidades bancar-
70 ias estatales. Fueron 75 en la capital y 583 en el resto del país; esto representa el 0,1% de los más de 347.000 trabajadores privados registrados, que son lo que se considera emprendedores en Cuba.

Todos estos son emprendedores cubanos que han sabido
75 sacar adelante sus pequeños negocios privados en medio de una economía estatal compleja y marcada por el burocratismo. Pero sobre todo han demostrado que los cubanos pueden encontrar nichos comerciales y posibilidades de negocios donde otros solo verían problemas, pues como
80 dice la frase popular: "El cubano es capaz de venderle hielo a un esquimal".

---

1. ¿Cuál es el propósito del artículo?

   (A) Para mostrar que Cuba ha tenido éxito a nivel mundial con iniciativas y emprendimientos

   (B) Para describir los negocios innovadores en Cuba y cómo han creado negocios con pocos recursos

   (C) Para ilustrar las idiosincrasias de los emprendedores

   (D) Para introducir un cambio fiscal para los emprendedores cubanos

2. ¿Por qué se menciona Orelvys Bormey Torres?

   (A) Para sugerir que todos los negocios como los de él van a tener éxito

   (B) Porque es ingeniero y también emprendedor

   (C) Para ilustrar los riesgos de crear un negocio innovador

   (D) Para dar un ejemplo de un emprendedor que involucra a su familia en su negocio

3. El impacto del gobierno cubano es uno de

   (A) apoyo

   (B) creatividad

   (C) destrucción

   (D) aislamiento

4. ¿Qué significa el título "Cuba ¿País de Emprendedores?"?

   (A) Cuba es un país improbable para crear negocios privados.

   (B) Los emprendedores no son legítimos.

   (C) Los emprendedores solamente tienen negocios que involucran sus parientes.

   (D) Es un país único y compuesto de emprendedores influyentes.

5. Se menciona "¿Y por qué el maní?" para

   (A) ilustrar que hay pocos recursos en Cuba

   (B) describir algunos legumbres que existen naturalmente en Cuba

   (C) mostrar como se involucra la familia en el negocio

   (D) comentar sobre los productos caros que existen en el mercado cubano

6. La última frase "El cubano es capaz de venderle hielo a un esquimal" significa que

   (A) todos los negocios cubanos tienen problemas a causa del burocratismo

   (B) los cubanos son los mejores emprendedores al nivel mundial

   (C) el emprendedor cubano es sabio y usa los recursos que tiene para crear su negocio

   (D) los cubanos y los esquimales hacen negocios a menudo

Translated Text and Questions, with Explanations

Introduction

The following article appeared in 2015 in an electronic magazine of Latin American culture.

Cuba: Country of Entrepreneurs?

Cuban men and women who create new businesses have little, if anything, to do with entrepreneurs at the world level. On this island in the Caribbean, the economy is very different from the rest of the world when speaking of initiatives, startups, and entrepreneurship.

In Cuba, when one is going to start an innovative business, the first thing to think about is the family: "My uncle will lend me part of the money; my brother will work with me; my cousin will look for the raw material, and my wife and I will be the vendors. Then, we will distribute all of the profit according to each person's contributions." This is how Cubans think when they are going to create a new business, from a simple guarapo stand to an inn. Orelvys Bormey Torres, a young industrial engineer, highly specialized in his field, who created a business together with his family, assumes the economic risks and is successful.

Of course this entrepreneur from Villa Clara is not a fool: the first thing that he did was register his brand with the Cuban Registry of Industrial Property. In addition, he organized the business in such a way that the whole family could participate. The objective is that the business would be easier to manage, having to pay less for externally contracted employees, among other advantages of working with relatives.

And why the peanut? They simply found that there was little product diversity made with this food base and those that existed were very expensive. Thus they made a gamut of products that can compete with those on the "official" market, but at lower prices.

An interesting detail in this business is that they shared in raw materials and technological productive practices that existed in the family for several generations: his grandparents and his parents always harvested the peanut on these grounds. That is, that they had the tools, know-how, and guaranteed raw material. Orelvys only needed a small bank credit and his savings, because in Cuba no one opts for crowdfunding, as those options are cut off because of the low level of digital penetration the country has.

Their results were so successful that it was the first, and until now the only, private Cuban initiative that won the 2014 Prize from the Cuban Office of Industrial Property for "Creativity and Technological Innovation in the category of Distinctive Signs."

One of the most profitable businesses is the double cell-phone balance refill from abroad. And what is this? It's a system that represents a grand influx of money to the business in little time and which is only accessed by those who have family and friends abroad.

This is one of the interesting niches that Cuban entrepreneurs have discovered, having created Internet sites from which to make these refills and physical services in Cuba. How does it work? At the local level one pays 23 or 25 CUC and from abroad they re-charge you 20 dollars, which here in Cuba converts to 40 CUC.

Since Cuba is different from the rest of the world, here no entrepreneur uses Kickstarter or Indiegogo. In Cuba the financing of entrepreneurial projects many times counts on help from family members, and other times on "foreign investments" from relatives and friends who reside in other countries. Yes, the managers of businesses in Cuba never recognize they received financial help from abroad, since it is still a "grey area" in Cuban law.

Another of the options that Cuban adventurers and entrepreneurs have is to ask for a bank loan. But it appears not to be widely used among Cubans, as recent reports of the Central Bank of Cuba have revealed that during the year 2014 only 658 of the so-called "self-employed" asked for loans from state banks. There were 75 in the capital and 583 in the rest of the country; this represents 0.1% of the more than 347,000 registered private workers, which are those considered to be entrepreneurs in Cuba.

All these are Cuban entrepreneurs who have managed to develop their small private businesses in the middle of a complex and highly bureaucratic state economy. But above all, they have demonstrated that Cubans can find commercial niches and business possibilities where others only would see problems, as goes the popular phrase: "The Cuban is capable of selling ice to an Inuit."

Here's How to Crack It

1. What is the main point of the article?

   (A) To show that Cuba has had success on the global level with entrepreneurial initiatives

   (B) To describe innovative businesses in Cuba and how people have created businesses with few resources

   (C) To illustrate the idiosyncrasies of entrepreneurs

   (D) To introduce a fiscal change for Cuban entrepreneurs

The main point of the article is to show some of the creativity and resourcefulness needed to grow a business in Cuba. It says the opposite of (A), and does not mention either (C) or (D). Therefore, (B) is the best response.

2. Why is Orelvys Bormey Torres mentioned?

   (A) To suggest that all businesses like his are going to be successful

   (B) Because he is an engineer as well as an entrepreneur

   (C) To illustrate the risks when one creates an innovative business

   (D) To give an example of an entrepreneur who involves his family in his business

Orelvys Bormey Torres is an engineer as well as an entrepreneur, but that is not why he is mentioned, eliminating (B). Choice (A) is extreme, while (C) is not the focus. The real reason he is mentioned is to show how he built his business and involves his family members in the business. Choice (D) is correct.

3. The impact of the Cuban government is one of

   (A) support

   (B) creativity

   (C) destruction

   (D) isolation

The Cuban government is isolating, hence the limited resources available to entrepreneurs. They struggle to compete on the global stage as a result. There certainly are many creative entrepreneurs in Cuba, but the question asks about the government, not the entrepreneurs. Therefore, (D) is the correct response.

4. What does the title "Cuba: Country of Entrepreneurs?" signify?

   (A) Cuba is an improbable country to create private businesses.

   (B) The entrepreneurs are not legitimate.

   (C) The entrepreneurs only have businesses that involve their relatives.

   (D) It is a unique country that is comprised of influential entrepreneurs.

The question mark in the title suggests that Cuba is an unlikely place for private businesses to grow and flourish, as (A) suggests. Choice (B) is not mentioned in the passage, and (C) is too extreme. Choice (D) is tempting, but goes too far by suggesting the whole country is made up of entrepreneurs. Therefore, (A) is the best response.

5. "And why the peanut?" is mentioned to

    (A) illustrate that there are few resources in Cuba

    (B) describe some legumes that exist naturally in Cuba

    (C) show how the family is involved in the business

    (D) comment on the expensive products that exist in the Cuban market

Choice (B) is too literal, and (D) recycles words that are in the passage but that are not relevant to why the peanut is mentioned. Choice (C) best encapsulates *why* the peanut is mentioned, and that is to show how Torres's family works together on different aspects of the business.

6. The last phrase, "The Cuban is capable of selling ice to an Inuit" means that

    (A) all Cuban businesses have problems because of the bureaucracy

    (B) Cubans are the best entrepreneurs on the world stage

    (C) Cuban entrepreneurs are wise and use the resources they have to create their businesses

    (D) Cubans and Inuits frequently do business together

Choice (C) is the best response because it best ties together the main idea of the passage. Choice (A) is too extreme, (B) is false according to the passage, and (D) is just silly.

PRACTICE PASSAGE 3

Introducción

El siguiente artículo fue escrito por Catalina Marzorati-Strauß en 2015.

Laguna Garzón: obra de arte en la naturaleza

Dos amantes del arte y de la arquitectura reconocidos internacionalmente se unieron para construir en Uruguay una obra prácticamente única en el mundo: un puente circular
Linea sobre la Laguna Garzón, ubicado a no más de 100 metros
5 de distancia del mar. El lugar se caracteriza por una belleza inigualable, lo agreste de su paisaje y sus famosos crepúsculos dorados en la época veraniega. Una verdadera obra maestra que cuando esté culminada pasará a ser parte del paisaje natural, pero que no ha estado exenta de polémica
10 especialmente de parte de grupos ecologistas.

Uruguay destaca por su arquitectura y puentes extravagantes como el ondular de Leonel Viera, el de Las Américas en Montevideo o incluso el aeropuerto de Carrasco. Hoy, el país da paso a un nuevo y singular proyecto: un desafío
15 contra las fuerzas naturales, de alta modernidad y control ecológico. Un puente circular, apoyado en una línea única de 28 columnas de 25 metros de altura.

El puente unirá los dos palmos de la Ruta 10 entre Maldonado y Rocha. Por el lado de adentro de la rotonda se
20 transitará con vehículos y por fuera por una terraza "volada", que tendrá una senda peatonal para los transeúntes. Incluso los pescadores tendrán su espacio con zonas para poder sentarse cómodamente y observar los crepúsculos dorados y la variedad de aves de la zona, dos cosas que
25 caracterizan a la laguna.

Según la crítica que se escucha en la zona, sí. La franja que divide el mar de la laguna no tiene más de 500 mt en su zona más ancha y está en este momento completamente loteada para ser vendida a inversores extranjeros.

30 Se debe reconocer que más allá de todo posible interés económico, se unieron dos amantes del arte con una visión en común: hacer una obra maestra que fluya en y con la naturaleza. Por un lado está el inversor, Costantini, de ojo artístico y director del Museo de Arte Malba de Argentina,
35 uno de los más famosos en Sudamérica. Por el otro está Rafael Viñoly, el arquitecto uruguayo que hizo el diseño del puente.

Viñoly se caracteriza por sus obras innovadoras a nivel internacional y según comenta, "el gran precio profesional
40 de un arquitecto es justamente el péndulo constante de verse a uno mismo como artista y al mismo tiempo tener que respetar los adelantos técnicos de cada obra."

El Ministerio de Transporte, luego de años de tratativas e intentos por lograr un paso sobre la Laguna Garzón, aceptó
45 el proyecto de este puente circular, como los hay pocos en el mundo.

Sin embargo, como toda nueva creación artística, aún no plasmada y difícil de imaginar, no está ausente de crítica. Es más, este puente vivió grandes temporales antes de ser con-
50 struido. Estos no fueron causados por los conocidos vientos de la zona, debido a la cercanía al mar, sino que provinieron de críticas de los lugareños y de la sociedad.

La mayoría de ellas están basadas en los temores ante la posible destrucción y contaminación del medio ambiente.
55 La Laguna Garzón fue declarada "Área de importancia para la conservación de aves", por la presencia de más de 700 variedades de pájaros de 32 especies diferentes. Entre ellas se encuentran especies amenazadas como el playerito canela y el bellísimo y elegante flamenco austral, así como peces y
60 crustáceos poco comunes.

Hoy la laguna tiene una población de 77 personas, según la intendencia local. Hasta el año 2035 se proyecta una población de 11.200. Hoy existen solo 17 casas y para 2035 se esperan 2089 casas.

65 Para esta última fecha, se tiene previsto la construcción de una docena de proyectos de urbanización para personas acaudaladas, en su mayoría extranjeros. Antes de la planificación del puente, los precios por hectárea no sobrepasaban los U.S. $3000; hoy van desde U.S. $30.000 hasta U.S.
70 $1.000.000 por ha.

1. Los dos amantes del arte y de la arquitectura

    (A) son destinados a tener éxito con el puente sobre la laguna

    (B) tienen las facultades necesarias para construir la obra prósperamente

    (C) tienen más recursos financieros que El Ministerio de Transporte

    (D) van a destruir el medio ambiente a causa de su obra maestra

2. Se menciona "el ondular de Leonel Viera, el de Las Américas en Montevideo o incluso el aeropuerto de Carrasco" en líneas 12–13 para

    (A) dar ejemplos de otras obras únicas de la arquitectura en Uruguay

    (B) inferir que los puentes en Uruguay son los mejores de Sudamérica

    (C) ilustrar las diferencias entre los puentes que ya existen

    (D) sugerir que el puente sobre la laguna debe ser como los otros diseños

3. Según la crítica, las siguientes consecuencias puedan pasar SALVO:

    (A) la urbanización de la zona

    (B) precios inflados para comprar lotes

    (C) los extranjeros controlarán la municipalidad

    (D) unas especies amenazadas estarán en peligro

4. Podemos inferir que

    (A) acabarán el puente en el año 2035

    (B) el puente puede poner en riesgo el medio ambiente

    (C) Costantini y Viñoly trabajaron con El Ministerio de Transporte para diseñar el puente

    (D) hoy en día un hectárea cuesta más de $30.000 dólares

5. ¿Por qué se menciona que la laguna tiene una población de 77 personas hoy en día?

    (A) Para introducir retórica en contra de la construcción del puente

    (B) Para cambiar el sujeto del párrafo

    (C) Para dar un ejemplo

    (D) Para demostrar un contraste

6. ¿Cuál es la idea principal de esta selección?

    (A) El puente está destinado a destruir la naturaleza con urbanización y contaminación.

    (B) La destrucción y la contaminación del medio ambiente son a causa de Costantini y Viñoly.

    (C) La Laguna Garzón fue declarada un área de importancia para la conservación de aves, y no se debe construir el puente.

    (D) El puente será una obra de arte significativa, pero hay riesgos ambientales y comerciales a la laguna.

Translated Text and Questions, with Explanations

Introduction

The following article was written by Catalina Marzorati-Strauß in 2015.

Garzón Laguna: Work of Art in Nature

Two internationally recognized art and architecture lovers united to construct a work in Uruguay that is practically one-of-a-kind in the world: a circular bridge over the Garzón Laguna, located no more than 100 meters from the sea. The location is characterized by an unequalled beauty, the wildness of its landscape, and its famous golden sunsets in the summer season. A true masterwork that, when it is finished, will become part of the natural landscape, but which has not been exempt from controversy, especially among ecological groups.

Uruguay stands out for its architecture and extravagant bridges, like Leonel Viera's stressed ribbon bridge, the Bridge of The Americas in Montevideo, or even the Carrasco airport. Today, the country gives rise to a new and singular project: a challenge against the natural forces, very modern and involving ecological control. A circular bridge, supported on a single line of 28 columns 25 meters high.

The bridge will unite the two spans of route 10 between Maldonado and Rocha. The inside of the rotunda will circulate vehicle traffic and on the outside the "flying" terrace will have a pedestrian pathway for passers-by. Even fishermen will have their space, with zones where they can sit comfortably and observe the golden sunsets and the variety of birds in the area, two things that characterize the laguna.

According to the criticism that one hears about the area, yes. The band that divides the sea from the laguna is not more than 500 meters in its widest place, and is at this moment completely divided into lots to be sold to foreign investors.

It should be recognized that beyond all the possible economic interest, the two art lovers united with a common vision to make a masterwork that flows in and with the nature around it. On one side is the investor, Costantini, with an artistic eye: the director of the Arte Malba Museum in Argentina, one of the most famous in South America. On the other side is Rafael Viñoly, the Uruguayan architect who designed the bridge.

Viñoly is known for his innovative works on an international level and according to his comment, "the great price, professionally, of being an architect is precisely the constant pendulum of seeing yourself as an artist and at the same time having to respect the technical specifications of each work."

The Ministry of Transportation, after years of negotiations and attempts to build a path over the Garzón Laguna, accepted this circular bridge project, as there are few in the world.

Nevertheless, as with all new artistic creations, even ones still unrealized and difficult to imagine, it's not free from criticism. Furthermore, this bridge lived through great storms before being constructed. Those were not caused by the well-known winds in the area, which are due to the close proximity to the sea, but rather by criticism from locals and from society.

The majority of critiques are based on fears of possible destruction and contamination of the environment. The Garzón Laguna was declared "an area of importance for bird conservation," because of the presence of over 700 varieties of birds from 32 different species. Among these, one encounters endangered species like the buff-breasted sandpiper and the beautiful and elegant Chilean flamingo, as well as uncommon fish and crustaceans.

Today the laguna has a population of 77 people, according to local administration. It is projected that by the year 2035 the population will be 11,200. Today there exist only 17 houses and by 2035 they expect 2,089 houses.

By this latter date, the construction of a dozen urbanization projects have been planned for the wealthy, the majority of whom are foreigners. Before the planning of the bridge, prices per hectare weren't over 3,000 U.S. dollars; today they range from $30,000 up to $1,000,000.

Here's How to Crack It

1. The two art and architecture lovers
   - (A) are destined to have success with the bridge over the laguna
   - **(B) have the necessary resources to successfully construct the work**
   - (C) have more financial resources than the Ministry of Transportation
   - (D) are going to destroy the environment with their masterwork

Choice (B) is correct because they have made a deal with the Ministry of Transportation to fund the project. The bridge is not "destined" for anything, eliminating (A) and (D). Choice (C) is unsupported by the passage.

2. The phrase "Leonel Viera's stressed ribbon bridge, the Bridge of The Americas in Montevideo, or even the Carrasco airport" is mentioned in lines 12–13 in order to
   - **(A) give examples of other unique architectural works in Uruguay**
   - (B) imply that the bridges in Uruguay are the best in South America
   - (C) illustrate the differences among the bridges that already exist
   - (D) suggest that the bridge over the laguna should be like the other designs

The phrase mentions other interesting architectural projects in Uruguay, as in (A). It does not say that the bridges are the best in South America or what the differences are among them, eliminating (B) and (C). It does not suggest anything about designs, eliminating (D) as well. Therefore, (A) is the correct response.

3. According to the critics, any of the following consequences could happen EXCEPT:
   - (A) the urbanization of the area
   - (B) inflated prices to buy land lots
   - **(C) foreigners will control the local government**
   - (D) some endangered species could be in danger

In the ninth paragraph, the article mentions risks to the environment and to the wildlife, and the last paragraph mentions the rapidly increasing prices for land in the area. Nowhere does the article say that foreigners will control the government, though they most likely will own land or businesses in the area once the commercial lots are developed. Therefore, (C) is correct.

4. We can infer that
   - (A) the bridge will be completed in the year 2035
   - **(B) the bridge could put the environment at risk**
   - (C) Costantini and Viñoly worked with the Ministry of Transportation to design the bridge
   - (D) today a hectare of land costs more than $30,000 dollars

Choice (B) is the only choice that can be supported by the text. Be careful to eliminate answer choices that are not written in the passage!

5. Why is it mentioned that the laguna has a population of 77 people today?

(A) To introduce rhetoric against the construction of the bridge

(B) To change the subject of the paragraph

(C) To give an example

(D) To demonstrate a contrast

The mention of the current population is to contrast with the possible increase to 11,200 people by 2035. It is not an example of a previous idea, nor does it change the subject of the paragraph, eliminating (B) and (C). It is a possible argument against the construction of the bridge, but it is not a rhetorical device in an argument, eliminating (A). Therefore, (D) is correct.

6. What is the main idea of this selection?

(A) The bridge is destined to destroy the environment with urbanization and pollution.

(B) The destruction and contamination of the environment are because of Costantini and Viñoly.

(C) The Garzón Laguna was declared an area of importance for bird conservation and so the bridge should not be constructed.

(D) The bridge will be a significant artwork, but there are environmental and commercial risks to the laguna.

Choice (A) predicts the future and is too extreme. Choice (B) attributes all of the bridge's potential destruction to the two art lovers, making it incorrect. Choice (C) contains a true statement and an unsupported opinion; regardless, it is not the main point of the passage. Only (D) is broad enough to encapsulate the main idea of the passage.

PRACTICE PASSAGE 4

Interpretive Communication: Print Texts

Introducción

El siguiente artículo apareció en 1993 en el periódico *La Cultura Latina*.

Panamá: el misterio de las calles sin nombre

Panamá es actualmente uno de los destinos turísticos más populares del continente y una de las economías más fuertes de la región. Sin embargo, el caos es parte natural de su hermosa ciudad capital. Casi no existe planificación urbana y tanto los propios panameños como los turistas sufren a diario tratando de encontrar una simple calle. Describir de forma visual la ubicación de un lugar puede ser complicado, algunos sin duda forma parte de la vida cotidiana de sus habitantes. Si te atreves, acompaña a nuestra periodista en esta misteriosa aventura a través de la ciudad, tratando de descifrar "el misterio de las calles sin nombre"…

A pesar de todos los avances logrados durante poco más de un siglo de vida republicana, los panameños todavía tenemos que convivir con algunos legados de nuestro pasado, como el no tener un sistema bien planificado y señalizado de calles. Hablar de cuadras, avenidas con nombres propios y edificios con numeración es muy extraño.

Después de la independencia, Panamá tuvo un gran crecimiento económico. Esto generó migraciones masivas desde áreas rurales del país y del extranjero, que obligaron a la ciudad a expandirse. De la noche a la mañana, esta urbe comenzó a crecer desordenadamente, sobrepasando la capacidad de planificación de las autoridades.

El crecimiento no se detuvo, incluso aumentó. La apertura del Canal y otros sucesos del siglo XX nos dejaron como herencia una ciudad no solamente llena de rincones, sino de calles que se quedaron sin nombre.

"Aquí cada quién hizo lo que le dio la gana, y no hubo autoridad interesada en poner orden", recuerda Carmen, docente retirada de 76 años de edad. "Hay unas calles que no tienen nombre, y otras que tienen hasta dos y tres", asegura.

Para Maru, argentina y miembro del cuerpo diplomático, este problema obedece a aspectos culturales arraigados en la mentalidad de los panameños. "La primera vez que intenté salir sola me aprendí la dirección y llamé un taxi. Cuando le di el nombre de la calle y el número de la embajada, el conductor no sabía de qué le estaba hablando. El hombre insistía en preguntarme sobre algún lugar de referencia que quedara cerca. Ningún taxista me pudo llevar."

Una cosa que le llama muchísimo la atención es que la gente utilice como puntos de referencia cosas que ya no existen y que dejaron incluso de existir mucho antes de que ellos nacieran, como "la Lechería", el Teatro Bella Vista, "el Casino", la estatua de Roosevelt o el antiguo Club de Golf, entre otros.

¿Solución?

Hace cerca de 15 años, la autoridad trató de señalizar casi todas las calles residenciales de la ciudad, asignándoles nombres de flores y plantas. Poco a poco los letreros fueron desapareciendo y con ellos, los nombres que se suponía que serían más fáciles de recordar. La fórmula de número, letra y punto cardinal ha vuelto a ser el sistema oficial utilizado por el Municipio de Panamá. Sin embargo, esto no parece haber hecho efecto en los habitantes de la ciudad, que están acostumbrados a su constante crecimiento y cambios.

Used by permission of VeinteMundos.com

1. ¿Cuál es el propósito del artículo?

   (A) Los habitantes de Panamá deben usar nombres para distinguir las calles.

   (B) La planificación urbana es un desafío para Panamá, que sigue cambiando con el crecimiento de la ciudad.

   (C) El nombramiento de las avenidas y calles es uno de los proyectos más importantes de la planificación urbana en Panamá.

   (D) Las personas entrevistadas tienen las soluciones para mejorar el sistema de nombrar las calles.

2. ¿Cuál es una explicación para las calles sin nombres?

   (A) Hay calles que no tienen nombre, y otras que tienen hasta dos y tres.

   (B) Es un destino turístico, y por lo tanto las calles no necesitan nombres.

   (C) Los extranjeros tenían sus propios nombres para ciertas calles, mientras que los panameños tenían otros para las mismas.

   (D) La ciudad creció desordenadamente, sobrepasando la capacidad de planificación de las autoridades.

3. Después de la independencia, todos los siguientes eventos sucedieron EXCEPTO:

   (A) Panamá tuvo un gran crecimiento económico

   (B) hubo una gran cantidad de migraciones a la ciudad desde áreas rurales del país

   (C) la planificación urbana nombró las cuadras, avenidas y calles con nombres propios

   (D) se abrió el Canal poco tiempo después

4. Según la entrevista de Maru, ¿por qué se menciona el taxi?

   (A) Era difícil comunicar su destino al taxista con solamente el nombre de calle.

   (B) El taxista no podía comprender el acento argentino de Maru.

   (C) Los lugares de referencia se convertían en distracciones para el taxista.

   (D) Maru debe obedecer las tradiciones y la mentalidad de los panameños.

5. Se menciona «"la Lechería"… entre otros» para

   (A) nombrar unos lugares donde muchas personas nacieron

   (B) mostrar que muchos de los lugares de referencia son antiguos

   (C) sugerir nombres para las calles en estos lugares

   (D) dar ejemplos de lugares de referencia que ya no existen

6. Según el último párrafo, ¿qué podemos inferir de los cambios que ha implementado el Municipio de Panamá?

   (A) Los cambios fueron un fracaso porque nadie usa los nombres propios de las calles.

   (B) El Municipio de Panamá ordenó a los panameños que usen los nombres propios de las calles.

   (C) No parecen haber hecho mucho efecto.

   (D) La fórmula de número, letra y punto cardinal mejorará la organización urbana de la ciudad.

Translated Text and Questions, with Explanations

Introduction

The following article appeared in 1993 in the periodical *The Latino Culture*.

Panama: The Mystery of the Nameless Streets

Nowadays, Panama is one of the most popular tourist destinations on the continent and one of the strongest economies in the region. Nevertheless, chaos is a natural part of its beautiful capital city. Urban planning hardly exists, and just as many native Panamanians as tourists suffer daily trying to find a simple street. Describing the visual aspects of the whereabouts of a location can be complicated; this without a doubt is already part of the daily lives of its inhabitants. If you dare, accompany our journalist on this mysterious adventure through the city, trying to decipher "the mystery of the nameless streets"....

Despite all the successful advances over more than a century of republican life, we Panamanians still have to live with some legacies of our past, such as not having a well-planned system of naming the streets. Referring to districts and avenues with proper names and buildings with numbers is very strange.

After its independence, Panama underwent great economic growth. This generated large migrations to the city from rural areas of the country and abroad, which forced the city to expand. Overnight, this metropolis began to grow in a disorganized fashion, surpassing the planning capacity of the authorities.

The growth did not stop or slow, but rather increased. The opening of the Canal and other events of the 20th century left us with the legacy of a city not only full of nooks and corners, but also streets without names.

"Here, everyone did what they felt like, and there was no authority interested in creating order," remembers Carmen, a 76-year-old retired teacher. "There are some streets that do not have names,, and others that have two or three," she maintains.

For Maru, an Argentinian and member of the diplomatic corps, this problem lies in aspects of culture rooted in the mentality of the Panamanians. "The first time I tried to go out by myself, I found the address and called a taxi. When I gave him the name of the street and number of the embassy, the driver did not know what I was talking about. The man insisted on asking me for some landmarks that were around there. No taxi driver could get me there."

One thing that is very noticeable is that people use points of reference that do not exist anymore, including many from before they were born, like "the Dairy," "the Bella Vista theater," "the Casino," the statue of Roosevelt, or the old Golf Club, among others.

Solutions?

About 15 years ago, the authorities tried to post signs naming almost all the residential streets of the city, assigning them names of flowers and plants. Little by little, the signs disappeared, and, with them, the names that were supposed to be easier to remember. The formula of number, letter, and geographic point has become the official system utilized by the Panama Municipality. Nevertheless, this does not appear to have had an effect on the inhabitants of the city, who are accustomed to its constant growth and change.

Here's How to Crack It

1. What is the purpose of the article?

   (A) The inhabitants of Panama should use names to distinguish their streets.

   (B) Urban planning is a challenge for Panama, which continues to change and grow.

   (C) The classification of avenues and streets is one of the most important urban planning projects in Panama.

   (D) The interviewees have solutions to improve the system of naming the streets.

Choice (B) is the correct answer. The main purpose of the article is to explain, through interviews, the phenomenon of Panama's unmarked streets, and the ways in which residents have substituted using landmarks as a means of coping with the problem. The urban planning system has had many challenges in naming and organizing the streets, due to the city's constant growth and change. The passage never mentions what Panamanians should or should not do (A), nor that the interviewees have solutions for the problem of naming the streets (D). Choice (C) is a trap because it is extreme.

2. What is one explanation for the streets without names?

   (A) There are some streets without names, while others have two or three.

   (B) It is a tourist destination, and, for the most part, it is not necessary to name the streets.

   (C) The foreigners had their own names for certain streets, while Panamanians had other names for the same ones.

   (D) The city grew in a disorderly fashion, surpassing the planning capacity of the authorities.

Choice (D) is the correct answer. After independence, the city grew at a rapid pace, a pace that the urban planners could not match. Therefore, the city expanded without adequate city planning and developed without official street names. While (A) is mentioned during an interview, it is merely an observation and not a real explanation for the nameless streets. Neither (B) nor (C) is true.

3. After independence, all of the following happened EXCEPT:

   (A) Panama experienced great economic growth

   (B) there were many people who migrated to the city from rural areas of the country

   (C) the urban planning department named the blocks, avenues, and streets with proper names

   (D) the Canal opened shortly thereafter

After independence, the city expanded economically (A) and attracted a lot of citizens from rural areas of the country (B). The Canal opened shortly after as well (D), but there is no mention that the urban planners named the streets, blocks, and avenues during that time. Therefore, (C) is correct.

4. According to Maru's interview, why is the taxi mentioned?

   (A) It was difficult to communicate her destination to the taxi driver using only the street name.

   (B) The taxi driver couldn't understand Maru's Argentinian accent.

   (C) The landmarks became distractions for the taxi driver.

   (D) Maru should abide by the traditions and mentality of the Panamanians.

Maru recounts her experience of trying to take a taxi in Panama to illustrate how difficult it was to communicate her destination with only a street address. The taxi driver did not seem to understand this type of address, but rather asked for landmarks around the destination. Choice (B) recycles phrases, and the text never says that the taxi driver cannot understand Maru's accent. Choice (D) is not mentioned anywhere in the text. Therefore, (A) is correct.

5. "'The Dairy,'…among others" is mentioned to

   (A) name some locations where many people were born

   (B) show that many of the landmarks are old

   (C) suggest names for the streets in those locations

   (D) give some examples of landmarks that do not exist anymore

The Dairy, the Casino, the Bella Vista theater, and others are examples of landmarks that no longer exist, yet native residents still refer to them. In fact, these landmarks disappeared before many residents were born. Though these landmarks are or were old (B), that is not the main reason for their mention here. They are certainly not locations in which residents were born, as in (A). Therefore, (D) is correct, as they are merely landmarks that residents refer to.

6. According to the last paragraph, what can we infer about the changes that have been implemented by the Municipality of Panama?

   (A) The changes were a failure because no one uses the proper names of the streets.

   (B) The Municipality of Panama mandated that the Panamanians use the proper names of the streets.

   (C) The changes do not appear to have had much effect.

   (D) The formula of number, letter, and geographic coordinate will improve the city's urban planning.

Choice (C) is the correct answer. Many changes implemented in the last 15 years in Panama have not been of much use, as some of the street signs have disappeared, and Panamanians still refer to landmarks instead of street names for directions. Choice (A) is too extreme, and (D) predicts the future. Choice (B) is not mentioned in the passage, so (C) must be correct.

PRACTICE PASSAGE 5

Introducción

El siguiente panfleto apareció en 2008 del Ministerio de Salud de la Universidad de Puerto Rico.

INFLUENZA A (H1N1)
Información, precauciones y acciones a tomar.

¿Qué es la influenza A(H1N1)?
Se trata de un nuevo virus de influenza capaz de producir la enfermedad en el ser humano, originado en el cerdo por el intercambio genético entre los virus porcinos, aviarios y humanos.

¿Cómo se transmite la influenza A(H1N1)?
De persona a persona (el virus entra al organismo por la boca, la nariz y los ojos), principalmente cuando las personas enfermas o portadoras de influenza A(H1N1) expulsan gotitas de saliva al estornudar o toser frente a otra sin cubrirse la boca y la nariz, al compartir utensilios o alimentos con una persona enferma o al saludar de mano, beso o abrazo a una persona enferma. También se puede transmitir a través del contacto con superficies previamente contaminadas con gotitas de saliva de una persona enferma de influenza A(H1N1), tales como las manos, mesas, teclados de computadora, manijas, barandales, pañuelos desechables y telas.

¿Cuáles son los síntomas de la influenza A(H1N1)?
Fiebre de 38°C o más, tos y dolor de cabeza, acompañados de uno o más de los siguientes síntomas: escurrimiento nasal, congestión nasal, dolor de articulaciones, dolor muscular, decaimiento, dolor al tragar, dolor de pecho, dolor de estómago y diarrea.

¿Cuál es la gravedad de la enfermedad?
No se conoce hasta el momento la verdadera mortalidad de la enfermedad. Resulta importante hacer notar que la influenza estacional también puede producir manifestaciones severas en pacientes que integran algunos grupos de riesgo (mayores de 65 y menores de 5 años, personas afectadas por enfermedades cardiorrespiratorias crónicas, inmunosuprimidos, y diabéticos).

¿Por cuánto tiempo puede una persona infectada propagar la influenza a otras?
Las personas infectadas por el virus de la influenza A(H1N1) pueden transmitir la enfermedad mientras tengan los síntomas y posiblemente hasta siete días después del inicio de la enfermedad. Los niños, especialmente los más pequeños, podrían ser contagiosos durante períodos más largos.

¿Existe un tratamiento efectivo?
El tratamiento con Tamiflu es efectivo especialmente si se administra en los primeros dos días de iniciados los síntomas y está recomendado en casos sospechosos o confirmados. Esta medicación será provista por el Ministerio de Salud con unas instrucciones que el médico comunicará al paciente.

¿Es útil la vacuna antigripal (influenza estacional)?
La vacuna antigripal no incluye al virus influenza A(H1N1) por lo que no es útil para prevenir esta enfermedad. Sin embargo, es importante cumplir con la vacunación anual en los grupos de riesgo.

¿Qué debe hacer una persona que presente síntomas?
Acudir a la unidad de salud que le corresponda para que el médico le realice el diagnóstico clínico y de laboratorio. Sólo el médico deberá indicar la administración de medicamentos antivirales para el tratamiento. NO AUTOMEDICARSE.

¿Cuáles son los signos de alarma que deben motivar una consulta urgente?
Además de los síntomas ya descritos debe realizarse una consulta de urgencia en caso de presentar los siguientes síntomas.

- Dificultad para respirar
- Color azul o gris de la piel (cianosis)
- Dolor de pecho o abdomen
- Desorientación
- Vómito

Medidas De Prevención

Para reducir la probabilidad de exposición y transmisión del virus es muy importante que TODOS realicemos las medidas de higiene personal y del entorno. Por eso es muy importante que adoptemos como hábitos las siguientes medidas:

- Lavarse las manos frecuentemente con agua y jabón o utilizar gel a base de alcohol al llegar de la calle, antes de comer o después de estar en contacto con espacios contaminados.
- Al toser o estornudar, cubrirse la nariz y boca con un pañuelo desechable o con el ángulo interno del brazo.
- No escupir. Si es necesario hacerlo, utilizar un pañuelo desechable, meterlo en una bolsa de plástico, cerrarla con un nudo y tirarla a la basura.
- No tocarse la cara con las manos sucias, sobre todo la nariz, la boca y los ojos.
- Limpiar y desinfectar superficies y objetos de uso común en casa, oficinas y escuelas, además de ventilar y permitir la entrada de luz solar.
- No compartir bebidas ni utensilios que pueden transmitir los virus y otros gérmenes.

1. ¿Cuál es el tono del panfleto?

   (A) Miedo

   (B) Entusiasmo

   (C) Curiosidad

   (D) Aviso

2. Se puede trasmitir la influenza H1N1 a través de

   (A) cubrirse la nariz y boca con un pañuelo desechable o con el ángulo interno del brazo

   (B) estar en contacto con los cerdos, el origen del virus

   (C) el contacto con superficies previamente contaminadas

   (D) ser mayor de 65 años o menor de 5 años, o ser de un grupo de riesgo elevado

3. Se menciona "mayores de 65… diabéticos" para

   (A) identificar unos grupos de riesgo elevado para las manifestaciones severas

   (B) recomendar que ellos tomen Tamiflu

   (C) identificar a personas que sienten fiebre de 38°C o más, tos y dolor de cabeza, acompañados de otros síntomas

   (D) nombrar los grupos de personas que contraerán la influenza

4. Según el panfleto, ¿es útil la vacuna antigripal para prevenir la influenza H1N1?

   (A) Es una vacunación anual que los grupos de riesgo deben tomar para evitarse la influenza H1N1.

   (B) La vacuna no tiene ningún beneficio para nadie.

   (C) Es importante cumplir con la vacunación anual para evitar la influenza.

   (D) Aunque la vacuna anual previene la influenza regular, no incluye el H1N1.

5. Desorientación, vómitos, y otros síntomas similares son ejemplos de

   (A) los que se presentan en los grupos de riesgo

   (B) síntomas normales de la influenza, que se presentan durante solamente tres días

   (C) los que deben ocasionar una consulta de urgencia

   (D) los que resultan de las medidas de prevención

6. Todas las siguientes son medidas de prevención de la influenza SALVO:

   (A) lavarse las manos frecuentemente con agua y jabón o utilizar gel a base de alcohol

   (B) al toser o estornudar, abrir la boca al aire libre

   (C) limpiar y desinfectar superficies y objetos de uso común

   (D) ventilar y permitir la entrada de luz solar

Translated Text and Questions, with Explanations

Introduction

The following pamphlet appeared in 2008 from the Ministry of Health of The University of Puerto Rico.

INFLUENZA A (H1N1)

Information, Precautions, and Actions to Take

What is influenza A(H1N1)?

It is a new flu virus capable of making humans sick, originating from pigs in a genetic exchange between the porcine, avian, and human viruses.

How is influenza A(H1N1) transmitted?

It is transmitted from person to person (the virus enters an organism through the mouth, nose, or eyes), primarily when sick persons or carriers of the influenza A(H1N1) expel droplets of saliva from sneezing or coughing in front of another without covering the mouth or nose, when one shares utensils or food with a sick person, or when shaking hands, kissing, or hugging a sick person. Also, it can be transmitted through contact with surfaces previously contaminated by droplets of saliva from a person sick with influenza A(H1N1) such as hands, tables, keyboards, handles, banisters, tissues, and fabrics.

What are the symptoms of influenza A(H1N1)?

Fever of 38°C or higher, cough, and headache, accompanied by one or more of the following symptoms: runny nose, nasal congestion, joint pain, muscular soreness, lack of energy, painful swallowing, chest pain, stomach pain, and diarrhea.

How serious is it?

At this point, the real severity of the disease is not known. It is important to note that the seasonal flu can also produce severe cases in patients in higher-risk groups (older than 65 and younger than 5 years of age, those affected by diseases such as chronic cardiorespiratory conditions, the immunosuppressed, and diabetics).

For how long can an infected person spread the flu to others?

Persons infected with the influenza A(H1N1) virus can spread the sickness while they have symptoms, and possibly up to seven days after its start. Children, especially the youngest, can be contagious for longer durations of time.

Is there an effective treatment?

The treatment Tamiflu is effective, especially if administered in the first two days after the onset of symptoms, and is recommended in suspected or confirmed cases. The Health Ministry will provide this medication with instructions that the doctor will communicate to the patient.

Is the flu vaccine useful (seasonal influenza)?

The flu vaccine does not include the influenza A(H1N1) virus, and therefore is not useful in preventing this disease. Nevertheless, it is important for groups at higher risk to get the annual vaccination.

What should a person who presents symptoms do?

Attend a health clinic in which a doctor can carry out clinical and laboratory diagnostics. Only a doctor can prescribe and administer antiviral medications for treatment. DO NOT TREAT YOURSELF.

What are some warning signs that should prompt you to seek urgent care?

In addition to the symptoms already described, one should seek urgent care if the following symptoms are present:

- Difficulty breathing
- Blue- or grey-colored skin (cyanosis)
- Chest or abdominal pain
- Disorientation
- Vomiting

Prevention Measures

To reduce the probability of exposure and transmission of the virus, it is important that EVERYONE carry out measures regarding personal hygiene and their surroundings. For this reason, it is very important that we adopt the following habits:

- Wash your hands frequently with soap and water or use alcohol-based gel upon arriving home, before eating, or after contact with contaminated spaces.

- When coughing or sneezing, cover your nose and mouth with a disposable tissue or the inside of your elbow.

- Do not spit. If it is necessary to do so, use a disposable tissue and put it in a plastic bag, tie it closed with a knot, and throw it in the trash.

- Do not touch your face with dirty hands: above all your nose, mouth, and eyes.

- Clean and disinfect commonly used surfaces and objects at homes, offices, and schools, along with ventilating and allowing in sunlight.

- Do not share beverages or utensils that can transmit viruses and other germs.

Here's How to Crack It

1. What is the tone of the pamphlet?
   (A) Fear
   (B) Enthusiasm
   (C) Curiosity
   (D) Advisory

Choice (D) is correct. The tone of the pamphlet is one of advice and warning to college students about the seriousness of the flu. Though fear (A) might be tempting, it is too extreme, and the others, enthusiasm (B) and curiosity (C), do not make sense.

2. One can transmit the H1N1 virus by
   (A) covering the nose and mouth with a disposable tissue or with the inside of the elbow
   (B) being in contact with pigs, the origin of the virus
   (C) being in contact with previously contaminated surfaces
   (D) being older than 65 years old, younger than 5 years old, or in a high-risk group

Choice (C) is correct. Covering your nose and mouth with a tissue or elbow is supposed to help stop the spread of the flu (A). However, having contact with previously contaminated surfaces that have bits of saliva from a sick person can contribute to the spread of the disease (C). Being in a high-risk group does not mean that one will get the flu, so it has nothing to do with transmitting the disease (D), and the pamphlet never mentions being around pigs as a means of transfer either (B).

3. "Those over 65...diabetics" are mentioned in order to
   (A) identify some groups at increased risk for severe cases
   (B) recommend that they take Tamiflu
   (C) identify some people who experience fevers of 38°C and higher, cough, and headache, along with other symptoms
   (D) name the groups of people who will get the flu

Persons over 65, diabetics, and the others mentioned are various groups with elevated risk for getting the flu, not those who already have the flu. Tamiflu is the drug one takes when one already has the flu (B), and one also would already have the flu if one were presenting with fevers and other symptoms (C). Choice (D) predicts the future as to who will get the flu, so (A) is correct.

4. According to the pamphlet, is the flu vaccine useful in preventing the H1N1 virus?

(A) It is an annual vaccination that at-risk groups should get to avoid the H1N1 virus.

(B) The vaccine does not have any benefits for anyone.

(C) It is important to get the annual vaccination to avoid influenza.

(D) Even though the annual vaccine prevents the regular flu, it does not include the H1N1 virus.

Choice (D) is correct. The flu vaccine, while useful in protecting against seasonal influenza, does not protect against the influenza A(H1N1) virus. Choice (A) contains recycled words that suggest that at-risk groups should get the vaccine; however, the passage states that it does not protect against the H1N1 virus; and (B) is extreme. Choice (C) is contained in the passage, but does not answer the question of whether or not the vaccine protects against influenza A(H1N1).

5. Disorientation, vomiting, and other similar symptoms are examples of

(A) those which are present in high-risk groups

(B) normal symptoms of the flu, which present themselves and only last three days

(C) those which should result in emergency care

(D) those which are the result of preventative measures

Choice (C) is correct. Disorientation, vomiting, and others are examples of symptoms that need urgent medical care. They are not normal symptoms that only last for three days, as in (B). These symptoms will not necessarily be present in at-risk groups (A), and they are certainly not the result of preventative measures (D).

6. All of the following are preventative measures for the flu EXCEPT:

(A) washing your hands frequently with soap and water or using alcohol-based gel

(B) while coughing or sneezing, opening your mouth to the open air

(C) cleaning and disinfecting commonly used surfaces and objects

(D) ventilating areas and allowing in sunlight

Choice (B) is correct. Opening your nose and mouth to the open air while sneezing or coughing is exactly the opposite of what the pamphlet advises. All other choices are in the "preventative measures" portion of the pamphlet.

PRACTICE PASSAGE 6

Introducción

El siguiente artículo apareció en 2005 en una revista de literatura juvenil.

La Aventura de don Quijote en la escuela

©BIRGIT RIEGER, KIKA SUPERBRUJA Y DON QUIJOTE DE LA MANCHA, BRUÑO, 2004.

En este Año del Quijote, el autor aprovecha para hablar de la lectura del clásico en la escuela y para analizar la gran cantidad de adaptaciones y recreaciones de la obra de Cervantes que están ‹colonizado› actualmente el mercado.

Como casi todo el mundo sabe, el 2005 es el año del *Quijote* ya que se coincide con los 400 años de su primera edición.
También coinciden —aunque ya no todo el mundo sabe— los
Línea doscientos años de nacimiento de Hans Christian Andersen, el
5 inmortal autor de cuentos tan universales como *El patito feo*, o los cien años de la muerte de Jules Verne, además los 50 años de la muerte de Albert Einstein, el de la teoría de la relatividad.

Es por ello que este año fue declarado oficialmente Año de la Lectura y del Libro. Hay muchos eventos conmemorativos que
10 celebrarán la historia del experto autor de la obra cervantina y muchos otros autores.

Versiones, adaptaciones, recreaciones del clásico

Lo primero que nos sorprende es la proliferación de diferentes versiones que lanzan las editoriales, con un esfuerzo
15 evidente de ocupar el mercado. Adaptaciones en las que hay supresión de partes o capítulos, o nuevas reescrituras intentando cambiar la historia, son las más fastidiosas.

Otra cosa son las versiones que llamamos ‹recreaciones o inclusiones libres›. Estas me parecen más honestas ya que no
20 hay interrupción en el personaje cervantino. Cuando se cambia el personaje, metido en otro mundo que no es el suyo, resulta demasiado esperpéntico y se le ‹infantiliza› demasiado, lo que a mi juicio, no es positivo para ganarse a corto plazo más lectores de la novela.

Darlo a conocer, sin imponerlo
25 Vistos todos estos argumentos, la pregunta clave es: ¿cómo se debe entonces proceder? ¿Cuál es la metodología adecuada? Es cierto que no hay soluciones fáciles porque el camino para consolidar hábitos de lectura está lleno de obstáculos.

Pero, dicho esto, lo que en primer lugar se debe hacer es ed-
30 ucar, sin prisas pero sin pausas. La mejor medicina es extender el conocimiento de los buenos libros infantiles, de la buena literatura infantil o juvenil. Una vez puestos estos cimientos, el camino estará mejor preparado. Solo queda dar prioridad a
35 la lectura placentera, darles la oportunidad de leer y de elegir, declarar la lectura patrimonio común de los escolares. Incluso depararles la oportunidad de hojearlo o de no leerlo.

No sea el caso que el exceso de celo produzca los efectos contrarios a los que proponemos: «La sombra del *Quijote*
40 —dice Ana María Matute— planeaba sobre nuestras vidas de escolares nacientes como una amenaza. Para decirlo claramente: nos hicieron odiarlo».

En fin: un *Quijote* en verso, otro expurgado, otro adaptado, otro modernizado. ¿Qué queda del verdadero *Quijote*?

Adapted from "La aventura de don Quijote en la escuela," by Juan José Lage Fernández, Biblioteca Virtual de Prensa Histórica.
http://prensahistorica.mcu.es

1. ¿Cuál de las siguientes afirmaciones resume mejor el artículo?

   (A) Las recreaciones y inclusiones libres son las mejores adaptaciones.

   (B) Cervantes es el autor más celebrado por los críticos de la literatura.

   (C) Hay dificultades para crear una adaptación destinada a los jóvenes, pero se les puede dar a conocer los libros clásicos.

   (D) Las versiones reescritas del *Quijote* resultaron en más lectores de corto plazo para la novela.

2. Se menciona "adaptaciones en las que hay supresión… nuevas reescrituras" para

   (A) describir las adaptaciones desconcertantes que intentan cambiar la historia

   (B) ganarse a corto plazo lectores de la novela por sus dibujos vibrantes

   (C) ilustrar una metodología adecuada de hacer las adaptaciones

   (D) promover la lectura placentera

3. Podemos inferir que las adaptaciones y libros condensados

   (A) producen los efectos contrarios, que hace los niños odiar los libros clásicos

   (B) son ridículos e inmaduros

   (C) pueden cultivar un agradecimiento de los libros clásicos

   (D) no pueden contener el "verdadero *Quijote*"

4. La imagen en el principio del artículo es uno que

   (A) ilustra el realismo de la historia del *Quijote*

   (B) muestra la sombra del *Quijote*

   (C) muestra un esfuerzo evidente de ocupar el mercado

   (D) puede acompañar las recreaciones o inclusiones libres

5. La siguiente frase se puede añadir al texto: "Los dibujos que acompañan estas ediciones también me parecen honestos por sus hermosos detalles que representan los personajes de una manera auténtica." ¿Dónde serviría mejor esta frase?

   (A) Después de las líneas 16–17: "nuevas reescrituras intentando cambiar la historia, son las más fastidiosas"

   (B) Después de la línea 20: "... interrupción en el personaje cervantino"

   (C) Después de las líneas 23–24: "... ganarse a corto plazo más lectores de la novela"

   (D) Después de las líneas 43–44: "en verso, otro expurgado, otro adaptado, otro modernizado"

6. ¿Cuál es el significado de la frase "la sombra del *Quijote*"?

   (A) El *Quijote* es una amenaza a los escolares nacientes.

   (B) Los niños obligados a leer el *Quijote* habían empezado a resentir el libro.

   (C) La sombra oscurece las palabras, que lo hace más difícil a leer.

   (D) *Don Quijote*, celebrando su aniversario de 400 años, es un libro monumental de la literatura clásica.

7. Podemos inferir que

   (A) al principio, el autor encontró las adaptaciones demasiado ‹infantiles›, pero al final concede que hay aspectos beneficiosos de estos libros

   (B) no hay solamente una manera de adaptar o condensar un libro de literatura clásica

   (C) los escolares deben leer los libros clásicos para ser más cultos

   (D) la literatura clásica no se debe ser adaptada porque se disminuye la importancia del texto

Translated Text and Questions, with Explanations

Introduction

The following article appeared in 2005 in a journal of youth literature.

The Adventure of Don Quixote in Schools

In this Year of Don Quixote, the author uses the opportunity to talk about classic literature in schools and to analyze the great quantity of adaptions and recreations of Cervantes's work, which are "colonizing" the market.

As almost all the world knows, 2005 is the year of Don Quixote, coinciding with the 400-year anniversary of the book's first edition. Also coinciding—even though not all the world knows—is the 200th anniversary of the birth of Hans Christian Andersen, the immortal author of such universal stories as *The Ugly Duckling*, and the 100th anniversary of the death of Jules Verne, in addition to the 50th anniversary of Albert Einstein's death (he of the Theory of Relativity).

For these reasons, this year was officially declared The Year of Reading and Books. There are many commemorative events that will praise Cervantes along with many other authors.

Versions, Adaptations, and Recreations of the Classic

The first thing that surprises us is the proliferation of different versions that publishers issue, with an evident effort to occupy the market. Adaptations which eliminate parts or chapters, or which rewrite them, intending to change the story, are the most bothersome.

Others are the versions that we call "recreations or free inclusions." They seem more honest to me, since they do not seem to be a departure from the Cervantine character. When one changes the character, involving it in another world that is not its own, it becomes too absurd and "infantilized," which, in my judgment, is not good as it only gains short-term readers for the novel.

Allow the Book to be Encountered, not Imposed

Seeing all these arguments, the key question is this: how should we now proceed? What is the appropriate methodology? Certainly, there are no easy solutions because the road to strengthen reading habits is full of obstacles.

But, that said, the first thing we should do is educate, without hurry or pause. The best medicine is to extend a knowledge of good children's books, of good children's and youth literature. Once these foundations are in place, the road will be more or less carved out ahead. All that remains is to give priority to reading for pleasure, giving schoolchildren the opportunity to read, choose, and claim the common wealth and heritage of reading. This includes allowing them the opportunity to leaf through a book and choose not to read it.

It may be the case that an excess of enthusiasm produces the opposite effect that we intend: "the shadow of *Don Quixote*," says Ana María Matute "soared over our lives as budding schoolchildren like a menace. To put it clearly, we were made to loathe it."

Anyhow, a *Don Quixote* in verse, another expurgated, another adapted, and another modernized: what remains of the real *Quixote*?

Here's How to Crack It

1. Which of the following statements best summarizes the article?

    (A) Recreations and "inclusive" editions are the best editions.

    (B) Cervantes is the author most celebrated by literary critics.

    (C) There are difficulties in creating adaptations for young people, though these can introduce them to classic literature.

    (D) The rewritten versions of *Don Quixote* have cultivated more short-term readers of the novel.

The article focuses on the many adaptations and recreations of *Don Quixote* and the difficulties that come with making such editions. While some editions are better than others, they allow children to experience the classics at a young age. Choice (A) is a superlative, and though the author likes these editions, we cannot choose this answer because of its language. Choice (B) contains a superlative as well, and we do not have proof that Cervantes is the author most celebrated amongst literary critics. Choice (D) is true according to the article, but is not a summary of its main points. Therefore, (C) is correct.

2. "Adaptations which eliminate…which rewrite them" are mentioned in order to

    (A) describe the disconcerting adaptations which intend to change the story

    (B) gain short-term readers of the novel through their vibrant pictures

    (C) illustrate an adequate methodology for making adaptations

    (D) promote reading for pleasure

Choice (A) is correct. The author explicitly says that he finds these types of adaptations to be the most bothersome because they leave out parts of the story and change other parts. There is no proof of pictures in these editions, though many children's books contain illustrations (B). Since these adaptations are not seen as satisfactory by the author, they would not be an adequate method of creating an adaptation (C), nor do these examples necessarily promote reading for pleasure (D).

3. We can infer that the adaptations and condensed books

    (A) produce contrary effects that make children hate classic literature

    (B) are ridiculous and immature

    (C) can cultivate an appreciation of classic books

    (D) cannot encompass the "real *Quixote*"

We can only infer that adaptations can cultivate an appreciation of classic books. We cannot prove that these editions will produce adverse effects (A), or that they will necessarily be ridiculous or immature (B). In addition, these adaptations do not always miss the true spirit of the "real *Quixote*" (D). Therefore, (C) is correct.

4. The illustration at the start of the article is one that

    (A) shows the realism of the story of *Don Quixote*

    (B) shows the shadow of *Don Quixote*

    (C) shows an evident effort to occupy the market

    (D) can accompany recreations and "inclusive" editions

The illustration characterizes *Don Quixote*'s charming madness, which remains true to the original book, and therefore the most authentic adaptations might contain these same sentiments, i.e., the recreations and inclusive editions. Choice (A) does not work because the illustration does not depict realism, nor does it show the "shadow of *Don Quixote*" (B), as this phrase is taken out of context and is not related to the illustration. The illustration does not show evidence of occupying the market (C), so (D) must be correct.

5. The following sentence may be added to the text: "The pictures that accompany these editions also appear to me to be honest in their beautiful details that represent the characters with authenticity." Where would this fit best?

    (A) After lines 16–17: "which rewrite them, intending to change the story, are the most bothersome"

    (B) After line 20: "…departure from the Cervantine character"

    (C) After lines 23–24: "gains short-term readers for the novel"

    (D) After lines 43–44: "in verse, another expurgated, another adapted, another modernized"

The insertion of a sentence about illustrations that seem "honest as well" should be paired with the recreations and "inclusive" editions because those are described in a similar manner, and seem in line with the protagonist's character. Choice (A) would be the opposite of the correct answer, describing the more irksome adaptations that change the story of *Don Quixote*. Choice (C) may seem tempting, but the illustration is described in a positive light, opposite of the "short-term" readers. Choice (D) would not create good flow or continuity for the inserted sentence, so (B) is correct.

6. What is the meaning of the phrase "the shadow of *Don Quixote*"?

    (A) *Don Quixote* is a menace to schoolchildren.

    (B) The schoolchildren who were obliged to read *Don Quixote* had started to resent it.

    (C) The shadow obscures the words, and makes it difficult to read.

    (D) *Don Quixote,* celebrating its 400-year anniversary, is a great book of classic literature.

Choice (B) is correct. Schoolchildren felt the "shadow of *Don Quixote*" because schools placed so much emphasis on the book that the students began to dread it, as Ana María Matute stated in her quote. Choice (D) is contained in the passage but does not answer the question about the given phrase, and (A) recycles words from the text, making it too literal. Choice (C) takes the word "shadow" too literally, so (B) must be correct, as the meaning of the phrase is metaphorical.

7. It can be inferred that

    (A) in the beginning, the author found the adaptations too "infantile," but later he concedes that there are some beneficial aspects to them

    (B) there is no one single way to adapt or condense a book of classic literature

    (C) schoolchildren should read classic books in order to be cultured

    (D) classic literature should not be adapted because it belittles the importance of the text

Choice (B) is correct. Choice (A) contains recycled words, which, placed next to one another, change the meaning of the phrases, as they are taken out of context. Choice (C) is offensive to the schoolchildren. Choice (D) is extreme, and does not go along with the main point of the article. Therefore, (B) is correct, as there is no one method of creating adaptations or condensations for pieces of classic literature.

PRACTICE PASSAGE 7

Introducción

La siguiente entrevista apareció en la revista TELOS en 2019.

Juliana Rueda es maestra de música con vocación de ingeniera de sonido, su profesión y su pasión. Se define como emprendedora "intensa", que significa, a la vista de su trayectoria, que lo que persigue, lo consigue. Viajó de Colombia a Barcelona para completar su formación durante seis meses y lleva más de quince años de aquí para allá, porque el mundo del audiolibro, del libro narrado, tiene y cobra más fuerza cada día.

Línea 5

Proclamas que vivimos en una nueva "era de la voz". Explícanos, por favor.

10

Vivimos un momento en el que la voz cobra un protagonismo muy importante en la manera de comunicarnos, de disfrutar de experiencias distintas, a nivel profesional y en el ámbito personal. Lo estoy viviendo intensamente en mi empresa. Nosotros somos un estudio de grabación y el formato estrella ahora mismo es el audiolibro; en realidad, el crecimiento ha sido exponencial desde el año 2012, y este año hemos producido casi el doble de lo que habíamos producido durante todo el año pasado. Vemos un interés creciente en los medios, en el público, en el mercado.

15

20

¿Qué tiene el audio que no tenga un buen texto?

Lo que a mí me apasiona de la voz es la conexión que crea, cómo da vida a las palabras de un texto. Cuando haces la grabación de un libro, lo sientes, sientes las palabras. Yo he llorado, reído, sufrido… he pasado miedo grabando. Y piensas: "Ya me he leído el libro, ¿cómo es posible que las palabras cobren tanta vida?" Todo es mucho más sentido, más vívido, con la voz. Ese es su poder: el poder de la conexión. Por eso la gente ha vuelto al audio: porque es más fácil, más rápido, pero también más cercano, más sentido, más emocional.

25

30

Se puede deducir que en este mundo tecnologizado necesitamos más emoción, sentir más, establecer conexiones más estrechas.

35

La voz genera emoción. Por eso los dispositivos electrónicos de voz están teniendo éxito. ¿Cuánta gente sola en casa ha encontrado en los robots a alguien con quien hablar? ¡A alguien que le escucha! Se está humanizando la relación con las máquinas gracias a la voz. ¿Qué hay más humano que la tradición oral? Si podemos hablar con las máquinas, las sentimos más cercanas: la voz mejora la relación. El audio, además, es más directo, es una forma de estar con alguien, es una forma de tener compañía.

40

¿Qué es lo mágico del audiolibro?

45

Tienes un autor y un lector—que en este caso es un oyente; el primero quiere contar algo, el segundo quiere que se lo cuenten. El actor es quien pone voz a ese autor, es quien los conecta a través de la historia; tiene que ser capaz de extraer cada una de las emociones que quiere expresar el autor con cada palabra. Para que la experiencia de escuchar esa voz sea placentera necesitamos crear técnicamente un entorno que funcione, que facilite el encuentro. Cuando escuchamos la narración, tenemos a una persona dentro de los oídos; es una experiencia tremendamente íntima. La tecnología crea ese ambiente de intimidad y emoción; nos acerca. La palabra es vital para conectar con el otro. Es lo que nos define como especie. El lenguaje verbal te puede decir todo sobre cómo se siente una persona y tú puedes percibir la ironía, la rabia, la risa, la emoción, la voz dice cómo respiran; necesitamos escuchar para saber cómo está el otro, para sentir, para sentirlo.

50

55

60

Escuché decir que "hablar es antiguo", pero conforme avanza la tecnología recuperamos la tradición oral, la base sobre la que se ha construido nuestra historia.

65

Sí. Narrar, contar, hablar es algo que se remonta en los tiempos y lo bonito de su antigüedad es que era capaz, y aún lo es, de unir a las personas alrededor de un fuego. La historia de la humanidad se ha contado a través de las palabras. La palabra nos hace humanos, conforma una cultura y la convierte en perpetua. La palabra es el mejor vehículo para conectar. La emoción que transmite la voz nos distingue como humanos.

70

1. ¿A qué se dedica la empresa de Juliana Rueda?

   (A) Unen a la gente alrededor de un fuego.

   (B) Son un estudio de grabación que se enfoca en hacer audiolibros.

   (C) Crean momentos íntimos para que las personas se conecten.

   (D) Construyen máquinas que usan audio para trabajar con humanos.

2. Según Juliana, ¿por qué la gente quiere volver al audio?

   (A) Porque el crecimiento del audiolibro ha sido exponencial

   (B) Porque hace que la gente sufra y tenga miedo

   (C) Porque las palabras cobran vida y es más fácil, rápido y significativo

   (D) Porque la gente conoce a la persona que está leyendo el audiolibro

3. ¿Cómo ha crecido la relación entre humanos y máquinas?

   (A) A través de la comunicación oral los humanos se sienten más cerca de las máquinas.

   (B) Los humanos han hecho que las máquinas se conviertan en sus sirvientes.

   (C) Las máquinas son iguales a los humanos en la comprensión de las emociones.

   (D) Tanto los humanos como las máquinas se brindan terapia y comodidad.

4. ¿Qué tipo de atmósfera crean la tecnología y las palabras?

   (A) Un ambiente académico que se centra en el aprendizaje

   (B) Un ambiente íntimo y emocional que acerca a las personas

   (C) Un ambiente rústico que ayuda a las personas a trabajar conectando con los demás

   (D) Un ambiente entretenido lleno de risas y alegría

5. ¿Por qué sigue siendo importante hablar, según la última pregunta de la entrevista?

   (A) Puede ayudar a las personas a liberar emociones.

   (B) Puede contectarnos con la antigüedad.

   (C) Puede conectar humanos a máquinas.

   (D) Puede unir a la gente alrededor de un fuego.

Translated Text and Questions, with Explanations

Introduction

The following interview appeared in TELOS magazine in 2019.

Juliana Rueda is a music teacher with a vocation as a sound engineer, her profession and her passion. She defines herself as an "intense" entrepreneur, which means, in view of her career, that what she pursues, she achieves. She traveled from Colombia to Barcelona to complete her training for six months and she has been going here and there for more than fifteen years, because the world of the audiobook, of the narrated book, has and gains more strength every day.

You proclaim that we live in a new "age of voice." Please explain this to us.

We live in a moment in which the voice takes on a very important role in the way we communicate, enjoy different experiences, professionally and personally. I am living it intensely in my company. We are a recording studio and the star format right now is the audiobook; in fact, the growth has been exponential since 2012, and this year we have produced almost double what we had produced during all of last year. We see a growing interest in the media, in the public, in the market.

What does audio have that good text doesn't?

What I love about the voice is the connection it creates, how it brings the words of a text to life. When you record a book, you feel it: you feel the words. I've cried, laughed, suffered…I've been scared recording. And you think: "I've already read the book, how is it possible that the words come to life so much?" Everything is much more meaningful, more vivid, with the voice. That is its power: the power of connection. That's why people have returned to audio: because it's easier, faster, but also closer, more meaningful, more emotional.

It can be deduced that in this technological world we need more emotion, to feel more, to establish closer connections.

The voice generates emotion. That's why electronic voice devices are succeeding. How many people alone at home have found someone to talk to in robots? Someone who listens to them! The relationship with machines is being humanized thanks to the voice. What is more human than oral tradition? If we can talk to the machines, we feel closer to them: the voice improves the relationship. Audio is also more direct: it's a way of being with someone; it's a way of having company.

What is the magic of the audiobook?

You have an author and a reader—who in this case is a listener; the first wants to tell something, the second wants to be told. The actor is the one who gives voice to that author, the one who connects them through history; the actor has to be able to extract each one of the emotions that the author wants to express with each word. For the experience of listening to that voice to be pleasant, we need to technically create an environment that works, that facilitates the encounter. When we listen to the narration, we have a person inside our ears; it is a tremendously intimate experience. Technology creates that atmosphere of intimacy and emotion; it brings us closer. The word is vital to connect with the other. It is what defines us as a species. Verbal language can tell you everything about how a person feels and you can perceive irony, anger, laughter, the emotion. The voice tells you how someone breathes; we need to listen to know how the other is: to feel, to feel it.

I have heard it said that "speaking is ancient," but as technology advances we recover the oral tradition, the basis on which our history has been built.

Yes. Narrating, telling, talking is something that goes back in time and the beauty of its antiquity is that it was capable, and still is, of uniting people around a fire. The history of humanity has been told through words. The word makes us human, forms a culture and makes it perpetual. The word is the best vehicle to connect. The emotion conveyed by the voice distinguishes us as humans.

Here's How to Crack It

1. What does Juliana Rueda's company do?

   (A) They unite people around a fire.

   (B) They are a recording studio that focuses on making audiobooks.

   (C) They create intimate moments for people to connect.

   (D) They build machines that use audio to work with humans.

The question asks what Juliana Rueda's company does. In the response to the first question, Juliana says *Nosotros somos un estudio de grabación y el formato estrella ahora mismo es el audiolibro,* so eliminate (D). While (A) and (C) are effects of creating audiobooks, this is not exactly what the company does, so eliminate both answers. The correct answer is (B).

2. According to Juliana, why are people wanting to return to audio?

   (A) Because growth for the audiobook has been exponential

   (B) Because it makes people suffer and be scared

   (C) Because words come to life and it is easier, faster, and more meaningful

   (D) Because people know the person who is reading the audiobook

The question asks why people are wanting to return to audio according to Juliana. In the response to the second question, Juliana states *Por eso la gente ha vuelto al audio: porque es más fácil, más rápido, pero también más cercano, más sentido, más emocional,* which directly matches answer choice (C). While Juliana does say *el crecimiento ha sido exponencial desde el año 2012,* that is not the direct reason for why people want to return to audio, so eliminate (A). Eliminate (B) because while Juliana says *Yo he llorado, reído, sufrido,* that is not why people want to return to audio. Eliminate (D) because nowhere in the passage does Juliana say that people know the person reading the audiobook. The correct answer is (C).

3. How has the relationship between humans and machines grown?

   (A) Through oral communication humans feel closer to machines.

   (B) Humans have made machines become their servants.

   (C) Machines are equal to humans in understanding emotion.

   (D) Both humans and machines give each other therapy and comfort.

The question asks how the relationship between humans and machines has grown. In the response to the third question, Juliana says *Si podemos hablar con las máquinas, las sentimos más cercanas,* which matches (A), so keep answer choice (A). Eliminate (B) because while some humans may treat machines as servants, this is not stated in the interview. Eliminate (C) because while Juliana says *Se está humanizando la relación con las máquinas gracias a la voz,* this does not directly say that machines can understand emotion as humans do. Eliminate (D) because therapy is not mentioned in the interview. The correct answer is (A).

4. What kind of atmosphere do technology and words create?

    (A) A scholarly atmosphere that is focused on learning

    (B) An intimate, emotional atmosphere that brings people closer together

    (C) A rustic atmosphere that helps people work connecting with others

    (D) An entertaining atmosphere that is full of laughter and joy

The question asks what kind of atmosphere technology and words create. Eliminate (A) because while audiobooks can be used to learn, that is not mentioned in the interview. Keep (B) because in the response to the fourth question, Juliana says *La technolgía crea ese ambiente de intimidad y emoción; nos acerca,* which matches that answer. Eliminate (C) and (D) because while these answers may be inferred from the passage, they are not exactly what Juliana states in the interview. The correct answer is (B).

5. Why is speaking still important, according to the last question in the interview?

    (A) It can help people to release emotion.

    (B) It can connect us to antiquity.

    (C) It can connect humans to machines.

    (D) It can unite people around a fire.

The question asks why speaking is still important according to the last question in the interview. Therefore, the answer must lie in the response to the last question. Juliana says *Narrar, contar, hablar es algo que se remonta en los tiempos y lo bonito de su antigüedad es que era capaz, y aún lo es, de unir a las personas alrededor de un fuego,* which directly matches (D). Eliminate (C) because that is not mentioned in response to the last question. Eliminate (A) because while that answer could be true, it is not stated in the interview. Eliminate (B) because, while Juliana says *hablar es algo que se remonta en los tiempos,* she goes on to say that *lo bonito de su antigüedad es que era capaz, y aún lo es, de unir a las personas alrededor de un fuego,* so it's not just the connection to antiquity that makes speaking important. The correct answer is (D).

Interpretive Communication: Print Texts Tips

- Choose the order in which you want to do the passages. Read a couple of sentences to see whether the writing style is easy to follow and the vocabulary is manageable. If so, go for it. If not, look ahead for something you find easier.

- Read the passage for topic and structure only. Don't read for detail, and don't try to memorize the whole thing. The first read is for you to get a sense of the general idea and the overall structure—that's all.

- Go straight to the general questions. Mark them as general questions with a "G" or any other mark of your choice and save them for last.

- Do the specific questions in order. For these, you're going to let the key terms in the question tell you where to look in the passage. Then, read the area that the question pertains to slowly and carefully. Find an answer choice that basically says the same thing. Answer choices are often paraphrases of the passage.

1. Specific Questions
2. General Questions

- Once you are finished with the specific questions, use your knowledge of the passage to answer the general questions. Ideally, you should be able to answer them without looking back at the passage. Most passages contain only a few general questions.

- Avoid specific answers on general questions, and on specific questions, avoid answers that are reasonable but go beyond the scope of the passage.

- Don't pick an answer choice just because you recall reading the word in the passage. Frequently that is a trick; correct answers will often use synonyms rather than the word originally used in the passage.

> Limit your knowledge only to the info in the passage. If you know more about the topic, leave that knowledge at the door.
>
> Beware of recycled words from the passage. Often, they are used out of context in these answer choices.

INTERPRETIVE COMMUNICATION: AUDIO TEXTS

The Audio Texts portion of the exam consists of audio recordings accompanied by multiple-choice questions. Your task is to listen to the audio carefully and answer the questions that are printed in your examination booklet. Each selection will be approximately three minutes in length and will be played twice. You will be given a designated amount of time to read a preview of the selection and skim the accompanying questions.

For each of the Audio Text samples in this section, you will find a translation of the selection with the answers and explanations that follow. Resist any urge you might have to sneak a peek while listening to the audio tracks. You'll get the most out of your practice just by listening carefully and taking notes. You can go online to PrincetonReview.com, where you may either download or stream the audio after registering your book (step-by-step instructions on how to do this are on page vi).

Here are the general directions for Part B, which also includes the Print and Audio Text (combined) questions. You will see these printed in your test booklet on test day, in both English and Spanish.

You will listen to several audio selections. The first two audio selections are accompanied by reading selections. When there is a reading selection, you will have a designated amount of time to read it.	Vas a escuchar varias grabaciones. Las dos primeras grabaciones van acompañadas de lecturas. Cuando haya una lectura, vas a tener un tiempo determinado para leerla.
For each audio selection, first you will have a designated amount of time to read a preview of the selection as well as to skim the questions that you will be asked. Each selection will be played twice. As you listen to each selection, you may take notes. Your notes will not be scored.	Para cada grabación, primero vas a tener un tiempo determinado para leer la introducción y prever las preguntas. Vas a escuchar cada grabación dos veces. Mientras escuchas, puedes tomar apuntes. Tus apuntes no van a ser calificados.
After listening to each selection the first time, you will have 1 minute to begin answering the questions; after listening to each selection the second time, you will have 15 seconds per question to finish answering the questions. For each question, choose the response that is best according to the audio and/or reading selection and mark your answer on your answer sheet.	Después de escuchar cada selección por primera vez, vas a tener un minuto para empezar a contestar las preguntas; después de escuchar por segunda vez, vas a tener 15 segundos por pregunta para terminarlas. Para cada pregunta, elige la mejor respuesta según la grabación o el texto e indícala en la hoja de respuestas.

Interpretive Communication: Audio Texts

Basic approach:

1. Preview the Questions
2. Take Notes as you Listen
3. POE

There are two main types of listening passages: lecture passages and informal passages or conversations. For both of these types, preview your questions to know what to listen for. Avoid previewing the answer choices too closely, as they may actually lead you astray. The test-makers often recycle words from the lectures and dialogues to throw you off, so just know which questions you need to listen for. When you listen, jot down notes in your test booklet, noting the speaker, the subject matter, and any transition words such as *sin embargo, pero, además, por otro lado*, etc. to discover how different points fit together in the lecture. Get your pencil in hand and be ready to write down a few quick words as you listen. Usually, there will be 2–3 key points that the lecturer tries to make, and the overall argument will be laid out at the beginning of the lecture as well as at the end to wrap up the important ideas.

Give it a try:

Ready? Here we go! Listen carefully to the recordings in the following three listening samples and answer the questions as best you can. Try jotting down notes as you listen. Even if it is just a word or a phrase, active listening will help you significantly here.

Sample Audio Text Selection 1

Primero tienes un minuto para prever las preguntas.

(1 minute)

Ahora escucha la selección.

PLAY AUDIO: Track 8

Ahora tienes un minuto para empezar a responder a las preguntas para esta selección. Después de un minuto, vas a escuchar la grabación de nuevo.

(1 minute)

Ahora escucha de nuevo.

PLAY AUDIO: Track 8

Ahora termina de responder a las preguntas para esta selección.

1. ¿Que es AeroEspaña?
   (A) Es la línea aérea.
   (B) Es la compañía de abogados.
   (C) Es el nombre del aeropuerto.
   (D) Es el nombre de la señora.

2. ¿Que trabajo tiene la Señora?
   (A) Es azafata.
   (B) Trabaja en el mostrador de la línea aérea.
   (C) Es abogada.
   (D) Es la jefa de administración.

3. ¿A dónde viaja la Señora?
   (A) Viaja a Londres.
   (B) Viaja a Barcelona.
   (C) Viaja a Burgos.
   (D) Viaja al mostrador de la línea aérea.

Apply Strategy!
Preview the questions and underline or circle any key terms to be listening for!

Remember the 5 W's here as well. What is happening? Who are the people? How did the conversation conclude?

Basic approach:

1. Preview the Questions
2. Take Notes as you Listen
3. POE

What key words did you notice in the questions? If you noticed *AeroEspaña, trabajo, viaja,* and *la Señora*, great job! Your notes should be organized in a way that makes sense to you; try to listen for the questions you previewed. From there, POE away!

Selection 1: Translated Text and Questions, with Explanations

(NARRATOR) In the airport

(MAN) Excuse me madam, but would you know where the ticket counter for AeroEspaña is?

(WOMAN) Where are you going?

(MAN) I am going to Barcelona, and I am in a big hurry because I believe the plane leaves within twenty minutes.

(WOMAN) That's right. There is a plane that leaves for Barcelona this morning. The ticket counter for AeroEspaña is at the end of this hallway on your right.

(MAN) Do you have the time?

(WOMAN) Yes, it is nine o'clock. I will accompany you to the counter if you wish. I am also going to Barcelona this morning.

(MAN) Well yes, of course, it would be my pleasure. I am Ricardo Herrero.

(WOMAN) Delighted to meet you. I am Teresa Vara.

(MAN) Are you by chance the attorney for the Arturo Águila Company?

(WOMAN) Yes, I am. And you are the chief financial officer. We have met before, haven't we?

(MAN)   Yes, I think we met at the annual meeting last year in London. What a coincidence!

(WOMAN)   I suppose that you are going to the meeting in Barcelona with the president of the company?

(MAN)   Of course; what a small world!

1. What is AeroEspaña?
   (A) It is the airline.
   (B) It is the law firm.
   (C) It is the name of the airport.
   (D) It is the woman's name.

AeroEspaña is the name of the airline, (A). We know this because once inside the airport, the man asks the woman where the ticket counter is for the airline he is taking to Barcelona.

2. What work does the woman do?
   (A) She is a flight attendant.
   (B) She works at the ticket counter.
   (C) She is an attorney.
   (D) She is the head of administration.

Choice (C) is the correct answer. The woman is an attorney for the Arturo Águila Company.

3. Where is the woman traveling to?
   (A) She is going to London.
   (B) She is going to Barcelona.
   (C) She is going to Burgos.
   (D) She is going to the ticket counter.

Barcelona is mentioned several times in the dialogue, so if you picked (B), you had your ears open! London is mentioned in the dialogue as well, but only in reference to the fact that the two had met there last year.

Sample Audio Text Selection 2

Primero tienes un minuto para prever las preguntas.

(1 minute)

Ahora escucha la selección.

> **PLAY AUDIO: Track 9**

Ahora tienes un minuto para empezar a responder a las preguntas para esta selección. Después de un minuto, vas a escuchar la grabación de nuevo.

(1 minute)

Ahora escucha de nuevo.

> **PLAY AUDIO: Track 9**

Ahora termina de responder a las preguntas para esta selección.

4. ¿Qué tienen en común las ciudades de Nueva York, Los Angeles, Chicago, Dallas, San Antonio y San Francisco?

   (A) Tienen una gran población de personas que hablan español.

   (B) Los nombres son de origen hispano.

   (C) Son ciudades crecientes.

   (D) Son ciudades con grandes compañías.

5. ¿Qué están haciendo con respecto al mercado hispano las compañías grandes como los productores de refrescos y zapatillas deportivas?

   (A) Están comprando más productos.

   (B) Están creciendo más y más.

   (C) Están comprando publicidad para el mercado hispano.

   (D) Están comprando productos hechos por hispanos.

6. ¿Cómo es el típico consumidor hispano?

   (A) Joven

   (B) Mayor

   (C) Liberal

   (D) Conservador

7. ¿Con cuáles marcas se identifica el consumidor hispano?

   (A) Marcas hispanas

   (B) Marcas de buena calidad

   (C) Marcas de mala calidad

   (D) Marcas que cuestan menos

Basic approach:

1. Preview the Questions
2. Take Notes as you Listen
3. POE

Since this is a lecture instead of a dialogue, use transitional words to help identify the structure of the passage and therefore the key points. Words like *sin embargo*, *además*, and the like can help you to organize the passage and take good notes.

What key words did you notice in the questions? There were certainly a lot more than there were for the previous passage. Underline these key words in the questions so you are on alert. You should have noticed words such as the cities in question 1, *zapatillos deportivos*, *típico consumidor*, and *marca*, among a couple of others. Your notes should be reflective of the structure of the passage, using transitional words to notice new points and paragraphs. Try to listen for the questions you previewed. From there, POE away!

When taking notes, note the structure of the speech. If you hear a pause, this might be a clue that you have a new paragraph, and thus a new example, a contrast, or something similar, will come next.

Selection 2: Translated Text and Questions, with Explanations

The Hispanic Market in the United States

The U.S. Hispanic market is a source of opportunity for many large companies. The U.S. Hispanic market is a market that is growing daily. There are Spanish speakers in almost all of the major U.S. cities, especially in New York, Los Angeles, Chicago, Dallas, San Antonio, and San Francisco, just to name a few. All of the large companies have seen the value of the Hispanic consumer in today's marketplace.

Many of these companies, such as beverage producers, fast-food restaurants, and athletic shoe producers, spend a lot of money on advertising directed at the Hispanic consumer. The typical Hispanic consumer is very traditional; he likes the family. He also likes traditional values. The Hispanic consumer is also one who is loyal to the brand names that he considers of good quality. He identifies very easily with the brands that he likes. It doesn't matter to him to spend more money on a product if it is of better quality. The Hispanic market will continue to grow. Companies that ignore the importance of the Hispanic market do so at their own risk. The Hispanic consumer is a strong force in the marketplace of the future.

4. What do the cities New York, Los Angeles, Chicago, Dallas, San Antonio, and San Francisco have in common?

   (A) They have large populations of Spanish speakers.

   (B) Their names are of Hispanic origin.

   (C) They are growing cities.

   (D) They are cities with large companies.

Choices (B), (C), and (D) may or may not be true, but they have nothing to do with the short narrative. Therefore, the correct answer is (A); each of those cities has a large Spanish-speaking population.

5. What are the large companies, such as beverage producers and sports-shoe producers, doing with respect to the Hispanic market?

   (A) They are buying more products.

   (B) They are growing more and more.

   (C) They are buying advertising for the Hispanic market.

   (D) They are buying products made by Hispanics.

The word for advertising is *publicidad*. The large companies are, in fact, buying advertising directed at the Hispanic market. Notice that incorrect choices (A) and (D) also include the verb *comprando* to see whether you can be easily fooled; don't fall into this trap.

6. What is the typical Hispanic consumer like?

   (A) Young

   (B) Old

   (C) Liberal

   (D) Conservative

The typical Hispanic consumer is *tradicional*, which is closest to *conservador*. If this isn't immediately apparent, you may use POE to rule out the other answer choices. The age range (*joven* or *mayor*) of the typical Hispanic consumer is impossible to identify without detailed demographic information, which is not discussed in the short narrative. *Liberal* doesn't really make any sense, so it is an obvious wrong answer.

7. With which brand names does the Hispanic consumer identify?

   (A) Hispanic brand names

   (B) Good-quality brand names

   (C) Bad-quality brand names

   (D) Economical brand names

Hispanic consumers identify with good-quality brands. In fact, we are told that they do not mind paying more for an item if it is of better quality. Therefore, you should use POE to rule out (C) and (D). Nothing in the narrative indicates that the Hispanic market identifies with only Hispanic brand names, so you can say *adiós* to (A) as well.

Sample Audio Text Selection 3

Primero tienes un minuto para prever las preguntas.

(1 minute)

Ahora escucha la selección.

PLAY AUDIO: Track 10

Ahora tienes un minuto para empezar a responder a las preguntas para esta selección. Después de un minuto, vas a escuchar la grabación de nuevo.

(1 minute)

Ahora escucha de nuevo.

PLAY AUDIO: Track 10

Ahora termina de responder a las preguntas para esta selección.

8. ¿A quién va dirigida la revista *Mujer Moderna*?

    (A) Las mujeres del mundo interior de la moda

    (B) Las mujeres que trabajan

    (C) La mujer que se ocupa de la familia y la casa

    (D) La mujer contemporánea del mundo actual

9. ¿Cómo se distingue *Mujer Moderna* de las otras revistas de moda?

    (A) Es una revista de muñecas.

    (B) Es una revista de fantasía.

    (C) Se dedica a cómo la moda forma parte de la vida en el mundo actual.

    (D) Se dedica exclusivamente al mundo interior de la moda.

10. ¿Por qué está metida la revista *Mujer Moderna* en la causa social de los niños que nacen con el virus del SIDA?

    (A) Quiere dar ejemplo de responsabilidad hacia los desafortunados.

    (B) Quiere ser más contemporánea.

    (C) Era la causa de la Princesa Diana.

    (D) Está de moda ayudar a los menesterosos.

11. ¿Qué hay de interés para el hombre moderno en *Mujer Moderna*?

    (A) Puede aprender de la moda para hombres.

    (B) Puede aprender de la moda para su madre, hermana, novia o esposa.

    (C) Puede aprender sobre la Princesa Diana.

    (D) Puede aprender sobre si mismo.

12. ¿Qué relación hay entre la moda y el deporte, según la entrevista?

    (A) Muchos deportes tienen una moda desarrollada a su alrededor.

    (B) Muchos deportistas son modelos.

    (C) Todos los deportistas tienen mucho estilo.

    (D) La moda y el deporte son sinónimos.

Remember, active listening is your best friend here! Jot down key terms and main ideas.

Basic approach:

1. Preview the Questions
2. Take Notes as you Listen
3. POE

This is a longer dialogue, so note transitions while you listen for key words and phrases. What key words did you notice as you previewed the questions? Hopefully, you noticed *Mujer Moderna, dirigida, distingue*, the entire phrase *niños que nacen con el virus del SIDA, hombre moderno*, and *la moda y el deporte*. Your notes should be organized in a way that shows changes in topic as well as cues from the questions you previewed. Use POE aggressively to eliminate answer choices.

Listening comprehension tests just that: listening comprehension! Most answers will not be terribly difficult conceptually.

Now let's take a look at the answers and explanations for Selection 3.

Selection 3: Translated Text and Questions, with Explanations

(NARRATOR) Now we are going to listen to an interview with someone very informed in the world of fashion, Ms. Luz Hurtado, editor of the magazine *Modern Woman*.

(MAN) Luz, to begin, can you describe for us the typical reader of *Modern Woman*? In other words, who is your target audience?

(WOMAN) Our magazine is directed at the woman of today, primarily between the ages of twenty and thirty-five years of age. Many of our readers work, but others devote themselves to caring for their families and homes. Almost all of them have in common a deep interest in fashion. They are not necessarily those who work in the fashion industry, although many women in the fashion world do read our magazine. Let's say that our magazine brings the insider world of fashion to the contemporary woman.

(MAN) How is *Modern Woman* different from other fashion magazines?

(WOMAN)   That is a very important question. When they offered me the job
of editor at this magazine, I asked myself, "Do I really want to
work for another fashion magazine?" I had worked in the past as a
reporter for other fashion magazines, and I was no longer interested
in working for another magazine like all of the others. But *Modern
Woman* is different because it is directed at the woman who lives
in the real world of today. It is not about silly dolls in a protected
world or fantasy world. Our readers live in the real world, they work
in the real world, and they care for their families in the real world.
We don't devote ourselves exclusively to fashion but rather to the
role of fashion in the complicated modern world.

(MAN)   I have read that *Modern Woman* is very involved in various social
causes, above all, children who are born with the AIDS virus. Can you
explain to us the relationship between fashion and this very important
social cause?

(WOMAN)   Although it may be a bit out of the ordinary in the world of fashion, I
think it is extremely important that we help those who are less fortunate. Is there a more innocent victim than a poor child who has been
born with the AIDS virus? *Modern Woman* tries to foster a relationship
with social causes to show our readers that it is the responsibility of
each and every one of us to contribute to the improvement of society.
Furthermore, there have been others who have cultivated a relationship between fashion and social causes; for example, let's remember
the image of Princess Diana.

(MAN)   That's true. Princess Diana was a symbol of fashion and of dedication
to social causes. She was a very admirable person, don't you think so?

(WOMAN)   Of course she was admirable. She was a very good person. The public
figure was only a part of Diana. I met her on various occasions and
was impressed by her sincerity and her genuine concern for those who
suffer.

(MAN)   Changing the topic a bit if I may, is your magazine valuable for the
modern man?

(WOMAN)   I think that there is a lot of value for the modern man who is interested
in social causes that affect us all. Of course, it will also be interesting
to the man who wants to find out about the latest fashion trends for his
female friends, his girlfriend, his wife, his mother, his sister, etc. In
short, it is a magazine directed primarily at those interested in feminine
fashion, based on a philanthropic philosophy. For that reason, it can
also be interesting to many men. However, we also have a very good
sports section. (She laughs.)

(MAN)   What relationship is there, if any, between fashion and sports?

(WOMAN) Of course there is a relationship between them. Fashion could be considered an attitude toward life. Fashion can be seen in everything that we do. We either do things with style or without style. It all depends on the mentality and the level of interest of the individual. For example, there is an entire fashion that has evolved precisely around sports. Tennis and golf are two very clear examples. They have a very determined fashion requirement that allows for individual styles as well. For example, the American tennis players Andre Agassi and the Williams sisters show their individuality with the unique clothing that they wear and their hairstyles. Whether or not we care for the styles they wear, we must admire their individualistic styles.

(MAN) Of course, all three are very original. But tell us Luz, how did you get started in the world of fashion?

(WOMAN) Always, ever since I was young, men's and women's fashions have interested me. My father worked in the Spanish Diplomatic Service, so we spent a lot of time abroad. We lived in Milan, Paris, Singapore, and New York. Perhaps because of the differences I observed between the styles of clothing of the various cultures, I leaned toward the field of fashion. I have also, since I was young, always felt a sense of responsibility for the less fortunate. My mother always dedicated herself to social causes. I learned a great deal from her.

(MAN) Well, Ms. Luz Hurtado, we've run out of time. Thank you very much for being here with us.

8. Who is the target audience of *Modern Woman*?

(A) Women from the inside world of fashion

(B) Women who work

(C) Women who care for their homes and families

(D) The contemporary women of the real world

The correct answer is (D). The target audience of the magazine *Modern Woman* is the contemporary woman of today. Luz Hurtado says that the magazine is directed at those women who work and those who stay home and take care of their families. It tries to appeal to as many groups as possible. Use POE to eliminate (A), (B), and (C).

9. How is the magazine *Modern Woman* different from other fashion magazines?

(A) It is a magazine about dolls.

(B) It is a fantasy magazine.

(C) It is devoted to the role of fashion in the real world today.

(D) It is devoted exclusively to the inside world of fashion.

Modern Woman is different from other magazines because, according to the interview, it tries to explore the relationship between fashion and life in the modern world of today. It is not a magazine about dolls (A), nor of fantasy (B), nor an insider fashion magazine (D). Choices (C) and (D) may seem close, but the word *exclusivamente* in (D) should clue you in to the correct answer, (C), since you already know that the magazine tries to encompass a wide audience.

10. Why is *Modern Woman* involved with children born with the AIDS virus?

    (A) It wants to provide an example of responsibility to the needy.

    (B) It wants to be more contemporary.

    (C) It was Princess Diana's cause.

    (D) It is fashionable to help the needy.

Even if you didn't know that SIDA means AIDS in Spanish, you should be able to identify the one reasonable response among these four choices. If you use POE, you would quickly eliminate (C) and (D): the magazine would not be involved with a social cause just because Princess Diana had been involved without talking in greater detail about her. To say that it is fashionable to help those in need is just plain silly. Choice (B) is more reasonable, but once you compare it with (A), you'll find the correct answer.

11. What is of interest to the modern man in *Modern Woman*?

    (A) He can learn about men's fashions.

    (B) He can learn of the fashion trends affecting his mother, sister, girlfriend, or wife.

    (C) He can learn about Princess Diana.

    (D) He can learn about himself.

Choice (B) is the correct answer. According to the interview, the modern man can learn about the fashion interests of his sister, female friends, mother, girlfriend, or wife by reading *Modern Woman*. You can rule out (A), since men's fashion is never discussed in the interview except for a mention of Andre Agassi's individuality on the tennis court. Choices (C) and (D) simply refer to topics mentioned in the interview but not thoroughly discussed.

12. What relationship exists between fashion and sports, according to the interview?

    (A) Many sports have a fashion developed around them.

    (B) Many sports figures are models.

    (C) All sports figures have a lot of style.

    (D) Fashion and sports are synonymous.

According to what is said in the interview, the relationship between sports and fashion is that many sports figures, such as those in golf and tennis, develop their own styles within the sport. Choice (D) is completely wrong; fashion and sports are not synonymous. Choices (B) and (C) may be true but are not discussed in the interview. POE eliminates these right away. Therefore, (A) is the correct answer.

INTERPRETIVE COMMUNICATION: PRINT AND AUDIO TEXTS (COMBINED)

Now that you've practiced with Print Texts and Audio Texts, it's time to combine them! Note that on the test itself, you'll encounter the Print and Audio Texts (combined) section *before* the Audio Texts in Part B. For our purposes here, however, it makes more sense to familiarize you with the other sections first. As you might expect, this section combines an authentic print text (e.g., journalistic or literary text, ad, letter, or table) with a real-world audio source (e.g., interview, podcast, public service announcement, or presentation).

You will have time to read a preview of the selection and skim the questions before listening to the audio. The questions will pertain to both the print and audio texts. The audio selection is approximately 3 minutes in length and will be played twice. As with the Audio Text samples, you can listen to this audio selection online at PrincetonReview.com.

> Basic approach:
>
> 1. Read the Introduction
> 2. Preview the Passage Questions
> 3. Work the Passage and Answers
> 4. Rinse and Repeat for the Listening Text
> 5. Take Notes
> 6. POE

Ready? Here we go again! Listen carefully to the recording and read with care. Answer the questions to the best of your ability.

Sample Print and Audio Texts (Combined) Selection

Here are the general directions for the Print and Audio Texts (combined) section. You will see these instructions printed in your test booklet on test day in English and Spanish.

You will listen to several audio selections. The first two audio selections are accompanied by reading selections. When there is a reading selection, you will have a designated amount of time to read it.	Vas a escuchar varias grabaciones. Las dos primeras grabaciones van acompañadas de lecturas. Cuando haya una lectura, vas a tener un tiempo determinado para leerla.
For each audio selection, first you will have a designated amount of time to read a preview of the selection as well as to skim the questions that you will be asked. Each selection will be played twice. As you listen to each selection, you may take notes. Your notes will not be scored.	Para cada grabación, primero vas a tener un tiempo determinado para leer la introducción y prever las preguntas. Vas a escuchar cada grabación dos veces. Mientras escuchas, puedes tomar apuntes. Tus apuntes no van a ser calificados.
After listening to each selection the first time, you will have 1 minute to begin answering the questions; after listening to each selection the second time, you will have 15 seconds per question to finish answering the questions. For each question, choose the response that is best according to the audio and/or reading selection and mark your answer on the answer sheet.	Después de escuchar cada selección por primera vez, vas a tener un minuto para empezar a contestar las preguntas; después de escuchar por la segunda vez, vas a tener 15 segundos por pregunta para terminarlas. Para cada pregunta, elige la mejor respuesta según la grabación o el texto e indícala en la hoja de respuestas.

Fuente número 1

Primero tienes 4 minutos para leer la fuente número 1.

Introducción

Este texto se trata de dos personajes e iconos de la cultura pop de Latinoamérica. El artículo original fue escrito por Joaquín Bode.

Condorito Y Mafalda—Iconos de la Cultura Pop

Hace más de 63 y 48 años, "Pepo" y "Quino" crearon Condorito y Mafalda, respectivamente, "para dar humor y reflexión al mundo; dos personajes universales de *Línea* la cultura pop", tal como se señala en la página Web
5 "Culturacomic.com".

Mientras que los dos son protagonistas muy represen-tativos de la cultura latina, también es cierto que ambos son muy diferentes entre sí: Condorito es inocente y hasta torpe; Mafalda es inteligente e irónica. El primero vive feliz
10 la vida, disfrutando los pequeños placeres; mientras que la segunda establece una crítica social constante, casi con un afán revolucionario.

Eso sí: los dos tienen una gran personalidad, única y llamativa. Mafalda es auténtica, inteligente, analítica, liberal
15 y revolucionaria. Por su parte, Condorito es muy alegre, di-vertido, ingenioso, ladino y trata de sobrevivir con el menor esfuerzo posible. Le gustan mucho a sus amigos y aunque a veces es pendenciero y vengativo, en el fondo, tiene un gran corazón.

20 ### *El mundo según Mafalda*
Mafalda es la tira cómica por excelencia de Argentina. Esta niña de 6 años se impone a sí misma una gran misión: cambiar al mundo. Acompañada de amigos, y enloqueciendo a sus padres, siempre reflexiona acerca de cómo mejorar el
25 planeta y cómo cambiarlo desde los pequeños detalles. Se puede decir, incluso, que fue una de las primeras ecologistas latinoamericanas.

Nacida en el seno de una familia argentina de clase media, Mafalda cuenta con un variado y ecléctico grupo de amigos.
30 Además de su pequeño hermano Guille, el inocente, también están: Miguelito, el ingenuo; Susanita, cuyo mayor deseo en la vida es casarse con un hombre guapo y rico; Manolito, el conservador de ideas capitalistas; y la pequeña Libertad, una gran filósofa. Cada uno de los personajes representa
35 un elemento propio de la realidad argentina. Esta historieta aporta fuertemente a la reflexión. Siempre queda un mensaje que puede ser aplicado a cualquier realidad.

María Paz Castillo, coordinadora en Chile de la exposición "El Mundo de Mafalda", sostiene que el éxito
40 de esta pequeña se basa en que pese a ser una historia con casi 40 años de antigüedad, sigue siendo muy actual. "El mundo sigue teniendo los mismos problemas que antes", asegura. "Queremos acercar esta historieta a los niños y educarlos respecto al mundo. Hoy viven en una especie de
45 burbuja, por eso resulta importante que sepan cómo pensaba Mafalda", añade.

Un pájaro humoristico
Condorito es otro personaje que ha ganado popularidad en muchos lados. Creado en 1949 por el chileno René Ríos
50 ("Pepo"), está inspirado en el ave nacional de ese país: el cóndor. Aunque al inicio su aspecto era predominantemente animal, con el paso de los años se volvió más "humano".

Una de las características más llamativas de esta historieta es que no aborda la dimensión política de su entorno, sino
55 que más bien describe el esfuerzo, la picardía, el ingenio y las aventureras de personajes populares.

Junto a Condorito aparecen diferentes personajes siendo los más típicos el astuto sobrino "Coné"; la eterna y atractiva novia "Yayita"; el torpe enemigo "Pepe Cortisona"; su com-
60 padre "Don Chuma"; el alcohólico "Garganta de Lata"; y el simpático "Huevoduro".

Su humor es siempre blanco y su sátira inofensiva. A través de historias sencillas, se representa la vida cotidiana de los sectores populares de América Latina. De esta mane-
65 ra, se logra generar una cercanía cultural con los lectores.

"Condorito rescata lo popular; por eso a la gente le gusta y se identifica con él", afirma Juan Plaza, dibujante de cómics y quien desde hace 25 años se dedica a hacer las viñetas de Condorito. "Si bien es un chileno típico, también es pro-
70 fundamente universal, porque los demás miembros de la comunidad latinoamericana lo ven como un igual", agrega. "Este personaje fue capaz de quedarse grabado en el subcons-ciente de la gente. El hecho de que sea gracioso y que a las personas les guste sus chistes, permite que muchos quieran
75 seguir leyéndolo", concluye Plaza.

Used by permission of VeinteMundos.com

Fuente número 2

Tienes dos minutos para leer la introducción y prever las preguntas.

Introducción

Esta grabación se trata de un dibujante, Joaquin Salvador Lavado, y su famosa tira cómica *Mafalda*. La grabación dura aproximadamente tres minutos.

Ahora escucha la fuente número dos.

PLAY AUDIO: Track 11

Ahora tienes un minuto para empezar a responder a las preguntas para esta selección. Después de un minuto, vas a escuchar la grabación de nuevo.

(1 minute)

Ahora escucha de nuevo.

PLAY AUDIO: Track 11

Ahora termina de responder a las preguntas para esta selección.

1. ¿Cuál es el propósito de este artículo?
   - (A) De convencer al lector que Condorito es más popular que Mafalda
   - (B) De convencer al lector que Mafalda es más popular que Condorito
   - (C) Informar al lector de dos personajes en la cultura Latina que son populares
   - (D) Informar al lector la razón por qué estas tiras cómicas son controversiales en Latinoamérica

2. Según la fuente auditiva, ¿cómo reaccionan los Argentinos a Mafalda?
   - (A) A algunos le gusta, y a otros no.
   - (B) Piensan que es espectacular.
   - (C) Es una historieta vieja e irrelevante.
   - (D) No la conocen.

3. Según la fuente auditiva, ¿qué tipo de humor tiene Mafalda?
   - (A) Chismosa
   - (B) Inteligente
   - (C) Satírico
   - (D) Irónico e inofensivo

4. Según el artículo, ¿que se puede deducir sobre los amigos de Mafalda?
   - (A) Es un grupo de amigos iguales.
   - (B) Es un grupo de amigos variados, pero piensan en la misma manera que piensa Mafalda.
   - (C) Es un grupo de amigos eclécticos que representan las ideas o realidades del público Argentino.
   - (D) Es un grupo de amigos iguales que se llevan bien.

5. Según la fuente auditiva, ¿que piensa Cristóbal Navarro de Mafalda?
   - (A) Ella es un personaje muy intelectual, pero a la misma vez muy idealista.
   - (B) No se merece tanta atención.
   - (C) Es popular pero complicada.
   - (D) Es muy chiquita para tener opiniones tan adultas.

6. ¿A que se refiere "no aborda la dimensión política" (línea 54)?
   - (A) Condorito no se preocupa por los temas políticos.
   - (B) La política no impacta a Chile.
   - (C) La política es importante en las tiras cómicas.
   - (D) Es la dimensión más importante de este personaje.

7. Según el texto, ¿qué representa Condorito?

    (A) Un personaje querido

    (B) La única manera de que los lectores se acerquen culturalmente

    (C) Las historietas simples y ejemplares de la vida cotidiana

    (D) El ave nacional de Argentina

8. Según el artículo, ¿cómo es la actitud de Juan Plaza sobre Condorito?

    (A) Despreciativo

    (B) Informativo

    (C) Sarcástico

    (D) Juguetona

9. Según la fuente auditiva, ¿qué es "El Mundo de Mafalda"?

    (A) Una revista de tiras cómicas

    (B) Una película

    (C) Una juguetería

    (D) Una exhibición interactiva

10. Según la fuente auditiva, ¿que representa Mafalda?

    (A) La idiosincrasía del latinoamericano

    (B) La cultura Argentina

    (C) La cultura Chilena

    (D) Los puntos de vista en la cultura latina

Read the introductions here to get a bit of context. What is the passage about? What is the recording about? Next, preview the questions for the passage and tackle those first. Find the window in the passage and work the answers just as you would in the other reading passages. Similarly, treat the audio passages exactly as you would the other listening passages, previewing the questions, taking notes, and using POE aggressively. Remember, listening passages are not going to ask terribly complicated questions!

Let's read the translation and take a look at each question more closely.

Preview, take notes, and tackle the answer choices.

Sample Print and Audio Selection: Translated Texts and Questions, with Explanations

Source 1

Introduction

This text has to do with two iconic characters of Latin American pop culture. The original article was written by Joaquin Bode.

Condorito and Mafalda—Pop Culture Icons

More than 63 and 48 years ago, "Pepo" and "Quino" created Condorito and Mafalda, respectively, "to give humor and reflection to the world; two universal characters of pop culture," as stated on the website Culturacomic.com.

While the two protagonists are very representative of Latino culture, it is also true that both are very different from each other: Condorito is innocent and even clumsy; Mafalda is clever and ironic. The first lives a happy life, enjoying the simple pleasures, while the second establishes a constant social criticism, with an almost revolutionary zeal.

It's true: they both have great personality, unique and striking. Mafalda is genuine, intelligent, analytical, liberal, and revolutionary. Meanwhile, Condorito is very cheerful, funny, witty, and sly and tries to survive with the least possible effort. Condorito is very fond of his friends and although he is sometimes quarrelsome and vindictive, in reality, he has a big heart.

The World According to Mafalda
Mafalda is the quintessential comic strip from Argentina. This 6-year-old girl imposes on herself a grand mission: to change the world. Accompanied by her friends, and driving her parents crazy, she always reflects on how to improve the planet and how to change it, starting from the smallest details. You can even say that Mafalda was one of the first Latin American environmentalists.

Born into a middle class family in Argentina, Mafalda counts on her varied and eclectic group of friends. In addition to her little brother Guille, the innocent one, there are also: Miguelito, the naïve one; Susanita, whose greatest desire in life is to marry a handsome and rich man; Manolito, the conservative capitalist; and the small Libertad, a great philosopher. Each of these characters represents an element of truth in Argentina's own reality. This cartoon brings forth strong reflection. There is always a message that can be applied to any reality.

María Paz Castillo, coordinator of the "The World of Mafalda" exhibition in Chile, maintains that the success of this little girl is based on a story that, despite being almost 40 years old, is still very current. "The world still has the same problems as before," she says. "We want to bring this story to the children and educate them about the world. Today they live in a kind of bubble, so it is important for them to know how Mafalda thought," she adds.

A Humorous Bird

Condorito is another character that has gained popularity in many places. Created in 1949 by the Chilean René Ríos ("Pepo"), Condorito is inspired by the national bird of Chile: the condor. Although at first his appearance was predominantly animal, over the years he became more "human."

One of the most striking features of this cartoon is that it does not address the political dimension of its environment, but rather describes the effort, mischief, ingenuity, and adventures of popular characters.

Alongside Condorito, different typical characters appear: the astute nephew "Coné"; the eternal and attractive girlfriend "Yayita"; the clumsy enemy "Pepe Cortisone"; his friend "Don Chuma"; the alcoholic "Garganta de Lata (tin throat)"; and the friendly "Huevoduro (hard-boiled egg)".

His humor is always simple and his satire is harmless. Through simple stories, the daily life of the popular sectors in Latin America is represented. In this manner, it is possible to generate a cultural closeness among readers.

"Condorito appeals to the general populace; this is why people like and identify with him," said Juan Plaza, cartoonist and the person who has dedicated 25 years to making Condorito vignettes. "While Condorito is a typical Chilean, he is also profoundly universal because the other members of the Latin American community see him as an equal," he adds. "This character was able to stay engraved in the people's subconscious. The fact that he is funny and that people like his jokes, means that people want to continue reading this comic," concludes Plaza.

Source 2

Introduction

This recording is about a cartoonist, Joaquin Salvador Lavado, and his famous comic strip, *Mafalda*.

(REPORTER) Joaquín Salvador Lavado, better known worldwide as Quino, was the creator of Mafalda. Mafalda appeared in the newspaper as a weekly comic strip from 1964 to 1973. Surely she was the queen of the world of cartoons, translated into different languages, including Japanese. Vignettes of Mafalda were published in books in South America and Europe.

If one finds an Argentinian and asks him about Mafalda, the reaction is always spectacular. Mafalda represents more than a great comic character; she represents the Latin American idiosyncrasy. This little girl, awake and observant, has made—and still makes—people of all ages, whether grandparents, adults, or children, laugh. Her humor—naïve, harmless, and full of irony—is the highlight of this cartoon. Her creator was able to perfectly capture the essence of Latino culture across borders and time barriers. In social networks and Internet blogs, many speak about the famous Mafalda. Besides being loved by the Argentine public, she is very funny. Mafalda has won the hearts and affection of many people over the years.

Why was it, and does it continue to be, one of the most famous cartoons? Mafalda has a great personality. She is genuine, intelligent, mature, liberal, revolutionary, a lover of justice and world peace, and above all, she hates soup. Apparently, as many say, Mafalda is a faithful copy of her creator.

Cristóbal Navarro is a guide in the exhibition "The World of Mafalda." This interactive exhibit can be seen today throughout South America.

(NAVARRO) What catches people's attention about this character is how such a little girl can have that type of worldview. This character also represents the Argentine people very well, with the picaresque nature they possess.

(REPORTER) Cristóbal says that Mafalda transcends genres and manages to keep its critical spirit over time. In that sense, he adds that Quino created Mafalda at the right time.

(NAVARRO) What people have told me during this exhibition, and what I also believe, is that Mafalda is a very idealistic, critical, and intellectual character.

(REPORTER) During the most difficult times in Argentina's economy and social life, Mafalda was always present in the perception of the great Argentine public. With humor and truth, Mafalda was able to go further than Quino ever could have imagined.

1. What is the purpose of this article?

   (A) To convince the reader that Condorito is more popular than Mafalda

   (B) To convince the reader that Mafalda is more popular than Condorito

   (C) To inform the reader about two characters in Latin culture that are very popular

   (D) To inform the reader of the reason these comic strips are controversial in Latin America

This article focuses on two pop culture icons that have been around for over 40 years. Each of these characters represents an important part of Latin American culture, and the article describes why both characters are so relatable and loved by the public. The purpose of the article is not to convince the reader that one character is better than the other; thus (A) and (B) are incorrect. Choice (D) is not mentioned in the article. Choice (C) is the correct answer.

2. According to the audio source, how do Argentinians react to Mafalda?

   (A) Some like her, some don't.

   (B) They think she is spectacular.

   (C) It's an old comic strip and not relevant anymore.

   (D) They don't know her.

The recording does not state that people don't know her or that some like her and some don't. Choices (A) and (D) can be eliminated. It is, in fact, an old comic strip, though it is still relevant to this day. Choice (C) is incorrect. The audio portion states that Argentinians have a spectacular reaction to Mafalda. Choice (B) is the correct answer.

3. According to the audio source, what type of humor does Mafalda have?

   (A) Gossipy

   (B) Intelligent

   (C) Satirical

   (D) Ironic and inoffensive

Mafalda is described as an intelligent character, but her sense of humor is not described in the same way. She is not satirical or gossipy in nature, thus the only plausible answer is (D), stated directly in the recording.

4. According to the article, what can be inferred about Mafalda's friends?

   (A) They are a group of friends that are the same.

   (B) They are a group of friends that are varied, but that think in the same manner as Mafalda.

   (C) They are a group of eclectic friends that represent the ideas or realities of the Argentine public.

   (D) They are a group of friends that are the same and that get along well.

The article describes both Mafalda's and Condorito's friends in detail. The article states that Mafalda counts on her varied and eclectic group of friends. Choices (A) and (D) can be eliminated. In that same paragraph, the author also states that each of these characters represents an element of truth in the Argentine reality. Choice (B) is not stated anywhere in the article; thus (C) is the correct answer.

5. According to the audio source, what does Cristóbal Navarro think of Mafalda?

(A) She is a very intellectual character, but at the same time very idealistic.

(B) She doesn't deserve such attention.

(C) She is popular, but complicated.

(D) She is too little to have such adult opinions.

According to the interview with Cristóbal Navarro, he states that the main reason Mafalda is well-liked by all is due to her precocious nature. Choice (D) should be eliminated. Navarro does not state (B) or (C), so they should be eliminated as well. Navarro states that many people who visit the exhibition tell him that she is very intellectual, but idealistic. He agrees with that statement. Choice (A) is the correct answer.

6. What does "it does not address the political dimension of its environment" refer to in line 54?

(A) Condorito does not preoccupy himself with political topics.

(B) Politics do not impact Chile.

(C) Politics is important in comic strips.

(D) It is the most important dimension of this character.

The comparison that the article is trying to make is that, although both Mafalda and Condorito are popular characters, they are very different from each other. Mafalda focuses more on the socio-economic aspect of life, and Condorito is concerned with the simpler things and representing daily life. Choice (B) is incorrect, and is talking about politics in a nation rather than the political view of Condorito. The article makes no mention of how politics impact comics, thus (C) should be eliminated. Choice (D) doesn't make sense. Choice (A) is the correct answer.

7. According to the text, what does Condorito represent?

(A) A loved character

(B) The only way that readers can become culturally close

(C) Simple comic strips exemplary of daily life

(D) The national bird of Argentina

The article states directly that Condorito is a comic strip that is full of simplicity and satire. The stories of Condorito represent the daily life of certain sectors in Latin America. The national bird of Chile inspired his character, but Condorito does not represent that. Choice (D) is incorrect. Although (A) is true, again this is not what Condorito represents in Latin American culture. Choice (B) is not correct; Condorito does not represent the only way that readers can be culturally close. Choice (C) is the correct answer.

8. According to the article, what is Juan Plaza's attitude toward Condorito?

   (A) Contemptuous

   (B) Informative

   (C) Sarcastic

   (D) Playful

The overall tone of the article is informative and positive. In Plaza's interview, he describes why the public relates to Condorito and so well. Choices (A) and (C) can be eliminated. Choice (D) is not applicable, since he does not make any joking remarks. Choice (B) is the correct answer.

9. According to the audio source, what is "The World of Mafalda"?

   (A) A comic strip magazine

   (B) A movie

   (C) A toy store

   (D) An interactive exhibition

The reporter introduces Cristóbal Navarro as a guide in the exhibition "The World of Mafalda." This interactive exhibit can be seen today throughout South America. Choice (D) is the correct answer.

10. According to the audio source, what does Mafalda represent?

    (A) The idiosyncrasies of Latin Americans

    (B) Argentinian culture

    (C) Chilean culture

    (D) The viewpoints in Latin American culture

Mafalda represents more than a funny character or famous comic strip. Choices (B), (C), and (D) are not mentioned specifically. According to the recording, she represents the idiosyncrasies of the Latin American person. Choice (A) is correct.

Chapter 2
How to
Approach the
Free-Response
Section

THE BASICS

The free-response section (Section II) of the AP Spanish Language and Culture Exam tests three important skills: writing, speaking, and listening. The Writing portion consists of two samples of writing: an Email Reply and an Argumentative Essay. The Speaking portion consists of a simulated conversation, as well as a cultural comparison, which is an integration of reading and listening skills. On the speaking part, you will be paced and prompted by a master recording for a total of 2 minutes.

WRITING

The Writing portion of the free-response section consists of two compositions. The first part tests your ability to write in the interpersonal mode. You will have 15 minutes to read a prompt and reply with your email response. The second part examines your ability to write in the presentational mode. Here, you will have 10 minutes to read a few printed sources and listen to an audio prompt. After this, you will have about 5 minutes to formulate your ideas and plan your response. Then, you will have 40 minutes to write your essay, for a total time allotment of 55 minutes.

Question 1: Email Reply

Let's take a look at a sample question. Typically, a response prompt will be an email from a professional offering you a study opportunity, a scholarship, a job, or an internship. It might also be a response to your request for a letter of recommendation. When presented with one of these situations, try to immerse yourself in the situation. Maybe you have never worked or traveled overseas before. It doesn't matter—you can make things up! Graders are looking to see how convincing you are in your writing piece. That's all.

Use your note-taking skills to make a quick outline for yourself. If you get stuck, make something up!

The key to this limited-time assignment is to read the prompt quickly, touching upon all the points required and expanding upon them as much as possible in a grammatically correct and stylistically advanced manner. Spend less than 5 minutes reading the prompt and planning your answer, and begin writing your answer directly after having done so.

As you write, be sure to vary your vocabulary and your grammar. Graders don't want to see you use "bueno" and "malo" throughout your writing, and they definitely don't want to see you use only the present tense. Think about your speaking pattern in English. You don't speak only in present tense. You use a variety of tenses. Try to use some idiomatic expressions as well to show that you are familiar with the intricacies of the language. Remember to use original ways to open and close your letter. Use appropriate structural indicators and transitional words like *por lo tanto*, *sin embargo*, *en primer lugar*, *para concluir*, *finalmente*, and *adicionalmente*. Also, because this writing sample is so short, do not repeat yourself. Some final tips are to avoid Anglicism and never, under any circumstance, use English in your writing. If you don't know the word for something, find a way to describe it.

This section is also testing your ability to write a formal letter using correct register, possessive pronouns, appropriate vocabulary, and correct openings and closings. Remember, a basic and grammatically correct essay will score no more than a 3. An essay with dynamism, upper-level structures, and depth will score much higher.

> Know who you are writing to! It is often best to err on the side of formality by using *usted* instead of *tú* on these responses.

Basic Approach:

1. Read Carefully
2. Brainstorm Vocab and Plan your Points
3. Write!

Try the following sample email reply question on your own.

Sample Question

You will write a reply to an email message. You have 15 minutes to read the message and write your reply.	Vas a escribir una respuesta a un mensaje electrónico. Vas a tener 15 minutos para leer el mensaje y escribir tu respuesta.
Your reply should include a greeting and a closing and should respond to all the questions and requests in the message. In your reply, you should also ask for more details about something mentioned in the message. Also, you should use a formal form of address.	Tu respuesta debe incluir un saludo y una despedida, y debe responder a todas las preguntas y peticiones del mensaje. En tu respuesta, debes pedir más información sobre algo mencionado en el mensaje. También debes responder de una manera formal.

Introducción

El siguiente correo electrónico le llegó de parte de la Señorita Ciara Duran de la Universidad Interamericana de Puerto Rico. Es una invitación para asistir a un Congreso juvenil durante el verano.

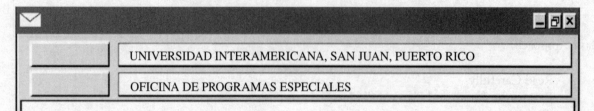

UNIVERSIDAD INTERAMERICANA, SAN JUAN, PUERTO RICO

OFICINA DE PROGRAMAS ESPECIALES

Estimado/a candidato/a:

Muchas gracias por haber expresado su interés en participar en nuestro Congreso Interamericano Juvenil que tendrá lugar el 14 de junio hasta el 5 de julio de este año en La Universidad Interamericana en San Juan, Puerto Rico. Me es muy grato ofrecerle un puesto como delegado representante este año.

Cada verano, nuestra universidad acoge a estudiantes visitantes de varios rincones del mundo hispano-hablante, lo cual nos aporta una perspectiva verdaderamente internacional ante los problemas que confrontan al joven de hoy. Como ya sabe, nuestra meta es alentar diálogo entre los jóvenes para definir cuáles son los problemas más contundentes que abarcan al joven. Y es de esperar que después de un intercambio de ideas, consigamos un mayor enfoque de cómo resolver la problemática regional que afecta a tantos jóvenes hoy en día.

Nosotros contamos con el esfuerzo y dedicación de los delegados voluntarios, ya que brindan una energía y espíritu servicial perspectiva única a las situaciones contundentes que confronta a nuestros países.

Para proveerle una experiencia de lo más agradable, además de confirmar su asistencia al Congreso, sería necesario que nos clarificara alguna información preliminar:

- Por favor díganos cuáles son algunos de los problemas actuales que confrontan a los jóvenes para que se incluyan en la agenda del Congreso. ¿Por qué le son importantes estos problemas?

- Durante su estadía aquí, puede optar por su alojamiento en un hotel o con una familia puertorriqueña. ¿Cuál sería su preferencia, y por qué?

- En el tiempo libre, habrá excursiones y oportunidades para intercambiar con la gente de Puerto Rico. ¿Qué actividades le interesarían a usted, y por qué?

Le pedimos que nos mande esta información de inmediato, ya que se aproxima la fecha límite para inscribirse en el programa.

Le saluda cordialmente,

Ciara Duran
Directora de Programas Estudiantes
Universidad Interamericana

Here's How to Crack It

Quickly brainstorm the vocabulary necessary for the task *(intercambiar, lograr, meta, en cuanto a, en cambio, por otra parte)*. Also, as it is a formal communication, have some generic lines in your back pocket that can be used for the opening and ending parts, for example: *Me dirijo a Usted (I am writing to you); Si fuera posible (If it were possible); Le doy las gracias de antemano por haberme atendido (I thank you in advance for your attention)*. And of course, don't forget all that great grammar: subjunctive, indirect object pronouns, transitional words, variety of tenses, and idiomatic expressions. Try to have several in each category prepared beforehand so you can refer to them and use them readily. It's almost like having your clothes picked out the night before school; it makes things a lot easier when you are under pressure. Also, don't forget the inverted exclamation points and question marks. Don't overdo commas and semicolons; Spanish uses them much more sparingly than English.

> Have some canned transitional phrases ready to go!

> A quick brainstorm before you write helps you organize your thoughts and avoid getting stuck mid-response.

Translation of the Question

Introduction

You received the following email from Ms. Ciara Duran of Inter-American University in Puerto Rico; it's an invitation to attend a Youth Congress during the summer.

> INTER-AMERICAN UNIVERSITY, SAN JUAN, PUERTO RICO
> SPECIAL PROGRAMS OFFICE

Dear candidate:

Many thanks for having expressed your interest in participating in our Inter-American Youth Congress that will take place from the 14th of June to the 5th of July of this year at the Inter-American University in San Juan, Puerto Rico. It is my great pleasure to offer you a position as representative delegate this year.

Each summer, our university welcomes visiting students from various corners of the Spanish-speaking world, which provides us a truly international perspective on the problems confronting today's youth. As you already know, our goal is to encourage dialogue between young people in order to define which are the toughest problems the youth are facing. It is the hope that after an interchange of ideas, we will achieve a better focus on how to resolve the regional problems that affect so many youth today.

We count on the spirit and dedication of the volunteer delegates, as they bring energy and the unique perspective of the spirit of service to the tough problems confronting our nations.

To ensure your experience is as pleasant as possible, along with confirming your attendance to the Congress, we need to clarify some preliminary information:

- Please tell us some of the current problems confronting youth so that they can be included in the agenda for the Congress. Why are these problems important to you?
- During your stay here, you can choose lodging in a hotel or with a Puerto Rican family. Which would be your preference, and why?
- In your free time, there will be excursions and opportunities for interchange with the people of Puerto Rico. What activities would interest you, and why?

We ask that you send us this information immediately, since the deadline to register for the program is approaching.

Warm regards,

Ciara Duran
Director of Student Programs
Inter-American University

Sample Student Response

Estimada Señorita Duran:

Me dirijo a usted con el propósito de informarle sobre mi deseo de participar en el Congreso. Siempre he soñado con participar en un evento así de importante, y espero con ganas la oportunidad de intercambiar ideas con diferentes jóvenes del mundo hispano. Ojalá podamos lograr nuestra meta de definir y lidiar con los problemas que afectan a los jóvenes de hoy. Con el esfuerzo y el positivismo, ¡todo es posible!

Usted me preguntó sobre mis ideas acerca de los temas más contundentes que afectan a los jóvenes del mundo hispanohablante. Yo diría que entre estos problemas se encuentran el desempleo, la falta de alfabetismo en las zonas rurales y el daño al medioambiente. Son problemas muy globales en el sentido que afectan a toda la sociedad, y creo que si podemos progresar en la lucha contra sus efectos, podemos desarrollar un mundo mejor para futuras generaciones. Estos problemas me son importantes ya que estoy al punto de emprender mi carrera universitaria, y la crisis global de muchas maneras me limita las oportunidades profesionales. En cuanto al alfabetismo, gracias a la tecnología, vivimos en un mundo donde nadie tiene que aislarse. La educación ayuda no solo a que la gente pueda participar en la sociedad, sino también les da una voz para votar y ayudar a los demás, así creando el sentido de igualdad entre todos los ciudadanos. Y finalmente, vivimos en un mundo comprometido por la industrialización, la deforestación y la explotación de los recursos naturales. Los ríos y lagos se ven cada día más contaminados, y el agua es tal vital a nuestra vida de tantas maneras. Espero poder informarles a mis compañeros la importancia de considerar estos problemas, pero al mismo tiempo, tengo muchas ganas de escuchar sus ideas también.

En cuanto al alojamiento, me gusta experimentar toda la cultura nativa, así que me encantaría vivir con una familia puertorriqueña. Es la mejor forma de entender y apreciar las perspectivas de otras culturas—¡ver el mundo a través de sus ojos!

Sé que Puerto Rico cuenta con muchos lugares turísticos. Si fuera posible, sería excelente visitar las zonas agrícolas de café y piñas para ver cómo se cosechan estos productos. También sé que la zona colonial de San Juan es muy histórica y pintoresca; y como soy fanática de la historia, tengo que visitar esa parte de la capital. Y claro está, ¡pasar un rato en sus lindas playas no vendría mal tampoco!

Nuevamente, le doy las gracias por esta oportunidad y espero mayor información sobre el evento. Si necesita más información de mi parte, sírvase de comunicarse conmigo a su conveniencia.

Un saludo cordial,

Victoria Hirsch

Translation of the Sample Student Response

Dear Ms. Duran:

I am writing to you to inform you of my desire to participate in the Congress. I have always dreamed of participating in an event of this importance, and I am looking forward to the opportunity to share ideas with different young people from the Hispanic world. I hope we can reach our goal of defining and dealing with the problems that affect the young people of today. With effort and positive thinking, anything is possible!

You asked me to share my ideas about the most pressing issues facing the youth of the Spanish-speaking world. I would say that among these problems we find unemployment, illiteracy in rural areas, and damage to the environment. These are worldwide problems in the sense that they affect all levels of society, and I think that if we can progress in fighting their effects, we can create a better world for future generations. These problems are important to me because I am at the beginning of my university career, and the global crisis in many ways has limited my professional opportunities. In terms of literacy, thanks to technology, we live in a world where no one has to be isolated. Education not only helps people participate in society, but also it gives them a voice to vote and help others, thus creating a sense of equality among all citizens. And finally, the world we live in is one compromised by industrialization, deforestation, and the exploitation of natural resources. The rivers and lakes are becoming more contaminated each day, and water is vital to our lives in so many ways. I hope to have the chance to inform my colleagues about the importance of considering these problems, but at the same time I am very interested in hearing their ideas as well.

In terms of lodging, I enjoy experiencing everything about the native culture, so I would love to live with a Puerto Rican family. That is the best way to understand and appreciate the perspectives of another culture—seeing the world through their eyes!

I know Puerto Rico has many tourist attractions. If it were at all possible, it would be wonderful to visit the agricultural zones of coffee and pineapples to see how these products are harvested. I also know that the colonial zone of San Juan is very historical and picturesque, and since I am a history fanatic, I have to visit that part of the capital. And of course, spending time on Puerto Rico's beautiful beaches would not be a bad idea either!

Once again, I thank you for this opportunity and I await further information about the event. If you need any more information from me, feel free to contact me at your convenience.

With cordial greetings,

Victoria Hirsch

Evaluation

This essay was organized, appropriate, and detailed; it would score a 5. The first paragraph clearly defined the writer's intention (to accept the invitation), the second paragraph talks about the topics that interest her, and the third and fourth paragraphs address specific questions from the email prompt. The closing makes the response even more cohesive. Notice also the breadth of vocabulary (*me dirijo a, contundentes, lidiar, cuenta con, fanática, claro está, sírvase de*) and grammar (subjunctive, *si* clauses, formal commands, preterite, conditional)—this is also an important aspect that graders examine. The response is well presented and not repetitive. Notice also that the writer showed she knew information about the country (coffee and pineapples, the beach, the colonial district). This is very important to demonstrate here and in the presentational speaking section. In order to write a native-sounding letter, you might want to view examples of formal writing online and try to incorporate several elements you observe in them that are not in your repertoire. Don't worry if you can't produce this lengthy a response. If you can duplicate parts of it and mimic some of the grammar and style, you will be in good shape.

> Check out how this student used some idioms and the subjunctive. Steal some phrases and use them in your own writing!

Question 2: Argumentative Essay

The second composition in the free-response section is the Argumentative Essay, which is a formal presentational writing sample. In this section, you will be required to read two sources and hear one audio piece and then respond to a written prompt. All resources will be related and must be referred to when you write your formal composition. You will have 6 minutes to read the essay topic and the text sources, and you will hear the audio selection twice. You should take notes while you listen. Finally, you will have 40 minutes to write your formal piece, for a total of 55 minutes.

> Basic Approach:
>
> 1. Read and Take Notes
> 2. Brainstorm Vocab and Plan your Points
> 3. Write!

This section of the exam requires more extensive preparation than the Email Reply prompt because we tend to have more experience with that form of communication in daily life. To do well on the Argumentative Essay, take plenty of time before the exam to expose yourself to a variety of media. Think of social and cultural topics that may appear on an exam. There could be questions on poverty, global warming, social unrest, or literacy implications across Latin America and Spain, or there could be questions based on music, food, and clothing trends.

Making yourself as well-rounded as possible and actively seeking Spanish printed and audio material will greatly help your score on this part.

So how do you plan for topics that are apparently limitless? Take the time to read newspapers from different areas of Latin America and Spain. You can find plenty of material on the Internet. Just do searches for *noticias latinoamericanas* or *periódicos chilenos* (*argentinos/españoles/peruanos*, and so on) and choose an article that is more challenging for you, grasping its message the best you can. It's not expected that you understand every word in an article, but if you can read the article's title, skim over it, and then read through it, you'll certainly be able to deduce its meaning. Read several articles and follow this procedure as you plan for the exam.

Keep it formal in the argumentative essay! Have some of those canned transitional phrases ready to go.

In order to train yourself for the audio prompt of this section, you will need to practice with dialects and with searching for meaning in a message. A fantastic and fun way to practice with dialects would be to turn on a Spanish soap opera *(telenovela)* or a movie in Spanish, lie back, and just listen. Some students choose an hour to watch television in Spanish and keep a notebook nearby. They jot down words they don't know or even full sentences they would like to include in their repertoire. Another way you can practice for this section is to download some podcasts. Set your Internet browser to Spanish so you can see and read what is happening in the Spanish-speaking world. Listen to Spanish-speaking radio stations; music is an amazing way to learn vocabulary and improve comprehension. Listen to speeches or interviews in Spanish—start somewhere in the middle of a selection and pay close attention to detail. Take notes as you listen. Be sure to get materials from both Spain and Latin America, as the AP loves to include listening passages with a Spanish accent, which can be a little difficult to understand if you are not used to hearing it.

> If you were learning vocabulary in English, you wouldn't gloss over words you don't know. Same idea here: write those words down, look them up, and learn to use them in context.

By reading various selections and listening to diverse audio samples, you begin to build vocabulary and you enhance your ability to make connections to meaning. These are essential tools to write a thorough formal composition. When you write the essay, be sure to make references to all three resources. Making references to the resources does not mean repeating something written or said in the selections; rather, you make an assertion or connection and use the materials to support your point of view. In your introduction you will explain your goal or position in reference to the topic question. In the paragraphs that follow, be sure to have a topic sentence in each to guide your thoughts and support your ideas with information from the sources. In your conclusion, do not repeat what you said in your introduction; rather, let it serve as a summation of your ideas throughout the essay. If you have time, proofread your composition and make sure you place accents where necessary and check your spelling. If you need to change a thought or idea, do not use correction fluid or try to erase what you wrote; just cross it out. You will not be penalized for doing this. Of course, this may sound silly, but try to be as neat as possible, as a well-presented essay is viewed favorably by graders.

Here's a sample argumentative essay prompt to try on your own.

Sample Question

You will write an argumentative essay to submit to a Spanish writing contest. The essay topic is based on three accompanying sources, which present different viewpoints on the topic and include both print and audio material. First, you will have 6 minutes to read the essay topic and the printed material. Afterward, you will hear the audio material twice; you should take notes while you listen. Then, you will have 40 minutes to prepare and write your essay.

In your argumentative essay, you should present the sources' different viewpoints on the topic, clearly indicate your own viewpoint, and defend it thoroughly. Use information from all of the sources to support your essay. As you refer to the sources, identify them appropriately. Also, organize your essay into clear paragraphs.

Vas a escribir un ensayo persuasivo para un concurso de redacción en español. El tema del ensayo se basa en las tres fuentes adjuntas, que presentan diferentes puntos de vista sobre el tema e incluyen material escrito y grabado. Primero, vas a tener 6 minutos para leer el tema del ensayo y los textos. Después, vas a escuchar la grabación dos veces; debes tomar apuntes mientras escuchas. Luego vas a tener 40 minutos para preparar y escribir tu ensayo.

En un ensayo persuasivo, debes presentar los diferentes puntos de vista de las fuentes sobre el tema, expresar tu propio punto de vista y apoyarlo. Usa información de todas las fuentes para apoyar tu punto de vista. Al referirte a las fuentes, identifícalas apropiadamente. Organiza también el ensayo en distintos párrafos bien desarrollados.

Tema del ensayo:

¿Por qué nos urge mejorar las condiciones de vivir de los niños latinoamericanos?

Fuente número 1

Introducción

Este artículo apareció en la revista mexicana *Auge* en 2009.

A través del continente americano, a pesar de los enormes avances tanto en la tecnología agrícola como en las mismas técnicas de arar la tierra, los niveles de nutrición de varios países siguen estancados a niveles tan reducidos que se ven comprometidas la estatura física, la habilidad de poder trabajar una jornada completa y, peor aún, las capacidades intelectuales de sus ciudadanos. La Organización de Desarrollo y Fomento Internacional reporta que, según cifras de los gobiernos latinoamericanos, el consumo de calorías de la región alcanza un promedio de unas 2680 por día (comparado con unas 3450 en los Estados Unidos), y peor aún en los países centroamericanos apenas sobrepasa las 2250 calorías diarias. En los países de mayor actividad económica, como Argentina, Brasil y México, las diferencias regionales han dejado a ciertas zonas marginadas en condiciones similares. La malnutrición se empeora por la falta de servicios de salud, el desempleo y la alta tasa de enfermedad que resulta de la escasez de debido a los escasos servicios sanitarios adecuados.

Los efectos de la modernización y la caída económica mundial requieren una mano de obra de tiempo completo listo para trabajar horas extensas, y a los niveles de nutrición actuales muchos adultos apenas contarán con la energía necesaria para trabajar las 40 o más horas necesarias semanalmente. Entre el 40% de la población adulta clasificada como "pobre" (con un ingreso diario equivalente a unos $2,50 estadounidenses), la falta de nutrición es un factor constante que les aqueja muy a menudo.

No faltan de los esfuerzos para aliviar el problema, sino que lo que ha variado es la magnitud de su alcance y su eficacia en condiciones sociales y económicas sumamente inhóspitas. Se han registrado victorias en algunas áreas (como el programa Salta de Vitarte en Perú, que se concentró en las personas más pobres y les facilitó 3 servicios básicos) pero el obstáculo más formidable es la irremediable realidad económica en la que vive la población. Los programas de bienestar público intentan repartir certificados a las familias de bajo ingreso—parecido al programa de Cupones de Alimentos en los Estados Unidos—pero no existen ni los recursos ni la infraestructura para sostener el programa a largo plazo. Otros programas tienen como meta enfatizar la educación de salud y nutrición, pero los esfuerzos se hacen en balde ya que los ingresos familiares no generan lo suficiente para sostener dietas mejor balanceadas. Ningún esfuerzo ha logrado tener el impacto necesario para lidiar con el problema en toda su magnitud.

Fuente número 2

Introducción

Este artículo apareció en *Páginas Escolares,* una revista juvenil colombiana.

EL CÍRCULO DE AMOR

Cuando uno piensa en Guatemala, tal vez le llegue a la mente la imagen de un país pobre donde predomina la agricultura, o tal vez recuerde a la famosa Rigoberta Menchú, ganadora del Premio Nobel de La Paz en 1992 y con ella la gran tradición indígena que por siglos ha representado un papel omnipresente en la historia guatemalteca. Pero si conoce a Maria Giammarino, de Mahwah, Nueva Jersey, entonces lo primero que sabrá de Guatemala es sobre El Círculo de Amor.

El Círculo de Amor fue fundado por Giammarino en 2001, pero su interés en los guatemaltecos proviene desde los años 90, cuando visitaba el país por su trabajo de aeromoza en una línea aérea americana. Así nos cuenta su experiencia: "Durante unas cuantas estadías en el país, tuve la oportunidad de recorrer muchas de las zonas rurales más pobres. Una vez hicimos una excursión en canoa cerca de Livingston, que nos llevó a una aldea prácticamente olvidada por el mundo. Vimos una pobreza que me partió el alma. Llegamos a un pueblo retirado, y de repente vi a unas niñas de edad escolar vendiendo caramelos y cigarrillos en el muelle. ¡Les correspondía estar en la escuela! Una me llamó la atención: llevaba su ropita harapienta y andaba pata pelada, pero me ofreció una sonrisa dulce e inocente. Una mirada hacia el pueblo me confirmó lo peor: unas covachas con techo de estaño, y el desagüe en la calle cuyo olor perduraba y perduraba. Ni Dante hubiera vislumbrado un mundo así".

Después de cultivar una amistad, Giammarino empezó por enseñarle a tejer a la niña. Le obsequió el material y pronto la novata creó chompas de algodón no sólo para su familia, sino también para la venta. Giammarino le alquiló un pequeño puesto donde vendían la mercancía. Y así se inició El Círculo de Amor. Su aerolínea también le dio la mano, lanzando el programa "Quédate con el vuelto", que les pide a pasajeros norteamericanos que vuelven a su tierra que donen los quetzales sobrantes de su estudía en Guatemala. La campaña ha recaudado más de 10.000 dólares desde su inicio. Ahora hay talleres de tejer, los cuales les ayudan a las mujeres a aprender un oficio ya que juegan éstas un papel esencial en la estrategia de la sobrevivencia de las familias. Hay una pequeña cantina que sirve almuerzos a los residentes del pueblo. Y este año, gracias a la bondadosa ayuda de varios auspiciadores, se presenció la apertura de un pequeño consultorio médico que otorga un servicio de salud básico a los 1200 habitantes del pueblo.

El Círculo de Amor tiene como meta principal procurar el bienestar de las niñas guatemaltecas, muchas veces las más explotadas y marginadas de la sociedad. Las contribuciones también se destinan a la educación femenina, porque según Giammarino "a la gente sin acceso a la educación básica se les priva la voz". Por sólo 30 dólares mensuales, un patrocinador puede mandar a una niña a la escuela. El Círculo de Amor pone atención especial en reclutar a las niñas más pequeñas de una familia para que asistan a la escuela, lo cual es un privilegio reservado mayormente para los niños varones. La estrategia de elegir a la niña menor viene de la perspectiva de que mientras más joven sea ella al iniciar los estudios, más probabilidad tendrá de continuarlos en el futuro.

Fuente número 3

Tienes 30 segundos para leer la introducción.

Introducción

El siguiente discurso lo ofreció Alesandro Dávila, decano de la escuela de Economía de la Pontificia Universidad Católica del Perú en La X Asamblea del Pacto Andino, celebrado en Cajamarca, Perú el año pasado. Se titula "Declive de inversiones gubernamentales con la crisis económica andina".

Ahora escucha la fuente número tres.

> **PLAY AUDIO: Track 12**

Ahora escucha de nuevo.

> **PLAY AUDIO: Track 12**

Ahora tienes cuarenta minutos para preparar y escribir un ensayo persuasivo.

(40 minutes)

Translation of the Question

Essay topic:

Why is improving the living conditions of Latin American children an urgent need?

Source 1

Introduction

This article appeared in the Mexican magazine *Auge* in 2009.

Throughout the American continents, despite enormous advances in agricultural technology and plowing techniques, the levels of nutrition in various countries continue to stagnate at levels so low that citizens are left compromised in terms of physical stature, ability to work full-time, and (even worse) intellectual capacity. The International Development and Promotion Organization reports that, according to figures from Latin American governments, the average calorie consumption for the region reaches around 2,680 per day (compared to about 3,450 in the United States); it's even worse in the Central American countries, where it barely exceeds 2,250 calories per day. In countries with more economic activity, such as Argentina, Brazil, and Mexico, regional differences have left certain marginalized areas in similar conditions. Malnutrition is exacerbated by the lack of health services, unemployment, and the high rate of sickness due to the scarcity of adequate sanitation services.

The effects of modernization and the global economic recession require a labor force ready to work extensive hours, and at current levels of nutrition many adults can barely count on getting the energy necessary to work the required 40 or more hours per week. Among the 40% of the adult population classified as "poor," (with a daily income equivalent to $2.50 in American dollars), lack of nutrition is a constant affliction.

Efforts to alleviate the problem are not lacking, but vary in the magnitude of their scope and their efficacy in extremely inhospitable social and economic conditions. Victories have been recorded in some areas (such as the Salta de Vitarte program in Peru, which concentrated on the poorest people and facilitated three basic services), but the most formidable obstacle is the irremediable economic reality in which the population lives. Public health programs try to distribute certificates to low-income families—similar to Food Stamp programs in the United States—but neither the resources nor the infrastructure exist to sustain the programs in the long run. Other programs aim to emphasize health and nutrition education, but their efforts are in vain since family incomes don't generate enough to sustain better-balanced diets. No endeavor has been successful in having the necessary impact to fight the problem in its whole magnitude.

Source 2

Introduction

This article appeared in *Páginas Escolares,* a Colombian youth magazine.

THE CIRCLE OF LOVE

When you think of Guatemala, maybe what comes to mind is an image of a poor country where agriculture predominates, or maybe you remember the famous Rigoberta Menchú, winner of the Nobel Peace Prize in 1992, and with her the great indigenous tradition that for centuries has played an omnipresent role in Guatemalan history. But if you know Maria Giammarino, of Mahwah, New Jersey, then the first thing you'll know about Guatemala is the Circle of Love.

The Circle of Love was founded by Giammarino in 2001, but her interest in Guatemalans began in the '90s, when she visited the country while working as a flight attendant for an American airline. She recounts her experience like this: "During a few stays in the country, I had the opportunity to travel through many of the poorest rural areas. Once we took a canoe excursion near Livingston, which brought us to a village practically forgotten by the world. We saw poverty that split open my soul. We came to a remote town, and suddenly I saw some school-age girls selling candy and cigarettes on a wharf. They should have been in school! One attracted my attention: She wore little ragged clothes and walked barefoot, but offered me a sweet and innocent smile. A look at the town confirmed the worst: a few hovels with tin roofs, and a drainage ditch in the street the smell of which lasted and lasted. Not even Dante would have imagined a world like that."

After cultivating a friendship, Giammarino began to teach the girl to knit. She gave her the materials and soon the novice was creating cotton sweaters not only for her family but also to sell. Giammarino rented her a tiny stall from which she sold the merchandise. And so began the Circle of Love. Her airline also lent a hand, launching the program "Keep the Change," which asked North American passengers returning home to donate the leftover *quetzales* (Guatemalan currency) from their stays in Guatemala. The campaign has collected more than 10,000 dollars since it began. Now there are knitting workshops, which help women learn a trade and so play an essential role in their families' survival. There is a small café that serves lunch to residents of the town. And this year, thanks to the kind-hearted help of various sponsors, witnessed the opening of a small doctor's office granting basic health services to the 1200 residents of the town.

The Circle of Love's principal goal is the well-being of Guatemala's young girls, often the most exploited and marginalized members of society. Contributions also go to education for females, because according to Giammarino, "people without access to basic education are deprived of their voice." For only 30 dollars per month, a sponsor can send a girl to school. The Circle of Love places special attention on recruiting families' youngest daughters for school, a privilege for the most part reserved for male children. The strategy of choosing the youngest daughter comes from the perspective that the younger a girl is upon beginning her studies, the more likely she is to continue them into the future.

Source 3

Introduction

The following discourse was offered by Alesandro Dávila, dean of the School of Economics of the Papal Catholic University of Peru in the 10th Assembly of the Andean Pact, celebrated in Cajamarca, Peru, last year. It is titled "Decline of Governmental Investments in the Andean Economic Crisis."

Audio Track 12

What I can predict with certainty is that the only thing that will change in Latin America is the climate. Our national problems have lots of ups and downs, but in the end come out the same: we are a poor country, and our most marginalized become more and more trapped in this vicious cycle that is poverty. The reality we are living is that our external debt suffocates us and almost robs us of the will to keep progressing. Almost 50% of our gross national product goes to satisfy payments to our European and North American creditors. Our problems are strongly rooted in our foreign relations, which leave a paltry amount for family planning, education, and vaccine programs. Our national budget is not enough for everything, and our children are suffering the worst. Investment in education has diminished 50%, and some precincts already in disrepair cannot even provide the minimum necessary for their classrooms: books, blackboards, floors, and potable water. And when it comes to survival, many choose to work rather than study. As a result, we as a region have one of the highest rates of illiteracy on the continent. One of the most sensitive problems the populations of our countries in general and specifically those most marginalized groups are going through right now is plummeting incomes. In Lima, the family shopping basket: basic necessities support less but cost more, and now La Leche League will suspend its deliveries of this valuable food to daycares due to exorbitant costs, and free lunches are already an endangered species. Ten years ago, every child in the Andean provinces received vaccines, dental exams, and school snacks. Now they are lucky to get one of the three. The data shows the sad reality. In Bolivia, the national budget for education programs diminished by 33% even though the student population grew by 8%. In Chile, falling income from exports resulted in the elimination of nutrition and family planning programs, scholarships, and four free clinics in the areas of greatest need. The conclusion we can extract reliably is that inequality and absolute poverty have grown with the economic crisis. Unfortunately, the world is blind to the problem. The "bailout," a first-world luxury, is not an option for us. In the future, based on what I see now, it's probable that the South American continent will experience negative growth, like the runaway inflation of the '80s, which will exacerbate the nutritional deficiencies, productivity problems, and sadly, the potential for growth and development for the future.

Sample Student Response

¿Por qué nos urge mejorar las condiciones de vivir de los niños latinoamericanos?

Es sumamente importante que mejoremos las condiciones de vivir de los niños latinoamericanos, ya que ellos son esenciales para el bienestar del futuro. Hoy en día, se puede decir que la falta de acceso a servicios básicos es uno de los problemas más grandes que confronta a los niños a través del mundo latinoamericano. Como resultado, los niños son atrapados en una problemática sin salida: la pobreza, la cual trae consigo un menor acceso a la educación, la medicina y la vivienda. El trabajo reemplaza la educación como la primera prioridad. Según la fuente #3, algunos niños latinoamericanos carecen de buena nutrición, vacunas y alfabetismo básico. Esto concuerda con otra triste realidad: el hecho preocupante que la inversión financiera en educación, según la fuente número 3, es mucho menor en América Latina, lo cual es claramente paradójico, ya que es donde más se necesita esta clase de inversión (Fuente 2).

,Pienso que si las necesidades básicas de la gente se satisficieran, entonces podrían preocuparse de los lujos como la educación. Como nos explica la fuente #1, la gente hambrienta no puede funcionar en el mundo laboral. Vivir, comer y estar libre de enfermedades son necesidades básicas del ser humano. Si esta gente no recibe los servicios básicos, ello puede causar epidemias tal como se presencia en México actualmente. Además, la educación, la planificación familiar, la nutrición y la vivienda adecuadas ayudan a la gente a que contribuyan más a sus países. Y hasta es posible que puedan aportar al futuro de su país al convertirse en políticos o doctores. Se dice que con el apoyo y el deseo todo es posible. El mundo está conectado social, económica y políticamente, entonces es nuestra responsabilidad ayudar a estas personas que, según la fuente 2, "se les priva de voz" en su futuro.

Hemos visto que nuestras acciones sí hacen una diferencia en las vidas de los niños latinoamericanos y, obviamente, se sabe que no hay soluciones rápidas y fáciles. Sin embargo, la señora Giammarino se empeñó en ayudar a una comunidad pequeña guatemalteca, demostrando que los esfuerzos pequeños pueden lograr milagros. Esperamos que otras personas reconozcan la urgencia de ayudar a estas personas necesitadas.

Translation of the Sample Student Response

Why is improving the living conditions of Latin American children an urgent need?

It is extremely important for us to improve the living conditions of Latin America's children, as they are essential to the wellbeing of the future. Nowadays, it can be said that the lack of access to basic services is one of the most formidable problems that confront children throughout the Latin American world. As a result, children are trapped in a problem without solution: poverty that brings with it reduced access to education, medicine, and shelter. Work replaces education as the first priority. According to source #3, some Latin American children lack good nutrition, vaccinations, and basic literacy. This goes hand in hand with another sad reality: the worrying fact that financial investment in education in Latin America is much less (source #3), which is clearly paradoxical as it is precisely where this type of investment is needed (source #2).

I believe that if the basic needs of the people were satisfied, then they would be able to concern themselves with luxuries such as education. As source #1 explains to us, hungry people cannot function in the workplace. Living, eating, and illness prevention are basic necessities of human beings. If these people don't receive basic services, it could cause epidemics as we have witnessed recently in Mexico. Moreover, education, family planning, nutrition, and adequate housing help people to contribute more to their respective countries. It's even possible they might contribute to the future of their countries by becoming politicians or doctors. It is said that with support and desire anything is possible. The world is connected socially, economically, and politically, and thus it is our responsibility to help those people, who, according to source #2, "are denied a voice" in their future.

We have seen that our actions do indeed make a difference in the lives of Latin American children. And obviously, we know there are no quick and easy solutions. However, Mrs. Giammarino gave of herself to help a small Guatemalan community, demonstrating that small efforts can produce miracles. We can only hope that other people recognize the urgency of helping these needy people.

Evaluation

This essay had strong vocabulary, grammar, and organization. One of the challenges with the argumentative essay section is to try to refer to all the sources, because the AP often includes sources that don't have a clear correlation to each other. It is your responsibility to try to find connections between them, however minor, in order to include all of them in your analysis, your synthesis, and ultimately, your composition. Mentioning ALL the sources will help you score higher. One weakness in this essay was that it needed a greater incorporation of the sources, and possibly a deeper analysis. The writer did make some connections among the materials which, although somewhat predictable, nonetheless carried ideas from start to finish and used data to back up the conclusions. The summary was kept to a minimum and statements referred to information in the readings, which are things to remember when writing your essay. This essay would probably score in the 4 range.

PRACTICE PROMPT 1

Introducción

El siguiente correo electrónico le llegó de parte del Señor Ramón Hector Ramos de la Organización de las Naciones Unidas. Es una entrevista electrónica por una práctica profesional este verano. Tendrá 15 minutos para leer la carta y escribir su respuesta.

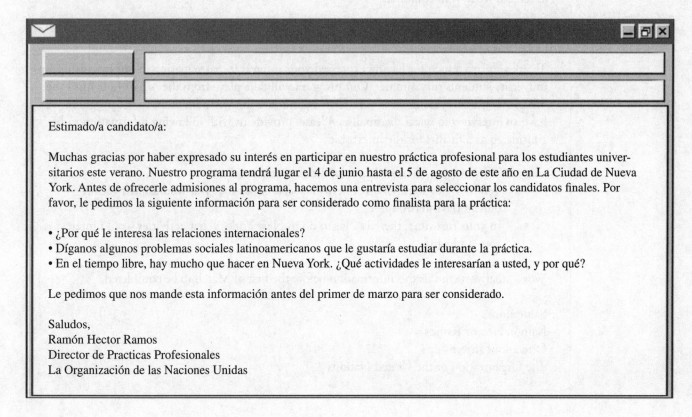

Estimado/a candidato/a:

Muchas gracias por haber expresado su interés en participar en nuestro práctica profesional para los estudiantes universitarios este verano. Nuestro programa tendrá lugar el 4 de junio hasta el 5 de agosto de este año en La Ciudad de Nueva York. Antes de ofrecerle admisiones al programa, hacemos una entrevista para seleccionar los candidatos finales. Por favor, le pedimos la siguiente información para ser considerado como finalista para la práctica:

• ¿Por qué le interesa las relaciones internacionales?
• Díganos algunos problemas sociales latinoamericanos que le gustaría estudiar durante la práctica.
• En el tiempo libre, hay mucho que hacer en Nueva York. ¿Qué actividades le interesarían a usted, y por qué?

Le pedimos que nos mande esta información antes del primer de marzo para ser considerado.

Saludos,
Ramón Hector Ramos
Director de Practicas Profesionales
La Organización de las Naciones Unidas

PRACTICE PROMPT 1 TRANSLATION

Introduction

You received the following email from Señor Ramón Hector Ramos of the United Nations. It is an electronic interview for an internship this summer. You will have 15 minutes to read the letter and write your response.

Esteemed candidate:

Thank you very much for having expressed your interest in participating in our internship for university students this summer. Our program will take place from the 4th of June until the 5th of August this year in New York City. Before offering you admission to the program, we have an interview to select the finalists. Please, provide us with following information to be considered as a finalist for the internship:

- Why are you interested in international relations?
- Tell us about some Latin American social issues that you would like to study during the internship.
- In your free time, there is a lot to do in New York. What activities would interest you, and why?

We ask that you send us this information before the first of March to be considered.

Salutations,
Ramón Hector Ramos
Director of Internships
The Organization of the United Nations

PRACTICE PROMPT 2

Introducción

Este mensaje es de Señora Elena Guzman, su profesora de literatura latinoamericana. Ha recibido este mensaje porque recientemente le había pedido que le escribiera una carta de recomendación para estudiar en el programa de su universidad en Puebla, México por el primer semestre. Tendrá 15 minutos para leer la carta y escribir su respuesta.

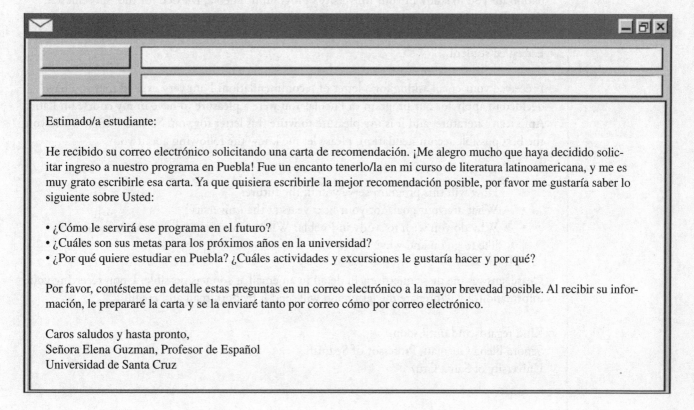

Estimado/a estudiante:

He recibido su correo electrónico solicitando una carta de recomendación. ¡Me alegro mucho que haya decidido solicitar ingreso a nuestro programa en Puebla! Fue un encanto tenerlo/la en mi curso de literatura latinoamericana, y me es muy grato escribirle esa carta. Ya que quisiera escribirle la mejor recomendación posible, por favor me gustaría saber lo siguiente sobre Usted:

• ¿Cómo le servirá ese programa en el futuro?
• ¿Cuáles son sus metas para los próximos años en la universidad?
• ¿Por qué quiere estudiar en Puebla? ¿Cuáles actividades y excursiones le gustaría hacer y por qué?

Por favor, contésteme en detalle estas preguntas en un correo electrónico a la mayor brevedad posible. Al recibir su información, le prepararé la carta y se la enviaré tanto por correo cómo por correo electrónico.

Caros saludos y hasta pronto,
Señora Elena Guzman, Profesor de Español
Universidad de Santa Cruz

PRACTICE PROMPT 2 TRANSLATION

Introduction

This message is from Señora Elena Guzman, your professor of Latin American Literature. You have received this message because recently you have asked her to write a letter of recommendation for you to study in your university's program in Puebla, Mexico for the Fall semester. You will have 15 minutes to read the letter and write your response.

Esteemed student,

I received your email asking for a letter of recommendation. I am very excited that you have decided to apply for our program in Puebla! You were a pleasure to have in my course on Latin American Literature, and it is my pleasure to write this letter for you. So that I might write you the best possible recommendation, please let me know the following about you:

- How will this program serve you in the future?
- What are your goals for your next years at the university?
- Why do you wish to study in Puebla? Which activities and excursions would you like to go on and why?

Please, answer me these questions in detail in an email as soon as possible. Upon receiving your information, I will prepare the letter and will send it by both mail and email.

Kind regards and until soon,
Señora Elena Guzman, Professor of Spanish
University of Santa Cruz

SPEAKING

The directions for the speaking part will be given to you by the master recording. You will be told when to open the booklet containing the material. You will be asked to respond to different prompts and to record your voice. Most directions will be spoken in English, but you will be asked different types of questions in Spanish in the Directed Response part of the exam. There are two sections in the speaking part: a role-play conversation in which the student listens to a speaker and responds to prompts, and an oral presentation of two minutes based on reading and listening passages. Together, these sections comprise 25 percent of your overall score.

Question 3: Conversation

This section integrates both listening and speaking skills in a role-play conversation. Students will be asked to interact with the recorded conversation. You will be required to answer either five or six times to various prompts. Each response will be 20 seconds long and will be timed by a beep on the recording. Before beginning, you will have the opportunity to read the outline of the simulated conversation and instructions.

Basic Approach:

1. Listen to the Scenario Carefully to Determine Context
2. Take Notes if Needed
3. Stay Relaxed and Have Some Phrases Ready

For the upcoming sample question, you may want to have a device on hand with which to record your spoken answers. This will allow you to compare your responses with the sample student responses that follow.

Ready to begin? Let's give it a try!

Sample Question

You will participate in a conversation. First, you will have 1 minute to read a preview of the conversation, including an outline of each turn in the conversation. Afterward, the conversation will begin, following the outline. Each time it is your turn to speak, you will have 20 seconds to record your response; a tone will indicate when you should begin and end speaking.	Vas a participar en una conversación. Primero, vas a tener un minuto para leer la introducción y el esquema de la conversación. Después, comenzará la conversación, siguiendo el esquema. Cada vez que te corresponda participar en la conversación, vas a tener 20 segundos para grabar tu respuesta; una señal te indicará cuando debes empezar y terminar de hablar.
You should participate in the conversation as fully and appropriately as possible.	Debes participar de la manera más completa y apropiada posible.

Introducción

Imagina que recibes un mensaje telefónico de parte del director del Departamento de Estudios para Extranjeros de una universidad latinoamericana. El director te llama para invitarte a acudir a su oficina para una entrevista sobre tu solicitud de beca. [You will hear the message on the recording.]

> **PLAY AUDIO: Track 13**

[The shaded lines reflect what you will hear on the recording.]

Entrevistador	Te saluda
Tú	Salúdalo y preséntate
Entrevistador	Te explica por qué te hace la entrevista y te hace una pregunta
Tú	Responde a la pregunta
Entrevistador	Continúa la conversación
Tú	Responde a la pregunta
Entrevistador	Continúa la conversación
Tú	Responde a la pregunta
Entrevistador	Continúa la conversación
Tú	Responde a la pregunta
Entrevistador	Continúa la conversación
Tú	Haz una pregunta

Here's How to Crack It

Use the introduction by the narrator to gain some context, jotting down a quick note or two of key vocabulary terms. This section is testing your ability to initiate, sustain, and conclude a conversation in a given situation as well as use language that is culturally, semantically, grammatically, and socially correct. In other words, are you using the correct *Usted* and *tú* forms? Are you being culturally appropriate in a social setting by using correct markers in your conversation, such as the subjunctive and formal commands, when necessary? Many of these situations involve traveling or studying overseas, or applying for jobs, internships, and scholarships. It would be smart to study up on some of the vocabulary involved in job applications, college courses, scholarships, internships, and so on.

Remember that you have only 20 seconds to respond to each prompt. Do not restate the question in your answer, as it wastes valuable time. Speak clearly and slowly. Don't worry if you get cut off in mid-sentence by the tone. Make it your goal to provide interesting and high-level answers that address the question or situation with correct grammar and pronunciation. Also, try not to use the simple way to say things; use higher-order vocabulary. For example, use *dirigirse* or *acudir* instead of *ir*. Try to incorporate certain phrases that can help you introduce your answers: *Lo que es importante, Quisiera, Si fuera posible,* for example.

Have these conversational phrases and relevant vocabulary ready! It will help with the entire exam, really.

The higher-level the structure and vocabulary you use, the higher your score will be. Try to use all 20 seconds, as it will enable you to give two solid, high-level sentences. Remember that if you are using the *Usted* form, which is probably more often than not, you need to have all of the verbs, possessive pronouns, and especially the object pronouns in the corresponding forms. Pay attention to the student answers in the Sample Script with Student Response, as these are the kinds of answers that will get you high scores.

> Try to fill the 20 seconds! If you have any pauses, try to convert your "uhs" into "ems," which is more common in Spanish-speakers' speech patterns.

Script with Sample Student Response and Translation

Narrador:	Imagina que recibes un mensaje telefónico de parte del director del Departamento de Estudios para Extranjeros de una universidad latino-americana. El director te llama para invitarte a acudir a su oficina para una entrevista sobre tu solicitud de beca.
	Imagine that you receive a phone message from the director of the Department of Foreign Student Studies at a Latin American university. The director calls you to invite you to his office for an interview about your scholarship application.
MA:	[Answering machine] [Beep] Buenos días, le habla el señor Guillermo Butrón, director del programa de Estudios para Extranjeros. Quisiera que pasara por mi oficina mañana para una entrevista sobre la solicitud que usted nos envió. Tengo algunas preguntas que quisiera hacerle.
	Good morning, this is Mr. Guillermo Butrón, director of the Foreign Student Studies program. I would like you to come by my office tomorrow for an interview concerning the application you submitted. I have a few questions I would like to ask you.
Narrador:	Ahora tienes un minuto para leer el esquema de la conversación.
	Now you have one minute to read the conversation outline.
	Ahora imagina que te encuentres en la oficina del señor Butrón para realizar una entrevista.
	Now imagine that you are in Mr. Butrón's office for an interview.
Entre:	Buenos días. Me es muy grato conocerle en persona. Soy Guillermo Butrón, director del programa de Estudios para Extranjeros y de becas en la región latinoamericana. Por favor, pase y siéntese.
	Good morning. It is a pleasure to meet you in person. I am Guillermo Butrón, director of the Foreign Student Studies program and scholarships in Latin America. Please, come in and sit down.

Tú:	Es un verdadero gusto conocerle también, Señor Butrón. Soy Michael Randello de Nueva York.
	It is real pleasure to meet you also, Mr. Butrón. I am Michael Randello, from New York.
Entre:	Tengo su solicitud para una beca de estudios y necesito hacerle algunas preguntas para saber un poco más sobre usted. ¿Por qué le interesa estudiar en Latinoamérica?
	I have your scholarship study application and I need to ask you some questions to find out a little more about you. Why are you interested in studying in Latin America?
Tú:	Siempre me han llamado la atención la cultura y el idioma de esa región. Como quisiera trabajar en un empleo relacionado con América Latina, necesito hablar mejor el español y entender más a fondo su cultura y costumbres.
	I have always been interested in both the culture and language of that region. Since I would like to work in a position that relates to Latin America, I need to speak Spanish better and understand in depth its culture and customs.
Entre:	Ah, muy interesante. Se nota que tiene un verdadero interés en estudiar en el extranjero. ¿Dónde en Latinoamérica le gustaría estudiar y vivir, y por qué?
	Ah, very interesting. I see that you have a real interest in studying abroad. Where in Latin America would you like to study and live, and why?
Tú:	Definitivamente me interesaría estar en Argentina. Encuentro tanto la historia como la cultura fascinante. Además, ahí podría perfeccionar el español.
	I would definitely like to be in Argentina. I find both the history and culture fascinating. In addition, there I would be able to perfect my Spanish.
Entre:	Si fuera a recibir la beca, ¿qué le gustaría estudiar y por qué?
	If you were to receive the scholarship, what would you like to study and why?
Tú:	Bueno, obviamente necesitaría estudiar el español, pero como quisiera trabajar en negocios internacionales, sería buena idea que estudiara comercio, relaciones internacionales e historia.
	Well, obviously I would need to study Spanish, but as I would like to work in international business, it would be a good idea to study commerce, international relations, and history.

Entre:	Además de sus responsabilidades académicas, los estudiantes que reciben becas deben participar en actividades culturales. ¿Qué aspectos de la cultura del país que visitará le interesan?

In addition to their academic responsibilities, the students who receive scholarships must participate in cultural activities. What aspects of the culture interest you in your country of choice?

Tú:	Siempre me ha fascinado el tango. La historia y el significado del tango me son muy interesantes. Siempre soñé con aprender a bailar el tango, así que tomaré clases.

The tango has always fascinated me. The history and meaning of the tango are very interesting. I always dreamed about learning to dance the tango, so I will take classes.

Entre:	¡Qué bien! Y para terminar, ¿qué preguntas tiene sobre la beca o sobre nuestro programa en general?

How nice! And to conclude, what questions do you have about the scholarship or about our program in general?

Tú	Por favor, dígame: ¿Cuándo empezará el programa? ¿Viviré con una familia o en una residencia estudiantil? ¿Cuándo me informarán sobre la beca?

Please tell me: When does the program begin? Will I live with a family or in a student residence? When will I be informed about the scholarship?

Evaluation

The responses by the student were rich, varied, and complete; he used excellent grammatical and vocabulary structures: conditional, subjunctive, and future tenses. The student also fulfilled the requirement of being socially appropriate by using the *Usted* command *Dígame* in the last response. Be sure to get one example of that in your response. The responses enriched and advanced the conversation; notice how the topics were addressed and developed with creative and interesting answers: the student showed an understanding of university courses, culture, and studying overseas. You should be sure to have an understanding of several Spanish-speaking countries, as you may need to discuss their culture in one of these types of questions. This response would very likely score in the 4 or 5 level.

> **Reflect**
> - Review idioms and phrases like *Dígame* to prepare for this section.
> - Use all the time available to continue talking. Don't worry if you get cut off!
> - Have a friend help you study by reading prompts from AP Students.

Question 4: Cultural Comparison

This section requires you to make a presentation on a specific topic. You are given 4 minutes to read the question and plan your answer, and then 2 minutes to actually deliver your presentation. Although you are not given any material on which to base your answer, you need to reflect on the cultural knowledge you have acquired

Brainstorm on paper and then decide how to order and structure your argument.

about the Spanish-speaking world, as well as the knowledge you have acquired about the community in which you live.

Try this sample question. As with the last section, you may want to have a device on hand with which to time yourself and record your presentation so that you can evaluate it later.

> Basic Approach:
>
> 1. Brainstorm Key Vocab and Order your Points
> 2. Have Specific Regions and Examples Ready to Pull From
> 3. Have Transitional Phrases Ready

Sample Question

You will make an oral presentation on a specific topic to your class. You will have 4 minutes to read the presentation topic and prepare your presentation. Then you will have 2 minutes to record your presentation. In your presentation, compare your own community to an area of the Spanish-speaking world with which you are familiar. You should demonstrate your understanding of cultural features of the Spanish-speaking world. You should also organize your presentation clearly.	Vas a dar una presentación oral a tu clase sobre un tema cultural. Vas a tener 4 minutos para leer el tema de la presentación y prepararla. Después vas a tener 2 minutos para grabar tu presentación. En tu presentación, compara tu propia comunidad con una región del mundo hispanohablante que te sea familiar. Debes demostrar tu comprensión de aspectos culturales en el mundo hispanohablante y organizar tu presentación de una manera clara.

Tienes cuatro minutos para leer el tema de la presentación y prepararla.

(4 minutes)

Tema de la presentación:

¿Cómo ha afectado la tecnología la vida de las personas en su comunidad?

Compara tus observaciones acerca de las comunidades en las que has vivido con tus observaciones de una región del mundo hispanohablante que te sea familiar. En tu presentación, puedes referirte a lo que has estudiado, vivido, observado, etc.

Tienes dos minutos para grabar tu presentación.

Here's How to Crack It

This section is challenging, since there are no prompts to use as a basis for your answer. It is testing your ability to produce an oral report for an extended period of time, to expound on familiar topics that require some sort of research, and to demonstrate and understand aspects of the target culture (geography, art, music, and social, economic, and political elements). There also should be some sort of comparing and contrasting going on in your response; this is an example of higher-order thinking, and the graders like to see that. The best way to prepare for this section is to become completely familiar with several countries in the Spanish-speaking world. Pick one from each major region: the Caribbean, Mexico and Central America, the Andean and Southern Cone regions of South America, and Spain. This way, you have knowledge of the different ethnic groups, history, and customs. Often, you will be asked to compare and contrast cultures, so practice doing that on your own by looking for similarities and differences when reading and comparing articles or other media. Use specific vocabulary to voice similarities and differences: *por otra parte, se parecen, se diferencian, vale mencionar que mientras una _____, la otra _____*, and so on.

> Check out these phrases! Learn them. Love them.

Translation of the Question

Presentation Topic:

How has technology affected the lives of the people in your community?

Compare your observations about the communities you have lived in to your observations of a Spanish-speaking region of the world with which you are familiar. In your presentation, you can refer to what you have studied, lived, observed, etc.

Sample Student Response

Les voy a hablar sobre cómo la tecnología ha empeñado un papel sumamente importante en las vidas de las personas tanto en mi comunidad como en la comunidad hispanohablante.

Yo diría que en mi comunidad la tecnología ha enriquecido la educación en las escuelas. Gracias al Internet, tenemos acceso a recursos para el estudio de idiomas —periódicos de cualquier país de Latinoamérica o España. Inclusive podemos escuchar noticieros y ver programas televisivos a cualquier hora. Hasta hemos abandonado los diccionarios, ya que podemos usar páginas de Web desde los teléfonos para descifrar palabras y entender su uso correcto en la gramática. Como resultado, mi rendimiento como estudiante ha mejorado.

En mi comunidad, veo que hay padres que pueden vigilar sus casas, empleados, niños —todo desde su teléfono celular. Los policías pueden usar tecnología especial para rastrear a niños perdidos o secuestrados a través de las torres de teléfonos celulares.

La tecnología también ha tenido efectos positivos en los países de América Latina. En Argentina, por ejemplo, la tecnología ha ayudado a conservar al medioambiente. Durante un viaje allá, presencié el uso de hidrógeno en los carros en vez de gasolina. Este uso especializado ha ayudado a que la gente use menos combustible y es económicamente beneficioso ya que combate el alto costo del petróleo. Argentina es uno de los pocos países de Sudamérica que no cuenta con vastos campos petrolíferos. También vi el uso de la tecnología en el campo médico. En Argentina hay muchas zonas retiradas y aisladas cuya población no puede acudir al servicio médico. Ahora hay trenes que viajan a través del paisaje y llevan equipo médico portátil y hasta usan el Internet para consultar con expertos en Buenos Aires, para diagnosticar al paciente por la Red. Ese programa se llama "El tren de la Esperanza" y fue creado por jóvenes médicos argentinos que se preocupaban por el bienestar de los niños. Hace 10 años nada de eso fue posible.

Hay centenares de ejemplos más; pero si tuviera que elegir un cambio tecnológico que ha revolucionado al mundo, diría que es el teléfono celular. Los teléfonos de hoy ahora nos hablan, nos guían, nos traducen, y nos conectan al Red. Gracias a la tecnología, los sueños de hace sólo un par de años de verdad pueden convertirse en realidad.

Translation of the Sample Student Response

I'm going to speak to you about how technology has played an extremely important role in the lives of people both in my community and in the Spanish-speaking community.

I would say that in my community, technology has enriched education in schools. Thanks to the Internet, we have access to resources for the study of language—newspapers from any Latin American country or Spain. We can even listen to news broadcasts or watch television at any time. We've stopped using dictionaries since we can use web pages from our phones to decipher words and understand their correct grammatical usage. As a result, my performance as a student has improved.

In my community, I see that parents can watch their homes, employees, children—all from a cell phone. The police can use special technology to track lost or kidnapped children through cell phone towers.

Technology has also had positive effects in Latin America. In Argentina, for example, technology has helped save the environment. During a trip there, I witnessed the use of hydrogen in cars instead of gasoline. This specialized use has helped people use less gasoline, and it is economically beneficial because it combats the high price of oil. Argentina is one of the few countries in South America that does not possess vast oil fields. I also saw the use of technology in the medical field. In Argentina there are many isolated areas where the population doesn't have access to medical services. There are now trains that travel through the countryside and bring portable medical equipment and even use the Internet to consult with experts in Buenos Aires to diagnose the patient over the Internet. This program is called the "Train of Hope" and was created by young Argentinean doctors who were concerned about the wellbeing of children. Ten years ago, none of this was possible.

There are hundreds more examples, but if I had to choose one technological change that has revolutionized the world, I would say it would have to be the cell phone. The phones of today speak to us, guide us, translate for us, and connect us to the Internet. Thanks to technology, dreams from just a few years ago can now become reality.

Evaluation

This was a tough question, as it was so open-ended. Although it seemed that the student was grasping at straws at first, it turned out to be a pretty good response. Overall, there was a lack of contrasting, and the two applications of technology didn't really have a common thread. However, the student clearly demonstrated knowledge of the target culture and did apply the variable of technology to both societies in a very creative way. The answer also flowed well and even gave a surprise at the end with a personal evaluation of technology's greatest contribution. It would probably score a 4, possibly a 5, given the strong grammar and organization it demonstrated.

> Make notes for yourself to talk from and organize yourself. Decide which point you will talk about first, second, and so on.

Essay Practice Prompt 1

Tienes cuatro minutos para leer el tema de la presentación y prepararla.

(4 minutes)

Tema de la presentación:

¿Cuáles son las aventajas y las desventajas del teléfono celular?

Compara tus observaciones acerca de las comunidades en las que has vivido con tus observaciones de una región del mundo hispanohablante que te sea familiar. En tu presentación, puedes referirte a lo que has estudiado, vivido, observado, etc.

Tienes dos minutos para grabar tu presentación.

Essay Practice Prompt 2

Tienes cuatro minutos para leer el tema de la presentación y prepararla.

(4 minutes)

Tema de la presentación:

¿Cómo le ha afectado a usted la educación?

La educación puede ocurrir por varias maneras, formales e informales. Compara tus experiencias acerca de las comunidades en las que has vivido con tus observaciones de una región del mundo hispanohablante que te sea familiar. En tu presentación, puedes referirte a lo que has estudiado, vivido, observado, etc.

Tienes dos minutos para grabar tu presentación.

> **Need More Help on Essays?**
> We've got just the book for that! *How to Write Essays for Standardized Tests* contains advice and examples of best practices on an assortment of AP exams, plus ACT, and others!

Essay Practice Prompt 3

Tienes cuatro minutos para leer el tema de la presentación y prepararla.

(4 minutes)

Tema de la presentación:

¿Cómo ha afectado los medios sociales las vidas de las personas en su comunidad?

Compara tus observaciones acerca de las comunidades en las que has vivido con tus observaciones de una región del mundo hispanohablante que te sea familiar. En tu presentación, puedes referirte a lo que has estudiado, vivido, observado, etc.

Tienes dos minutos para grabar tu presentación.

REFLECT

Think about what you've learned in Part IV, and respond to the following questions:

Be sure to download our special supplement, "Using Time Effectively to Maximize Points," when your register your book online!

- What is your pace for an average passage of 6–8 questions? Your average pace per question?

- How will you change your approach to multiple-choice questions?

- What is your multiple-choice guessing strategy? Should you guess?

- How should you use the multiple-choice questions to help you through the listening portions?

- How should you listen to the audio recordings? What should you do as you listen?

- How will you change your approach to the interpersonal response? The argumentative essay? The conversation? The spoken presentation?

- What kinds of salutatory phrases might be useful to keep in mind for the conversation?

- What kinds of transitional phrases might come in handy for the interpersonal response, the essay, and the spoken presentation?

- What kinds of tenses should you be using for the spoken and written portions?

- Which parts of this section are you going to re-review?

- Will you seek further help, outside this book (such as from a teacher, tutor, or AP Students), on how to approach multiple-choice questions, the essay, or a pacing strategy?

Study Break!
Before you dive into Part V, be sure to give yourself some down-time to let your brain absorb the information you've been studying.

Part V
Grammar Review for the AP Spanish Language and Culture Exam

HOW TO USE THIS REVIEW

In the following chapter, we'll highlight the grammar topics you should master by test day. In addition to our review, we strongly urge you to study your textbook and class notes as well. If there is a topic that you don't fully understand or is not covered here, be sure to go through your textbook and ask your teacher about it well before test day.

Remember, a careful review of verb and grammar forms now can translate into higher-quality responses on the exam. At the end of the chapter, you'll have an opportunity to reflect on what you've absorbed and what you may need to re-review.

Chapter 3
Review of
Spanish Verb and
Grammar Forms

BASIC TERMS

Although you won't see the following terms on the test, they are important because they will come up later in the chapter. Knowing these terms will allow you to understand the rules of grammar that you're about to review.

Noun: a person, place, thing, or idea

EXAMPLES: Abraham Lincoln, New Jersey, a taco, a thought

Pronoun: a word that replaces a noun

EXAMPLES: Abraham Lincoln would be replaced by *he*, New Jersey by *it*, and a taco or thought by *it*. You'll see more about pronouns later.

Adjective: a word that describes a noun

EXAMPLES: cold, soft, colorful

Verb: an action—a word that describes what is being done in a sentence

EXAMPLE: Ron *ate* the huge breakfast.

Infinitive: the original, unconjugated form of a verb

EXAMPLES: to eat, to run, to laugh

Auxiliary Verb: the verb that precedes the past participle in the perfect tense

EXAMPLE: He *had* eaten his lunch.

Past Participle: the appropriate form of a verb when it is used with the auxiliary verb

EXAMPLE: They have *gone* to work.

Adverb: a word that describes a verb, an adjective, or another adverb, just as an adjective describes a noun

EXAMPLES: slowly, quickly, happily (In English, adverbs often, but don't always, end in -*ly*.)

Subject: the person or thing (noun) in a sentence that is performing the action

EXAMPLE: *John* wrote the song.

Compound Subject: a subject that's made up of two or more subjects or nouns

EXAMPLES: *John and Paul* wrote the song together.

Object: the person or thing (noun or pronoun) in the sentence that the action is happening to, either directly or indirectly

EXAMPLES: Mary bought *the shirt*. Joe hit *him*. Mary gave *a gift* to *Tim*.

Direct Object: the thing that receives the action of the verb

EXAMPLE: I see *the wall*. (The wall "receives" the action of seeing.)

Indirect Object: the person who receives the direct object

EXAMPLE: I wrote *her* a letter. (She receives a letter.)

Preposition: a word that marks the relationship (in space or time) between two other words

EXAMPLES: He received the letter *from* her. The book is *below* the chair.

Article: a word (usually a very small word) that precedes a noun

EXAMPLES: *a* watch, *the* room

That wasn't so bad, was it? Now let's put all those terms together in a few examples.

Dominic	spent	the	entire	night	here.
subject	verb	article	adjective	dir. obj.	adverb

Margaret	often	gives	me	money.
subject	adverb	verb	indir. obj. pronoun	dir. obj.

Alison and Rob	have	a	gorgeous	child.
compound subject	verb	article	adjective	dir. obj.

PRONOUNS

You already learned that a pronoun is a word that takes the place of a noun. Now you'll review what pronouns look like in Spanish. There are three basic types.

SUBJECT PRONOUNS

These are the most basic pronouns and probably the first ones you learned. Just take a moment to look them over to make sure you haven't forgotten them. Then spend some time looking over the examples that follow until you are comfortable using them.

yo	I	**nosotros/as**	we
tú	you (singular)	**vosotros/as**	you (plural)
él, ella, Ud.	he, she, you (singular)	**ellos, ellas, Uds.**	they, you (plural)

When to Use Subject Pronouns

A subject pronoun replaces a noun (like any other pronoun). In the case of the subject pronoun, the noun replaced is the subject of the sentence.

Marco no pudo comprar el helado.

Marco couldn't buy the ice cream.

Who performs the action of this sentence? Marco—so he is the subject. If we wanted to use a subject pronoun in this case, we'd replace **Marco** with **él.**

Él no pudo comprar el helado.

He couldn't buy the ice cream.

Direct Object Pronouns

A direct object pronoun replaces (you guessed it) the direct object in a sentence.

me	me	**nos**	us
te	you (*tú* form)	**os**	you (*vosotros* form)
lo/la	him, it (masc.)/ you (*Ud.* form)/ her, it (fem.)	**los/las**	them (masc./fem.)/ you (*Uds.* form)

When to Use Direct Object Pronouns

Now let's see what it looks like when we replace the direct object with a pronoun in a sentence.

> *Marco no pudo comprar el helado.*

What couldn't Marco buy? Ice cream. Since ice cream is what's receiving the action, it's the direct object. To use the direct object pronoun, you'd replace **helado** with **lo:**

> *Marco no pudo comprar**lo**.*   or   *Marco no **lo** pudo comprar.*

When the direct object pronoun is used with the infinitive of a verb, it can either be tacked on to the end of the verb (the first example), or it can come before the conjugated verb in the sentence (the second example). Here is another example.

> *Voy a ver**lo**.*   I'm going to see it.
>
> ***Lo** voy a ver.*   (Both sentences mean the same thing.)

The direct object pronoun also follows the verb in an affirmative command, for example:

> *¡Cómelo!*   Eat it!
>
> *¡Escúchame!*   Listen to me!

Indirect Object Pronouns

These pronouns replace the indirect objects in sentences. Keep in mind that in Spanish, when the object is indirect, the preposition is often implied, not explicitly stated. So how can you tell the difference? In general, the indirect object is the person who receives the direct object.

me	me	**nos**	us
te	you (*tú* form)	**os**	you (*vosotros* form)
le	him, her, you (*Ud.* form)	**les**	them, you (*Uds.* form)

When to Use Indirect Object Pronouns

This may seem a bit strange, but in Spanish the indirect object pronoun must be present even in a sentence that contains the indirect object noun.

> *Juan **le** da el abrigo al viejo.*
>
> Juan gives the old man the coat.

Notice that the sentence contains the indirect object noun (**viejo**) and the indirect object pronoun (**le**). Including the noun is often necessary to clarify the identity of the indirect object pronoun, or to emphasize that identity. Typically, an expression of clarification is used with the pronouns **le** and **les** and **se** (see below), but is not used with other pronouns.

> *María **nos** ayudó.*   María helped us.
>
> *Juan **me** trae el suéter.*   Juan brings me the sweater.

The identity of the indirect object is obvious with the choice of pronoun in these examples and so is not necessary for clarification. It may be used, however, to emphasize the identity of the indirect object.

> *No **me** lo trajeron a mí; **te** lo trajeron a ti.*
>
> They didn't bring it to **me**; they brought it to **you.**

We would change our intonation to emphasize these words in English. This doesn't happen in Spanish; the expressions **a mí** and **a ti** serve the same function.

Se is used in place of **le** and **les** whenever the pronoun that follows begins with **l.**

¿Le cuentas la noticia a María?	Are you telling Maria the news?
*Sí, **se** la cuento **a María.***	Yes, I'm telling it to her.
¿Les prestas los guantes a los estudiantes?	Do you lend gloves to the students?
*No, no **se** los presto **a ellos.***	No, I don't lend them to them.

Notice that **le** changes to **se** in the first example and **les** to **se** in the second because the direct object pronouns that follow begin with **l.** Notice also the inclusion of **a María** and **a ellos** to clarify the identity of **se** in each example.

Prepositional Pronouns

As we mentioned earlier, there are some pronouns that take explicitly stated prepositions, and they're different from the indirect object pronouns. The prepositional pronouns are as follows.

mí	me	**nosotros/nosotras**	us
ti	you (*tú* form)	**vosotros/vosotras**	you (*vosotros* form)
él/ella/Ud.	him/her/you (*Ud.* form)	**ellos/ellas/Uds.**	them/you (*Uds.* form)

When to Use Prepositional Pronouns

Consider the following examples:

1. *Cómprale un regalo de cumpleaños.* Buy him a birthday present.

2. *Vamos al teatro sin él.* We're going to the theater **without** him.

Notice that in the first example, "him" is translated as **le,** whereas in the second, "him" is translated as **él.** What exactly is the deal with that?! Why isn't it the same word in Spanish, as it is in English? In Spanish, the different pronouns distinguish the different functions of the word within the sentence.

In the first example, *him* is the indirect object of the verb *to buy* (buy the gift for whom? For him—*him* receives the direct object), so we use the indirect object pronoun **le.** In the second example, however, *him* is the object of the preposition *without,* so we use the prepositional pronoun **él.** Here are some more examples that involve the prepositional pronouns. Notice that they all have explicitly stated prepositions.

*Las flores son **para** ti.* The flowers are **for** you.

*Estamos enojados **con** él.* We are angry **with** him.

*Quieren ir de vacaciones **sin** Uds.* They want to go on vacation **without** you.

In two special cases, when the preposition is **con** and the object of the preposition is **mí** or **ti**, the preposition and the pronoun are combined to form **conmigo** (with me) and **contigo** (with you).

*¿Quieres ir al concierto **conmigo**?* Do you want to go to the concert **with me**?

*No, no puedo ir **contigo**.* No, I can't go **with you.**

When the subject is **él, ella, ellos, ellas, Ud.,** or **Uds.,** and the object of the preposition is the **same** as the subject, the prepositional pronoun is **sí,** and is usually accompanied by **mismo/a** or **mismos/as:**

> *Alejandro es muy egoísta. Siempre habla de **sí mismo.***
>
> Alejandro is very egotistical. He always talks about **himself.**
>
> *Ellos compran ropa para **sí mismos** cuando van de compras.*
>
> They buy clothes for **themselves** when they go shopping.

POSSESSIVE ADJECTIVES AND PRONOUNS

Possessive adjectives and pronouns are used to indicate ownership. When you want to let someone know what's whose, use the following pronouns or adjectives:

Stressed Possessive Adjectives

mío/mía	mine	**nuestro/nuestra**	ours
tuyo/tuya	yours (*tú* form)	**vuestro/vuestra**	yours (*vosotros* form)
suyo/suya	his, hers, yours (*Ud.* form)	**suyo/suya**	theirs, yours (*Uds.* form)

Unstressed Possessive Adjectives

mi	my	**nuestro/nuestra**	our
tu	your (*tú* form)	**vuestro/vuestra**	your (*vosotros* form)
su	his/her/your (*Ud.* form)	**su**	their, your (*Uds.* form)

When to Use Possessive Adjectives

The first question is, "When do you use an unstressed adjective, and when do you use a stressed adjective?" Check out these examples, and then we'll see what the rule is.

> *Ésta es **mi** casa.*
> This is **my** house.
>
> *Esta casa es **mía.***
> This house is **mine.**
>
> *Aquí está **tu** cartera.*
> Here is **your** wallet.
>
> *Esta cartera es **tuya.***
> This wallet is **yours.**

The difference between stressed and unstressed possessive adjectives is emphasis, as opposed to meaning. Saying "This is my house" puts emphasis on the house, while saying "This house is mine" takes the focus off of the house and stresses the identity of its owner—me. To avoid getting confused, just remember that unstressed is the Spanish equivalent of *my* and stressed is the Spanish equivalent of *mine.*

In terms of structure, there is an important difference between the two types of adjectives, but one you should be able to remember: stressed adjectives come after the verb, but unstressed adjectives come before the noun. Notice that neither type agrees with the possessor; they agree with the thing possessed.

If it's not clear to you why these are adjectives when they look so much like pronouns, consider their function. When you say *my house,* the noun *house* is being described by *my.* Any word that describes a noun is an adjective, even if that word looks a lot like a pronoun. The key is how it's being used in the sentence.

Possessive Pronouns

Possessive pronouns look like stressed possessive adjectives, but they mean something different. Possessive pronouns *replace* nouns; they don't *describe* them.

When to Use Possessive Pronouns

This type of pronoun is formed by combining the article of the noun that's being replaced with the appropriate stressed possessive adjective. Just as stressed possessive adjectives must agree with the nouns they describe, possessive pronouns must agree in gender and number with the nouns they replace.

> ***Mi** bicicleta es azul.*
> **My** bicycle is blue.
>
> ***La mía** es azul.*
> **Mine** is blue.

Notice how the pronoun not only shows possession, but also replaces the noun. Here are some more examples.

Mis zapatos son caros.	*Los míos* son caros.
My shoes are expensive.	**Mine** are expensive.
Tu automóvil es rápido.	*El tuyo* es rápido.
Your car is fast.	**Yours** is fast.
No me gustaban los discos que *ellos* trajeron.	No me gustaban *los suyos*.
I didn't like the records they brought.	I didn't like **theirs**.

Reflexive Pronouns

Remember those reflexive verbs you learned about in class (**ponerse, hacerse,** and so on)? Those all have a common characteristic, which is that they indicate the action is being done to or for oneself. When those verbs are conjugated, the reflexive pronoun (which is always **se** in the infinitive) changes according to the subject.

me	myself	**nos**	ourselves
te	yourself (*tú* form)	**os**	yourselves (*vosotros* form)
se	himself/herself/yourself (*Ud.* form.)	**se**	themselves/ yourselves (*Uds.* form)

A reflexive pronoun is used when the subject and indirect object of the sentence are the same. This may sound kind of strange, but after you see some examples it ought to make more sense.

> *Alicia se pone el **maquillaje**.*
>
> **Alicia** puts on makeup.
>
> What does she put on? **Makeup**—direct object.
>
> Who receives the makeup? **Alicia**—indirect object; she's also the subject.

The action is thus *reflected* back upon itself: Alicia does the action and then receives it. No outside influences are involved.

Another meaning for reflexive verbs is literally that the person does something directly to or for themselves/themself.

> *Rosa **se cortó** con el cuchillo.*
>
> Rosa **cut herself** with the knife.
>
> *Roberto tiene que **comprarse** una libreta nueva.*
>
> Roberto has to **buy himself** a new notebook.

The Relative Pronouns (Que, Quien, and Quienes)

A relative pronoun connects a noun or pronoun to a clause that describes the noun or pronoun. Relative pronouns may represent people, things, or ideas, and they may function as subjects, direct or indirect objects, or as objects of prepositions. Unlike in English, the relative pronouns cannot be omitted in Spanish.

Let's look at some examples with relative pronouns in their various functions.

Remember that **que** is used to refer to people and things. **Quien(es)** is used to refer only to people.

1. As a subject:

   Busco el libro **que** *estaba en mi mochila.*

   I am looking for the book **that** was in my bookbag.

2. As a direct object:

   Hicimos la tarea **que** *la profesora nos asignó.*

   We did the assignment **that** the professor gave us.

3. As an indirect object:

   No conozco a la prima a **quien** *le mandé la invitación.*

   I don't know the cousin to **whom** I sent the invitation.

4. As an object of a preposition:

   Ud. no conoce a los alumnos de **quienes** *hablo.*

   You don't know the students **whom** I am talking about.

The relative pronoun **cuyo** acts as an adjective and agrees with the noun it introduces, not the possessor.

El alumno, **cuyas** *notas son excelentes, es un chico muy simpático.*

The student, **whose** grades are excellent, is a very nice boy.

Interrogative Words

You probably know most of your interrogative words in Spanish by this time, but it wouldn't hurt for you to review them. Remember that they all have accents when used as parts of questions. Let's look briefly at one interrogative that students commonly misuse: **cuál** (meaning *which* or *what*) is used when a choice is involved. It's used in place of **qué** before the verb **ser**, and it has only two forms: singular (**cuál**) and plural (**cuáles**). Both **cuál** and the verb **ser** must agree in number with the thing(s) being asked about.

*¿**Cuál** es tu ciudad favorita?*	**What** is your favorite city?
*¿**Cuáles** son nuestros regalos?*	**Which** presents are ours?

Demonstratives

First, learn the construction and meaning.

este/esta	this (one)	**estos/estas**	these
ese/esa	that (one)	**esos/esas**	those
aquel/aquella	that (one over there)	**aquellos/aquellas**	those (over there)

Adjective or Pronoun—Which Is It?

If the demonstrative word comes before a noun, then it is an adjective.

***Este** plato de arroz con pollo es mío.*	**This** plate of chicken and rice is mine.
***Ese** edificio es de mi hermano.*	**That** building is my brother's.

If the demonstrative word takes the place of a noun, then it's a pronoun.

> *Dije que **este** es mío.* I said that **this one** is mine.
>
> *Sabemos que **ese** es de mi hermano.* We know **that one** is my brother's.

When used as adjectives, these words mean *this*, *that*, and so on. When used as pronouns, they mean *this one*, *that one*, and so on.

Pronoun Summary

You should know the following types of pronouns: subject, object (direct and indirect), possessive, prepositional, reflexive, and demonstrative. Don't just memorize what the different pronouns look like! Recognizing them is important, but it's just as important that you understand how and when to use them.

Are You a Visual Learner?

If you're getting overwhelmed by all of the concepts for an AP course, consider looking at our *Fast Track* or *ASAP* books, available for some AP subjects. These handy guides focus on the most-tested content or present it in a friendly, illustrated fashion.

Drill 1: How Well Do You Know Your Pronouns?

1. El libro es _____.

   (A) mi
   (B) mío
   (C) mía
   (D) me

2. A mí _____ gusta ir al cine.

   (A) te
   (B) mío
   (C) me
   (D) tu

3. Laura _____ ayudaba a los estudiantes con la tarea.

   (A) les
   (B) se
   (C) lo
   (D) tu

4. Ana _____ dio un premio al perro por hacer un truco.

   (A) la
   (B) lo
   (C) se
   (D) le

5. A Yamil _____ gustaban todas sus clases el año pasado.

   (A) le
   (B) les
   (C) las
   (D) la

6. José _____ dio el regalo a su novia.

   (A) le la
   (B) se le
   (C) se la
   (D) se lo

7. ¿_____ aquí es la persona famosa?

   (A) Qué
   (B) Cuál
   (C) Quién
   (D) Quienes

8. ¿Para pintar el cuarto, _____ color prefieres?

   (A) qué
   (B) cuyo
   (C) quién
   (D) por qué

Drill 2: How Well Do You Know Your Pronouns?

1. ¿Maya, quieres ir de compras _____?

    (A) conmigo
    (B) contigo
    (C) con yo
    (D) con mí

2. El automóvil es _____.

    (A) su
    (B) suya
    (C) suyo
    (D) suyos

3. ¡Tu bicicleta es nueva, pero _____ es muy vieja!

    (A) la mia
    (B) la mía
    (C) el mío
    (D) el mio

4. ¿_____ prefieres? ¿Tacos o enchiladas?

    (A) Cuál
    (B) Por qué
    (C) Quién
    (D) Cual

5. _____ casa es nuestra.

    (A) Esta
    (B) Esto
    (C) Este
    (D) Está

6. Este barco no es mío. El mío es _____.

    (A) aquella
    (B) aquellas
    (C) aquel
    (D) aquellos

7. El doctor, _____ paciente está enfermo, le recetó antibióticos.

    (A) cuya
    (B) cuyas
    (C) cuyos
    (D) cuyo

8. Alessandra _____ puso el maquillaje.

    (A) le
    (B) lo
    (C) la
    (D) se

Drill 3: How Well Do You Know Your Pronouns?

1. ¿_____ es tu comida favorita?

    (A) Cual
    (B) Cuáles
    (C) Cuál
    (D) Quién

2. ¿Son _____ aquellos guantes que están sobre la butaca?

    (A) mío
    (B) mía
    (C) míos
    (D) mías

3. Teresa compró almuerzo por _____ porque estaba sola.

    (A) si mismo
    (B) sí misma
    (C) sí mismo
    (D) si misma

4. Mis libros están aquí, pero _____ están allí.

    (A) vuestra
    (B) vuestro
    (C) vuestros
    (D) vuestras

5. Caminé desde mi casa al trabajo simplemente porque _____ dio la gana.

    (A) se mi
    (B) se me
    (C) se le
    (D) se lo

6. ¿_____ dieron los lápices correctos a los estudiantes para el exámen?

    (A) Los
    (B) Les
    (C) Las
    (D) Se

7. Me gustaría hacer_____ abogado.

    (A) sí
    (B) mi
    (C) se
    (D) me

8. Carolina _____ cortó el pelo.

    (A) le
    (B) se
    (C) la
    (D) lo

VERBS

You probably learned what felt like a zillion different verbs and tenses in Spanish class. That knowledge will be essential on the AP Spanish Language and Culture Exam, not just for comprehending verbs in passages and questions, but also for exercising dynamism, breadth of vocabulary and grammar, a variety of tenses, and appropriate register in the written and spoken portions of your free response section. Review verbs, conjugation, and tenses if you feel less than confident here.

The Present Tense (aka the Present Indicative)

The present tense is the easiest, and probably the first, tense that you ever learned. It is used when the action is happening in the present, as in the following example:

> *Yo **hablo** con mis amigos cada día.*
>
> I **speak** with my friends each day.

You should know the present tense inside and out if you are enrolled in an AP Spanish class, but take a quick glance at the following verb conjugations just to refresh your memory:

	trabajar	vender	escribir
yo	trabaj**o**	vend**o**	escrib**o**
tú (fam.)	trabaj**as**	vend**es**	escrib**es**
él/ella/Ud.	trabaj**a**	vend**e**	escrib**e**
nosotros/nosotras	trabaj**amos**	vend**emos**	escrib**imos**
vosotros/vosotras (fam.)	trabaj**áis**	vend**éis**	escrib**ís**
ellos/ellas/Uds.	trabaj**an**	vend**en**	escrib**en**

The Future Tense

The future tense is used to describe things that will *definitely* happen in the future. The reason we stress *definitely* is that there is a different tense (the conditional), as well as a whole other verbal mode (the dreaded subjunctive), both of which can be used to describe things that *may* happen in different contexts. In Spanish, just as in English, there is a difference between being certain *(I will go)* and being uncertain *(I may go)*, and different forms are used for the different degrees of certainty. You'll see the fancier stuff later. First take a look at the regular future tense.

> *Mañana yo **hablaré** con mis amigos.*
>
> Tomorrow I **will speak** with my friends.

Notice that what takes two words to say in English *(will speak)* takes only one word to say in Spanish (**hablaré**). The future is a nice, simple tense (no auxiliary verb, only one word), which should be easy to spot thanks to the accents and the structure. The future is formed by tacking on the appropriate ending to the infinitive of the verb *without dropping the -ar, -er, or -ir*.

	trabajar	vender	escribir
yo	trabajar**é**	vender**é**	escribir**é**
tú (fam.)	trabajar**ás**	vender**ás**	escribir**ás**
él/ella/Ud.	trabajar**á**	vender**á**	escribir**á**
nosotros/nosotras	trabajar**emos**	vender**emos**	escribir**emos**
vosotros/vosotras (fam.)	trabajar**éis**	vender**éis**	escribir**éis**
ellos/ellas/Uds.	trabajar**án**	vender**án**	escribir**án**

Back to the Future: the Conditional

Remember the future tense? (It's the one that is used to describe actions that are *definitely* going to happen in the future.) Well, now we'll review a tense that is used to describe things that *may* happen in the future, *if* certain other conditions are met.

The conditional describes what could, would, or might happen in the future.

> Me **gustaría** hablar con mis amigos cada día.
>
> I **would like** to talk to my friends each day.
>
> Con más tiempo, **podría** hablar con ellos el día entero.
>
> With more time, I **could** speak with them all day long.
>
> Si gastara cinco pesos, solamente me **quedarían** tres.
>
> If I spent (were to spend) five pesos, I **would have** only three left.

It can also be used to make a request in a more polite way.

> ¿**Puedes** prestar atención?   ¿**Podrías** prestar atención?
>
> **Can you** pay attention?   **Could you** pay attention?

The conditional is formed by taking the future stem of the verb (which is the infinitive) and adding the conditional ending.

	trabajar	vender	escribir
yo	trabajar**ía**	vender**ía**	escribir**ía**
tú (fam.)	trabajar**ías**	vender**ías**	escribir**ías**
él/ella/Ud.	trabajar**ía**	vender**ía**	escribir**ía**
nosotros/nosotras	trabajar**íamos**	vender**íamos**	escribir**íamos**
vosotros/vosotras (fam.)	trabajar**íais**	vender**íais**	escribir**íais**
ellos/ellas/Uds.	trabajar**ían**	vender**ían**	escribir**ían**

The accented í is in the conditional, but not in the future.

To avoid confusing the conditional with the future, concentrate on the conditional endings. The big difference is the accented **í,** which is in the conditional, but not in the future.

FUTURE	CONDITIONAL
trabajaré	trabajaría
venderán	venderían
escribiremos	escribiríamos

The Past Tense (aka the Preterite)

There are many different tenses that are considered past tenses—all of which describe actions that took place at various points in the past. There are, for example, different tenses for saying *I spoke, I was speaking, I have spoken,* and so on. Let's start by reviewing the most basic of these: the simple past tense.

The past tense is used to describe an action that had a *definite beginning and ending in the past* (as opposed to an action that may be ongoing), as in the following example:

*Ayer yo **hablé** con mis amigos.*

Yesterday I **spoke** with my friends. (The action began and ended.)

	trabajar	vender	escribir
yo	trabajé	vendí	escribí
tú (fam.)	trabaj**aste**	vend**iste**	escrib**iste**
él/ella/Ud.	trabaj**ó**	vend**ió**	escrib**ió**
nosotros/nosotras	trabaj**amos**	vend**imos**	escrib**imos**
vosotros/vosotras (fam.)	trabaj**asteis**	vend**isteis**	escrib**isteis**
ellos/ellas/Uds.	trabaj**aron**	vend**ieron**	escrib**ieron**

To decide preterite vs. imperfect, ask yourself whether you have a "one-time" event or an ongoing one.

The easiest forms to spot are the first and third person singular (**yo** and **él/ella/Ud.** forms) because of the accents.

The Imperfect

The imperfect is another past tense. It is used to describe actions that occurred continuously in the past and exhibited no definitive end at that time. This is different from the preterite, which describes "one-time" actions that began and ended at the moment in the past being described. Look at the two together, and the difference between them will become clearer.

> *Ayer **yo hablé** con mis amigos y luego **me fui.***
>
> Yesterday **I spoke** with my friends and then **left.**
>
> (The act of speaking obviously ended, because I left afterward.)
>
> ***Yo hablaba** con mis amigos mientras **caminábamos.***
>
> **I spoke** with my friends while **we walked.**
>
> (The act of speaking was **in progress** at that moment, along with walking.)

The imperfect is also used to describe conditions or circumstances in the past, since these are obviously ongoing occurrences.

> ***Era** una noche oscura y tormentosa.*
>
> **It was** a dark and stormy night.
>
> *Cuando **tenía** diez años…*
>
> When **I was** ten years old…

In the first example, it didn't just start or just stop being a stormy night, did it? Was the dark and stormy night already a past event at that point? No. The dark and stormy night was **in progress** at that moment, so the imperfect is used, not the preterite.

In the second example, did I start or stop being ten years old at that point? Neither. Was being ten already a past event at the moment I am describing? No. I was simply in the process of being ten years old at that moment in the past, so the imperfect is the more precise tense to use.

Make sense? Good: now check out the conjugation.

	trabajar	**vender**	**escribir**
yo	trabaj**aba**	vend**ía**	escrib**ía**
tú (fam.)	trabaj**abas**	vend**ías**	escrib**ías**
él/ella/Ud.	trabaj**aba**	vend**ía**	escrib**ía**
nosotros/nosotras	trabaj**ábamos**	vend**íamos**	escrib**íamos**
vosotros/vosotras (fam.)	trabaj**abais**	vend**íais**	escrib**íais**
ellos/ellas/Uds.	trabaj**aban**	vend**ían**	escrib**ían**

Although the imperfect is similar to the other past tenses you've seen (e.g., the preterite and the present perfect) because it speaks of past actions, it looks quite different. That's the key, since half of your job is just to know what the different tenses look like. The toughest part will be distinguishing the preterite from the imperfect.

The Present Perfect

The present perfect is used to refer to an action that began in the past and is continuing into the present (and possibly beyond). It is also used to describe actions that were completed very close to the present. Compare these sentences.

1. *Ayer **hablé** con mis amigos.*
   Yesterday **I spoke** with my friends.

   ***Decidiste** no ir al cine.*
   You decided not to go to the movies.

2. ***He hablado** mucho con mis amigos recientemente.*
   I have spoken a lot with my friends lately.

   ***Has decidido** hacerte abogado.*
   You have decided (recently) to become a lawyer.

The first examples are just the plain past tense: I started and finished talking with my friends yesterday, and you completed the process of deciding not to go to the movies. In the second examples, the use of the present perfect tense moves the action to the very recent past instead of leaving it in the more distant past. The present perfect, then, is essentially a more precise verb form of the past, used when the speaker wants to indicate that an action happened very recently in the past or that it has continued from an unspecified point in the past *up until* the present.

Look for words like **ayer** or **recientemente** to help decide which tense to use.

Spotting the perfect tenses can be rather easy. These are compound tenses, meaning that they are formed by combining two verbs: a tense of the auxiliary (or helping) verb **haber** (present, imperfect, future, conditional) and the past participle of the main verb.

	trabajar	**vender**	**escribir**
yo	**he** trabaj**ado**	**he** vend**ido**	**he** escr**ito**
tú (fam.)	**has** trabaj**ado**	**has** vend**ido**	**has** escr**ito**
él/ella/Ud.	**ha** trabaj**ado**	**ha** vend**ido**	**ha** escr**ito**
nosotros/nosotras	**hemos** trabaj**ado**	**hemos** vend**ido**	**hemos** escr**ito**
vosotros/vosotras (fam.)	**habéis** trabaj**ado**	**habéis** vend**ido**	**habéis** escr**ito**
ellos/ellas/Uds.	**han** trabaj**ado**	**han** vend**ido**	**han** escr**ito**

> Any time there is a helping verb, no matter the tense, the participle will be the same.

The Subjunctive

Don't give up now! Just two more verb modes (not tenses—the subjunctive is a different *manner* of speaking) and you'll be done with all this verb business (give or take a couple of special topics).

The Present Subjunctive

The present subjunctive is used in sentences that have *two distinct subjects* in *two different clauses*, generally (on this test, at least) in four situations.

> For the subjunctive, look for expression of desire or emotion.

1. When a *desire* or *wish* is involved.
    *Quiero que **comas** los vegetales.*
    I want you **to eat** the vegetables.
    *Ordenamos que Uds. nos **sigan**.*
    We order you (pl.) **to follow** us.
2. When *emotion* is involved.
    *Me alegro que **haga** buen tiempo hoy.*
    I am happy that the weather **is** nice today.
    *Te enoja que tu novio nunca te **escuche**.*
    It makes you angry that your boyfriend never **listens** to you.
3. When *doubt* is involved.
    *Ellos no creen que **digamos** la verdad.*
    They don't believe that **we are telling** the truth.
    *Jorge duda que su equipo **vaya** a ganar el campeonato.*
    Jorge doubts that his team **is going** to win the championship.
4. When an *impersonal expression* or *subjective commentary* is made.
    *Es ridículo que no **pueda** encontrar mis llaves.*
    It's ridiculous that **I can't** find my keys.
    *Es importante que los estudiantes **estudien** mucho.*
    It's important that students **study** a lot.

The subjunctive is formed by taking the **yo** form of the present tense, dropping the **-o**, and adding the appropriate ending.

	trabajar	**vender**	**escribir**
yo	trabaj**e**	vend**a**	escrib**a**
tú (fam.)	trabaj**es**	vend**as**	escrib**as**
él/ella/Ud.	trabaj**e**	vend**a**	escrib**a**
nosotros/nosotras	trabaj**emos**	vend**amos**	escrib**amos**
vosotros/vosotras (fam.)	trabaj**éis**	vend**áis**	escrib**áis**
ellos/ellas/Uds.	trabaj**en**	vend**an**	escrib**an**

The Present Perfect Subjunctive

The important thing to remember about Spanish grammar is that grammar builds upon itself. To understand this next concept, you should have a strong knowledge of the previous one. Do you remember the present perfect from the previous section? Hope so! As you know, it is a compound tense made up of the auxiliary verb **haber** and the past participle of the main verb. You can apply this to the present subjunctive, and it becomes the *present perfect subjunctive*. Just be sure you know all the forms of **haber** in present subjunctive: **haya, hayas, haya, hayamos, hayáis, hayan.** The past participles are the same in all the perfect tenses: **dicho, hecho, hablado, roto,** and so on. So memorize them! On the AP exam, graders want to see diversity in the tenses you use, and utilizing an advanced form of a perfect tense will look impressive.

Here are a few examples of the present perfect subjunctive using some examples you saw previously.

> 1. **Present subjunctive**
>   *Te enoja que tu novio nunca te **escuche**.*
>   It makes you angry that your boyfriend never **listens** to you.
>   **Present perfect subjunctive**
>   *Te enoja que tu novio nunca te **haya escuchado**.*
>   It makes you angry that your boyfriend **has** never **listened** to you.
> 2. **Present subjunctive**
>   *Ellos no creen que **digamos** la verdad.*
>   They don't believe that **we are telling** the truth.
>   **Present perfect subjunctive**
>   *Ellos no creen que **hayamos dicho** la verdad.*
>   They don't believe that **we have told** the truth.

Still the same participle!

Commands

Commands are very similar to the present subjunctive form, perhaps because they are an obvious attempt to tell someone what to do. Let's look briefly at the formation of the regular commands.

	hablar	**comer**	**subir**
tú (fam.)	habla, no hables	come, no comas	sube, no subas
Ud.	hable	coma	suba
nosotros/nosotras	hablemos	comamos	subamos
vosotros/vosotras (fam.)	hablad, no habléis	comed, no comáis	subid, no subáis
Uds.	hablen	coman	suban

Remember: the affirmative **tú** form derives from the third person present singular tense, except for the verbs that are irregular in the **tú** form. The affirmative **vosotros** form comes from the infinitive: the 'r' is dropped and the 'd' is added. All other command forms come from the subjunctive. *¡Muy fácil!*

¡**Trabaja** con tu padre!	¡**Vende** el coche!	¡**Escribe** la carta!
Work with your father!	**Sell** the car!	**Write** the letter!

The Imperfect Subjunctive

This version of the subjunctive is used with the same expressions as the present subjunctive (wish or desire, emotion, doubt, impersonal commentaries), but it's used in the past tense.

*Quería que **comieras** los vegetales.*
I wanted you **to eat** the vegetables.
*Me alegré que **hiciera** buen tiempo ayer.*
I was happy that the weather **was** nice yesterday.
*No creían que **dijéramos** la verdad.*
They didn't believe that **we told** the truth.
*Era ridículo que no **pudiera** encontrar mis llaves.*
It was ridiculous that **I couldn't** find my keys.

One very important thing to notice in the examples above is that because the *expression* is in the past, you use the imperfect subjunctive. If you're looking at a sentence that you know takes the subjunctive, but you're not sure whether it's present or imperfect, focus on the expression. If the expression is in the present, use the present subjunctive. If the expression is in the past, use the imperfect subjunctive.

The imperfect subjunctive is also always used after the expression **como si,** which means "as if." This expression is used to describe hypothetical situations.

> *Él habla como si **supiera** todo.*
>
> He speaks as if **he knew** it all.
>
> *Gastamos dinero como si **fuéramos** millonarios.*
>
> We spend money as if **we were** millionaires.

The imperfect subjunctive is formed by taking the **ellos/ellas/Uds.** form of the preterite (which you already know, right?), removing the **-on,** and adding the correct ending.

	trabajar	**vender**	**escribir**
yo	trabajar**a**	vendier**a**	escribier**a**
tú (fam.)	trabajar**as**	vendier**as**	escribier**as**
él/ella/Ud.	trabajar**a**	vendier**a**	escribier**a**
nosotros/nosotras	trabaj**ár**amos	vendi**ér**amos	escrib**iér**amos
vosotros/vosotras (fam.)	trabajar**ais**	vendier**ais**	escribier**ais**
ellos/ellas/Uds.	trabajar**an**	vendier**an**	escribier**an**

The Past Perfect Subjunctive

As with the present perfect subjunctive, you can extend your knowledge of the imperfect subjunctive to apply to a more advanced grammar point that graders like to see from time to time on the exam. Just one correct use of the past perfect subjunctive can elevate your score. Just be sure you know all the forms of **haber** in the imperfect subjunctive: **hubiera, hubieras, hubiera, hubiéramos, hubierais, hubieran.** Again, the past participles are the same in all the perfect tenses: **dicho, hecho, hablado, roto,** and so on. So be sure to memorize them!

Here are a few examples of the past perfect subjunctive from previous examples.

> This is a tricky one: ask yourself whether there was a question in the past about whether or not it would happen. If there was ever question, use the past perfect subjunctive.

1. **Imperfect subjunctive**
    *No creían que **dijéramos** la verdad.*
    They didn't believe that **we told** the truth.
    Past perfect subjunctive
    *No creían que **hubiéramos dicho** la verdad.*
    They didn't believe that **we had told** the truth.

2. **Imperfect subjunctive**
    *Era ridículo que no **pudiera** encontrar mis llaves.*
    It was ridiculous that **I couldn't** find my keys.
    Past perfect subjunctive
    *Era ridículo que no **hubiera podido** encontrar mis llaves.*
    It was ridiculous that **I hadn't been able** to find my keys.

Special Topics

Preterite versus Imperfect

This may be the bout of the century, amigos! By now you probably have spent a long time in class (and in your head) debating which to use. When we study grammar, we learn how to form the verb and when to use the tense. One reason this concept confuses students is because the preterite, with all of its irregulars and exceptions, can be difficult to form—whereas the imperfect can seem a little easier to form, with **-aba** and **-ía** as a base and only 3 irregulars. However, when we think about when to use them, the preterite wins the round with its simplicity.

> Remember, is it a one-time event or an ongoing one?

Generally speaking, you use the preterite to express an action that happened once in the past. More specifically,

*   For actions that can be viewed as single events
    *Ellos **vinieron** a las ocho.*
    They **came** at eight o'clock.
*   For actions that were repeated a specific number of times
    *Ayer **escribí** cinco cartas.*
    Yesterday **I wrote** five letters.

- For actions that occurred during a specific period of time
  Vivimos allí por tres años.
  We lived there for three years.
- For actions that were part of a chain of events
  *Ella **se levantó**, **se bañó** y **salió** de la casa.*
  She **got up**, **bathed**, and **left** the house.
- To state the beginning or the end of an action
  Empezó a llover a las siete de la mañana.
  It began to rain at seven in the morning.

The imperfect is a bit more diverse in its application.

- For actions that were repeated habitually
  Cenábamos juntos todos los días.
  We would eat dinner together every day.
- For actions that "set the stage" for another past action
  *Yo **jugaba** cuando entró mi papá.*
  I **was playing** when my papa entered. (Note that *entered* is preterite.)
- For telling time
  Eran las seis de la noche.
  It was six o'clock at night.
- For stating one's age
  *La niña **tenía** siete años.*
  The little girl **was** seven years old.
- For mental states (usually)
  *José **tenía** miedo de estar en público.*
  José **was** afraid to be in public.
- For physical sensations (usually)
  *Me **gustaba** el libro.*
  I **liked** the book. (The book **was pleasing** to me.)
- To describe the characteristics of people, things, or conditions
  (usually more permanent features of the objects described)
  Era una señorita muy alta.
  She was a tall young lady.

Ser versus *Estar*

The verbs **ser** and **estar** both mean *to be* when translated into English. You may wonder, "Why is it necessary to have two verbs that mean exactly the same thing?" Good question. The answer is that in Spanish, unlike in English, there is a distinction between temporary states of being (e.g., *I am hungry*) and fixed, or permanent states of being (e.g., *I am Cuban*). Although this difference seems pretty simple and easy to follow, there are some cases when it isn't so clear. Consider the following examples:

> *El señor González _____ mi doctor.*
>
> *Cynthia _____ mi novia.*

Would you use **ser** or **estar** in these two sentences? After all, Cynthia may or may not be your girlfriend forever, and the same goes for Mr. González's status as your doctor. You may get rid of both of them tomorrow (or one of them may get rid of you)! So which verb do you use?

In both cases, the answer is **ser,** because in both cases there is no *foreseeable* end to the relationships described. In other words, even though they may change, nothing in either sentence gives any reason to think they will. So whether you and Cynthia go on to marry or she dumps you tomorrow, you would be correct if you used **ser.** When in doubt, ask yourself, "does this action/condition have a definite end in the near or immediate future?" If so, use **estar.** Otherwise, use **ser.** Try the following drill.

> **Ser** = permanent states of being
>
> **Estar** = temporary states of being

Drill 1: Ser vs. Estar

Fill in each blank with the correct form of **ser** or **estar.**

1. El regalo _____ para ti.

2. _____ enojados con el profesor. (nosotros)

3. _____ un tipo muy simpático.

4. Él ____ muy alto y _____ encima del techo.

5. La computadora _____ funcionando.

6. _____ listos para el examen. (ellos)

7. Las manzanas _____ en la bolsa.

8. Los estudiantes _____ jóvenes.

Answers: 1) es 2) Estamos 3) Es 4) es....está 5) está 6) Están 7) están 8) son

Don't assume that certain adjectives (like **enfermo**, for example) necessarily take **estar.** If you're saying someone is sick as in *ill,* then **estar** is appropriate. If you're saying that someone is sick, as in *a sickly person,* then **ser** is correct.

Unfortunately, usage is not the only tough thing about **ser** and **estar.** They are both irregular verbs. Spend a little time reviewing the conjugations of **ser** and **estar** before you move on.

> **estar**
>
> **present:** estoy, estás, está, estamos, estáis, están
>
> **preterite:** estuve, estuviste, estuvo, estuvimos, estuvistéis, estuvieron
>
> **pres. subj.:** esté, estés, esté, estemos, estéis, estén
>
> **imp. subj.:** estuviera, estuvieras, estuviera, estuviéramos, estuvierais, estuvieran

The other tenses of **estar** follow the regular patterns for **-ar** verbs.

> **ser**
>
> **present:** soy, eres, es, somos, sois, son
>
> **imperfect:** era, eras, era, éramos, erais, eran
>
> **preterite:** fui, fuiste, fue, fuimos, fuistéis, fueron
>
> **pres. subj.:** sea, seas, sea, seamos, seáis, sean
>
> **imp. subj.:** fuera, fueras, fuera, fuéramos, fuerais, fueran

The other tenses of **ser** follow the regular patterns for **-er** verbs.

Drill 2: Ser vs. Estar

1. Mi película favorita _____ dirigida por Guillermo del Toro.

   (A) estuve
   (B) es
   (C) era
   (D) fue

2. Las enchiladas _____ muy ricas, y ahora me duele el estómago.

   (A) son
   (B) estaban
   (C) fueran
   (D) eran

3. Yo _____ de los Estados Unidos pero ahora _____ en México.

   (A) estoy…fui
   (B) soy…estoy
   (C) sería…estoy
   (D) soy…estaba

4. La falda de ella ____ muy bonita.

   (A) son
   (B) esté
   (C) está
   (D) es

5. Camilla _____ triste cuando su gato se murió.

   (A) está
   (B) era
   (C) estaba
   (D) es

6. Ella _____ rubia y _____ contenta.

    (A) está…es
    (B) es…sea
    (C) es…está
    (D) era…está

7. _____ una noche gloriosa y tranquila.

    (A) Estaba
    (B) Eran
    (C) Está
    (D) Era

8. Fernando _____ mi esposo.

    (A) es
    (B) son
    (C) está
    (D) estuve

Answers: 1) fue 2) estaban 3) soy…estoy 4) es 5) estaba 6) es…está 7) Era 8) es

Drill 3: Ser vs. Estar

1. ¿Dónde _____ ellos?

    (A) están
    (B) son
    (C) eran
    (D) estaba

2. ¿_____ él aburrido o cansado?

    (A) Era
    (B) Es
    (C) Está
    (D) Esté

3. Puerto Rico _____ una isla en el Mar Caribe.

    (A) era
    (B) es
    (C) fue
    (D) está

4. Fútbol _____ el deporte nacional de México.

    (A) era
    (B) fue
    (C) está
    (D) es

5. Mis padres _____ muy sabios.

    (A) es
    (B) son
    (C) están
    (D) está

6. Este momento puede _____ lo más importante del juego.

   (A) ser
   (B) estar
   (C) es
   (D) está

7. He _____ enferma por tres días.

   (A) soy
   (B) estoy
   (C) sido
   (D) estado

8. Los zapatos _____ míos.

   (A) son
   (B) están
   (C) es
   (D) soy

Answers: 1) están 2) Está 3) es 4) es 5) son 6) ser 7) estado 8) son

Conocer versus Saber

As you probably remember from Spanish I, there is another pair of verbs that have the same English translation but are used differently in Spanish. However, don't worry; knowing when to use them is really very straightforward.

The words **conocer** and **saber** both mean *to know*. In Spanish, knowing a person or a thing (basically, a noun) is different from knowing a piece of information. Compare the uses of **conocer** and **saber** in these sentences.

> **Conocer** is for knowing people.
>
> **Saber** is for knowing facts.

> *¿**Sabes** cuánto cuesta la camisa?*
>
> **Do you know** how much the shirt costs?
>
> *¿**Conoces** a mi primo?*
>
> **Do you know** my cousin?
>
> ***Sabemos** que Pelé era un gran futbolista.*
>
> **We know** that Pelé was a great soccer player.
>
> ***Conocemos** a Pelé.*
>
> **We know** Pelé.

When what's known is a person, place, or thing, use **conocer.** It's like the English *to be acquainted with.* When what's known is a fact, use **saber.** The same basic rule holds for questions.

> *¿Sabe a qué hora llega el presidente?*
>
> **Do you know** at what time the president arrives?
>
> *¿Conoce al presidente?*
>
> **Do you know** the president?

Now that you know how they're used, take a look at their conjugations.

---

conocer

present: conozco, conoces, conoce, conocemos, conocéis, conocen

pres. subj.: conozca, conozcas, conozca, conozcamos, conozcáis, conozcan

---

The other tenses of **conocer** follow the regular **-er** pattern.

---

saber

present: sé, sabes, sabe, sabemos, sabéis, saben

preterite: supe, supiste, supo, supimos, supistéis, supieron

future: sabré, sabrás, sabrá, sabremos, sabréis, sabrán

conditional: sabría, sabrías, sabría, sabríamos, sabríais, sabrían

pres. subj.: sepa, sepas, sepa, sepamos, sepáis, sepan

imp. subj.: supiera, supieras, supiera, supiéramos, supiéráis, supieran

---

Drill 1: Saber vs. Conocer

In the following drill, fill in each blank with the correct form of **conocer** or **saber**:

1. Yo _____ a un músico ayer durante el ensayo.

2. Ellos _____ que necesitan trabajar más para obtener mejores notas.

3. Ellos no les _____.

4. Me gustaría _____ a Marc Anthony.

5. Yo _____ ayer que vivimos en la misma ciudad.

6. Ella _____ que debe estudiar mucho para la clase de química.

7. Tú no _____ a los jugadores de quienes hablo.

8. Yo no _____ la respuesta correcta.

Answers: 1) conocí 2) saben 3) conocen 4) conocer 5) supe 6) sabe 7) conoces 8) sé

Drill 2: Saber vs. Conocer

1. No _____ al director del departamento. (yo)

2. No _____ si voy a ir a la playa este fin de semana.

3. Nosotros no _____ si el profesor está enfermo o de vacaciones.

4. Vosotros _____ bien a los profesores de filosofía.

5. ¿_____ usted dónde está el restaurante nuevo?

6. Espero que yo _____ el presidente de Argentina.

7. ¡Él _____ cocinar muy bien!

8. Sí, ella y yo nos _____ bien.

Answers: 1) conozco 2) sé 3) sabemos 4) conocéis 5) Sabe 6) conozca 7) sabe 8) conocemos

Drill 3: Saber vs. Conocer

1. ¿_____ tú cuál es la ciudad más poblada?

2. Nosotros _____ la diferencia entre las dos lenguas.

3. Sí, yo _____ a Juanita. Ella es muy simpática.

4. Todos mis amigos _____ cocinar.

5. ¿_____ (vosotros) esta ciudad?

6. Nadia _____ nadar.

7. Antonio _____ bailar salsa y merengue.

8. Yo no _____ a nadie que me puede ayudar ahora.

9. ¿_____ usted el programa de televisión, *Amor Clandestino*?

10. Sí, yo _____ cocinar tamales.

Answers: 1) Sabes 2) sabemos 3) conozco 4) saben 5) Conocéis 6) sabe 7) sabe 8) conozco 9) Conoce 10) sé

Verb Summary

The tenses you need to know are the present, past, future, and perfect tenses; you also need to know the subjunctive mode (both present and imperfect) as well as the commands. In terms of memorizing and reviewing them, we think the best approach is to lump them together in the following way:

Present Tense	Past Tenses	Future Tenses	Subjunctive	Commands
Present	Preterite	Future	Present	
	Imperfect	Conditional	Imperfect	
	Present perfect			

As you continue preparing for your exam, keep the following in mind:

- There are certain expressions (wish or desire, emotion, doubt, and impersonal commentaries) that tell you to use the subjunctive and whether the expression is in the present or the past will tell you which subjunctive form to use.
- To distinguish between future and conditional, focus on the certainty of the event's occurrence.
- The three past tenses are differentiated by the end (or lack thereof) of the action and when that end occurred. If the action had a clear beginning and ending in the past, use the regular past. If the action was a continuous action in the past, use the imperfect. If the action began in the past and is continuing into the present, or ended very close to the present, use the present perfect.
- Certain tenses have accents, while others do not.
- Review all the verb forms by studying your textbook.

Drill 1: How Well Do You Know Your Verbs?

1. Ojalá que _____ mañana.

   (A) lloverá
   (B) llueve
   (C) llueva
   (D) llovió

2. _____ un barco nuevo ayer.

   (A) Compraste
   (B) Compres
   (C) Comprarías
   (D) Comprares

3. ¡_____ la tarea!

   (A) Haces
   (B) Haz
   (C) Hiciste
   (D) Harías

4. Eduardo _____ mucho tiempo jugando el fútbol.

   (A) pasado
   (B) he pasado
   (C) ha pasado
   (D) pasaron

5. Esperaba que nosotros _____ un paseo por el parque, pero llueve ahora.

   (A) dábamos
   (B) dimos
   (C) damos
   (D) diéramos

6. Mañana _____ el partido de fútbol.

   (A) asistí
   (B) asisto
   (C) asistiré
   (D) asistía

7. No creo que _____ odiarte nunca.

   (A) pueda
   (B) puedo
   (C) pudiera
   (D) podré

8. El fin de semana pasado, nosotros _____ a Cancún.

   (A) iremos
   (B) iríamos
   (C) fuiste
   (D) fuimos

Drill 2: How Well Do You Know Your Verbs?

1. _____ una noche oscura y nublado cuando él llegó a casa.

   (A) Fue
   (B) Era
   (C) Es
   (D) Estaba

2. Me gustaría que me _____ al concierto de Tito Puentes.

   (A) acompañaste
   (B) acompañaras
   (C) acompañas
   (D) acompañes

3. Es importante lavar los dientes. _____ los dientes, por favor. (tú)

   (A) Lavas
   (B) Lávese
   (C) Lávate
   (D) Lavarse

4. Era triste que Javier no _____ el premio.

   (A) gana
   (B) gane
   (C) ganó
   (D) ganara

5. ¡Estoy alegre de que usted _____ venir!

   (A) puede
   (B) podrá
   (C) pueda
   (D) podría

6. Es cierto que ella _____ pelo rojo.

   (A) tiene
   (B) tenga
   (C) tuve
   (D) tuviera

7. Es la mejor película que _____ en mi vida.

   (A) he visto
   (B) ha visto
   (C) haya visto
   (D) hubiera visto

8. Por supuesto que _____ a la escuela mañana.

   (A) irías
   (B) irás
   (C) fuiste
   (D) fuera

Drill 3: How Well Do You Know Your Verbs?

1. Por favor, _____ la cama. (tú)

   (A) haz
   (B) haga
   (C) hiciste
   (D) hará

2. Paso mucho tiempo _____ por el parque.

   (A) corro
   (B) correr
   (C) corriendo
   (D) corre

3. Me _____ conocerse mejor.

   (A) gusto
   (B) gustaría
   (C) gusta
   (D) gustaba

4. Sus padres dijeron que _____ mejor comer la cena antes del postre.

   (A) ha sido
   (B) haya sido
   (C) he sido
   (D) hubiera sido

5. Gabriela _____ a la sala mientras sus hermanos _____ televisión.

   (A) entró…miraban
   (B) entraba…miraban
   (C) entraba…miraron
   (D) entró…miraron

6. Julio no quiere que ella _____ la verdad.

   (A) dice
   (B) diga
   (C) dirá
   (D) diría

7. Es importante _____ eficazmente.

   (A) sabe escribir
   (B) saber a escribir
   (C) saber escribiendo
   (D) saber escribir

8. No sé si Rodrigo _____ cocinar.

   (A) sabe
   (B) sepa
   (C) supiera
   (D) sabía

PREPOSITIONS

A preposition is a little word that shows the relationship between two other words. In English, prepositions are words such as *to, from, at, for, about,* and so on. In Spanish, they're words like **a, de, sobre,** and so on.

Part of what you need to know about prepositions is what the different ones mean. The other thing you need to know is how and when to use them. You need to know which verbs and expressions take prepositions and which prepositions they take. This shouldn't be too difficult to learn, but it can be tricky.

Common Prepositions and Their Uses

- **a:** to; at

  ¿Vamos a la obra de teatro esta noche?   *Llegamos a las cinco.*

  Are we going to the play tonight?   We arrived at 5:00.

- **de:** of; from

  Son las gafas de mi hermano.   *Soy de la Argentina.*

  Those are my brother's glasses.   I am from Argentina.
  (Literally, the glasses of my brother.)

- **con:** with

  Me gusta mucho el arroz con pollo.

  I like chicken with rice a lot.

- **sobre:** on; about; over

  La chaqueta está sobre la mesa.

  The jacket is on the table.

  La conferencia es sobre la prevención del SIDA.

  The conference is about AIDS prevention.

  Los Yankees triunfaron sobre los Braves en la serie mundial.

  The Yankees triumphed over the Braves in the World Series.

- **antes de:** before

  Antes de salir quiero ponerme un sombrero.

  Before leaving I want to put on a hat.

- **después de:** after

  Después de la cena me gusta caminar un poco.

  After dinner I like to walk a little.

Common Prepositions and Their Uses (continued)

- **en:** in

  Regresan en una hora.

  They'll be back in an hour.

  Alguien está en el baño.

  Someone is in the bathroom.

- **entre:** between

  La carnicería está entre la pescadería y el cine.

  The butcher shop is between the fish store and the cinema.

  La conferencia duró entre dos y tres horas.

  The conference lasted between two and three hours.

- **durante:** during; for

  Durante el verano me gusta nadar cada día.

  During the summer I like to swim each day.

  Trabajé con mi amigo durante quince años.

  I worked with my friend for fifteen years.

- **desde:** since; from

  He tomado vitaminas desde mi juventud.

  I've been taking vitamins since childhood.

  Se pueden ver las montañas desde aquí.

  The mountains can be seen from here.

Para versus *Por*

The prepositions **para** and **por** both mean *for* (as well as other things, depending on context), but they are used for different situations, and so they tend to cause a bit of confusion. Luckily, there are some pretty clear-cut rules as to when you use **para** and when you use **por,** because they both tend to sound fine even when they're being used incorrectly. Try to avoid using your ear when choosing between these two.

When to Use *Para*

The following are examples of the most common situations in which **para** is used. Instead of memorizing some stuffy rule, we suggest that you get a feel for what types of situations imply the use of **para,** so that when you see those situations come up on your AP Spanish Language and Culture Exam, you'll recognize them.

The preposition **para,** in very general terms, expresses the idea of *destination,* but in a very broad sense.

- **Destination in time**
  *El helado es **para** mañana.*
  The ice cream is for tomorrow. (Tomorrow is the ice cream's destination.)
- **Destination in space**
  *Me voy **para** el mercado.*
  I'm leaving for the market. (The market is my destination.)
- **Destination of purpose**
  *Compraste un regalo **para** Luis.*
  You bought a gift for Luis. (Luis is the destination of your purchase.)
  *Estudiamos **para** sacar buenas notas.*
  We study to get good grades. (Good grades are the destination of our studies.)
- **Destination of work**
  *Trabajo **para** IBM.*
  I work for IBM. (IBM is the destination of my work.)

Two uses of **para** do not indicate a sense of destination.

- **To express opinion**
  ***Para** mí, el lunes es el día más largo de la semana.*
  For me, Monday is the longest day of the week.
- **To qualify or offer a point of reference**
  ***Para** un muchacho joven, tiene muchísimo talento.*
  For a young boy, he has a lot of talent.

When to Use *Por*

Chances are, if you're not discussing destination in any way, shape, or form, and you're not engaging in the other two uses of **para,** then you'll need to use **por.** If this general rule isn't enough for you, however, study the following possibilities and you should have all the bases covered.

- **To express how you got somewhere (by)**
  *Fuimos a Italia **por** barco.*
  We went to Italy by boat.
  *Pasamos **por** esa tienda ayer cuando salimos del pueblo.*
  We passed by that store yesterday when we left the town.

- **To describe a trade (in exchange for)**
  *Te cambiaré mi automóvil **por** el tuyo este fin de semana.*
  I'll trade you my car for yours this weekend.

- **To lay blame or identify cause (by)**
  *Todos los barcos fueron destruidos **por** la tormenta.*
  All the boats were destroyed by the storm.

- **To identify gain or motive (for; as a substitute for)**
  *Ella hace todo lo posible **por** su hermana.*
  She does everything possible for her sister.
  *Cuando Arsenio está enfermo, su madre trabaja **por** él.*
  When Arsenio is ill, his mother works (as a substitute) for him.

Drill 1: Por vs. Para

1. Caminaba _____ el parque con mi esposo.

2. _____ obtener notas buenas, necesitas estudiar más.

3. ¿_____ cuánto tiempo dura la película?

4. _____ mí, prefiero pasar tiempo con mis amigos.

5. Tenéis que comprar verduras frescas _____ la fiesta.

6. _____ el Día de los Muertos, vamos a celebrar con nuestra familia.

7. Los automóviles fueron construidos _____ los alemanes.

8. Cambiaré mi pieza de chocolate _____ tu galleta.

Answers: 1) por 2) Para 3) Por 4) Para 5) para 6) Para 7) por 8) por

Drill 2: Por vs. Para

1. La canción fue escrita _____ ella.

2. Tengo que comprar un regalo _____ el cumpleaños de mi prima.

3. Necesito un motor nuevo _____ reparar el coche.

4. Él fue a la oficina de correos _____ mandar una tarjeta de cumpleaños.

5. El grupo de estudiantes caminaban _____ los pasillos de la escuela.

6. Prefiero ir a Nueva York _____ tren.

7. _____ comenzar, gracias _____ asistir la reunión.

8. Debemos gastar dinero _____ comprar una casa.

Answers: 1) por 2) para 3) para 4) para 5) por 6) por 7) Para...por 8) para

Drill 3: Por vs. Para

1. Compré el regalo _____ Adelina.

2. Voy a correr _____ treinta minutos.

3. Estamos aquí _____ estudiar _____ el exámen.

4. Fue al mercado _____ comprar manzanas y bananas.

5. La cita es _____ el jueves por la tarde.

6. Sí, _____ supuesto, puedo ayudarse.

7. _____ mí, es importante saber la diferencia entre los dos.

8. El precio de la chaqueta incluye un descuento del 30 ____ ciento.

9. ¡Gracias _____ invitarme al concierto!

Answers: 1) para 2) por 3) para...por 4) para 5) para 6) por 7) Para 8) por 9) por

Ir a and *Acabar de*

Ir a is used to describe what the future will bring, or, in other words, what is going to happen. The expression is formed by combining the appropriate form of **ir** in the present tense (subject and verb must agree) with the preposition **a.**

> *Mañana **vamos a** comprar el árbol de Navidad.*
>
> Tomorrow we are going to buy the Christmas tree.
>
> *¿**Vas a** ir a la escuela aun si te sientes mal?*
>
> You're going to go to school even if you feel ill?

Acabar de is the Spanish equivalent of *to have just* and is used to talk about what has just happened. It is formed just like **ir a,** with the appropriate form of **acabar** in the present tense followed by **de.**

> ***Acabo de** terminar de cocinar el pavo.*
>
> I have just finished cooking the turkey.
>
> *Ellos **acaban de** regresar del mercado.*
>
> They have just returned from the supermarket.

Other Prepositions to Remember

Other prepositions and prepositional phrases you should know follow. Notice that many of these are merely adverbs with **a** or **de** tacked on to the end to make them prepositions.

hacia	toward
enfrente de	in front of
frente a	in front of
dentro de	inside of
fuera de	outside of
a la derecha de	to the right of
a la izquierda de	to the left of
debajo de	underneath
encima de	above, on top of
alrededor de	around, surrounding
en medio de	in the middle of
hasta	until
tras	behind
cerca de	near
lejos de	far from
detrás de	behind
(a)delante de	in front of
al lado de	next to

Preposition Summary

- Much of your work with prepositions boils down to memorization: which expressions and verbs go with which prepositions, and so on.
- You should concentrate on the boldfaced examples at the beginning of the preposition section, since those are the most common. Once you're comfortable with them, the subsequent list should be a snap because many of those expressions are merely adverbs with **a** or **de** after them.
- Some verbs take prepositions all the time, some never do, and others sometimes do. This isn't as confusing as it may sound, however, because prepositions (or lack thereof) change the meanings of verbs. Consider the following:

Voy a tratar _____ despertarme más temprano.

(A) a
(B) de
(C) con
(D) sin

Which one of these goes with **tratar**? Actually, each of them does, depending on what you are trying to say. In this case you want to say *try to*, so **de** is the appropriate preposition. **Tratar con** means *to deal with*, and **tratar sin** means *to try/treat without*, while **tratar a** doesn't mean anything unless a person is mentioned afterward; in which case it means *to treat*. Only one of them makes sense in this sentence. The moral of the story is: don't try to memorize which verbs go with which prepositions; concentrate on meaning.

Drill 1: How Well Do You Know Your Prepositions?

1. Tenemos una reservación de restaurante _____ las ocho.

   (A) en
   (B) por
   (C) a
   (D) de

2. Ana va a casarse _____ Raul.

   (A) con
   (B) de
   (C) a
   (D) por

3. Estoy enamorado _____ ti.

   (A) de
   (B) con
   (C) a
   (D) por

4. Ellos _____ regresar a casa.

   (A) fueron de
   (B) acaban a
   (C) acaban de
   (D) hacia

5. El techo está _____ la casa.

   (A) dentro de
   (B) encima de
   (C) al lado de
   (D) frente a

6. Sigue derecho _____ al norte hasta que llegues a la ciudad.

   (A) hasta
   (B) frente
   (C) tras
   (D) hacia

7. El jardín está _____ la casa.

   (A) para
   (B) debajo de
   (C) fuera de
   (D) acabar de

8. Maya y Alejandro fueron de compras _____ obtener nueva ropa.

   (A) de
   (B) a
   (C) por
   (D) para

Drill 2: How Well Do You Know Your Prepositions?

1. El perro se escondió _____ la aspiradora.

   (A) al lado de
   (B) dentro de
   (C) lejos de
   (D) encima de

2. Olivia toca el piano muy bien _____ una chica joven.

   (A) por
   (B) para
   (C) a
   (D) que

3. Es un juego _____ niños, pero a mí me encanta el escondite en el parque.

   (A) para
   (B) por
   (C) con
   (D) de

4. Argentina es _____ Rusia.

   (A) al lado
   (B) en frente de
   (C) cerca de
   (D) lejos de

5. _____ ahora, he estudiado mucho.

   (A) Acabo de
   (B) Hacia
   (C) Hasta
   (D) Tras de

6. La película _____ la vida de un hombre buscando su destino.

   (A) sobre de
   (B) durante
   (C) en vez de
   (D) trata de

7. _____ nosotros, tenemos un compromiso.

   (A) Entre
   (B) Encima de
   (C) Con
   (D) Sin

8. _____ mí, hay demasiado drama entre las chicas adolescentes.

   (A) Adelante de
   (B) Hacia
   (C) Para
   (D) Por

Drill 3: How Well Do You Know Your Prepositions?

1. La cena está _____ la mesa.

    (A) debajo de
    (B) encima de
    (C) dentro de
    (D) enfrente de

2. Busco _____ unos platos para la cena.

    (A) a
    (B) por
    (C) para
    (D) no se necesita una preposición

3. Me gusta relajar un poco cuando estoy _____ casa.

    (A) dentro de
    (B) en
    (C) a
    (D) en frente de

4. Escuchaba a una lectura _____ tomaba apuntes.

    (A) sobre
    (B) para
    (C) durante
    (D) mientras

5. Fui al parque _____ completar el día de trabajo.

    (A) después de
    (B) al lado de
    (C) en frente de
    (D) acababo de

6. A Caterina le gusta andar _____ las montañas.

    (A) por
    (B) para
    (C) a
    (D) encima de

7. El cuarto de baño está _____ dormitorio.

    (A) dentro del
    (B) encima del
    (C) al lado del
    (D) acaba del

8. _____ salir, Eva se puso el maquillaje.

    (A) Antes de
    (B) Hasta
    (C) Durante de
    (D) En medio de

ANSWERS AND EXPLANATIONS FOR QUIZZES

Drill 1: How Well Do You Know Your Pronouns? (Page 218)

1.   The book is _____.

   (A) mi
   (B) mío
   (C) mía
   (D) me

The correct word should mean *mine* and should agree with **el libro**, which is masculine. Therefore, the correct answer is (B).

2.   I enjoy going to the movies.

   (A) te
   (B) mío
   (C) me
   (D) tu

The verb **gustar** is used in a reflexive form to show that something is pleasing to the person. Since the sentence says **A mí,** the answer should be in the **yo** form. Eliminate (A) and (D). The answer should be an indirect object pronoun, so the correct answer is (C).

3.   Laura _____ helped the students with their homework.

   (A) les
   (B) se
   (C) lo
   (D) tu

The pronoun here refers to the students, who are the indirect object in the sentence. Eliminate (C) (direct object) and (D) (**tú** form). Remember that **se** is only used when it is followed by a direct object pronoun beginning with **l.** Since that's not the case here, eliminate (B). The correct answer is (A).

4.   Ana _____ gave a treat to the dog for doing a trick.

   (A) la
   (B) lo
   (C) se
   (D) le

The pronoun refers to the dog, which is the indirect object in the sentence. Eliminate (A) and (B) because they are direct object pronouns. Remember that **se** is only used when it is followed by a direct object pronoun beginning with **l.** Since that's not the case here, eliminate (C). The correct answer is (D).

5. Yamil _____ enjoyed all his classes last year.

    (A) le
    (B) les
    (C) las
    (D) la

The verb **gustar** has a backward construction: its subject is that which pleases, and its object is the person who is pleased. So the subject of **gustar** here is **todas sus clases,** and the indirect object (with which this pronoun must agree) is **Yamil**. Since he is singular, choose **le.** The correct answer is (A).

6. José _____ gave the present to his girlfriend.

    (A) le la
    (B) se le
    (C) se la
    (D) se lo

In this sentence, there are both an indirect and a direct object pronoun. When both are present and the direct object pronoun begins with **l,** use **se** for the indirect, so eliminate (A). The indirect object pronoun will come first and then the second will be a direct object pronoun, so eliminate (B) because **le** is indirect. José's girlfriend is the indirect object (a great way to tell which object is the indirect is that it's the object after a preposition such as *to, from, for, with,* etc.) and **el regalo** is the masculine direct object. Since the direct object is masculine, the correct response is (D).

7. _____ here is the famous person?

    (A) Qué
    (B) Cuál
    (C) Quién
    (D) Quienes

Since the question refers to a person, eliminate (A) and (B), which both refer to things. The famous person is singular, so the correct answer is (C).

8. To paint the room, _____ color do you prefer?

    (A) qué
    (B) cuyo
    (C) quién
    (D) por qué

In English, *what* or *which* would be acceptable. Eliminate (B), *whose,* (C), *who,* and (D), *why.* The correct answer is (A).

Drill 2: How Well Do You Know Your Pronouns?
(Page 219)

1. Maya, would you like to go shopping _____?

    (A) conmigo
    (B) contigo
    (C) con yo
    (D) con mí

The correct pronoun for *with me* in Spanish is **conmigo:** one word, rather than two. The correct answer is (A).

2. The car is _____.

    (A) su
    (B) suya
    (C) suyo
    (D) suyos

The car is singular and masculine, so the correct answer is (C).

3. Your bicycle is new, but _____ is ancient!

    (A) la mia
    (B) la mía
    (C) el mío
    (D) el mio

La bicicleta is singular and feminine, so eliminate (C) and (D). The pronoun needs an accent, so (B) is correct.

4. _____ do you prefer? Tacos or enchiladas?

    (A) Cuál
    (B) Por qué
    (C) Quién
    (D) Cual

The question is asking *which* the person prefers, so eliminate (B) and (C) because they ask *why* and *who* respectively. When asking a question, there needs to be an accent on **cuál,** so (A) is correct.

5. _____ house is ours.

    (A) Esta
    (B) Esto
    (C) Este
    (D) Está

Casa is feminine, so the answer must also be feminine. Eliminate (B) and (C). Choice (D) is a verb form of **estar,** not a pronoun, so eliminate this choice as well. The correct answer is (A).

6. This boat is not mine. Mine is _____.

   (A) aquella
   (B) aquellas
   (C) aquel
   (D) aquellos

The boat is singular and masculine. Therefore, (C) is the correct answer.

7. The doctor, _____ patient is sick, gave him/her antibiotics.

   (A) cuya
   (B) cuyas
   (C) cuyos
   (D) cuyo

El paciente is singular and masculine (even though the noun can be feminine): you can tell because the adjective **enfermo** is used later in the sentence. Therefore (D) is the correct response.

8. Alessandra _____ put on makeup.

   (A) le
   (B) lo
   (C) la
   (D) se

Ponerse is a reflexive verb and here it is used in the third person, so **se** is the correct form of the pronoun. Choice (D) is the correct answer.

Drill 3: How Well Do You Know Your Pronouns? (Page 220)

1. _____ is your favorite food?

   (A) Cual
   (B) Cuáles
   (C) Cuál
   (D) Quién

When asking a question, there should be an accent on the question word, so eliminate (A). The subject is singular and a thing (not a person), so eliminate (B) and (D). The correct answer is (C).

2. Are those _____ gloves that are on the armchair?

   (A) mío
   (B) mía
   (C) míos
   (D) mías

Guantes is masculine and plural (which you can also tell by looking at **aquellos**), so (C) is correct.

3. Teresa bought lunch for _____ because she was alone.

   (A) si mismo
   (B) sí misma
   (C) sí mismo
   (D) si misma

The correct idiom to express *him-* or *herself* is **sí mismo/misma.** Teresa is a feminine name and the adjective **sola** is used, so eliminate (A) and (C). There should be an accent on **sí,** so the correct answer is (B).

4. My books are here, but _____ are there.

   (A) vuestra
   (B) vuestro
   (C) vuestros
   (D) vuestras

The pronoun needs to match **libros,** which is plural and masculine. Therefore, the correct answer is (C).

5. I walked from my house to work simply because it pleased _____ to.

   (A) se mi
   (B) se me
   (C) se le
   (D) se lo

Darse la gana is a reflexive verb phrase. Since this sentence is in first person, there should be a first-person pronoun in the sentence. Eliminate (C) and (D). **Mi** is a possessive pronoun and **me** is reflexive, so (B) is the correct answer.

6. Did they give the correct pencils to the students for the exam?

    (A) Los
    (B) Les
    (C) Las
    (D) Se

This sentence contains both a direct object **(los lápices)** and an indirect object **(los estudiantes)**. The one that must be accompanied by a pronoun is the indirect object, so eliminate (A) and (C), the direct object pronouns. Since **se** is only used when both the indirect and direct object pronouns are present (and the direct object pronoun begins with **l**), the correct answer is (B).

7. I would like to become a lawyer.

    (A) sí
    (B) mi
    (C) se
    (D) me

The verb **hacerse** is reflexive and is used in the context of becoming a member of a profession. Since the subject is *I*, a first-person pronoun is needed, so eliminate (A) and (C). **Me** is the reflexive pronoun, so the correct answer is (D).

8. Carolina _____ cut her hair.

    (A) le
    (B) se
    (C) la
    (D) lo

Cortarse is a reflexive verb, and Carolina is a third-person subject. Since this is the case, **se** is the correct pronoun. The correct answer is (B).

Drill 1: How Well Do You Know Your Verbs? (Page 242)

1. Hopefully it will _____ tomorrow.

   (A) lloverá
   (B) llueve
   (C) llueva
   (D) llovió

The expression **ojalá** indicates subjunctive, so the correct answer must be (C).

2. _____ a new boat yesterday.

   (A) Compraste
   (B) Compres
   (C) Comprarías
   (D) Comprares

The clue for time in this sentence is **ayer,** meaning *yesterday,* so the verb must be in past tense. Choice (A) is the simple preterite, so keep this choice. Choice (B) is simple present, so eliminate it. **Comprarías** is conditional and **comprares** is future, so eliminate these choices as well. The correct answer is (A).

3. _____ the homework!

   (A) Haces
   (B) Haz
   (C) Hiciste
   (D) Harías

This is a command, so the verb must be in the command form, whether formal or informal. Therefore, the correct verb must be **Haz** (tú), **Haga** (Ud.), **Hagamos** (nosotros), **Haced** (vosotros), or **Hagan** (Uds.). Only one of these is present, so (B) is the correct response.

4. Eduardo _____ a lot of time playing soccer.

   (A) pasado
   (B) he pasado
   (C) ha pasado
   (D) pasaron

The sentence is not very clear about the tense, but the subject is singular and third person. Eliminate (A) because this is only the participle without a helping verb that is conjugated. In (B), **he** is first person, so eliminate this choice too. Choice (C) is in the third person, so keep it, and eliminate (D) because it is a plural form. The correct answer is (C).

5. I hoped that we _____ a walk through the park, but now it's raining.

   (A) dábamos
   (B) dimos
   (C) damos
   (D) diéramos

The clue here is **Esperaba que,** which indicates desire and therefore must be followed by the subjunctive. Since **Esperaba** is imperfect, the imperfect subjunctive is necessary. Therefore, (D) is the correct answer.

6. Tomorrow _____ the soccer game.

   (A) asistí
   (B) asisto
   (C) asistiré
   (D) asistía

There is a time trigger here: **Mañana.** Therefore, the verb must be in the future tense. Choice (A) is first person preterite, so eliminate this choice. Choice (B) is in the present tense, which is incorrect as well. Choice (C) is in the future, so keep this choice. Choice (D) is in the imperfect, so eliminate this one as well. The correct answer is (C).

7. I don't believe _____ ever hate you.

   (A) pueda
   (B) puedo
   (C) pudiera
   (D) podré

The phrase **No creo que** needs subjunctive because it expresses doubt. Eliminate (B) and (D) since they are indicative. **Creo** is present tense, so the subjunctive should also be present. Therefore, (A) is correct.

8. Last weekend, we _____ to Cancún.

   (A) iremos
   (B) iríamos
   (C) fuiste
   (D) fuimos

The time trigger here is **El fin de semana pasado,** which indicates past tense. Eliminate (A) and (B). Choice (C) is in the tú form, but the sentence contains **nosotros.** Only (D) agrees.

Drill 2: How Well Do You Know Your Verbs? (Page 243)

1. _____ a dark and cloudy night when he returned home.

   (A) Fue
   (B) Era
   (C) Es
   (D) Estaba

There is a preterite verb at the end of the sentence, so there must also be a past tense verb at the beginning of the sentence. Eliminate (C). When setting the stage, as in this sentence, use the imperfect tense. Eliminate (A), which is preterite. Between **ser** and **estar, ser** is the correct verb to use here. Therefore, (B) is the correct answer.

2. I would like that _____ me to the Tito Puentes concert.

   (A) acompañaste
   (B) acompañaras
   (C) acompañas
   (D) acompañes

The beginning of the sentence expresses desire, so use the subjunctive. Eliminate (A) and (C). The sentence uses the conditional, indicating that the concert is in the future, so use the present subjunctive. Therefore, (D) is the correct answer.

3. It is important to brush your teeth. _____ your teeth, please. (tú)

   (A) Lavas
   (B) Lávese
   (C) Lávate
   (D) Lavarse

This sentence needs the informal form, so eliminate (B) and (D). The sentence is a command, so eliminate (A), which is the simple present tense. The correct answer is (C).

4. It was sad that Javier did not _____ the prize.

   (A) gana
   (B) gane
   (C) ganó
   (D) ganara

Since this sentence expresses emotion, use the subjunctive. Since the first part of the sentence uses the imperfect **era,** you need the imperfect subjunctive **ganara,** so the correct answer is (D).

5.   I am happy that you _____ come!

    (A) puede
    (B) podrá
    (C) pueda
    (D) podría

This sentence shows emotion, so use the subjunctive here. The only option for subjunctive is (C).

6.   It is certain that she _____ red hair.

    (A) tiene
    (B) tenga
    (C) tuve
    (D) tuviera

Since the sentence shows certainty, do not use the subjunctive, but rather use the indicative. The sentence is in the present, so use the simple present tense. The correct answer is (A).

7.   It is the best movie that _____ in my life.

    (A) he visto
    (B) ha visto
    (C) haya visto
    (D) hubiera visto

The clue here is **mi vida,** so the verb needs to be first person. Eliminate (B). Since it is clear that the person saw the movie, the indicative is needed. Eliminate (C) and (D), and the correct answer is (A).

8.   Of course _____ to school tomorrow.

    (A) irías
    (B) irás
    (C) fuiste
    (D) fuera

The sentence has a trigger word **mañana,** so eliminate the past tense choices (C) and (D). Choice (A) contains the conditional and (B) contains the future tense. Since there is not a **si** clause in the sentence, there is no need for the conditional. Choice (B) is correct.

Drill 3: How Well Do You Know Your Verbs? (Page 244)

1. Please, _____ the bed. (tú)

   (A) haz
   (B) haga
   (C) hiciste
   (D) hará

This is a command, and it must be in the informal form. Therefore, (A) is correct.

2. I spend a lot of time _____ through the park.

   (A) corro
   (B) correr
   (C) corriendo
   (D) corre

There is already a conjugated verb in the sentence without a **que:** usually this means the sentence will use an infinitive or a progressive tense. Eliminate (A) and (D). It does not make sense to use the infinitive; the meaning would be *I spend a lot of time to run,* so the progressive is the correct choice. Choice (C) is correct.

3. I would like to know you better. (formal)

   (A) gusto
   (B) gustaría
   (C) gusta
   (D) gustaba

The conditional is used as a formality with the verb **gustar** to express want or desire. Therefore, (B) is correct.

4. Their parents said that _____ better to eat dinner before dessert.

   (A) ha sido
   (B) haya sido
   (C) he sido
   (D) hubiera sido

The parents expressed preference in the past, though it is not certain that the children did what the parents suggested they do. Therefore, use the subjunctive; eliminate (A) and (C). Since the first part of the sentence is in past tense, use a past subjunctive. Choice (D) is correct.

5. Gabriela _____ the room while her brothers _____ television.

    (A) entró...miraban
    (B) entraba...miraban
    (C) entraba...miraron
    (D) entró...miraron

Gabriela did a singular action while her brothers did a continual action, both in the past. The singular action should be expressed with the preterite, while the continual action should be expressed with the imperfect. Therefore, (A) is correct.

6. Julio does not want for her _____ the truth.

    (A) dice
    (B) diga
    (C) dirá
    (D) diría

Julio expresses desire in the first part of the sentence, so use the subjunctive. The only option here is (B).

7. It is important _____ effectively.

    (A) sabe escribir
    (B) saber a escribir
    (C) saber escribiendo
    (D) saber escribir

There is already a conjugated verb in the sentence, not followed by **que**: this usually indicates the need for an infinitive or a progressive tense. Eliminate (A) since **sabe** is conjugated. In English, the sentence is trying to say *It is important to know how to write effectively,* so there are two infinitives needed. Eliminate (C) because it contains a progressive tense instead. Since the infinitive already includes the *to* in it, the **a** in Spanish is not necessary. Choice (D) is correct.

8. I don't know whether Rodrigo _____ to cook.

    (A) sabe
    (B) sepa
    (C) supiera
    (D) sabía

Since the sentence is expressing doubt, use the subjunctive. Eliminate (A) and (D). Since the first part of the sentence is in the present tense, (B) is correct.

Drill 1: How Well Do You Know Your Prepositions? (Page 253)

1. We have a restaurant reservation _____ eight o'clock.

    (A) en
    (B) por
    (C) a
    (D) de

When talking about a meeting time, use **a** to replace the English *at.* Choice (C) is correct.

2. Ana is going to marry _____ Raul.

    (A) con
    (B) de
    (C) a
    (D) por

The correct idiom is **casarse con,** which is a bit counterintuitive to English speakers. Therefore, (A) is correct.

3. I am in love ____ you.

    (A) de
    (B) con
    (C) a
    (D) por

The correct idiom for *in love with* is **enamorada/o de.** The correct answer is (A).

4. They _____ returned home.

    (A) fueron de
    (B) acaban a
    (C) acaban de
    (D) hacia

This sentence is a bit tricky. The infinitive **regresar** comes right after the blank, so there must be a conjugated verb in the blank. Eliminate (D), since there is not a verb there. **Fueron** means *they went,* which does not make sense in the sentence, so eliminate (A) as well. The correct idiom between (B) and (C) is **de,** meaning *to have just* done something. The correct answer is (C).

5. The roof is _____ the house.

    (A) dentro de
    (B) encima de
    (C) al lado de
    (D) frente a

The roof of a house should be above the house. Choice (A) means *inside,* so eliminate this choice. Choice (B) works, so keep it. Choice (C) means *next to,* and (D) means *in front of,* so eliminate these too. Choice (B) is correct.

6. Continue straight _____ the north until you arrive at the city.

   (A) hasta
   (B) frente
   (C) tras
   (D) hacia

The meaning of the word should be along the lines of *toward* the north. **Hasta** means *until,* so eliminate (A). Choice (B) is close, *facing,* but it is not idiomatically correct, so eliminate this choice as well. **Tras** means *through,* which does not make sense in context: eliminate (C). The only word that means *toward* is **hacia.** The correct answer is (D).

7. The garden is _____ the house.

   (A) para
   (B) debajo de
   (C) fuera de
   (D) acabar de

The garden is most likely *outside* the house, though there may be some exceptions. **Para** does not work here because with it, the sentence means *The garden is in order to the house,* so eliminate (A). The garden would not be *underneath* the house, so eliminate (B) as well. Keep (C) since it matches the prediction of *outside* the house. Choice (D) does not make sense grammatically, roughly translating to *to have just the house.* Choice (C) is correct.

8. Maya and Alejandro went shopping _____ get new clothes.

   (A) de
   (B) a
   (C) por
   (D) para

Maya and Alejandro went shopping *in order to* get new clothes. Whenever it works to use *in order to* in the sentence, use **para.** The correct answer is (D).

Drill 2: How Well Do You Know Your Prepositions? (Page 254)

1. The dog hid itself _____ the vacuum.
   (A) al lado de
   (B) dentro de
   (C) lejos de
   (D) encima de

If the dog is hiding from the vacuum, it wants to get *away* from the vacuum. Only **lejos de** puts space between the dog and the vacuum, so the correct answer is (C).

2.   Olivia plays the piano very well _____ a young child.

   (A) por
   (B) para
   (C) a
   (D) que

The English translation would be *for a young child*. Therefore, this is a **por** vs. **para** question. The correct idiom for this type of sentence is **para,** so (B) is correct.

3.   It is a game _____ children, but I love hide-and-seek in the park.

   (A) para
   (B) por
   (C) con
   (D) de

It is a game for children; the word *for* here tells you that this is a **por** vs. **para** question. The correct idiom here is **para** because it is *intended for* children. The correct answer is (A).

4.   Argentina is _____ Russia.

   (A) al lado
   (B) en frente de
   (C) cerca de
   (D) lejos de

Argentina is not *next to* Russia, so eliminate (A), which is also missing a word **(de).** It is not *in front of* Russia either, so eliminate (B). Since it is not *near* or *around* Russia, eliminate (C) as well. The correct answer is (D), meaning *far from* Russia.

5.   _____ now, I have studied a lot.

   (A) Acabo de
   (B) Hacia
   (C) Hasta
   (D) Tras de

The sentence intends to say *until now,* so the correct idiom to express this in Spanish is **Hasta ahora.** Choice (A) does not make sense in context (*to have just now),* and neither does (B), *toward now.* Choice (D) means *behind,* so this is incorrect as well. The correct answer is (C).

6.   The movie _____ the life of a man in search of his destiny.

   (A) sobre de
   (B) durante
   (C) en vez de
   (D) trata de

To express that a movie, book, play, etc. is *about* something, use the idiom **tratar de.** The correct answer is (D).

7. _____ us, we have an agreement.

    (A) Entre
    (B) Encima de
    (C) Con
    (D) Sin

We have an agreement *between* us. Therefore, the proper preposition is **entre.** The correct answer is (A).

8. _____ me, there is too much drama amongst adolescent girls.

    (A) Adelante de
    (B) Hacia
    (C) Para
    (D) Por

The phrase *For/to me* to express *in my opinion* in Spanish is **para mí.** Therefore, (C) is correct.

Drill 3: How Well Do You Know Your Prepositions? (Page 255)

1. The dinner is _____ the table.

    (A) debajo de
    (B) encima de
    (C) dentro de
    (D) enfrente de

Hopefully dinner is not *under, inside,* or *in front of* the table, eliminating (A), (C), and (D), respectively. Choice (B) is correct.

2. I am in search of _____ some plates for dinner.

    (A) a
    (B) por
    (C) para
    (D) no se necesita una preposición

The verb **buscar** means *to look for,* so there is no preposition needed. The preposition is already part of the verb itself. Choice (D) is correct.

3. I enjoy relaxing a bit when I am _____ home.

   (A) dentro de
   (B) en
   (C) a
   (D) en frente de

To express *at home,* the correct idiom is **en casa,** making (B) correct. The idiom is not *inside the house,* so eliminate (A). Choice (C) is used when a person is going home, not when a person is already at home. Choice (D) does not make much sense in context *(in front of house).* Choice (B) is correct.

4. I was listening to a lecture _____ I was taking notes.

   (A) sobre
   (B) para
   (C) durante
   (D) mientras

Sobre means *over,* which does not make sense in this context, since one thing is happening while another thing is also happening in this sentence. **Para** does not work either, since one does not listen to a lecture *in order to* take notes, eliminating (B). **Durante** is tempting, but the correct idiom is **mientras.** The correct answer is (D).

5. I went to the park _____ completing the workday.

   (A) después de
   (B) al lado de
   (C) en frente de
   (D) acababo de

There are only a few clues here, though there is most likely a time trigger since the workday is complete. **Después de** works because one could go to the park *after* the workday. Keep (A). Choice (B) does not make sense because one could not go to the park *next to* completing the workday. Eliminate (B). Choice (C) makes the same error as (B), showing spatial orientation, so eliminate this one as well. Choice (D) carries the right intention, but it is idiomatically and grammatically incorrect, conjugating a second verb without a **que** in the sentence. Choice (A) is correct.

6. Caterina enjoys walking _____ the mountains.

   (A) por
   (B) para
   (C) a
   (D) encima de

This is a **por** vs. **para** question. Here, the idiom is to *walk through* the mountains, so use **por** to express this. The correct answer is (A).

7.   The bathroom is _____ bedroom.

   (A) dentro del
   (B) encima del
   (C) al lado del
   (D) acaba del

The bathroom hopefully is not *inside* or *on top of the* bedroom, so eliminate (A) and (B) respectively. Choice (C) makes sense: *next to the* bedroom. Choice (D) does not make sense in the sentence: *to have just the* bedroom. The correct answer is (C).

8.   _____ leaving, Eva put on makeup.

   (A) Antes de
   (B) Hasta de
   (C) Durante de
   (D) En medio de

One would assume that Eva put on makeup *before* leaving, so the correct answer is (A).

REFLECT

Respond to the following questions:

- Of which topics discussed in this chapter do you feel you have achieved sufficient comprehension to use effectively in an essay?

- On which topics discussed in this chapter do you feel you need more work before you can use them effectively in an essay?

- Of which topics discussed in this chapter do you feel you have achieved sufficient comprehension to use effectively in a spoken response?

- On which topics discussed in this chapter do you feel you need more work before you can use them effectively in a spoken response?

- Which parts of this chapter are you going to re-review?

- Will you seek further help, outside this book (such as from a teacher, tutor, or AP Students), on any of the content in this chapter—and if so, on what content?

Part VI
Practice Test 2

Practice Test 2

Following are the audio track numbers for **Practice Test 2**. You can find them in your online Student Tools to stream or download.

- Track 14: Selección 1 (Fuente 2)

- Track 15: Selección 2 (Fuente 2)

- Track 16: Selección 3

- Track 17: Selección 4

- Track 18: Selección 5

- Track 19: Question 2: Argumentative Essay (Fuente 3)

- Track 20: Question 3: Conversation

Again, make sure you have a device handy with which to record and time yourself for the speaking sections.

Good luck!

AP® Spanish Language and Culture

SECTION I: Multiple-Choice Questions

DO NOT OPEN THIS BOOKLET UNTIL YOU ARE TOLD TO DO SO.

<table>
<tr><td>

At a Glance

Total Time
1 hour and 35 minutes
Number of Questions
65
Percent of Total Grade
50%
Writing Instrument
Pencil required

</td></tr>
</table>

Instructions

Section I of this examination contains 65 multiple-choice questions. Fill in only the ovals for numbers 1 through 65 on your answer sheet.

Indicate all of your answers to the multiple-choice questions on the answer sheet. No credit will be given for anything written in this exam booklet, but you may use the booklet for notes or scratch work. After you have decided which of the suggested answers is best, completely fill in the corresponding oval on the answer sheet. Give only one answer to each question. If you change an answer, be sure that the previous mark is erased completely. Here is a sample question and answer.

Sample Question   Sample Answer

Chicago is a
(A) state
(B) city
(C) country
(D) continent

Use your time effectively, working as quickly as you can without losing accuracy. Do not spend too much time on any one question. Go on to other questions and come back to the ones you have not answered if you have time. It is not expected that everyone will know the answers to all the multiple-choice questions.

About Guessing

Many candidates wonder whether or not to guess the answers to questions about which they are not certain. Multiple-choice scores are based on the number of questions answered correctly. Points are not deducted for incorrect answers, and no points are awarded for unanswered questions. Because points are not deducted for incorrect answers, you are encouraged to answer all multiple-choice questions. On any questions you do not know the answer to, you should eliminate as many choices as you can, and then select the best answer among the remaining choices.

GO ON TO THE NEXT PAGE.

Part A

Interpretive Communication: Print Texts

You will read several selections. Each selection is accompanied by a number of questions. For each question, choose the response that is best according to the selection and mark your answer on your answer sheet.	Vas a leer varios textos. Cada texto va acompañado de varias preguntas. Para cada pregunta, elige la mejor respuesta según el texto e indícala en la hoja de respuestas.

Selección número 1

Introducción

La siguiente infografía apareció en el sitio web de las Naciones Unidas.

CIUDADES SOSTENIBLES:
POR QUÉ SON IMPORTANTES

11 CIUDADES Y COMUNIDADES SOSTENIBLES

¿Cuál es el objetivo en este caso?

Lograr que las ciudades y los asentamientos humanos sean inclusivos, seguros, resilientes y sostenibles

¿Por qué?

La mitad de la humanidad, esto es, unos 3.500 millones de personas, viven actualmente en ciudades, y esta cifra seguirá en aumento. Dado que para la mayoría de personas el futuro será urbano, las soluciones a algunos de los principales problemas a que se enfrentan los seres humanos —la pobreza, el cambio climático, la asistencia sanitaria y la educación— deben encontrarse en la vida de la ciudad.

¿Cuáles son los retos más urgentes a que se enfrentan actualmente las ciudades?

La desigualdad es motivo de gran preocupación. Hay 828 millones de personas que viven en barrios marginales y esta cifra sigue aumentando. Los niveles de consumo de energía y de contaminación en las zonas urbanas son también preocupantes. Aunque las ciudades ocupan solo el 3% de la superficie terrestre, representan entre un 60% y un 80% del consumo de energía y el 75% de las emisiones de carbono.

En los próximos decenios, el 95% de la expansión urbana tendrá lugar en países en desarrollo.

GO ON TO THE NEXT PAGE.

1. ¿Cuál es el tono del panfleto?

   (A) Informativo

   (B) Confundido

   (C) Espantoso

   (D) Cansado

2. ¿Cuántas personas viven en las ciudades y ese número aumentará o disminuirá en el futuro?

   (A) 3.500 millones, disminución

   (B) 95 mil millones, aumento

   (C) 3.500 millones, aumento

   (D) 95 mil millones, disminución

3. ¿Cuál NO es un problema al que se enfrentan los seres humanos mencionado en el folleto?

   (A) Cambio climático

   (B) Pobreza

   (C) Depresión

   (D) Falta de asistencia sanitaria

4. Según el panfleto, ¿cuáles son algunos de los problemas más urgentes que tienen las ciudades?

   (A) Vivir en las mansiones, expansión de mansiones y recursos escasos

   (B) Desigualdad, contaminación y nivel de consumo de energía

   (C) Cambio climático, reciclaje y basura

   (D) Construir nuevas ciudades, ser sostenibles y controlar la población

5. Se menciona "Hay 838 millones de personas" para

   (A) mostrar cuanto más uso de energía es debido a las personas que viven en barrios marginales

   (B) mostrar que hay tanta gente viviendo en este planeta

   (C) mostrar cuántas personas están contribuyendo al problema de la contaminación

   (D) monstrar la desigualdad entre los habitantes de los barrios marginales y el resto del los habitantes de las ciudades

GO ON TO THE NEXT PAGE.

Selección número 2

Introducción

La siguiente selección es un fragmento de *Como Agua Para Chocolate*.

INGREDIENTES:
1 lata de sardinas
½ chorizo
1 cebolla
orégano
1 lata de chiles serranos
10 teleras

Manera de hacerse:

La cebolla tiene que estar finamente picada. Les sugiero ponerse un pequeño trozo de cebolla en la mollera[1] con el fin de evitar el molesto lagrimeo que se produce cuando uno la está cortando. Lo malo de llorar cuando uno pica cebolla no es el simple hecho de llorar, sino que a veces uno empieza, como quien dice, se pica, y ya no puede parar. No sé si a ustedes les ha pasado pero a mí la mera verdad sí. Infinidad de veces. Mamá decía que era porque yo soy igual de sensible a la cebolla que Tita, mi tía abuela.

Dicen que Tita era tan sensible que desde que estaba en el vientre de mi bisabuela lloraba y lloraba cuando ésta picaba cebolla; su llanto era tan fuerte que Nacha, la cocinera de la casa, que era medio sorda, lo escuchaba sin esforzarse. Un día los sollozos[2] fueron tan fuertes que provocaron que el parto se adelantara. Y sin que mi bisabuela pudiera decir ni pío, Tita arribó a este mundo prematuramente, sobre la mesa de la cocina, entre los olores de una sopa de fideos que estaba cocinando, los del tomillo, el laurel, el cilantro, el de la leche hervida, el de los ajos y, por supuesto, el de la cebolla. Como se imaginarán, la consabida nalgada no fue necesaria, pues Tita nació llorando de antemano, tal vez porque ella sabía que su oráculo determinaba que en esta vida le estaba negado el matrimonio. Contaba Nacha que Tita fue literalmente empujada a este mundo por un torrente impresionante de lágrimas que se desbordaron sobre la mesa y el piso de la cocina.

En la tarde, ya cuando el susto había pasado y el agua, gracias al efecto de los rayos del sol, se había evaporado, Nacha barrió el residuo de las lágrimas que había quedado sobre la loseta roja que cubría el piso. Con esta sal rellenó un costal de cinco kilos que utilizaron para cocinar bastante tiempo.

[1]*crown of head*
[2]*sobs or wailing*

---

6. ¿Por qué el autor recomienda poner cebolla cerca de tu cara?

   (A) Para hacerte llorar y estar triste

   (B) Para evitar las lágrimas molestas que se produce al cortar cebollas

   (C) Para unirte a tu familia mientras cortas cebollas

   (D) Para ver los surcos en la cebolla para cortar mejor la cebolla

7. ¿Quién es sensible a las cebollas como la autora?

   (A) La madre del autor

   (B) La bisabuela del autor

   (C) La tía abuela del autor

   (D) El padre del autor

GO ON TO THE NEXT PAGE.

8. ¿Qué detalle mostró que Tita lloró muy fuerte?

    (A) Tita lloró desde el vientre y Nacha que es medio sorda pudo oírla.

    (B) Tita lloró cuando la bisabuela del autor picó cebollas.

    (C) Tita nació en medio de los olores de la sopa de fideos, como el laurel.

    (D) Tita es tan sensible a las cebollas como el autor.

9. ¿Qué ingrediente NO se describió en el olor de la sopa de fideos?

    (A) Hojas de laurel

    (B) Leche hervida

    (C) Hojuelas de chile

    (D) Cebolla

10. ¿Cómo describe Nacha la razón por la que nació Tita?

    (A) Tita tenía tantas lágrimas que la empujaron al mundo.

    (B) Tita odiaba tanto la cebolla que se escapó de su vientre.

    (C) Tita amaba tanto la comida que dejó el útero para probar la comida.

    (D) Tita tenía tantas ganas de ver a su madre que nació.

11. ¿De qué color era la loseta del piso donde Nacha barrió las lágrimas?

    (A) Azul

    (B) Rojo

    (C) Marrón

    (D) Negro

12. ¿Qué quedó después de que se evaporaron las lágrimas y para qué lo usaron?

    (A) Los rayos del sol que usaban para calentar la casa

    (B) El amor que solían unir entre sí

    (C) La sal con la que solían cocinar

    (D) Cebollas que usaban en su comida

GO ON TO THE NEXT PAGE.

Selección número 3

Introducción

La siguiente selección es una carta de Ana a su abuelo.

---

25 de Marzo de 2014
Londres, Inglaterra
Reino Unido

Querido Abuelo:

¡Hola! ¡Tanto tiempo que no te escribo! Espero que te sientas bien y que tu pierna ya se haya curado. ¡Cuidado con el hielo abuelo! Es muy resbaladizo.

Los estudios van muy bien y realmente me gusta mucho Óxford. Es una universidad muy popular pero los profesores dan mucho trabajo, y eso no me gusta. El fin de semana pasado, me tomé un tren a Londres. ¡Que lindo que es! Visité los grandes museos, el palacio de Buckingham, el río Támesis y las Casas de Parlamento. Realmente fue una experiencia. Las cafeterías son bastante caras, pero sin embargo me he juntado con muchos amigos para cenar. Me gusta mucho la comida. Espero poder volver el próximo año por última vez antes de volver para casa. ¿Están planeando en visitarnos el próximo año? Me gustaría verte a vos y a la abuela. Ya sé que el viaje de Alaska a Oregón no es nada fácil. A lo mejor podemos planear en encontrarnos en California.

Mañana empiezo una nueva clase de arte. Quería otro curso de arte artesanal, pero no tenían espacio. Me anoté en un curso de arte moderno. ¡Estoy muy entusiasmada! Te voy a mandar unos de mis grandes dibujos— ¡algún día los podrás vender!

¡Te mando muchos abrazos y besos! Espero verte pronto. ¡Te quiero mucho!

Ana

---

13. ¿Por qué Ana le advierte a su abuelo sobre el hielo?

    (A) Porque hace mucho frio

    (B) Porque nunca ha estado en Londres

    (C) Porque es resbaladizo

    (D) Porque su pierna todavía está rota

14. ¿A dónde va Ana a la universidad?

    (A) La Universidad Óxford

    (B) la Universidad de Cambridge

    (C) Alaska

    (D) El palacio de Buckingham

15. ¿Qué lugar NO visitó Ana en Londres?

    (A) Las Casas del Parlamento

    (B) El río Támesis

    (C) Los museos

    (D) La catedral de San Pablo

16. ¿Qué piensa Ana de la cafetería?

    (A) Que son baratas, pero la comida sabe mal

    (B) Que son caras, pero le gusta mucho la comida

    (C) Que son caras, pero la comida sabe mal

    (D) Que son baratas, pero la comida es deliciosa

17. ¿Dónde sugiere Ana que su abuelo la encuentre el próximo año?

    (A) California

    (B) Alaska

    (C) Londres

    (D) Oregón

18. ¿Por qué Ana no ingresó al curso de arte artesenal?

    (A) Porque quería tomar un curso de arte moderno

    (B) Porque la clase no tenía espacio

    (C) Porque quería cambiar de carrera

    (D) Porque la clase era aburrida

19. Se puede inferir que Ana enviará más cartas en el futuro porque

    (A) menciona que va a enviar dibujos

    (B) menciona que visitará el Palacio de Buckingham

    (C) menciona que las cafeterías tienen buena comida

    (D) menciona que extraña a su abuelo

GO ON TO THE NEXT PAGE.

Selección número 4

Introducción

El siguiente sitio de Internet trata de El Sistema, el programa nacional de Venezuela que comparte la música con niños desfavorecidos. El sitio apareció en mayo de 2003.

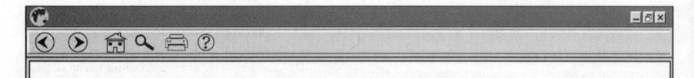

Tocar, Cantar y Luchar

Fundado en 1975 por maestro Dr. José Antonio Abreu, El Sistema Nacional de Orquestas y Coros Juveniles e Infantiles de Venezuela empezó en un garaje con 11 niños. Hoy en día, el programa, afectuosamente llamado "El Sistema", sirve a más que 500 mil estudiantes desfavorecidos en Venezuela y continúa crecer. Además, más de 42 países habían creado programas inspirados por El Sistema, entre ellos Argentina, Australia, Austria, Bolivia, Brasil, Canadá, Chile, Colombia, Corea del Sur, Costa Rica, Cuba, Ecuador, El Salvador, Escocia, los Estados Unidos, Francia, Guatemala, Honduras, India, Inglaterra, Italia, Jamaica, Japón, México, Nicaragua, Panamá, Paraguay, Perú, Portugal, Puerto Rico, la República Dominicana, Trinidad y Tobago, y Uruguay.

El Sistema en Venezuela enseña la música a través de instrucción individual y colectiva a niños tan jóvenes como 2 y 3 años de edad, y combina estas lecciones con participación en orquestas o coros infantiles y juveniles. En cada programa, las orquestas tienen más importancia que solamente compartir la música clásica: son dedicadas a la prevención de deserción escolar y la reducción del crimen en las ciudades. En un estudio, la tasa de abandono escolar ha disminuido desde 6,9% en estudiantes involucrados en El Sistema, comparado al 26,4% del grupo de control. También, se puede ver el gran impacto de El Sistema en las tasas reducidas de analfabetismo, marginalidad y exclusión en la población joven e infantil en Venezuela.

Los niños y sus padres son parte de la comunidad social en El Sistema que enfatiza la importancia del desarrollo del ser humano. Esta población de 500 mil niños y jóvenes venezolanos se distribuye en aproximadamente 285 orquestas preinfantiles (entre 4 y 6 años), 220 orquestas infantiles (entre 7 y 16 años), 180 orquestas juveniles (entre 16 y 22 años), 30 orquestas profesionales, 360 agrupaciones corales, 1.355 agrupaciones corales afiliadas y más de 15.000 profesores en todas partes del país. Los profesores les enseñan a los niños a "tocar, cantar y luchar" para vencer los obstáculos de la pobreza y perseguir la educación formal.

Aquí en los Estados Unidos, hay muchos programas extracurriculares inspirados por El Sistema en Venezuela que promueven el cambio social en lugares con pocos recursos. El NAESIP (National Alliance of El Sistema-Inspired Programs) da a los niños en estas comunidades las herramientas para superar los obstáculos de la pobreza y para descubrir la importancia de educación. "He pensado siempre que la enseñanza de la música desde la más tierna infancia es una tarea hermosísima y crucial de toda sociedad. Esto es un ideal de la educación desde hace muchísimos siglos: la música forma parte del desarrollo espiritual y la conciencia y la formación estética del hombre", dice el maestro Abreu.

GO ON TO THE NEXT PAGE.

20. ¿Qué significa el título "Tocar, Cantar y Luchar"?

(A) El Sistema enseña a los niños a luchar por su derecho a la educación y para superar la pobreza.

(B) El Sistema enseña a los niños a luchar entre sí.

(C) "Tocar y cantar" es una metáfora de la lucha en los países latinoamericanos.

(D) Muchas veces los niños se pelean con sus padres.

21. ¿De qué se trata este artículo?

(A) Hay un gran problema del analfabetismo, la pobreza y la marginalidad en Venezuela y en otras partes del mundo.

(B) El Sistema ha creado un ambiente positivo para los niños involucrados, y otros países han creado programas de afiliados con el fin de mejorar las vidas de los niños desfavorecidos.

(C) Todos los niños que participan en El Sistema tienen éxito con los estudios de música.

(D) El NAESIP es la extensión de El Sistema en los Estados Unidos, también fundado por Maestro Abreu.

22. ¿Cómo ha cambiado la tasa de deserción escolar en Venezuela?

(A) La tasa de deserción escolar ha aumentado en los estudiantes que no participan en El Sistema.

(B) La tasa de abandono escolar ha crecido mientras la tasa de analfabeto ha disminuido.

(C) La tasa de deserción escolar ha disminuido mientras la tasa de criminalidad ha aumentado en las zonas urbanas.

(D) La tasa de deserción escolar ha disminuido, en comparación con los estudiantes que no están involucrados en El Sistema.

23. Se menciona las 285 orquestas pre-infantiles, 220 orquestas infantiles, 180 orquestas juveniles y otras para

(A) demostrar cómo El Sistema ha crecido en Venezuela con más de 500 mil participantes

(B) enfatizar que a los estudiantes les gustan las orquestas y los coros

(C) ilustrar que los programas en otros países han crecido muchísimo como resultado de su inspiración de El Sistema

(D) contrastar cómo El Sistema comenzó en un garaje y explicar cómo sus orquestas han reducido las tasas del analfabetismo

24. En el último párrafo, incluye la cita de Abreu para

(A) demostrar que Dr. Abreu fue el maestro del año en 2013 porque ha dado oportunidades a muchos niños en Venezuela

(B) probar que los niños de El Sistema han cambiado el mundo

(C) ilustrar la importancia de la educación a través de música

(D) dar un ejemplo de una tarea hermosísima que es parte de la educación spiritual

GO ON TO THE NEXT PAGE.

Selección número 5

Introducción

Las siguientes son unos anuncios clasificados en la prensa peruana.

LA COCINA DE TOMAS
RESTAURANTE * CLUB DE BAILE

28 Elf Street, Lee, MA * 432-888-9090

El lugar mas lindo, original y lujoso de Massachusetts.

Comida Hispana con especialidad en: ¡empanadas y margaritas!

¡Venga a probar uno o todos los platos en el menú y quédese a bailar! ¡Música Latina para todos y mucho mas!

¡Abierto todo los días desde las 12 P.M. hasta amanecer!

¡Tenemos muchos grupos musicales que tocan todos los viernes!

La Cocina de Tomas presenta:

Junio 13: Orquesta Orlando—música de Argentina y Colombia
Junio 20: Los Lobos Locos—Mariachi
Junio 27: María Luz Roca—la Cantante Mejicana
Julio 4: Los Independientes—¡un grupo local que viene a festejar el día de la Independencia Americana!
¡Compre 2 entradas antes del 4 de julio y reciba una margarita gratis!

¡Reserve hoy!
Mesas y asientos limitados.

---

25. ¿Que tipo de lugar es La Cocina de Tomas?

   (A) Cocina

   (B) Restaurante

   (C) Restaurante y bar

   (D) Restaurante y lugar de baile

26. ¿Quiénes son Los Independientes?

   (A) Grupo musical de Argentina

   (B) Grupo musical de los Estados Unidos

   (C) Grupo musical local

   (D) Grupo musical que festeja todo

27. ¿Cuándo hay que reservar y por que?

   (A) Cuando se pueda porque hay muchas mesas

   (B) Después de amanecer porque si no están cerrados

   (C) Después de el 4 de julio porque es un día feriado

   (D) Inmediatamente porque no hay mucho lugar

28. ¿Cómo se describe el establecimiento?

   (A) Lujoso

   (B) Feo

   (C) Famoso

   (D) Lejano

29. ¿A que hora cerraría La Cocina de Tomas?

   (A) 12:00 A.M.

   (B) 2:00 A.M.

   (C) 6:00 A.M.

   (D) 12:00 P.M.

30. ¿Hay alguna ventaja por comprar las entradas temprano?

   (A) Si, pero hay que comprarlas el 4 de julio.

   (B) Si, pero hay que comprarlas antes del 4 de julio.

   (C) No, no hay ventaja.

   (D) No, no hay ninguna oferta especial.

GO ON TO THE NEXT PAGE.

Part B

Interpretive Communication: Print and Audio Texts (combined)

You will listen to several audio selections. The first two audio selections are accompanied by reading selections. When there is a reading selection, you will have a designated amount of time to read it.

For each audio selection, first you will have a designated amount of time to read a preview of the selection as well as to skim the questions that you will be asked. Each selection will be played twice. As you listen to each selection, you may take notes. Your notes will not be scored.

After listening to each selection the first time, you will have 1 minute to begin answering the questions; after listening to each selection the second time, you will have 15 seconds per question to finish answering the questions. For each question, choose the response that is best according to the audio and/or reading selection and mark your answer on your answer sheet.

Vas a escuchar varias grabaciones. Las dos primeras grabaciones van acompañadas de lecturas. Cuando haya una lectura, vas a tener un tiempo determinado para leerla.

Para cada grabación, primero vas a tener un tiempo determinado para leer la introducción y prever las preguntas. Vas a escuchar cada grabación dos veces. Mientras escuchas, puedes tomar apuntes. Tus apuntes no van a ser calificados.

Después de escuchar cada selección por primera vez, vas a tener un minuto para empezar a contestar las preguntas; después de escuchar por segunda vez, vas a tener 15 segundos por pregunta para terminarlas. Para cada pregunta, elige la mejor respuesta según la grabación o el texto e indícala en la hoja de respuestas.

GO ON TO THE NEXT PAGE.

Selección número 1

Fuente número 1

Primero tienes 4 minutos para leer la fuente número 1.

Introducción

Solo cerca de 20% de los estudiantes en los Estados Unidos elijen aprender un segundo idioma mientras que, en lugares como Europa, la cifra es cerca a 90% de los estudiantes. El siguiente blog apareció en el sitio de internet oficial de la red de universidades Anáhuac.

¿Por qué es importante dominar un segundo idioma?

Hablar un segundo idioma abre la puerta a muchas oportunidades personales y profesionales, por eso, hoy las personas que dominan más de un idioma reciben más y mejores ofertas laborales.

La globalización de la educación, los mercados y el mundo en general exige a las personas a prepararse mucho más que hace tan solo unas décadas y el dominio de otro idioma diferente al materno se ha vuelto indispensable para desarrollarse y destacar a nivel profesional.

Además de brindar beneficios en el ámbito laboral, se ha comprobado que las personas bilingües presentan habilidades superiores a aquellas personas que solo se comunican en un solo idioma. Aunque el inglés es la lengua preferida por los estudiantes, hay otros idiomas que también han comenzado a volverse relevantes en el plano mundial.

¿Cuáles son las ventajas y desventajas de estudiar los siguientes idiomas?

- Inglés: hablado en los cinco continentes y por las naciones potencia, el inglés es considerado el idioma internacional, ya que es el más usado en los negocios y el comercio internacional. La mayoría de las universidades piden como requerimiento para graduarse el manejo avanzado de esta lengua.

- Francés: con más de 200 millones de personas francófonas en todo el mundo, esta es la segunda lengua más estudiada después del inglés. Su importancia radica en que organismos internacionales, como la ONU, el Comité Olímpico y la FIFA, lo consideran como idioma oficial. Considera que como hablante del español, este idioma es más fácil de aprender.

- Chino Mandarín: el acelerado crecimiento de China en el plano de los negocios a nivel mundial ha convertido a este idioma en una indispensable herramienta de intercambio profesional y se coloca como el idioma del futuro laboral. Al ser hablado por más de mil millones de personas es el idioma más hablado en el mundo.

- Portugués: el portugués es el sexto idioma más hablado en el mundo y por su historial político resulta una de las lenguas más interesantes de aprender. Además de abrir puertas laborales a mercados de Latinoamérica y Europa, el portugués ayuda a explorar una cultura muy amplia que a veces es olvidada.

Beneficios de hablar un segundo idioma

No importa a qué edad se aprende un idioma, si desde la niñez o ya siendo adulto, se ha comprobado que ser bilingüe es beneficial para el desarrollo cognitivo de las personas, ya que mejora la flexibilidad, memoria y habilidad del cerebro.

Los principales beneficios de aprender un nuevo idioma son:

Mejor toma de decisiones. Un cerebro que sabe moverse rápidamente entre dos idiomas es uno que tiene facilidad para analizar varias situaciones simultáneas, una habilidad indispensable para tomar mejores decisiones.

Aumento de la memoria. Conocer dos o más idiomas requiere de mucha dedicación, atención a los detalles y, más importante, una memoria activa y eficiente que logre retener una gran cantidad de información.

Reduce la posibilidad de enfermedades mentales. Los médicos han descubierto que las personas bilingües fortalecen su cerebro, lo cual provoca que se reduzca la posibilidad y los efectos de padecer enfermedades mentales como Alzheimer y demencia.

Crecimiento profesional. Uno de los requisitos más demandados en el ámbito laboral es el dominio de un segundo idioma. Los profesionales bilingües son reconocidos por su preparación con mejores puestos y mayores salarios.

GO ON TO THE NEXT PAGE.

Fuente número 2

Tienes 2 minutos para leer la introducción y prever las preguntas.

Introducción

Esta grabación trata del aprendizaje en línea. Los siguientes entrevistados comparten sus opiniones sobre aprender segundo idioma. La grabación dura aproximadamente tres minutos.

Ahora escucha la fuente número dos.

> **PLAY AUDIO: Track 14**

Ahora tienes un minuto para empezar a responder a las preguntas para esta selección. Después de un minuto, vas a escuchar la grabación de nuevo.

(1 minute)

Ahora escucha de nuevo.

> **PLAY AUDIO: Track 14**

Ahora termina de responder a las preguntas para esta selección.

31. ¿Cuál es uno de los beneficios principales de hablar un segundo idioma de acuerdo con el artículo?

    (A) Mejora la habilidad de retener grandes cantidades de información eficientemente.

    (B) Te hace una persona más interesante en el trabajo.

    (C) Te garantiza un trabajo con un mejor puesto y un mejor salario.

    (D) Siempre tomarás las mejores decisiones, rápidamente, en cualquier situación.

32. El artículo menciona que el idioma preferido por los estudiantes es

    (A) el inglés

    (B) el francés

    (C) el italiano

    (D) el chino mandarín

33. Se menciona "la globalización" para

    (A) hablar sobre los diferentes países en el mundo, y todos sus diferentes idiomas

    (B) demostrar que el inglés es el idioma mas usado en los negocios internacionalmente

    (C) ilustrar que la globalización es la causa por la cual es requisito aprender un segundo idioma en las escuelas

    (D) enfatizar lo indispensable que es el dominio de un idioma diferente al materno para el desarrollo a nivel profesional

34. ¿Por qué se menciona "la ONU, el Comité Olímpico, y la FIFA"?

    (A) Muestra organismos internacionales que sólo hablan francés.

    (B) Muestra organismos internacionales que consideran el francés como su idioma oficial.

    (C) Muestra que el francés es el idioma más importante en la lista.

    (D) Muestra que las personas que saben francés también aman los deportes.

GO ON TO THE NEXT PAGE.

35. ¿Cuál de las afirmaciones mejor resume este artículo?

    (A) Si no aprendes segundo idioma, no podrás participar en negocios internacionales.

    (B) Las personas que dominan más de un solo idioma tendrán más éxito en el mundo laboral que las personas que dominan solo un idioma.

    (C) Aprender segundo idioma provee muchos beneficios como mejores oportunidades laborales y mejor memoria, y puede reducir la posibilidad de enfermedades mentales.

    (D) Aprender un segundo idioma debería ser requisito en todas las escuelas alrededor del mundo.

36. Según la fuente auditiva, ¿cuál es la opinión de los entrevistados?

    (A) Los que conocen otro idioma lo aprecian, y aprovechan de sus beneficios, mientras que los que hablan un solo idioma no sienten que es necesario aprender otro idioma.

    (B) Todos los entrevistados opinan que aprender segundo idioma debería ser obligatorio.

    (C) Todos los entrevistados prefieren aprender inglés.

    (D) Ninguno de los entrevistados es bilingüe.

37. Según la fuente auditiva, cuando Edgar Suárez era niño, intentó aprender

    (A) francés

    (B) italiano

    (C) inglés

    (D) chino mandarín

38. Ana Cálix prefiere enfocarse en

    (A) conseguir un trabajo

    (B) cursos relevantes a lo que estudiará en la universidad

    (C) aprender muchos idiomas

    (D) pasar más tiempo con sus amigos y familia

39. ¿Quién aprendió japonés?

    (A) Jonathan Castro

    (B) Edgar Suárez

    (C) Ana Cálix

    (D) Paola Hernández

GO ON TO THE NEXT PAGE.

Selección número 2

Fuente número 1
Primero tienes 4 minutos para leer la fuente número 1.

Introducción
Este artículo apareció en el sitio de Web theconversation.com, y trata de la reciente popularidad de los "booktubers", y su efecto positivo en las comunidades de lectores de libros.

Hablar de libros en video: una habilidad con un futuro brillante

Los *booktubers* se encargan de hacer vídeos sobre libros y lecturas con diferentes formatos: *Book hauls* (compras de libros), *Wrap ups* (resúmenes de libros), *Shelf tours* (recorridos por los libros disponibles). Es decir, exponen los libros que poseen, exhiben sus últimas adquisiciones, formulan sus recomendaciones, lanzan sus críticas, etc. De esta forma, despiertan el gusto e interés por la lectura en una generación muy acostumbrada a recibir este tipo de contenido prescriptivo en forma de video.

¿Aprender a ser *booktuber*?

El proyecto se estructuró en tres grandes bloques:
Fase 1. Los estudiantes debían asumir el papel de booktubers
Fase 2. En la segunda parte del proyecto los estudiantes pasaron de ser booktubers a ser narradores digitales.
Fase 3. Trabajo escrito que engloba la totalidad del proceso de aprendizaje.

Alta satisfacción y motivación

Tras el desarrollo de este proyecto, se analizaron las respuestas de 145 estudiantes que, de forma anónima, contestaron un cuestionario creado ad hoc.

De acuerdo con los datos, el 80% de los encuestados no conocía el fenómeno del booktubing y más del 90% afirmó que su interés por este tipo de recursos se había incrementado. Más del 90% de los participantes terminó muy satisfecho con el resultado de su práctica y les gustó compartir sus vídeos con el grupo de clase. Todo ello repercutió en que más del 95% de los estudiantes manifestara que el gusto por la lectura de literatura infantil se había incrementado.

Competencias de comunicación

Además de la competencia específica sobre literatura, nuestros estudiantes también desarrollaron con esta actividad sus competencias lingüísticas y comunicativas.

Así, más del 90% expresó que con la elaboración de ambos vídeos prestó más atención de la habitual a la forma de expresarse verbalmente. Más del 85% explicó que también observaron con detalle su lenguaje no verbal.

Aliados digitales, no enemigos

En este caso, gracias a las actividades planteadas a partir de creación de contenido en vídeo, los estudiantes no solo han mejorado su competencia literaria, sino que también han desarrollado habilidades de expresión y comprensión (oral y escrita), y han activado su creatividad. Asimismo, han ampliado sus conocimientos sobre narraciones infantiles y han leído, comprendido, interpretado y valorado textos narrativos literarios para este ciclo.

De esta manera, no solamente podemos respondernos que sí, queda espacio para la lectura en la vida actual, sino que además podemos ampliar y mejorar ese espacio con vídeo (vídeorreseña o videonarración). El vídeo puede ser la llave de entrada al mundo apasionante de la literatura.

GO ON TO THE NEXT PAGE.

Fuente número 2

Tienes 2 minutos para leer la introducción y prever las preguntas.

Introducción

Esta grabación auditiva es de una conversación entre Melvin y Regina sobre el tema de los booktubers.

Ahora escucha la fuente número dos.

PLAY AUDIO: Track 15

Ahora tienes un minuto para empezar a responder a las preguntas para esta selección. Después de un minuto, vas a escuchar la grabación de nuevo.

(1 minute)

Ahora escucha de nuevo.

PLAY AUDIO: Track 15

Ahora termina de responder a las preguntas para esta selección.

40. ¿Cuál es el propósito del artículo y de las estadísticas?

(A) Hablar sobre como las redes digitales han destruido el interés por los libros y la lectura

(B) Demostrar un método de aprendizaje que puede aumentar la motivación, el interés, y el gusto por el hábito de la lectura en los participantes

(C) Demostrar que recibir contenido en forma de video siempre es mejor que leer un libro

(D) Hablar sobre cómo ser un booktuber profesional

41. ¿Cuál de las siguientes afirmaciones mejor describe a los "booktubers"?

(A) Son personas que leen libros mientras se graban.

(B) Personas que recrean escenas enteras de libros en un video estilo película.

(C) Son personas que consumen libros en forma audiovisual exclusivamente.

(D) Son personas que, en forma de video, exponen los libros que poseen, exhiben sus últimas adquisiciones, formulan recomendaciones, lanzan críticas, etc.

42. De acuerdo con los datos, ¿qué efecto tuvo el proyecto de "aprender a ser booktuber"?

(A) Sólo 20% de los participantes demostraron un aumento en interés por este tipo de recurso.

(B) Más de 90% de los participantes demostró un aumento en interés por este tipo de recurso.

(C) No se observó ningún efecto significativo al culminar este proyecto.

(D) Más de 90% de los participantes pasaron a ser booktubers profesionales luego de culminar este proyecto.

43. De acuerdo con el artículo, ¿sigue quedando espacio para la lectura?

(A) Si, queda espacio para la lectura, pero solo en escuelas y grupos de lecturas.

(B) No, ya que el video ha reemplazado la lectura.

(C) Si, queda espacio para la lectura, y podemos mejorar ese espacio con video.

(D) No, los libros ocupan mucho espacio, y es muy inconveniente leer en forma digital.

GO ON TO THE NEXT PAGE.

44. De acuerdo con la fuente auditiva, ¿qué efecto tuvieron los booktubers para Melvin?

   (A) Los libros le parecen más interesantes a Melvin, los lee más a menudo, ylos booktubers lo ayudan a descubrir libros nuevos.

   (B) Los encuentra aburridos ya que a Melvin no le gusta leer libros.

   (C) Melvin se divierte haciendo asignaciones, y las completa más rápidamente.

   (D) No tuvieron ningún efecto para Melvin.

45. ¿Cuál es el género de libros que prefiere leer Regina?

   (A) Ciencia Ficción

   (B) Romance

   (C) Aventura

   (D) Misterio

46. ¿Cómo podrían ayudar los booktubers para completar asignaciones de lecturas?

   (A) Te pueden brindar una perspectiva diferente sobre el libro.

   (B) Te permiten completar las asignaciones sin tener que leer el libro.

   (C) Puedes copiar las palabras de los booktubers en tu asignación sin brindar referencias.

   (D) Son una buena distracción para cuando necesitas un descanso de las asignaciones.

47. ¿Cuál es la intención de Melvin en la fuente auditiva?

   (A) Intenta convencer a Regina a consumir el contenido de los booktubers.

   (B) Comparte su experiencia personal con los booktubers para ayudar a Regina a descubrir cómo pueden ser útil en su vida.

   (C) Sólo busca hacer conversación; a Melvin no le importan mucho los booktubers.

   (D) Expresa cómo los libros de misterio también son sus favoritos.

GO ON TO THE NEXT PAGE.

Interpretive Communication: Audio Texts

Selección número 3

Introducción

Primero tienes un minuto para leer la introducción y prever las preguntas.

La siguiente grabación trata sobre como un grupo de mujeres en Lima, Perú se organizó para brindar alimentos a una comunidad con pocos recursos.

Ahora escucha la selección.

PLAY AUDIO: Track 16

Ahora tienes un minuto para empezar a responder a las preguntas para esta selección. Después de un minuto, vas a escuchar la grabación de nuevo.

(1 minute)

Ahora escucha de nuevo.

PLAY AUDIO: Track 16

Ahora termina de responder a las preguntas para esta selección.

48. ¿Qué es "Mi ángel poderoso"?

    (A) Una entidad divina que protege a los habitantes de Cerrito La Libertad

    (B) Apodo que se le dio al esposo de una de las cocineras que las ayuda a levantar las bolsas de arroz

    (C) Una olla común que alimenta a cerca de 100 personas de la comunidad

    (D) Un hospital en Perú

49. ¿Qué características resaltan en esta comunidad?

    (A) Hay mucha riqueza y abundancia.

    (B) Es un lugar muy plano, no hay colinas.

    (C) Carece de recursos como electricidad, desagüe, y luz.

    (D) Allí solo viven 100 personas.

50. ¿Para qué se organizó "Mi ángel poderoso"?

    (A) Para recaudar fondos que pagarán los estudios de los hijos de Giovanna

    (B) Para poner en marcha una solución que frenara la carencia alimentaria de la comunidad

    (C) Para ser el mejor restaurante de Perú

    (D) Se organizó con la intención de vender el negocio.

51. ¿Quién es Giovanna Ávila Ñaupari?

    (A) Alcaldesa de Chosica

    (B) La única que cocina entre las mujeres de "Mi ángel poderoso"

    (C) Una donadora independiente de "Mi ángel poderoso"

    (D) Presidenta de "Mi ángel poderoso"

52. ¿Cuál es el propósito de esta grabación?

    (A) Atraer el turismo a Cerrito La Libertad

    (B) Promover a la olla común "Mi ángel poderoso" y sus contribuciones a la comunidad

    (C) Vendernos comida típica

    (D) Informarnos sobre las condiciones de Cerrito La Libertad

GO ON TO THE NEXT PAGE.

Selección número 4

Introducción

Primero tienes un minuto para leer la introducción y prever las preguntas.

La siguiente grabación trata sobre los beneficios de la terapia y varias personas comparten sus experiencias.

Ahora escucha la selección.

PLAY AUDIO: Track 17

Ahora tienes un minuto para empezar a responder a las preguntas para esta selección. Después de un minuto, vas a escuchar la grabación de nuevo.

(1 minute)

Ahora escucha de nuevo.

PLAY AUDIO: Track 17

Ahora termina de responder a las preguntas para esta selección.

53. ¿Por qué la terapia era un tema tabú en el pasado?

  (A) La terapia es solo para personas con traumas graves.

  (B) La terapia no funciona para muchas personas.

  (C) Los terapeutas son muy extremos con sus filosofías y prácticas.

  (D) Las personas se sentían avergonzadas de buscar ayuda profesional para sus problemas emocionales o de relación.

54. ¿Cómo se ha vuelto más accesible y menos tabú la terapia para el mundo en general?

  (A) El avance de la ciencia y las investigaciones sobre la salud mental han logrado mas aceptación de la terapia.

  (B) Las celebridades y personalidades públicas que comparten sus experiencias han hecho más claro el proceso.

  (C) La disponibilidad de la terapia vía videollamadas permite sesiones de terapia remotamente.

  (D) Todas estas respuestas son correctas.

55. De acuerdo con Dave, ¿qué es un malentendido común sobre la terapia?

  (A) Los terapeutas no entienden tus problemas.

  (B) La terapia es sólo para casos emocionales.

  (C) La terapia es difícil para los pacientes.

  (D) Los pacientes pierden el tiempo.

56. ¿Cuál es el tono de María cuando habla sobre su experiencia?

  (A) Nostalgia

  (B) Frustración

  (C) Arrepentimiento

  (D) Agradecimiento

57. ¿Qué recomienda Matt a todos sus amigos?

  (A) Que escojan la misma oficina de terapia que él

  (B) Que escojan específicamente a Dave como terapeuta

  (C) Que intenten terapia, aunque no piensen que lo necesiten

  (D) Que intenten resolver sus propios problemas sin ayuda profesional

GO ON TO THE NEXT PAGE.

Selección número 5

Introducción

Primero tienes un minuto para leer la introducción y prever las preguntas.

La siguiente grabación trata del Día de los Reyes Magos y los costumbres diferentes respeto a este día que en algunos paises hispanohablantes se llama "la segunda Navidad".

Ahora escucha la selección.

> **PLAY AUDIO: Track 18**

Ahora tienes un minuto para empezar a responder a las preguntas para esta selección. Después de un minuto, vas a escuchar la grabación de nuevo.

(1 minute)

Ahora escucha de nuevo.

> **PLAY AUDIO: Track 18**

Ahora termina de responder a las preguntas para esta selección.

58. ¿Cuál mejor resume esta grabación?
    - (A) Provee detalles y tradiciones relacionados al Día de los Reyes Magos con la intención de educar.
    - (B) Intenta ilustrar que el Día de los Reyes Magos es una copia de la Navidad.
    - (C) Indica que los niños malos no reciben regalos.
    - (D) Habla sobre la Navidad en países hispanos.

59. De acuerdo con la grabación, ¿qué es el Día de los Reyes Magos?
    - (A) Un día en el cual se conmemora la llegada de los tres Reyes Magos a Belén para adorar y traer regalos al niño Jesús
    - (B) Un día para comer y festejar
    - (C) Un día para celebrar los reyes del pasado de España
    - (D) Un día para prolongar las celebraciones de la Navidad hasta el año nuevo

60. ¿Dónde se celebra comúnmente el Día de los Reyes Magos?
    - (A) En Europa
    - (B) En los Estados Unidos
    - (C) En las iglesias
    - (D) En países de habla hispana

61. Tradicionalmente, ¿cómo se preparan los niños para la llegada de los Reyes Magos?
    - (A) Abren todas las ventanas de la casa para que puedan entrar los Reyes Magos.
    - (B) Dejan zapatos vacíos en la ventana o debajo de la cama.
    - (C) Dejan leche y galletas en la sala de la casa.
    - (D) Decoran el patio con luces de muchos colores diferentes.

62. ¿En qué fecha se celebra el Día de los Reyes?
    - (A) El 26 de diciembre
    - (B) El primer sábado de enero
    - (C) El 6 de enero
    - (D) El 2 de enero

63. ¿Dónde dejan los regalos los Reyes Magos?
    - (A) En la entrada de la casa
    - (B) En el cuarto de los padres
    - (C) Dentro y alrededor de los zapatos
    - (D) En la chimenea

GO ON TO THE NEXT PAGE.

64. ¿Qué descripción brinda el audio para el roscón de reyes?

 (A) Una tuerca que le dejan los reyes a los niños malos en vez de regalos

 (B) Un pastel dulce hecho con harina, azúcar, y esencias de limón y anís

 (C) El nombre de uno de los camellos

 (D) Un banquete especial para los reyes

65. ¿Por qué se le llama al Día de los Reyes Magos "segunda Navidad"?

 (A) Porque Santa regresa el 6 de enero con mas regalos navideños

 (B) Por que es exactamente como la Navidad

 (C) Por que hay mucha nieve y comida navideña

 (D) Por las similitudes a algunas tradiciones navideñas, y porque los niños reciben regalos una segunda vez dentro de dos semanas

END OF SECTION I

IF YOU FINISH BEFORE TIME IS CALLED, YOU MAY CHECK YOUR WORK ON THIS SECTION.

SPANISH LANGUAGE AND CULTURE

SECTION II

Time—88 minutes

50% of total grade

Question 1: Email Reply

| You will write a reply to an email message. You will have 15 minutes to read the message and write your reply. | Vas a escribir una respuesta a un mensaje electrónico. Vas a tener 15 minutos para leer el mensaje y escribir tu respuesta. |
| Your reply should include a greeting and a closing, and should respond to all the questions and requests in the message. In your reply, you should also ask for more details about something mentioned in the message. Also, you should use a formal form of address. | Tu respuesta debe incluir un saludo y una despedida, y debe responder a todas las preguntas y peticiones del mensaje. En tu respuesta, debes pedir más información sobre algo mencionado en el mensaje. También debes responder de una manera informal. |

Introducción

Este mensaje trata sobre planes para vacaciones con un grupo de amigos. Ha recibido este correo electrónico por una reciente conversación con un grupo de tus amigos sobre viajar a un lugar nuevo para las vacaciones.

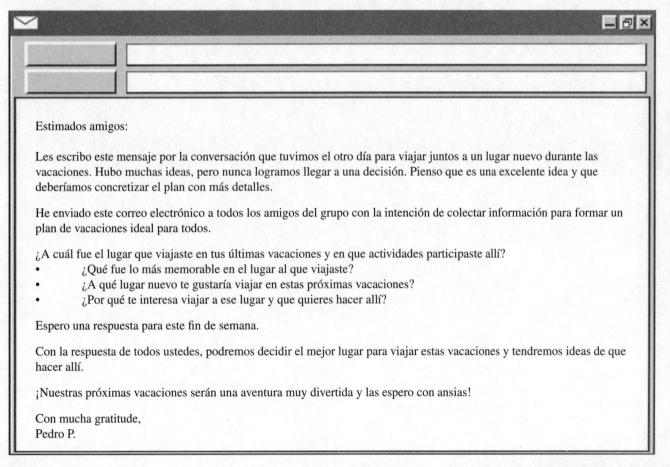

Estimados amigos:

Les escribo este mensaje por la conversación que tuvimos el otro día para viajar juntos a un lugar nuevo durante las vacaciones. Hubo muchas ideas, pero nunca logramos llegar a una decisión. Pienso que es una excelente idea y que deberíamos concretizar el plan con más detalles.

He enviado este correo electrónico a todos los amigos del grupo con la intención de colectar información para formar un plan de vacaciones ideal para todos.

¿A cuál fue el lugar que viajaste en tus últimas vacaciones y en que actividades participaste allí?
- ¿Qué fue lo más memorable en el lugar al que viajaste?
- ¿A qué lugar nuevo te gustaría viajar en estas próximas vacaciones?
- ¿Por qué te interesa viajar a ese lugar y que quieres hacer allí?

Espero una respuesta para este fin de semana.

Con la respuesta de todos ustedes, podremos decidir el mejor lugar para viajar estas vacaciones y tendremos ideas de que hacer allí.

¡Nuestras próximas vacaciones serán una aventura muy divertida y las espero con ansias!

Con mucha gratitude,
Pedro P.

GO ON TO THE NEXT PAGE.

Question 2: Argumentative Essay

You will write an argumentative essay to submit to a Spanish writing contest. The essay topic is based on three accompanying sources, which present different viewpoints on the topic and include both print and audio material. First, you will have 6 minutes to read the essay topic and the printed material. Afterward, you will hear the audio material twice; you should take notes while you listen. Then, you will have 40 minutes to prepare and write your essay.

In an argumentative essay, you should present the sources' different viewpoints on the topic, and also clearly indicate your own viewpoint and defend it thoroughly. Use information from all of the sources to support your essay. As you refer to the sources, identify them appropriately. Also, organize your essay into clear paragraphs.

Vas a escribir un ensayo persuasivo para un concurso de redacción en español. El tema del ensayo se basa en las tres fuentes adjuntas, que presentan diferentes puntos de vista sobre el tema e incluyen material escrito y grabado. Primero, vas a tener 6 minutos para leer el tema del ensayo y los textos. Después, vas a escuchar la grabación dos veces; debes tomar apuntes mientras escuchas. Luego vas a tener 40 minutos para preparar y escribir tu ensayo.

En un ensayo persuasivo, debes presentar los diferentes puntos de vista de las fuentes sobre el tema, expresar tu propio punto de vista y apoyarlo. Usa información de todas las fuentes para apoyar tu punto de vista. Al referirte a las fuentes, identifícalas apropiadamente. Organiza también el ensayo en distintos párrafos bien desarrollados.

Tema del ensayo:

Cuál es la importancia de la alfabetización cultural y cómo podemos educarnos más en esta área?

GO ON TO THE NEXT PAGE.

Fuente número 1

Introducción

Este artículo apareció en el sitio web theconversation.com en enero de 2023.

Alfabetización Cultural en la Era Digital

Cada vez es más frecuente utilizar internet para una gran diversidad de actividades. Antes, lo más común era pagar un café con monedas. Hoy nuestro móvil tiene NFC (Near Field Communicaction) y una aplicación de pago que facilita esta acción. Incluso el móvil es el pasado: ahora se utiliza un reloj inteligente (smartwatch). La cultura digital se impone, cambia la vida personal y colectiva.

La alfabetización es el proceso de aprender a leer y escribir. La cultura es el "conjunto de modos de vida y costumbres, conocimientos y grado de desarrollo artístico, científico, industrial, en una época, grupo social".

La alfabetización cultural se refiere a la adquisición de las habilidades necesarias para comprender una determinada cultura los códigos culturales compartidos en sociedad.

Umberto Eco, refiriéndose a la cultura en De la estupidez a la locura, afirmó que "no es solo una acumulación de datos, es también el resultado de su filtrado". Es decir, "la cultura es asimismo la capacidad de desprenderse de lo que no es útil o necesario".

La alfabetización cultural se propone incentivar el acceso a la cultura en condiciones de igualdad. Es un planteamiento que busca reforzar y afianzar una ciudadanía más responsable. Tras él está la idea de una sociedad comprometida, culta y crítica que ponga en valor su libertad.

GO ON TO THE NEXT PAGE.

Fuente número 2

Introducción

Los siguientes datos aparecieron en el sitio web ine.es.

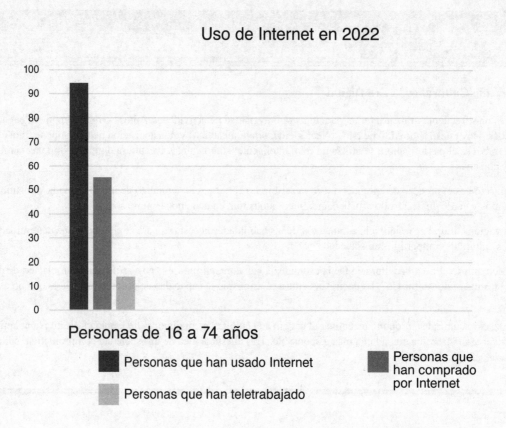

Uso de Internet en 2022

Personas de 16 a 74 años

- ■ Personas que han usado Internet
- ■ Personas que han teletrabajado
- ■ Personas que han comprado por Internet

Fuente número 3

Tienes 30 segundos para leer la introducción.

Introducción

La siguiente grabación es de un "podcast" llamado "Marco Talks" donde el anfitrión Marco tiene una conversación con su invitada Alexandra Melendez sobre la alfabetización cultural.

Ahora escucha la fuente número tres.

PLAY AUDIO: Track 19

Ahora escucha de nuevo.

PLAY AUDIO: Track 19

Ahora tienes cuarenta minutos para preparar y escribir un ensayo persuasivo.

(40 minutes)

GO ON TO THE NEXT PAGE.

Question 3: Conversation

You will participate in a conversation. First, you will have 1 minute to read a preview of the conversation, including an outline of each turn in the conversation. Afterward, the conversation will begin, following the outline. Each time it is your turn to speak, you will have 20 seconds to record your response. You should participate in the conversation as fully and appropriately as possible.	Vas a participar en una conversación. Primero, vas a tener un minuto para leer la introducción y el esquema de la conversación. Después, comenzará la conversación, siguiendo el esquema. Cada vez que te corresponda participar en la conversación, vas a tener 20 segundos para grabar tu respuesta. Debes participar de la manera más completa y apropiada posible.

Tienes un minuto para leer la introducción.

Introducción

Estás hablando con tu amiga Carla acerca de mudarse juntos. Carla está buscando entre las opciones y tiene unas preguntas que le ayudarán a escoger la casa o apartamento ideal para mudarse.

PLAY AUDIO: Track 20

Carla	Te saluda
Tú	Contesta la pregunta
Carla	Te hace una pregunta
Tú	Responde a la pregunta
Carla	Continúa la conversación
Tú	Responde a la pregunta
Carla	Continúa la conversación
Tú	Responde a la pregunta
Carla	Continúa la conversación
Tú	Contesta que no es posible y ofrece una alternativa
Carla	Continúa la conversación
Tú	Despídete

GO ON TO THE NEXT PAGE.

Question 4: Cultural Comparison

You will make an oral presentation on a specific topic to your class. You will have 4 minutes to read the presentation topic and prepare your presentation. Then you will have 2 minutes to record your presentation.	Vas a dar una presentación oral a tu clase sobre un tema cultural. Vas a tener 4 minutos para leer el tema de la presentación y prepararla. Después vas a tener 2 minutos para grabar tu presentación.
In your presentation, compare your own community to an area of the Spanish-speaking world with which you are familiar. You should demonstrate your understanding of cultural features of the Spanish-speaking world. You should also organize your presentation clearly.	En tu presentación, compara tu propia comunidad con una región del mundo hispanohablante que te sea familiar. Debes demostrar tu comprensión de aspectos culturales en el mundo hispanohablante y organizar tu presentación de una manera clara.

Tienes cuatro minutos para leer el tema de la presentación y prepararla.

(4 minutes)

Tema de la presentación:

Se sabe que las costumbres familiares son diferentes en cada cultura. Algunas familias son más estrictas, otras menos. En algunas familias los hijos se independizan mucho mas temprano, mientras que en otras familias a los hijos no les molesta vivir con sus padres por mas tiempo, y prefieren mantenerse cerca a su familia.

Compara tus observaciones sobre el comportamiento en general de las familias en el lugar donde vives con tus observaciones sobre el comportamiento de las familias en una región del mundo hispanohablante donde hayas observado, estudiado, o visitado personalmente.

Tienes dos minutos para grabar tu presentación.

STOP

END OF EXAM

Practice Test 2:
Answers and Explanations

ANSWER KEY

Section I

1. A	23. A	45. D
2. C	24. C	46. A
3. C	25. D	47. B
4. B	26. C	48. C
5. D	27. D	49. C
6. B	28. A	50. B
7. C	29. C	51. D
8. A	30. B	52. B
9. C	31. A	53. D
10. A	32. A	54. D
11. B	33. D	55. B
12. C	34. B	56. D
13. C	35. C	57. C
14. A	36. A	58. A
15. D	37. B	59. A
16. B	38. B	60. D
17. A	39. A	61. B
18. B	40. B	62. C
19. A	41. D	63. C
20. A	42. B	64. B
21. B	43. C	65. D
22. D	44. A	

Section II

See explanations beginning on page 338.

SECTION I

Note: These explanations make use of some of the strategies introduced in Part IV. Please refer to pages 93–200 to make the most of this section!

Interpretive Communication: Print Texts (Page 280)

Selection 1: Translated Text and Questions, with Explanations

Introduction

The following infographic appeared on the United Nations' website.

11 SUSTAINABLE CITIES AND COMMUNITIES

SUSTAINABLE CITES:
WHY ARE THEY IMPORTANT

What is the objective in this case?

To make cities and human settlements inclusive, safe, resilient, and sustainable.

Why?

Half of humanity, that is, about 3.5 billion people, currently live in cities, and this figure will continue to increase. Given that for most people, the future will be urban, solutions to some of the major problems human beings are facing —poverty, climate change, healthcare, and education— must be found in the life of the city.

What are the most urgent challenges cities face today?

Inequality is a matter of great concern. There are 838 million people who live in slums, and this number continues to rise. The levels of energy consumption and pollution in urban areas are also concerning. Although cities occupy only 3% of Earth's surface, they represent between 60% and 80% of energy consumption and 75% of carbon emissions.

In the coming decades, 95% of urban expansion will take place in developing countries.

Infographic appeared on United Nations website: www.un.org/sustainabledevelopment
"The content of this publication has not been approved by the United Nations and
does not reflect the views of the United Nations or its officials or Member States."

1. What is the tone of the pamphlet?

(A) **Informational**

(B) Confused

(C) Frightening

(D) Tired

The question is asking what the tone of the pamphlet is. Phrases throughout the pamphlet, such as *POR QUÉ SON IMPORTANTES* and *las soluciones a algunos de los principales problemas,* present information in a clear way, so eliminate (B) and keep (A). Eliminate (C) because, while the pamphlet highlights prevalent problems, *espantoso* is too extreme a word to describe the concerns it raises. Eliminate (D) because it doesn't make sense. The correct answer is (A).

2. How many people live in cities and will that number increase or decrease in the future?

(A) 3.5 billion, decrease

(B) 95 billion, increase

(C) **3.5 billion, increase**

(D) 95 billion, decrease

The question is asking how many people live in cities and whether that number will increase or decrease in the future. Under the question *¿Por qué?*, the pamphlet states *La mitad de la humanidad, esto es, unos 3.500 millones de personas, viven actualmente en ciudades, y esta cifra seguirá en aumento. 3.500 millones* indicates 3.5 billion, and the word *aumento* indicates an increase, so eliminate (A), (B), and (D). The correct answer is (C).

3. What is NOT a problem humans face mentioned in the pamphlet?

(A) Climate change

(B) Poverty

(C) **Depression**

(D) Lack of healthcare

The question is asking what is *not* a problem humans face mentioned in the pamphlet. The pamphlet states *algunos de los principales problemas a que se enfrentan los seres humanos—la probeza, el cambio climático, la asistencia sanitaria, y la educación,* which eliminates answers (A), (B), and (D). The correct answer is (C).

4. According to the pamphlet, what are some of the most urgent issues cities have?

(A) Living in the mansions, expansion of mansions, and scarce resources

(B) **Inequality, pollution, and level of energy consumption**

(C) Climate change, recycling, and littering

(D) Building new cities, being sustainable, and population control

The question asks what some of the most urgent issue cities face are. Looking at the last paragraph of the pamphlet, it states *La desigualdad es motivo de gran preocupación,* which mentions inequality. Further in the paragraph, the pamphlet also states *Los niveles de consumo de energía y de contaminación en las zonas urbanas son también preocupantes,* which mentions the levels of energy consumption and pollution. Eliminate (A) because mansions are not mentioned. Eliminate (C) because recycling and littering are not mentioned. Eliminate (D) because population control is not mentioned and being sustainable is a goal, not an issue. The correct answer is (B).

5. "There are 838 million people" is mentioned in order to
    (A) show how much energy use is due to slum-dwellers
    (B) show that there are so many people living on this planet
    (C) show how many people are contributing to the pollution problem
    (D) show inequality between slum-dwellers and the rest of the city-dwellers

The question asks why the phrase "There are 838 million people" is mentioned. Looking at the sentence before that phrase, the pamphlet states *La desigualdad es motivo de gran preocupación.* Then the pamphlet states *Hay 828 milliones de personas que viven en barrios marginales y esta cifra sigue aumentado.* The given phrase is an illustration of the *desigualdad* mentioned in the previous sentence. Eliminate (A) because the phrase is mentioned to show a comparison, rather than just give the number of people living in slums. Eliminate (B) because it's too broad: the pamphlet is talking about city-dwellers, not everyone on the planet. Eliminate (C) because living in slums does not mean that these people, in particular, are contributing more to the energy use or pollution problems. The correct answer is (D).

Selection 2: Translated Text and Questions, with Explanations

Introduction
The following selection is an excerpt from *Like Water For Chocolate*.

    INGREDIENTS:
    1 can of sardines
    ½ sausage
    1 onion
    oregano
    1 can of serrano peppers
    10 large loaves of bread (telera)

Manera de hacerse:

The onion has to be finely chopped. I suggest you put a small piece of onion near your face in order to avoid the annoying tearing up that occurs when you are cutting it. The bad thing about crying when you chop onions is not the simple act of crying, but sometimes you start, as they say, you chop, and you can't stop. I don't know if it has happened to you but it is true for me. Infinite times. Mom said it was because I'm just as sensitive to onions as Tita, my great-aunt.

They say that Tita was so sensitive that ever since she was in my great-grandmother's womb she cried and cried when she chopped onions; her crying was so loud that Nacha, the house cook, who was half deaf, heard her with no effort. One day the sobs were so strong that they caused the labor to begin early. And without my great-grandmother being able to say a peep, Tita arrived in this world prematurely, on the kitchen table, amid the smells of a noodle soup that she was cooking, those of thyme, bay leaves, cilantro, boiled milk, the garlic and, of course, the onion. As you can imagine, the usual spanking was not necessary, because Tita was born crying beforehand, perhaps because she knew that her oracle determined that marriage was denied her in this life. Nacha used to say that Tita was literally pushed into this world by an impressive torrent of tears that overflowed onto the kitchen table and floor.

In the afternoon, when the scare had passed and the water, thanks to the effect of the sun's rays, had evaporated, Nacha swept up the residue of tears that had remained on the red tile that covered the floor. With this salt she filled a five-kilo sack that they used to cook for a long time.

6. Why does the author recommend putting onion near your face?

(A) To make yourself cry and be sad

(B) To avoid the annoying tears that occur when cutting onions

(C) To bond with your family while cutting onions

(D) To see the grooves in the onion in order to cut the onion better

The question asks why the author recommends putting onion near your face. In the text, the author states *Les sugiero ponerse un pequeño trozo de cebolla en la mollera con el fin de evitar el molesto lagrimeo que se produce cuando uno la está cortando.* Eliminate (A) because the author says *evitar el molesto,* which means she is not recommending crying on purpose. Eliminate (C) because family is not mentioned here. Eliminate (D) because putting onion near the face should be done to avoid crying, not to observe the onion. The correct answer is (B).

7. Who is sensitive to onions like the author?

(A) The author's mother

(B) The author's great-grandmother

(C) The author's great-aunt

(D) The author's father

The question asks who is sensitive to onions just like the author. In the last sentence of the first paragraph, the author states *Mamá decía que era porque yo soy igual de sensible a la cebolla que Tita, mi tía abuela.* Eliminate (A), (B), and (D) because the author's mom states that the author cries like Tita, her great aunt. The correct answer is (C).

8. What detail showed that Tita cried very loudly?

(A) Tita cried from the womb and Nacha who is half deaf could hear her.

(B) Tita cried when the author's great-grandmother chopped onions.

(C) Tita was born amid the smells of noodle soup, such as bay leaf.

(D) Tita is just as sensitive to onions as the author is.

The question asks what detail showed that Tita cried very loudly. The passage states in the beginning of the second paragraph that *su llanto era tan fuerte que Nacha, la cocinera de la casa, que era medio sorda, lo escuchaba sin esforzarse.* Eliminate (B) because while the very beginning of the second paragraph states *Dicen que Tita era tan sensible que desde que estaba en el vientre de mi bisabuela lloraba y lloraba cuando ésta picaba cebolla,* this only mentions Tita crying but not how loud she was crying. Eliminate (C) and (D) because while these answers are true, they do not mention how loud Tita was when she cried either. The correct answer is (A).

9. Which ingredient was NOT described in the smell of noodle soup?

(A) Bay leaves

(B) Boiled milk

(C) Chili flakes

(D) Onion

The question asks what ingredient was not described in the smell of the noodle soup. Therefore, any ingredient mentioned in the passage cannot be the answer. The third paragraph states *Tita arribó a este mundo prematuramente, sobre la mesa de la cocina, entre los olores de una sopa de fideos que estaba cocinando, los del tomillo, el laurel, el cilantro, el de la leche hervida, el de los ajos y, por supuesto, el de la cebolla*. Eliminate (A), (B), and (D), as these are all mentioned in the passage. The correct answer is (C).

10. How does Nacha describe the reason Tita was born?

(A) Tita had so many tears that she was pushed into the world.

(B) Tita hated onions so much that she escaped her womb.

(C) Tita loved food so much she left the womb to try the food.

(D) Tita wanted to see her mother so badly that she was born.

The question asks how Nacha describes the reason Tita was born. At the end of the second paragraph, the passage states *Contaba Nacha que Tita fue literalmente empujada a este mundo por un torrente impresionante de lágrimas que se desbordaron sobre la mesa y el piso de la cocina*. The passage does not say that Tita hates onions, so eliminate (B). Eliminate (C) because it is not stated whether Tita loved food. Eliminate (D) because Tita wanting to see her mother is not mentioned in the passage. The correct answer is (A).

11. What was the color of the tiles on the floor that Nacha swept the tears from?

(A) Blue

(B) Red

(C) Brown

(D) Black

The question asks what color the tiles on the floor that Nacha swept the tears from were. The last paragraph states *Nacha barrió el residuo de las lágrimas que había quedado sobre la loseta roja que cubría el piso*. The word *roja* means red, so eliminate (A), (C), and (D). The correct answer is (B).

12. What was left after the tears evaporated, and what did they use it for?

(A) The Sun's rays that they used to heat the house

(B) The love that tended to bind them together

(C) Salt that they used to cook with

(D) Onions that they used in their food

The question asks what was left behind after the tears evaporated, and how was it used. In the last paragraph of the passage, the author states *En la tarde, ya cuando el susto había pasado y el agua, gracias al efecto de los rayos del sol, se había evaporado, Nacha barrió el residuo de las lágrimas que había quedado sobre la loseta roja que cubría el piso. Con esta sal rellenó un costal de cinco kilos que utilizaron para cocinar bastante tiempo.* This tells us that the residue is salt, so eliminate (A), (B), and (D). The correct answer is (C).

Selection 3: Translated Text and Questions, with Explanations

Introduction

The following selection is a letter from Ana to her grandfather.

25 March 2014
London, England
United Kingdom

Dear Grandpa:

Hello! It's been a long time since I wrote you. I hope you are feeling good and that your leg has healed. Careful with the ice, Grandpa! It's very slippery.

My studies are going really well and I really like Oxford. It's a very popular university, but the professors give a lot of work, and I don't like that. Last weekend, I took a train to London. It's so pretty! I visited the big museums, Buckingham Palace, the Thames River, and the Houses of Parliament. It really was an experience. The cafés are very expensive, but nevertheless I met up with a lot of my friends for dinner. I really love the food. I hope to be able to go back once more next year before returning home. Are you planning to visit us next year? I would like to see you and Grandma. I know that the trip from Alaska to Oregon is not easy. Maybe we can plan to meet up in California.

Tomorrow I start a new art class. I wanted another course on craft art, but there was no room. I signed up for a course on modern art. I am very excited! I will send you some of my grand drawings—someday you might be able to sell them!

I send you lots of hugs and kisses! I hope to see you soon. I love you very much!

Ana

13. Why does Ana warn her grandfather about the ice?

   (A) Because it is very cold
   (B) Because he has never been to London
   (C) Because it is slippery
   (D) Because his leg is still broken

The question asks why Ana warns her grandfather about the ice. In the first paragraph of the letter, Ana writes *¡Cuidado con el hielo abuelo! Es muy resbaladizo.* This specifically says that the ice is slippery, so eliminate (A), (B), and (D) because those are not written in the letter. The correct answer is (C).

14. Where does Ana go to college?

   (A) Oxford University
   (B) University of Cambridge
   (C) Alaska
   (D) Buckingham Palace

The question asks where Ana goes to college. In the first sentence of the second paragraph, Ana writes *Los estudios van muy bien y realmente me gusta mucho Óxford*. Given that she says that her studies are going well and then she mentions that she likes Oxford, it can be inferred that she is taking her classes at Oxford. Eliminate (B) because Cambridge is never mentioned. Eliminate (C) and (D) because she does not study near those locations. The correct answer is (A).

15. Which place did Ana NOT visit in London?
    (A) The Houses of Parliament
    (B) The Thames River
    (C) The museums
    (D) St. Paul's cathedral

The question asks which place Ana did not visit in London. In the fifth sentence of the second paragraph, Ana writes *Visité los grandes museos, el palacio de Buckingham, el río Támesis y las Casas de Parlamento*. Since the question is asking which place she did not visit, eliminate (A), (B), and (C), which are mentioned in this sentence. The correct answer is (D).

16. What does Ana think about the cafeterias?
    (A) That they are cheap, but the food tastes bad
    (B) That they are expensive, but she likes food a lot
    (C) That they are expensive, but the food tastes bad
    (D) That they are cheap, but the food is delicious

The question asks what Ana thinks about the cafeterias. About midway through the second paragraph, Ana writes *Las cafeterías son bastante caras, pero sin embargo me he juntado con muchos amigos para cenar. Me gusta mucho la comida*. Since she said that the cafeterias were expensive, eliminate (A) and (D). Since she liked the food, eliminate (C). The correct answer is (B).

17. Where does Ana suggest that her grandfather meet her next year?
    (A) California
    (B) Alaska
    (C) London
    (D) Oregon

The question asks where Ana suggests that her grandfather meet her the next year. In the last sentence of the second paragraph of the letter, she writes *A lo mejor podemos planear en encontrarnos en California*. Eliminate (B) and (D) because although she writes *Ya sé que el viaje de Alaska a Oregón no es nada fácil,* she does not say to meet there. Eliminate (C) because London is where she is writing from, not where they will meet next year. The correct answer is (A).

18. Why did Ana not get into the craft art course?

    (A) Because she wanted to take a modern art course

    (B) Because the class did not have space

    (C) Because she wanted to change majors

    (D) Because the class was boring

The question asks why Ana did not get into the craft art course. In the third paragraph, Ana writes *Quería otro curso de arte artesanal, pero no tenían espacio.* Eliminate (A) because she takes the modern art course only because she couldn't get into the craft art course. Eliminate (C) and (D) because she doesn't say that she wants to change her major or that the class is boring anywhere in the letter. The correct answer is (B).

19. It can be inferred that Ana will send more letters in the future because

    (A) she mentions that she will send drawings

    (B) she mentions that she will visit Buckingham Palace

    (C) she mentions that the cafeterias have good food

    (D) she mentions that she misses her grandfather

The question asks how it can be inferred that Ana will send more letters in the future. In the third paragraph of the letter, Ana writes *Te voy a mandar unos de mis grandes dibujos—¡algún día los podrás vender!* Right after this sentence she concludes the letter. Eliminate (B), (C), and (D) because, while these things are all mentioned in her letter (that she went to Buckingham Palace, that she liked the food at the cafeterias, and that she hasn't written to her grandfather for a while and loves him a lot), none of them provides proof that she will write more letters. Her only mention of sending any more mail is *Te voy a mandar unos de mis grandes dibujos.* The correct answer is (A).

Selection 4: Translated Text and Questions, with Explanations

Introduction

The following website is about *El Sistema*, Venezuela's national program that shares music with underprivileged children. The site appeared in May 2003.

To Play, Sing, and Struggle

Founded in 1975 by teacher Dr. José Antonio Abreu, the National System of Children's and Youth Orchestras and Choruses of Venezuela started in a garage with 11 young children. Today, the program, affectionately known as *El Sistema* (The System), serves more than 500 thousand disadvantaged students in Venezuela and continues to grow. Additionally, more than 42 countries have created programs inspired by *El Sistema*, among them Argentina, Australia, Austria, Bolivia, Brazil, Canada, Chile, Colombia, Costa Rica, Cuba, the Dominican Republic, Ecuador, El Salvador, England, France, Guatemala, Honduras, India, Italy, Jamaica, Japan, Mexico, Nicaragua, Panama, Paraguay, Peru, Portugal, Puerto Rico, Scotland, South Korea, Trinidad and Tobago, the United States, and Uruguay.

El Sistema in Venezuela teaches music through individual and group instruction to children as young as 2 or 3 years old, combining these lessons with participation in children's and youth orchestras and choruses. In every program, the orchestras have more significance than merely that of sharing classical music: they are dedicated to preventing school dropouts and reducing crime in the cities. In one study, the school dropout rate diminished to 6.9% amongst students participating in *El Sistema*, as compared to 26.4% in a control group. One can also see the great impact of *El Sistema* in reduced rates of illiteracy, marginality, and exclusion among the young population in Venezuela.

The children and their parents are part of the social communities of *El Sistema*, which emphasizes the importance of developing the human being. This population of 500,000 young Venezuelans is distributed across approximately 285 young children's orchestras (between 4 and 6 years old), 220 children's orchestras (7 to 16 years), 180 youth orchestras (16 through 22 years), 30 professional orchestras, 360 choral groups, 1,355 associated choral groups, and more than 15,000 teachers in all parts of the country. The teachers teach the students to "play, sing, and struggle" in order to overcome the obstacles of poverty and pursue formal education.

Here in the United States, there are multitudes of extracurricular programs inspired by *El Sistema* in Venezuela, which encourage social change in areas with limited resources. The NAESIP (National Alliance of *El Sistema*-Inspired Programs) gives children in these communities the tools to overcome the obstacles of poverty and discover the importance of education. "I've always thought that music education, from the most tender infancy, is a most beautiful task and is crucial to all society. It is an ideal of education that has existed for many centuries: music forms part of the spiritual development, conscience, and aesthetic formation of mankind," says Maestro Abreu.

20. What is the meaning of the title, "To Play, Sing, and Struggle"?

   (A) ***El Sistema* teaches children to fight for their right to education and to overcome poverty.**

   (B) *El Sistema* teaches children to fight with each other.

   (C) "To play and sing" is a metaphor for fighting in Latin American countries.

   (D) Many times, children fight with their parents.

Choice (A) is the correct answer. *El Sistema* teaches the children, through music, to fight for their rights to education and opportunity, and hopefully to overcome the obstacles they face with regard to illiteracy, lack of resources, and marginality. Choice (B) is way too literal; the program does not teach the children to fight with each other, nor does the passage say that children often fight with their parents, though that is a common occurrence (D). Choice (C) is not true and misinterprets the phrase "to play, sing, and struggle."

21. What is the article about?

   (A) There is a large problem of illiteracy, poverty, and marginality in Venezuela and in other parts of the world.

   (B) ***El Sistema* has created a positive environment for involved students, and other countries have created affiliated programs in order to better the lives of disadvantaged children.**

   (C) All the children who participate in *El Sistema* have success in music studies.

   (D) The NAESIP is the extension of *El Sistema* in the United States, also founded by Maestro Abreu.

Choice (B) is the correct answer. *El Sistema* is a program that creates a positive environment for disadvantaged children in Venezuela, and the programs it has inspired do the same in all parts of the world. Though (A) is true and is one of the main reasons for Dr. Abreu founding *El Sistema*, it is not the main focus of the article. Choice (C) is too extreme and goes beyond the scope of the passage. Choice (D) is not true, though Maestro Abreu is involved to some extent in the growth of these programs in the United States.

22. How has the school dropout rate changed in Venezuela?

   (A) The school dropout rate has risen in students who do not participate in *El Sistema*.

   (B) The school dropout rate has grown while the illiteracy rate has declined.

   (C) The school dropout rate has declined while the crime rate has risen in urban areas.

   (D) The school dropout rate has declined, compared to the students who are not involved in *El Sistema*.

Choice (D) is the correct answer. The school dropout rate has declined in students involved with *El Sistema* as compared to those outside the program. We cannot know from the passage that dropout rates have risen among students who do not participate in the program (A). Choices (B) and (C) are both half-right: we expect that the illiteracy rate has declined, as (B) states, but this correct information is paired with growth in the dropout rate. Similarly, the decline in the dropout rate is paired with a rise in crime rates in urban areas, a statistic not mentioned in the passage (C).

23. The 285 young children's orchestras, 220 children's orchestras, 180 youth orchestras, and others are mentioned in order to

    (A) **demonstrate how *El Sistema* has grown in Venezuela with more than 500,000 participants**

    (B) emphasize that the students enjoy the orchestras and choruses

    (C) illustrate that the programs in other countries have grown a lot as a result of inspiration from *El Sistema*

    (D) contrast how *El Sistema* started in a garage and explain how its orchestras have lowered illiteracy rates

Choice (A) is the correct answer. Listing the number of the orchestras and choruses in Venezuela adds weight to how much *El Sistema* has grown since its humble beginnings. Choice (D) is a trap answer, as the orchestras are contrasted with *El Sistema's* beginnings in a garage, but their numbers alone do not explain lowered illiteracy rates in the country. The orchestras and choruses are specific to Venezuela, and do not have anything to do with the programs in other countries (C). Lastly, the passage does not mention whether the students enjoy the groups or not (B).

24. In the last paragraph, Abreu's quote is included in order to

    (A) demonstrate that Dr. Abreu was the teacher of the year in 2013 because he has given opportunities to many children in Venezuela

    (B) prove that the children in *El Sistema* have changed the world

    (C) **illustrate the importance of education through music**

    (D) give an example of a beautiful task that is part of a spiritual education

Choice (C) is the correct answer. Dr. Abreu calls music one of the most important and beautiful gifts one can teach children. It combines life lessons needed to help them out of poverty and to pursue their educations. While (A) is true because Dr. Abreu was named teacher of the year in 2013 by multiple organizations, it is never mentioned in the passage, nor is it the reason for his quote at the end of the article. The quote does not prove anything, as (B) states, and (D) extracts words, changing the meaning from that in the passage.

Selection 5: Translated Texts and Questions, with Explanations

Introduction

The following are some classified ads in the Peruvian press.

THOMAS'S KITCHEN
RESTAURANT * DANCE CLUB

28 Elf Street, Lee, MA * 432-888-9090

The most beautiful, original, and luxurious place in Massachusetts.

Hispanic cuisine specializing in empanadas and margaritas!

Come try one or all of our menu items and stay for dancing! Latin music for everyone and much more!

Open every day from 12 P.M. until dawn!!

We have a lot of musical groups that play every Friday!

Thomas's Kitchen presents:

June 13: Orlando's Orchestra—Music from Argentina and Colombia
June 20: The Crazy Wolves—Mariachi
June 27: María Luz Roca—the Mexican singer
July 4: The Independents—a local group that is coming to celebrate American Independence Day!
Buy 2 tickets before the 4th of July and get a free margarita!

Reserve Today!
Tables and seats are limited.

25. What kind of place is Thomas's Kitchen?

   (A) A kitchen

   (B) A restaurant

   (C) A restaurant and bar

   (D) A restaurant and place for dancing

The title of the announcement below the restaurant name describes Thomas's as a restaurant and dance club. Choice (D) is the correct answer.

26. Who are The Independents?

   (A) A music group from Argentina

   (B) A music group from the United States

   (C) A local music group

   (D) A music group that celebrates everything

The flier lists the music groups that are playing at the venue. The Independents are a local group of musicians who are playing on the Fourth of July to celebrate American Independence Day. Therefore, (C) is the correct answer.

27. When do you have to make a reservation and why?

   (A) Whenever, because there are a lot of tables

   (B) After dawn, because if not the restaurant will be closed

   (C) After the 4th of July, because it's a holiday

   (D) Immediately, because there is not a lot of available space

The flier says to reserve today, as tables and seating are limited. Choice (A) contradicts this statement, (B) contradicts the passage, and (C) doesn't match the prediction, making (D) the correct answer.

28. How is the establishment described?

   (A) Luxurious

   (B) Ugly

   (C) Famous

   (D) Far

The flier states that the venue is the most beautiful, original, and luxurious place in Massachusetts. Choice (A) is correct.

29. At what time would Thomas's kitchen be closed?

   (A) 12:00 A.M.

   (B) 2:00 A.M.

   (C) 6:00 A.M.

   (D) 12:00 P.M.

According to the flier, Thomas's Kitchen is open from 12:00 P.M. until dawn. The only time that's close to the end of that range (dawn) in the given answer choices is 6:00 A.M., so (C) is the correct answer.

30. Is there an advantage to buying the entries early?

   (A) Yes, but you have to buy them on the 4th of July.

   (B) Yes, but you have to buy them before the 4th of July.

   (C) No, there isn't an advantage.

   (D) No, there's no special offer.

This one requires you to read carefully! Choice (A) may seem correct, but the flier states that you will receive a free margarita if you buy your entries before July 4th. So (B) is correct.

Interpretive Communication: Print and Audio Texts (Combined) (Page 289)

Selection 1: Translated Texts and Questions, with Explanations

Source 1

Introduction: Only about 20% of the students in the United States choose to learn a second language while the number is closer to 90% in places like Europe. The following blog appeared on the official website of the "Network of Anáhuac universities."

Why is it important to be fluent in a second language?

Speaking a second language opens the door to many opportunities both personal and professional, which is why today, people who are fluent in more than one language receive more and better job offers.

Globalization of education, the markets, and the world in general requires people to prepare much more than only a few decades ago and being fluent in another language different from our native one has become indispensable for us to develop and distinguish ourselves at a professional level.

Along with bilingualism providing benefits in the work environment, it has been proven that bilingual people exhibit abilities superior to those who only communicate in one language. Even though English is the preferred language of students, there are other languages that have also started to become relevant on the global plane.

What are the advantages and disadvantages of studying the following languages?

- English: Spoken on all seven continents and by powerful nations, English is considered the international language, since it is the most used in business and commerce internationally. Most universities have advanced proficiency in this language as a requirement to graduate.

- French: With more than 200 million French-speaking people in the world, this is the second most studied language after English. Its importance lies in that international organizations, like the UN, The Olympic Committee, and FIFA, consider it their official language. Consider that as a speaker of Spanish, this language is easier to learn.

- Mandarin Chinese: The accelerated growth of China on the business plane at a global level has turned this language into an indispensable tool of professional exchange and it is positioned to be the language of the future in work environments. As it is spoken by more than a billion people, it is the most spoken language in the world.

- Portuguese: Portuguese is the sixth most spoken language in the world, and because of its political history, it turns out to be one of the most interesting languages to learn. Besides just opening doors in the Latin American and European markets, Portuguese helps to explore a broad culture that is sometimes forgotten.

Benefits of speaking a second language

It doesn't matter at what age a second language is learned, whether from childhood or as an adult: it has been proven that being bilingual is beneficial for a person's cognitive development, since it improves flexibility, memory, and the ability of the brain.

The main benefits of learning a new language are:

Better decision making. A brain that knows how to move rapidly between two languages is one that can analyze various situations simultaneously with ease, an indispensable skill in making better decisions.

Increase in memory. Knowing two or more languages requires a lot of dedication, attention to detail, and, more importantly, an active and efficient memory that can retain a great amount of information.

Reduces the possibility of mental diseases. Doctors have discovered that bilingual people strengthen their brains, which causes a reduction in the possibility and effects of acquiring mental diseases like Alzheimer's and dementia.

Professional growth. One of the most in-demand qualifications in the work environment is knowing a second language. Professionals who are bilingual are recognized for their preparation with better positions and bigger salaries.

Source 2

Introduction: This recording is about learning a second language. The following interviewees share their opinions about learning a second language. The recording is approximately 3 minutes long.

(Narrator)	Source: The opinions of people of various ages about the topic of learning another language.
(Narrator)	Jonathan Castro, a 35-year-old Puerto Rican graphic designer, talks about his recent experience learning Japanese:
(Jonathan Castro)	A few years ago I decided to learn Japanese. I was always interested in learning about Japanese culture, and I thought, what better way than to learn their language? At first it seemed a little intimidating. Everything was new and strange, but with time and practice, I learned enough to have short and simple conversations. I didn't know that there's three different ways to write in Japanese, that was very impressive. When I went on vacation to Tokyo, I was able to ask the price of products that I was interested in buying, ask directions, and order food.
(Narrator)	Paola Hernández, Mexican, is 24 years old, and has just found a job in tourism.
(Paola Hernández)	I think that learning a second language is very important. I've been bilingual since I was little, so I can't remember if it was hard to learn. I just graduated from Anáhuac University Cancun, it hasn't even been a year, and I already found a job in the tourism industry thanks to me being bilingual. Tourism is very important here in Cancun, and being bilingual is a requisite for many jobs, so learning a second language can increase your opportunities of finding a job.
(Narrator)	Edgar Suárez is a mechanic, lives in Argentina, and is 51 years old.
(Edgar Suárez)	I've been working as a mechanic for 28 years, and never has a client walked into my workshop speaking another language. I don't see it as necessary to learn a second language if I'll be living my entire life in the same place. Sure, a lot of my friends speak Italian, but I never had to learn. When I was a kid, I tried to learn Italian but I had a lot of difficulty with the practice, so I didn't last long before I gave up. Of course I know all of the names of the different car parts in English as well as in Spanish, but that's all I need to know.
(Narrator)	Ana Cálix is a student at Dr. Gilberto Concepción de Gracia High School.
(Ana Cálix)	I think that learning a second language should not be a requirement for me to graduate. It might be useful at some time in my life, but right now I have other interests, and prefer to focus on courses more relevant to what I'll study in college. I'm willing to learn in the future if necessary!

31. What is one of the main benefits of speaking a second language according to the article?

   (A) Improves the ability to retain large quantities of information efficiently.

   (B) It makes you a more interesting person at work.

   (C) It guarantees you a job with a better position and a better salary.

   (D) You will always make the best decisions, quickly, in any situation.

The article lists the different benefits of knowing a second language and mentions *Aumento de la memoria. Conocer dos o más idiomas requiere de mucha dedicación, atención a los detalles y, más importante, una memoria activa y eficiente que logre retener una gran cantidad de información.* So keep (A). The article says nothing about making you a more interesting person at work, so eliminate (B). Even though the article does suggest that knowing a second language helps with professional growth and job opportunities, it does NOT say that a job with better position and salary is guaranteed, so eliminate (C). The article does mention better and quicker decision making as one of the main benefits of speaking a second language; however, it does not say that you will *always* make the best decisions, so eliminate (D). Choice (A) is the correct answer.

32. The article mentions that the language preferred by students is

   (A) English
   (B) French
   (C) Italian
   (D) Mandarin Chinese

Before listing the four different languages, the article says *Aunque el inglés es la lengua preferida por los estudiantes, hay otros idiomas que también han comenzado a volverse relevantes en el plano mundial.* Italian is not on the list of languages, so eliminate (C). Even though the other languages are also listed, English is preferred, so the correct answer is (A).

33. "Globalization" is mentioned to

   (A) speak about the different countries in the world, and all their different languages
   (B) show that English is the language most used in businesses internationally
   (C) illustrate that globalization is the reason why learning a second language is required in schools
   (D) emphasize how indispensable it is to be fluent in a language different from our native tongue for development at a professional level

The second paragraph mentions globalization in the following sentence: *La globalización de la educación, los mercados y el mundo en general exige a las personas a prepararse mucho más que hace tan solo unas décadas y el dominio de otro idioma diferente al materno se ha vuelto indispensable para desarrollarse y destacar a nivel profesional.* It doesn't really mention different countries and only lists a few languages later on, so eliminate (A). The article does mention that English is the most-used language in business internationally; however, this is not the reason why the term "*globalization*" is mentioned, so eliminate (B). The sentence does not say anything about globalization being the reason why learning a second language is required in schools, so eliminate (C). By process of elimination, (D) is correct, and it is mentioned word for word that being fluent in a second language has become indispensable for development at a professional level.

34. Why does it mention "the UN, the Olympic Committee, and FIFA"?

   (A) It shows international organizations that only speak French.
   (B) It shows international organizations that consider French their official language.
   (C) It shows that French is the most important language on the list.
   (D) It shows that people who speak French also love sports.

In the list of languages, referring to French, the article says: *Su importancia radica en que organismos internacionales, como la ONU, el Comité Olímpico y la FIFA, lo consideran como idioma oficial.* Eliminate (A) because even though these organizations do speak French, it's not necessarily the ONLY language they speak. Choice (B) matches the statement from the article, so keep it. Even though we are given a list of reasons that make French an important language internationally, it does not say that French is the MOST important language on the list, so eliminate (C). Even though the Olympic Committee and FIFA are indeed sports organizations, this does not imply that all people who speak French also love sports, and is not why these organizations are mentioned, so eliminate (D). Choice (B) is correct.

35. Which of the following statements best summarizes this article?
    (A) If you don't learn a second language, you will not be able to participate in international businesses.
    (B) People who are fluent in more than one language will have more success in the work environment than people who are only fluent in one language.
    (C) Learning a second language provides many benefits, such as better job opportunities and better memory, and can reduce the possibility of mental diseases.
    (D) Learning a second language should be a requirement in all the schools around the world.

Nothing in the article says that you will not be able to participate in international business if you only know one language, so eliminate (A). Choice (B) sounds like a guarantee of more success, whereas the article talks about how learning a second language *can* increase your chances of more *success* (*will* is extreme), so eliminate (B). Choice (C) is supported by the article, so keep it. The article does mention learning a second language as a requirement in the case of Universidad Anáhuac specifically, but does not state that this should be a requirement in all schools, so eliminate (D). Choice (C) is the correct answer.

36. According to the audio source, what are the opinions of the interviewees?
    (A) Those who know another language appreciate it, and take advantage of its benefits, while those who only speak one language don't feel it is necessary to learn another language.
    (B) All the interviewees have the opinion that learning a second language should be mandatory.
    (C) All the interviewees prefer to learn English.
    (D) None of the interviewees is bilingual.

Jonathan Castro and Paola Hernández both express positive opinions and benefits from learning a second language, while Edgar Suárez and Ana Cálix don't think it's necessary, so keep (A), since it matches the opinions expressed. Choice (B) is false: the opinion of Ana Cálix was the exact opposite, that it should NOT be a requirement to learn a second language. Choice (C) contradicts the passage as well: Jonathan Castro learned Japanese and Edgar Suárez mentioned he tried to learn Italian once, so eliminate (C). Eliminate (D) because Ana Cálix mentioned that she has been bilingual since she was a child. The correct answer is Choice (A).

37. According to the audio source, when Edgar Suárez was a child, he tried to learn

    (A) French

    (B) Italian

    (C) English

    (D) Mandarin Chinese

In the audio source, Edgar Suárez mentions that *Cuando era niño intenté aprender italiano, pero tuve mucha dificultad con la práctica, así que no duré mucho antes de rendirme.* Choice (B) is the correct answer.

38. Ana Cálix prefers to focus on

    (A) finding a job

    (B) courses relevant to what she will study in college

    (C) learning many languages

    (D) spending more time with her friends and family

In the audio source, Ana Cálix mentions nothing about finding a job, or spending time with friends and family, so eliminate (A) and (D). She says: *¡Estoy dispuesta a aprender en el futuro de ser necesario!* implying she is willing to learn a second language in the future if necessary, but this is not her focus right now, so eliminate (C). Choice (B) is correct and matches what she said: *prefiero enfocarme en cursos más relevantes a lo que estudiaré en la universidad.*

39. Who learned Japanese?

    (A) Jonathan Castro

    (B) Edgar Suárez

    (C) Ana Cálix

    (D) Paola Hernández

Jonathan Castro starts by mentioning: *Hace unos años decidí aprender japonés.* Paola Hernández doesn't mention what her second language is. Ana Cálix and Edgar Suárez don't know a second language. Choice (A) is correct.

Selection 2: Translated Texts and Questions, with Explanations

Source 1
Introduction: This article appeared on the website theconversation.com, and it talks about the recent popularity of "booktubers," and their positive effect in communities of book readers.

Talking About Books on Video: A Skill with a Bright Future

Booktubers undertake the making of videos about books and readings with different formats: Book Hauls (book purchases), Wrap Ups (book summaries), Shelf Tours (tours of available books). That is to say, they present the books they own, display their latest acquisitions, formulate their recommendations, deliver their criticisms, etc. In this way, they awaken a taste for and an interest in reading in a generation that is very accustomed to receiving this type of prescriptive content in the form of video.

Learn to be a booktuber ?
The project was structured in three large blocks:
Phase 1. The students had to assume the role of booktubers.
Phase 2. In the second part of the project, the students went from being booktubers to being digital storytellers.
Phase 3. Written assignment that encompasses the entire learning process.

High satisfaction and motivation

After the development of this project, the responses of 145 students, who anonymously answered a questionnaire created ad hoc, were analyzed.

According to the data, 80% of those surveyed were unaware of the booktubing phenomenon and more than 90% stated that their interest in this type of resource had increased. More than 90% of the participants ended up very satisfied with the result of their practice and they liked sharing their videos with the class group. All this had had the effect that more than 95% of the students stated that their interest in reading children's literature had increased.

Communication skills

In addition to specific competence in literature, our students also developed their linguistic and communication skills with this activity.

Thus, more than 90% expressed that when making both videos they paid more attention than usual to how they expressed themselves verbally. More than 85% explained that they also observed their nonverbal language in detail.

Digital allies, not enemies

In this case, thanks to the activities proposed based on the creation of video content, students not only have improved their literary competence, but also have developed expression and comprehension skills (oral and written), and have activated their creativity. Likewise, they have expanded their knowledge of children's stories and have read, understood, interpreted, and valued literary narrative texts for this cycle.

In this way, we can not only answer that yes, there is room for reading in modern life, but we can also expand and improve that space with video (video review or video narration). The video can be the entry key to the exciting world of literature.

Source 2
Introduction: This recording is of a conversation between Melvin and Regina about the topic of booktubers.

(Melvin) Hey Regina, do you know what booktubers are? I discovered them recently and it really gets my attention; I've already subscribed to three booktubers of different styles.

(Regina) No, it's the first time I've heard that word. What is a booktuber?

(Melvin) Well, they're people who prepare videos where they talk about a book that they've recently acquired, present their opinions or criticisms, and summarize the topics that had the most personal impact to them. Usually, they upload videos to social platforms like Youtube, hence the name "booktuber."

(Regina) Sounds interesting, but I don't read many books unless they are mystery or reading homework for school, although it sounds like a good way to develop a reading habit.

(Melvin) Yes, personally it has helped me read more often. Books seem more interesting to me when I see the different perspectives that booktubers have, and with the way they present them, they manage to plant the seed of interest in people who watch the video and still haven't read the book. Sometimes you also discover new books through their videos that you might have not discovered otherwise. Booktubers have different personalities and video styles. Some of them are dedicated to a specific genre like mystery, and if you have reading homework, it might benefit you to see a different perspective.

(Regina) Now that I think about it, I have a book that I still haven't read and maybe some booktuber has made an interesting video about it that will motivate me to read it soon. Additionally, it sounds useful for homework, so I'll explore it. Thank you for sharing your experience with me, I've discovered something new.

(Melvin) You're welcome Regina, let me know how it goes!

(Narrator) After two weeks, Melvin and Regina meet in the school cafeteria, and Regina tells Melvin her experience with booktubers.

(Regina) Hi, Melvin. After our last conversation I decided to explore different booktubers, and you were right! They were very useful for homework in my literature class, and I also discovered some very interesting videos about the book that I was interested in reading. I'll send you the links so that you can watch them; maybe you'll find them interesting and we'll be able to get together and talk about the book after reading it.

(Melvin) Excellent idea! I also think it's good to have a reading partner. I'm very happy that you have benefited from booktubers, as I have.

40. What is the purpose of the article and the statistics?

(A) To talk about how digital media have destroyed interest in books and reading

(B) To show a learning method that can increase motivation for, interest in, and enjoyment of the habit of reading in its participants

(C) To show that receiving content in video form is always better than reading a book

(D) To talk about how to be a professional booktuber

The article talks about how to combine digital media with learning to increase interest in books, not destroy it, so eliminate (A). The article does present a learning method and statistics showing an increase in reading, so keep (B). The article does not mention that receiving content in video form is better than reading a book, and the word *always* is extreme, so eliminate (C). The project, or learning method, presented in the article is about learning how to be a booktuber for educational purposes, not necessarily for going on to be a professional booktuber, so eliminate (D). Choice (B) is correct.

41. Which of the following statements best describes "booktubers"?

(A) They are people who record themselves reading books.

(B) They are people who recreate whole scenes from books in movie-style videos.

(C) They are people who consume books in exclusively audiovisual form.

(D) They are people who, in video form, present the books that they own, show their latest acquisitions, make recommendations, give critiques, etc.

Booktubers might read parts of books on video, but this does not fully encompass what they do, so eliminate (A). Some more elaborate booktubers might recreate scenes, but this is not supported by the article, so eliminate (B). Booktubers share some details of the book with their viewers, but the article shows booktubers to be audiovisual content creators—their viewers would be the consumers—so eliminate (C). The article does say: *"Es decir, exponen los libros que poseen, exhiben sus últimas adquisiciones, formulan sus recomendaciones, lanzan sus críticas,"* which supports (D), which is correct.

42. According to the data, what effect did the project "learning how to be a booktuber" have?

(A) Only 20% of the participants showed an increase in interest for this type of resource.

(B) More than 90% of the participants showed an increase in interest for this type of resource.

(C) No significant effect was observed at the end of this project.

(D) More than 90% of the participants went on to be professional booktubers after finishing this project.

The article states that *"más del 90% afirmó que su interés por este tipo de recursos se había incrementado,"* so eliminate (A) and (C), since these are not supported by the data. Choice (D) seems to be a trap answer: it includes the correct percentage (90%), but since there is no data about participants going on to become professional booktubers and this was not the purpose of the project, eliminate (D). Choice (B) is correct and is supported by the data.

43. According to the article, is there still room for reading?
    (A) Yes, there is still room for reading, but only in schools and reading groups.
    (B) No, since video has replaced reading.
    (C) Yes, there is still space for reading, and we can improve that space with video.
    (D) No, books occupy too much space, and it is very inconvenient to read in digital form.

This is a two-by-two question where the answer is either *yes* or *no*. The article states *"De esta manera, no solamente podemos respondernos que sí, queda espacio para la lectura en la vida actual, sino que además podemos ampliar y mejorar ese espacio con vídeo (vídeorreseña o videonarración)."* This answers the question "is there still room for reading?" with a yes, so eliminate (B) and (D). Choice (A) is not supported by the article, so eliminate it. Choice (C) is correct and is supported by the article.

44. According to the audio source, what effect did booktubers have on Melvin?
    (A) Books are more interesting to Melvin, he reads them more often, and booktubers help him discover new books.
    (B) He finds them boring, since Melvin doesn't like books.
    (C) Melvin has fun doing homework assignments and completes them rapidly.
    (D) They had no effect at all on Melvin.

In the audio source, Melvin says, *"Yes, personally it has helped me read more often. Books seem more interesting to me when I see the different perspectives that booktubers have…"* and later says, *"Sometimes you also discover new books through their videos that you might have not discovered otherwise."* These statements support (A), so keep it. Choice (B) is not supported, so eliminate it. Melvin does talk about the possible benefits booktubers can have on reading homework, but does not mention that he has fun doing homework, so eliminatechoice (C). Choice (D) is incorrect based on Melvin's statements, so eliminate it. Choice (A) is the correct answer.

45. What genre of books does Regina prefer to read?
    (A) Science Fiction
    (B) Romance
    (C) Adventure
    (D) Mystery

Regina says *"I don't read many books unless they are mystery or reading homework for school."* Choice (D) is the correct answer.

46. How could booktubers help you finish your reading homework?
    (A) They can give you a different perspective on the book.
    (B) They allow you to finish homework assignments without having to read the book.
    (C) You can copy the booktubers' words in your homework without providing references.
    (D) They're a good distraction for when you need a break from homework.

The reason Melvin gave as to why booktubers can help you with reading homework was *"Some of them are dedicated to a specific genre like mystery, and if you have reading homework, it might benefit you to see a different perspective."* This supports (A), so keep it. Melvin did not mention anything to support (B), (C), or (D), so eliminate them. Choice (A) is correct.

47. What is Melvin's intention in the audio source?

    (A) He tries to convince Regina to consume booktubers' content.

    (B) He shares his personal experience with booktubers to help Regina discover how they can be useful in her life.

    (C) He's only trying to make conversation; Melvin doesn't care about booktubers too much.

    (D) He explains that mystery books are also his favorite.

Even though Melvin is speaking about booktubers in a positive light, he is only sharing his personal experience: he's not necessarily trying to convince Regina to consume the content of booktubers, so eliminate (A). He is sharing his personal experience with booktubers, and he gives a few reasons why they might be useful to other people, which supports (B), so keep it. Nothing in the conversation supports (C) or (D), so eliminate them. Choice (B) is correct.

Interpretive Communication: Audio Texts (Page 295)

Selection 3: Translated Text and Questions, with Explanations

Introduction

The following recording is about how a group of women in Lima, Peru came together to bring food to a community with few resources.

(Narrator) In the heights of Lurigancho Chosica in Lima, Peru, there exists a common pot called "Mi Ángel Poderoso" as part of which a group of women from the community of Cerrito la Libertad wake up at five in the morning to start their shift. Day to day, they bring and cook enough food so that close to 100 people can have lunch for S/.2,50 in soles, (the currency of Peru). To bring the ingredients that they need to cook, such as bags of rice and vegetables, the women must work as a team to climb a steep hill every morning, but this does not stop them from achieving their work for the day.

(Narrator) In the heights of Sector Carapongo live 250 families in small and humble houses. Most of the families arrived there to work for a better future. There, the lack of resources such as electricity, drainage systems, and light stand out. In fact, since they had no water, they had to build a big water well in the lower parts to pump the water they need. They take turns among themselves to bring water.

(Narrator) The common pot "Mi Ángel Poderoso" was organized during the COVID-19 pandemic when the absence of basic services caused a food shortage, which motivated the president of the common pot, 52-year-old Giovanna Ávila Ñaupari, to put forth a solution that would put a stop to the food shortage in her community. The president and a group of women from Cerrito La Libertad organized to create the common pot. In the beginning, sometimes they would cook up to 200 plates a day, since the people weren't working because of the pandemic, so they had time to have lunch at the common pot.

(Narrator) In "Mi Ángel Poderoso," everyone takes turns on rotation to cook, buy groceries, prepare the ingredients, cut the vegetables, etc. It is a well-organized team effort, and this way they manage to have everything ready by ten in the morning. Giovanna has a dream to turn the common pot into a popular cafeteria. She has lots of experience in popular cafeterias in her area, and this is one of the reasons why she helped to organize "Mi Ángel Poderoso" and is president.

(Narrator) "Mi Ángel Poderoso," and many other common pots like it, were made possible by the resources provided by the "Ollas Que Desarrollan" initiative, a project of Alicorp. They provide materials like tomato sauce, noodles, oil, flour, and other things that really help the common pot. The recipients are really grateful for this help.

48. What is "Mi Ángel Poderoso"?

(A) A divine entity that protects the inhabitants of Cerrito La Libertad

(B) A nickname that was given to the husband of one of the cooks, who helps them carry the bags of rice

(C) A common pot that feeds close to 100 people in the community

(D) A hospital in Peru

Nothing in the audio supports (A), (B), or (C), so eliminate them. The correct answer is (C).

49. What characteristics stand out in this community?

    (A) There is a lot of wealth and abundance.

    (B) It is a very flat location: there are no hills.

    (C) It lacks resources such as electricity, drainage systems, and light.

    (D) Only 100 people live there.

The audio mentions that *"There, the lack of resources such as electricity, drainage systems, and light stand out."* This contradicts (A) and supports (C), so eliminate (A) and keep (C). The audio mentions that *"the women must work as a team to climb a steep hill every morning"* and repeats the word *"heights"* often, which implies the existence of hills, so eliminate (B). Choice (D) is a trap answer because even though they do feed close to 100 people a day, the audio also mentions that 250 families live there (way more than 100 people), so eliminate (D). Choice (C) is the correct answer.

50. Why was "Mi Ángel Poderoso" organized?

    (A) To collect funds to pay for the education of Giovanna's children

    (B) To implement a solution that would counter the food shortage in the community

    (C) To be Peru's best restaurant

    (D) It was organized with the intention of being sold.

The audio does not mention Giovanna's children, and nothing in the audio supports that her intentions were for monetary gain, so eliminate (A). The audio does mention that *"the absence of basic services caused a food shortage, which motivated the president of the common pot, 52-year-old Giovanna Ávila Ñaupari, to put forth a solution that would put a stop to the food shortage in her community."* This supports (B), so keep it. The audio mentions that Giovanna has a dream to turn the common pot into a popular cafeteria, but not *"Peru's best restaurant,"* so eliminate (C). Nothing in the audio supports (D), so eliminate it. Choice (B) is correct.

51. Who is Giovanna Ávila Ñaupari?

    (A) Mayor of Chosica

    (B) The only person who cooks among the women of "Mi Ángel Poderoso"

    (C) An independent donor to "Mi Ángel Poderoso"

    (D) President of "Mi Ángel Poderoso"

The audio states: *"The common pot 'Mi Ángel Poderoso' was organized during the COVID-19 pandemic when the absence of basic services caused a food shortage, which motivated the president of the common pot, 52-year-old Giovanna Ávila Ñaupari, to put forth a solution that would put a stop to the food shortage in her community,"* which names Giovanna as the president of "Mi Ángel Poderoso." Choice (D) is the correct answer.

52. What is the purpose of this recording?

    (A) To attract tourism to Cerrito La Libertad

    (B) To promote the common pot "Mi Ángel Poderoso" and its contributions to the community

    (C) To sell us local foods

    (D) To inform us about the conditions of Cerrito La Libertad

In the recording, the narrator describes the "Mi Ángel Poderoso" initiative and explains how it has helped people in the community around it. There is never any mention of tourism (A) or local foods (C), so eliminate those. While the recording does tell us about some conditions in Cerrito la Libertad, the main point is to explain the solution to those problems through "Mi Ángel Poderoso." Eliminate (D); the correct answer is (B).

Selection 4: Translated Text and Questions, with Explanations

Introduction

The following recording is about the benefits of therapy, and various people share their experiences.

(Narrator) In the past, therapy was a taboo topic in many cultures. People felt ashamed to seek professional help for their emotional problems, or problems in their relationships. But as science has advanced, and more investigations into mental health have been conducted, therapy has gained more acceptance and has become more common.

(Narrator) Therapy has become more accessible to the general public, and the process has become more clear thanks, in part, to celebrities and public personalities speaking openly about their experiences.

(Narrator) Today therapy is considered an important form of personal care and is promoted as a useful tool to improve mental health and wellness in general.

(Narrator) One of the most important benefits of therapy is that it provides a secure and confidential space to talk about your thoughts and feelings. Often, it is difficult to share these things with your friends and family, but a therapist offers you an impartial perspective and helps you to see things in a different way.

(Narrator) Therapy can also be beneficial for physical health. Studies have shown that therapy can reduce arterial pressure and the risk of cardiac diseases and can improve the quality of sleep and digestion.

(Narrator) Now Dave, Maria, and Matthew will share some of their experiences and opinions.

(Dave) Hello, my name is Dave, I'm 54 years old and I'm a therapist. I think that a common misunderstanding is that therapy is only for emotional cases, but in reality, it has many different uses. Some people leave my office with a new appreciation for their jobs, while others discover that they need a new job, or a change in environment. There are also different therapists with different specialties such as couples, families, eating disorders, and professional development.

(María) Hi, my name is María and I'm 25 years old. A few years ago, I was going through difficulties at my job and in my personal life. I decided to seek professional help, and what a difference it made! It was during the quarantine of 2020, so I had to use an application that allowed me to meet with my therapist through video call. We had one session per week, and I always felt noticeably better every time after the call was finished. I'm very grateful for the experience. Today I have found a balance in my life that I attribute to that experience, and coincidentally I now work at a therapist's office, and they treat me very well!

(Matthew)   Greetings, my name is Matt and I'm 26 years old. A few years ago, I got out of toxic relationship that left me in a state of mild depression, and I also had problems controlling my mood: I got angry easily. After the process of therapy, I discovered many things about myself that I decided to improve on, and my mood has been much more positive and productive since then. I discovered that I'm happy working with wood and creating wooden furniture, so I found a job in that, which I like, and I don't regret it. I just finished creating a gift that I plan to send to my therapist as a thank you; we developed a good relationship, he and I. I have recommended to all my friends to try it out, even if they don't think they need it; there's always some benefit in talking to someone that wants to hear and help you and has the professional knowledge to do so.

53. Why was therapy a taboo topic in the past?

(A)   Therapy is only for people with serious trauma.

(B)   Therapy does not work for many people.

(C)   Therapists are too extreme with their philosophies and practices.

(D)   People felt ashamed of seeking professional help for their emotional and relationship problems.

Although serious trauma is one of the problems that therapy can help solve, it is not ONLY reserved for people with serious trauma, so eliminate (A). Nothing in the recording supports (B) or (C), so eliminate them. The audio recording mentions that *"In the past, therapy was a taboo topic in many cultures. People felt ashamed to seek professional help for their emotional problems, or problems in their relationships,"* which supports (D). Choice (D) is correct.

54. How has therapy become more accessible and less taboo for the world in general?

(A)   Advances in science and research into mental health have made it so that therapy is more widely accepted.

(B)   Celebrities and public personalities who share their experiences have made the process clearer.

(C)   The availability of therapy via video calls allows for remote therapy sessions.

(D)   All of the above answers are correct.

The recording mentions *"But as science has advanced, and more investigations into mental health have been conducted, therapy has gained more acceptance and has become more common. Therapy has become more accessible to the general public, and the process has become more clear thanks, in part, to celebrities and public personalities speaking openly about their experiences."* This supports (A) and (B). Maria talks about having therapy sessions through video call, which made it more accessible to her. This supports (C). Since (A), (B), and (C) are all supported by the recording, (D) is the correct answer.

55. According to Dave, what is a common misunderstanding about therapy?

(A)   Therapists don't understand your problems.

(B)   Therapy is only for emotional cases.

(C)   Therapy is difficult for patients.

(D)   Patients are wasting their time.

Dave says, *"I think that a common misunderstanding is that therapy is only for emotional cases, but in reality it has many different uses,"* so (B) is correct.

56. What is Maria's tone when speaking of her experience?

(A) Nostalgia

(B) Frustration

(C) Regret

(D) Gratitude

Maria says, *"I'm very grateful for the experience,"* which supports (D). Choice (D) is correct.

57. What does Matt recommend to all his friends?

(A) That they choose the same therapy office as him

(B) That they specifically pick Dave as their therapist

(C) That they try therapy, even if they don't think they need it

(D) That they try to solve their own problems without professional help

Matt says, *"I have recommended to all my friends to try it out, even if they don't think they need it; there's always some benefit in talking to someone that wants to hear and help you and has the professional knowledge to do so."* This supports (C). Nothing in the recording supports (A), (B), or (D). Choice (C) is the correct answer.

Selection 5: Translated Text and Questions, with Explanations

Introduction

The following audio recording is about Three Kings Day, and the different customs related to this day that some Spanish speaking countries call "second Christmas."

(Narrator) Three Kings Day is an important holiday in many Spanish-speaking countries. It is celebrated on January 6th, and it commemorates the arrival of the Three Wise Kings to Bethlehem to adore and bring gifts to baby Jesus. Some call this day "second Christmas," since many Spanish-speaking countries celebrate both Christmas on the 25th of December and Three Kings Day on the 6th of January.

(Narrator) In many families, kids anxiously await Three Kings Day, since it is customary that the Wise Kings bring gifts to kids that are nice. Kids usually leave shoes, with a card on which they write down the gifts they want, near a window or under the bed the day before, to find that the Wise Kings have left gifts inside and around their shoes. It is said that this way, the Kings can identify how many kids there are and what ages they are, so they know what gifts they should leave. In countries such as Puerto Rico, it is customary to "extend Christmas" until January 6th. This way, families can leave their Christmas trees up in the house, and by January 6th, the Wise Kings can leave their gifts under the Christmas tree. In this way it is mixed a little with the traditions of Christmas. Another tradition is to fill a shoebox with grass and to leave it under the bed or close to the window. This way the Three Kings' camels can eat, and in the morning the shoebox is empty. This is similar to the tradition of leaving cookies and milk for Santa the day before Christmas.

(Narrator) Additionally, Three Kings Day is also an opportunity to enjoy candy and special foods. A typical dessert is called "Roscón de Reyes" (***"Kings Cake" would be a rough translation, since "rosca" technically means a circular shape with hole in the middle like a screw nut***), and it's a sweet cake made with flour, sugar, and lemon and anise essences. It is also customary to eat traditional foods of the season, which vary from country to country.

(Narrator)   In some parts of the world, Three Kings Day is celebrated with parades and processions. Kids dress up as the Kings and together they walk through the streets, singing and spreading candy. In some malls and public plazas, you can find the Three Kings during that day and take pictures with them. This is also similar to Christmas, when you can find Santa and take pictures with him during Christmas days. All these similarities are why many people call this holiday "second Christmas," and Hispanic/Latine kids receive gifts twice in a 2-week period, if they are nice.

(Narrator)   Three Kings Day is a holiday that is loved in many parts of the world and is an opportunity to celebrate friendship, family, and kindness. Happy Three Kings Day!

58. Which best summarizes this recording?

   (A) It provides details and traditions related to the Three Kings Day with the intention to educate.

   (B) It tries to show that Three Kings Day is a copy of Christmas.

   (C) It indicates that kids who are naughty don't receive gifts.

   (D) It speaks about Christmas in Spanish-speaking countries.

Choice (A) is supported by the recording, so keep it. The recording mentions that there are similarities between Christmas and Three Kings Day; however, it does not imply that it is a *copy;* eliminate (B). The recording does mention that kids who are nice receive gifts, but does not mention naughty kids, and this is not the general topic of the recording, so eliminate (C). The recording does speak about Christmas, but this does not summarize the entire recording, so eliminate (D). Choice (A) is the correct answer.

59. According to the recording, what is Three Kings Day?

   (A) A day which commemorates the arrival of the Three Wise Kings to Bethlehem to adore and bring gifts to baby Jesus

   (B) A day to eat and celebrate

   (C) A day to celebrate the kings of the past in Spain

   (D) A day to prolong Christmas festivities into the New Year

The recording starts by saying *"Three Kings Day is an important holiday in many Spanish speaking countries. It is celebrated on January 6th, and it commemorates the arrival of the Three Wise Kings to Bethlehem to adore and bring gifts to baby Jesus."* This supports (A), so keep it. The recording does mention that people eat typical foods and celebrate, but this is not the main reason Three Kings Day exists, so eliminate (B). The recording does not mention Spain specifically, nor the kings of its past, and since Three Kings Day refers to only the Kings that visited Bethlehem, eliminate (C). Eliminate (D) as well because, though the recording does say that *"in some countries it is customary to 'extend Christmas' until January 6th,"* that's only a regional variation and isn't a defining feature of Three Kings Day. Choice (A) is the correct answer.

60. Where is Three Kings Day commonly celebrated?

   (A) In Europe

   (B) In the United States

   (C) In churches

   (D) In Spanish-speaking countries

The recording does not directly mention Europe, the United States, or churches, and even though it might be celebrated by some people in those countries or churches, the passage does not support this, so eliminate (A), (B), and (C). The recording does say that *"Three Kings Day is an important holiday in many Spanish-speaking countries,"* which directly supports (D). Choice (D) is correct.

61. Traditionally, how do children prepare for the arrival of the Three Kings?
    (A) They open all the windows of the house so that the Three Kings can get in.
    (B) They leave empty shoes near the window or under the bed.
    (C) They leave milk and cookies in the living room of the house.
    (D) They decorate the yard with lights of many different colors.

They might open windows, but the recording more specifically says they leave shoes by the window so the Three Kings can leave gifts for them, not so that they can get in, so eliminate (A). The recording does mention that children leave shoes by the window or under the bed: this supports (B), so keep it. Choice (C) is what children do to prepare for Santa Claus, not the Three Kings, so eliminate it. Choice (D) is not mentioned in the recording, so eliminate it. Choice (B) is the correct answer.

62. What day is Three Kings Day celebrated on?
    (A) The 26th of December
    (B) The first Saturday in January
    (C) The 6th of January
    (D) The 2nd of January

The recording mentions neither the 26th of December nor the 2nd of January, so eliminate (A) and (D). Nowhere in the recording does it mention the first Saturday in January, so eliminate (B) as well. Choice (C) is supported by the recording and is the correct answer.

63. Where do the Three Kings leave their gifts?
    (A) In the entrance of the house
    (B) In the parents' room
    (C) Inside and around the shoes
    (D) In the chimney

The recording says that *"Kids usually leave shoes, with a card on which they write down the gifts they want, near a window or under the bed the day before, to find that the Wise Kings have left gifts inside and around their shoes."* Choice (C) is correct here.

64. What description does the audio provide for the *"Roscón de reyes"*?
    (A) A screw nut that the kings leave instead of presents for the children who have been naughty
    (B) A sweet cake made with flour, sugar, and lemon and anise essences
    (C) The name of one of the camels
    (D) A special feast for the Kings

The recording doesn't mention what happens when kids are naughty, so eliminate (A). The recording does say that *"A typical dessert is called 'Roscón de Reyes' and it's a sweet cake made with flour, sugar, and lemon and anise essences."* This supports (B), so keep it. The recording does not mention the names of the camels, so eliminate (C). Choice (D) is a description of the holiday in general, not the *"Roscón de Reyes,"* so eliminate it. Choice (B) is the correct answer.

65. Why is Three Kings Day called "second Christmas"?

   (A)   Because Santa returns on the 6th of January with more Christmas presents

   (B)   Because it is exactly like Christmas

   (C)   Because there is a lot of snow and Christmas foods

   (D)   Because of the similarities to some of the Christmas traditions, and because children receive presents a second time within two weeks

It is the Three Kings who come on the 6th of January, not Santa, so eliminate (A). The recording does mention a few similarities to Christmas, but it is not *exactly* like Christmas—(B) is too extreme, eliminate it. The recording does not mention *snow,* and even though there are special foods eaten in that season, this is not why it is called "second Christmas," so eliminate (C). Choice (D) is correct by process of elimination, and it is also supported by the recording.

SECTION II
Question 1: Email Reply (Page 299)

Translation of the Question

Introduction: This message is about plans for vacations with a group of friends. You have received this email because of a recent conversation with a group of your friends about traveling to a new place for vacations.

Dear Alexis:

I'm writing this message because of the conversation that we had the other day about traveling together to a new place on vacation. There were many ideas, but we never managed to reach a decision. I think it is an excellent idea and that we should make the plan more concrete with more details.

I've sent this email to all the friends in the group with the intention of collecting information to form an ideal vacation plan for all of us.

Please send a response to this email as soon as possible in which you include the answers to the following questions:

- What place did you travel to on your last vacations and what activities did you participate in there?

- What was the most memorable thing about the place you traveled to?

- Which new place would you like to travel to on these upcoming vacations?

- Why are you interested in traveling to that place and what would you like to do there?

I expect an answer by this weekend.

With all of your responses, we'll be able to decide the best place to travel to on these vacations and we'll have ideas of what to do there.

Our next vacations will be a very fun adventure and I anxiously await them!

With much gratitude,
Pedro P.

Sample Student Response

Hola Pedro,

Yo también pienso que es una excelente idea y estoy de acuerdo que debemos formar un plan.

Aquí te dejo las respuestas a tus preguntas:

Mis últimas vacaciones fueron a California con un grupo de amigos. Decidimos rentar un vehículo y guiar a todos los diferentes destinos que nos interesaban. Primero fuimos a San Diego y vimos las focas en la playa "La Jolla". Luego fuimos a Los Ángeles y vimos las colinas "Twin Peaks", el signo de "Hollywood", visitamos las diferentes estrellas de varios actores en la calle de Downtown, y cenamos en un restaurante italiano muy delicioso. Luego visitamos "Santa Monica Pier" y fuimos a la playa. Luego guiamos hasta el "Sequoia Forest" donde vimos los árboles mas grandes del mundo incluyendo "General Sherman", el árbol más grande del mundo. El próximo destino que visitamos fue Sacramento donde visitamos la vida nocturna. Finalmente visitamos San Francisco donde fuimos al "Pier 31", Japan Town, comimos burritos, etc.

Tuve varios detalles muy memorables en mi viaje. El primer detalle memorable fue los hermoso que es San Diego. Luego la lasaña muy deliciosa que probé en el restaurante italiano en Los Ángeles fue muy memorable. Otra experiencia memorable fue lo pequeño que te sientes al pararte al lado del árbol "General Sherman" en el "Sequoia Forest". Y por último, nos rompieron la ventana del vehículo que rentamos y nos robaron unas cosas en San Francisco. Esas fueron mis experiencias más memorables en mis últimas vacaciones a California.

El próximo lugar que me interesaría visitar es Italia. Si visitamos Italia, me gustaría visitar el gran Coliseo en Roma. También quiero estar en un pequeño bote en Venecia, caminar en Sicilia, y visitar el museo "Louvre". Siempre he querido visitar Europa, específicamente Italia, así que, por todas esas razones, esa es mi selección de lugar de vacaciones.

Espero que esto te ayude a planear nuestras vacaciones en grupo. Será interesante ver todas las posibles opciones para visitar.

¡Que tengas buen día!

Alexis.

Translation of the Sample Student Response

Hi Pedro,

I also think it's a great idea and agree that we should make a plan.

Here are my responses to your questions:

My last vacation was to California with a group of friends. We decided to rent a car and drive to all the different destinations we were interested in. First, we went to San Diego where we visited "La Jolla" beach and saw the seals. Then we went to Los Angeles and saw the "Twin Peaks" hills, the Hollywood sign, we visited the different stars of various actors in the street Downtown, and we had dinner at a very delicious Italian restaurant. Then we visited the Santa Monica Pier and went to the beach. Next, we drove to Sequoia Forest where we saw the biggest trees in the world including "General Sherman", the biggest tree in the world. The next destination we visited was Sacramento where we visited the nightlife. Finally, we visited San Francisco where we went to Pier 31, Japan Town, ate burritos, etc.

I had various memorable details in my trip. The first memorable detail was how beautiful San Diego is. Then the very delicious lasagna that I tried in the Italian restaurant in Los Angeles was very memorable. Another memorable experience was how tiny you feel when standing next to the tree "General Sherman" at the Sequoia Forest. And finally, they broke a window on our rental car and stole some things in San Francisco. Those were my most memorable experiences in my last vacations to California.

The next place I would like to visit is Italy. If we visit Italy, I would like to visit the great Colosseum in Rome. I would also like to be on a small boat in Venice, walk around in Sicily, and visit the Louvre Museum. I've always wanted to visit Europe, Specifically Italy, so for all those reasons, that is my selection for our vacations.

I hope this helps you plan our group vacations. It Will be interesting to see all the possible options to visit.

Have a great day!

Alexis.

Evaluation

This email response included a greeting, closing, and a reply to each of the questions asked in the original email. The student did a good job fulfilling all of the requirements with a well-organized response and would earn a high score as a result. Keep in mind, you can also improve your chances at a high score by including additional questions in your response. This response would probably earn a 5.

Question 2: Argumentative Essay (Page 300)

Essay topic:

How does global warming affect our lives?

Translation for Source 1

Introduction

This article appeared on the website theconversation.com in January 2023.

Cultural Literacy in the Digital Age

It is increasingly common to use the internet for a wide variety of activities. Before, the most common thing was to pay for a coffee with coins. Today, our mobile phone has NFC (Near Field Communication) and a payment application that facilitates this action. Even the mobile phone is becoming obsolete: now a smartwatch is used. Digital culture is prevailing, changing personal and collective life.

Literacy is the process of learning to read and write. Culture is the "set of ways of life and customs, knowledge and degree of artistic, scientific, industrial development, in a time, social group."

Cultural literacy refers to the acquisition of the necessary competencies to understand a certain culture to interpret the cultural codes shared in society.

Umberto Eco, referring to culture in "From Stupidity to Madness," stated that "it is not just an accumulation of data, it is also the result of its filtering." That is, "culture is also the ability to let go of what is not useful or necessary."

Cultural literacy aims to promote access to culture under conditions of equality. It is a proposal that seeks to reinforce and strengthen a more responsible citizenship. Behind it is the idea of a committed, cultured, and critical society that values its freedom.

Translation for Source 2

Introduction

The following data appeared on the website ine.es.

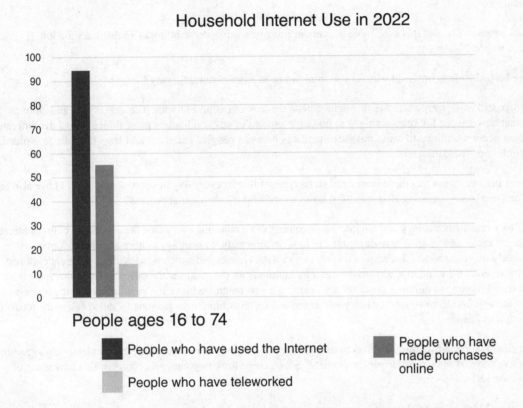

Household Internet Use in 2022

People ages 16 to 74

■ People who have used the Internet

■ People who have made purchases online

■ People who have teleworked

Translation for Source 3 (Audio Track 19)

Introduction

The following recording is of a podcast called "Marco Talks" where the host, Marco Moreno has a conversation with his guest Alexandra Melendez about cultural literacy.

MM: Last time we talked here in this podcast we briefly talked about cultural literacy, and I'm interested in continuing that conversation. For the benefit of those people who didn't listen to our last podcast, could you explain cultural literacy?

AM: Of course, Marco. Cultural literacy refers to the ability to understand and navigate different cultures, which is an essential ability in the interconnected world of today.

MM: And why is cultural literacy so important?

AM: The ability to understand and respect different cultures can help individuals to communicate more effectively, create relationships, and avoid misunderstandings. For example, understanding cultural differences can help people to work effectively in multicultural teams or help travelers to navigate different customs and expectations. For example, in certain countries it is disrespectful to point with your finger, so they use open hand expressions to point at people, objects, or directions. You don't want to disrespect a person trying to help you. Another example was some trains in Japan, where it is expected to maintain silence or escalators where people who go up standing stand on the right side of the escalator, and those who go up walking walk up the left side of the escalator. In other places, you greet people with a kiss on the cheek. It would be good to know those details before visiting.

MM: I understand. I can imagine, for example, a situation like the International Space Station. There are astronauts of many different cultures working in that station and they need to be able to communicate effectively to work as a team, so understanding the cultural differences must be very important for communication and mutual understanding.

AM: Yes, in a situation like that it is even more important. Imagine a misunderstanding in a sensitive situation. It wouldn't be good Marco.

MM: In space? No, definitely not. And why do you think we need more cultural literacy?

AM: Well, there still exist many examples that demonstrate the lack of cultural literacy. The stereotypes and cultural biases that have existed for years continue to make the process of cultural literacy more difficult. And the differences in communication continue to cause misunderstandings between people. These are problems that can be avoided with a little more education.

MM: It's true. I personally see that these biases and stereotypes still exist every day in social media sites. I have also felt the effects personally for being Hispanic. And how can we help accelerate that process?

AM: Thanks to access to technology and the internet becoming more common every day, the process of cultural literacy has become easier and faster. These days you can look up information about any culture and find information immediately on your phone. This helps a lot. We can also read books and watch movies about different cultures; this helps us enter the mind of a person of a different culture from ours and see the different situations from their perspective. Traveling to different countries and learning a new language make the most impact on the process of cultural literacy. You learn so much when you can see and feel the differences personally and speak to the locals in their native language.

MM: Yes, I can also support that traveling to countries drastically different from your own can completely change your perspective and make you a better person. Sometimes you come back to your own country with a new sense of appreciation and perspective.

AM: Yes, I agree, Marco. We should continue growing and developing ourselves personally in cultural literacy, learning more and educating ourselves in this area.

MM: And thanks to mediums like this one, we can deliver this message to many people. Thank you, Alexandra, for participating in this podcast; it is always a pleasure talking to you. And to our audience, if you have ideas or suggestions that could help us all to improve in this area, I invite you to share your experiences in the comment section, and that way, we can all learn a little more.

MZ: If only it were so simple. The risks to human health, to society in general, and to the environment increase as much with the rate as with the magnitude of climate changes. The fault for global warming undoubtedly belongs with human beings. The documents put out by the EPA suggest that climate extremes and illnesses transmitted by fleas and other organisms can kill more people as temperatures rise. Likewise, allergies may worsen because the climatic changes will produce more pollen. Smog, a principal cause of respiratory and pulmonary ailments, also counts among the threats to the world's population. At the same time, however, global warming may mean fewer sicknesses and deaths due to the cold.

LH: What has been the biggest obstacle to adopting legislation to prevent the dangers of global warming?

MZ: While scientists point to the connection between health and climate change, the government, for its part, has not done so—has not even recognized it. This recognition, many believe, would obligate the government to regulate greenhouse gases. This certainly would open a Pandora's box in the search for the governmental effort and support necessary to lend weight and importance to the necessity of embarking on the task of understanding and preventing the devastating consequences of global warming.

Sample Student Response

La alfabetización cultural ha sido tema de discusión durante décadas, y con el surgimiento de la era digital, el debate sobre su importancia se ha vuelto aún más relevante. La alfabetización cultural es la capacidad de entender y participar en referencias culturales, incluyendo literatura, historia y arte. En la era digital de hoy, donde la tecnología y los medios de comunicación se han vuelto ubicuos, la necesidad de alfabetización cultural se ha vuelto más importante que nunca.

Un argumento a favor de la alfabetización cultural en la era digital es que fomenta el pensamiento crítico y la comprensión. Cuando las personas poseen un amplio conocimiento de las referencias culturales, son capaces de hacer conexiones y entender el mundo que les rodea. Por ejemplo, alguien que es alfabetizado culturalmente podría identificar los temas de una novela en particular, comprender el contexto histórico en el que fue escrita y establecer conexiones con problemas contemporáneos. Este tipo de pensamiento puede ayudar a las personas a convertirse en ciudadanos más informados y comprometidos, capaces de tomar mejores decisiones y contribuir a sus comunidades.

Además, la alfabetización cultural puede ser una herramienta para superar las divisiones culturales. En un mundo cada vez más globalizado e interconectado, entender y respetar diferentes culturas se ha vuelto esencial. A través de la alfabetización cultural, las personas pueden aprender sobre la historia, valores y tradiciones de diferentes culturas y obtener una mayor apreciación por la diversidad. Esto puede ayudar a romper estereotipos y promover la comprensión, lo que es esencial para construir un mundo más armonioso y equitativo.

Sin embargo, algunos argumentan que la alfabetización cultural está perdiendo importancia en la era digital, ya que la tecnología ha facilitado el acceso a la información y la comunicación con personas de diferentes culturas. Con unos pocos clics de un botón, las personas pueden acceder a una gran cantidad de información sobre cualquier tema que les interese. Además, las plataformas de redes sociales como Twitter y Facebook ofrecen oportunidades para que personas de diferentes culturas se conecten y compartan sus experiencias.

Si bien es cierto que la tecnología ha facilitado el acceso a la información, es importante tener en cuenta que no toda la información se crea igual. Internet está lleno de información errónea y fuentes sesgadas, y puede ser difícil para las personas navegar en este paisaje sin una base sólida de conocimiento cultural. Además, las plataformas de redes sociales pueden convertirse en cámaras de eco, reforzando las creencias y prejuicios existentes en lugar de promover la comprensión y el diálogo.

En conclusión, la alfabetización cultural es una habilidad esencial en la era digital que fomenta el pensamiento crítico, la comprensión, y el respeto por la diversidad. Mientras que el crecimiento de la tecnología y los medios ha facilitado el acceso a la información, una fundación sólida de conocimiento cultural es crucial para navegar el mundo digital. Es nuestra responsabilidad como individuos y como sociedad priorizar la alfabetización cultural en nuestros sistemas educativos y en nuestra vida personal. De esta manera podemos construir un mundo más armonioso y equitativo donde las personas pueden conectarse entre sí, apreciar diferentes perspectivas, y tomar decisiones informadas.

Translation of the Sample Student Response

Cultural literacy has been a topic of discussion for decades, and with the rise of the digital age, the debate surrounding its importance has become even more relevant. Cultural literacy is the ability to understand and engage with cultural references, including literature, history, and art. In today's digital age, where technology and media have become ubiquitous, the need for cultural literacy has become more important than ever before.

One argument in favor of cultural literacy in the digital age is that it fosters critical thinking and understanding. When individuals possess a broad knowledge of cultural references, they are better able to make connections and understand the world around them. For example, someone who is culturally literate might be able to identify the themes of a particular novel, understand the historical context in which it was written, and make connections to contemporary issues. This kind of thinking can help individuals to become more informed and engaged citizens, able to make better decisions and contribute to their communities.

Additionally, cultural literacy can be a tool for bridging cultural divides. In a world that is increasingly globalized and interconnected, understanding and respecting different cultures has become essential. Through cultural literacy, individuals can learn about the history, values, and traditions of different cultures and gain a greater appreciation for diversity. This can help to break down stereotypes and promote understanding, which is essential for building a more harmonious and equitable world.

However, some argue that cultural literacy is becoming less important in the digital age, as technology has made it easier to access information and communicate with people from different cultures. With a few clicks of a button, individuals can access a wealth of information about any topic they are interested in. Furthermore, social media platforms like Twitter and Facebook provide opportunities for people from different cultures to connect and share their experiences.

While it is true that technology has made it easier to access information, it is important to note that not all information is created equal. The internet is full of misinformation and biased sources, and it can be difficult for individuals to navigate this landscape without a solid foundation of cultural knowledge. Furthermore, social media platforms can be echo chambers, reinforcing existing beliefs and biases rather than promoting understanding and dialogue.

In conclusion, cultural literacy is an essential skill in the digital age that promotes critical thinking, understanding, and respect for diversity. While the rise of technology and media has made it easier to access information, a solid foundation of cultural knowledge is crucial to navigate the digital landscape effectively. It is our responsibility as individuals and as a society to prioritize cultural literacy in our education systems and personal lives. By doing so, we can build a more harmonious and equitable world where individuals can connect with each other, appreciate different perspectives, and make informed decisions.

Evaluation

This response does define cultural literacy and present multiple viewpoints on its importance. However, the student does not identify the sources appropriately in their essay. They successfully demonstrate an understanding of the topic but because they do not explicitly refer to each of the sources, it is unclear how they are woven into their argument. Remember, it is your responsibility to try and find connections between the sources and include all of them in your analysis. To earn a higher score, the student should have used data and information that came directly from the sources. This essay would probably score in the 3 range.

Question 3: Conversation (Page 36)

Script with Sample Student Response and Translation

Carla: Bueno, si vamos a mudarnos juntos, debemos hablar sobre nuestras preferencias de vivienda. tenemos tiempo para elegir una casa o apartamento perfecto para rentar, pero debemos considerar unas preguntas primero. Primero la localización. Es más caro vivir en la ciudad, pero todo está más cerca. El costo de vivir cerca de la ciudad es menos y aún podemos guiar un poco y disfrutar los beneficios de la ciudad. Vivir alejado de la ciudad sería la opción más barata. ¿Prefieres vivir en la ciudad, cerca de la ciudad, o más alejado de la ciudad? ¿Y por qué?

Well, if we are moving in together, we need to talk about our living preferences. We have time to pick the perfect house or apartment to rent, but we should consider some questions first. First is location. It is more expensive to live in the city, but everything is closer. The cost of living close to the city is a bit less and we can still drive a little bit and enjoy the benefits of the city. Living further away from the city would be the cheapest option. Do you prefer living in the city, close to the city, or further away from the city? And why?

Tú: Bueno, yo prefiero vivir cerca de la ciudad porque me gusta la idea de tener la opción de guiar a la ciudad y llegar dentro de 30 minutos. Así nos podemos ahorrar un poco de dinero extra, sin sacrificar el acceso a la ciudad y las conveniencias del área urbana. Otra razón es que vivir dentro de la ciudad sería muy abrumante para mí, es muy ocupado con tráfico y sonidos. Prefiero un área más tranquila.

Well, I prefer living close to the city because I like the idea of having the option to drive to the city and get there within 30 minutes. That way we can save a little extra money without sacrificing access to the city and the conveniences of the urban area. Another reason is that living inside the city would be too overwhelming for me, it's too busy with traffic and sounds. I prefer more tranquil area.

Carla: ¡Bien, estoy de acuerdo! Ahora debemos decidir si queremos vivir en una casa o en un complejo de apartamentos. Esto también puede afectar el precio de la renta. Dependiendo la casa, podría ser más barato que un complejo de apartamentos. Aunque en un complejo de apartamentos podrías tener acceso a una piscina, un gimnasio, y estacionamiento seguro. ¿Qué prefieres rentar una casa o un apartamento y por qué?

Great, I agree! Now we should decide if we want to live in a house or an apartment complex. This can also affect the price of rent. Depending on the house, it could be cheaper than an apartment complex. Although in an apartment complex we could have access to a pool, a gym, and secure parking. What would you prefer to rent, a house or an apartment, and why?

Tú: No me molestaría vivir en una casa. Quizás de esa manera podemos ahorrar un poco dinero extra porque tengo amigos que tienen que pagar $100 dólares al mes por estacionamiento, y la renta es un poco más cara para vivir en algunos apartamentos. También el estacionamiento en apartamentos a veces queda muy lejos de tu puerta, hay que caminar mas y muchas veces subir un elevador compartido. Si vienes solo con muchas compras, será difícil sin tomar múltiples viajes. También tendremos más privacidad en una casa, y quizás un patio solo para nosotros.

I wouldn't mind living in a house. Maybe that way we can save a little extra money because I have friends that have to pay $100 dollars a month for parking, and rent is a little more expensive in some apartments. Also, the parking at apartments sometimes is too far from your door; you have to walk more and many times you have to go up a shared elevator. If you're coming in with many groceries it will be difficult to do without taking multiple trips. We would also more privacy in a house, and maybe a backyard just for us.

Carla: Algunos lugares no aceptan mascotas, y los lugares que aceptan mascotas cobran renta adicional por cada mascota. ¿Tienes mascota o quieres una mascota en el futuro? ¿Te molestaría si yo adopto una mascota?

Some places do not accept pets, and the places that do charge additional rent for each pet. Do you have a pet or want one in the near future? Would you mind if I adopt a pet?

Tú: Me gustaría un lugar que acepta mascotas porque quiero adoptar un gato en el futuro. No me molestaría si adoptas una mascota, nuestras mascotas pueden ser amigos y así no están solos cuando estemos fuera de la casa.

I would like a place that accepts pets because I want to adopt a cat in the future. I wouldn't be bothered if you adopt a pet; our pets could be friends, and that way, they are not alone when we are out of the house.

Carla: Algunos lugares no tienen su propio estacionamiento y requieren que te estaciones en la calle frente a, o cerca del hogar. Algunos complejos de apartamento tienen estacionamiento, pero cobran mensualmente por acceso. ¿Prefieres un lugar con estacionamiento seguro, o no te molesta estacionarte en la calle?

Some places do not have their own parking spots and require you to park on the street in front of or close to the home. Some apartment complexes have secure parking, but they charge monthly for the access. Would you prefer a place with a secure parking space, or do you not mind just parking on the street?

Tú: Me gustaría que la casa tenga entrada de coches que podemos compartir, o por lo menos un área no muy ocupada donde siempre tenemos acceso a estacionamiento en la calle frente a la casa.

I would like the house to have a driveway we can share, or at least an area that isn't too busy where we always have access to street parking in front of the house.

Carla: Es importante que ambos estemos disponibles para mudarnos el mismo mes. ¿Estarás disponible para mudarte en el mes de Julio?

It is important that we are both available to move in on the same month. Would you be available to move in together in July?

Tú: Desafortunadamente no será posible para mí en el mes de Julio ya que mi alquiler actual termina el primer día de Agosto.

Unfortunately, it will not be possible for me in the month of July since my current rental lease ends on the first day of August.

Carla: No hay problema, puedo quedarme con mi familia por un mes adicional mientras llega agosto. Gracias por esta conversación, me ayudará muchísimo a escoger un lugar ideal para nosotros. Voy a comenzar mi búsqueda y te mantendré informado/a. ¡Te veo luego, adiós!

No problem, I can stay with my family for an additional month while I wait for August. Thanks for this conversation, it will help me a lot in choosing an ideal place for us. I will begin my search and will keep you informed. See you soon, goodbye!

Tú: Suena bien, déjame saber que encuentras. Que tengas buen día y te veo luego. ¡Adiós!

Sounds good, let me know what you find. Have a good day and I'll see you soon. Goodbye!

Evaluation

The responses the student gave were clear, appropriate, and made for a meaningful conversation. They made sure to use varied vocabulary and grammar while answering Carla's questions with ease. This is an example of a strong response; they would likely earn a 5.

Question 4: Cultural Comparison (Page 37)

Translation of the Question

We know that family customs are different in each culture. Some families are stricter, others less so. In some families the sons and daughters become independent much sooner. While in other families the sons and daughters don't mind living with their parents for more time and prefer staying close to the family.

Compare your observations about the behavior in general of families in the place you live with your observations about the behavior of families in a Spanish speaking region of the world where you have observed, studied, or visited personally.

Sample Student Response

Yo vivo ahora en Michigan en los Estados Unidos pero nací y viví casi toda mi vida en Puerto Rico, así que he podido observar muchas diferencias entre Puerto Rico y Estados Unidos en cómo se comportan las familias. En Puerto Rico los hijos se quedan con las familias hasta mucho mas tarde que la costumbre en los Estados Unidos. Pienso que esto tiene que ver con el tamaño geográfico. Puerto Rico es una isla muy pequeña, así que cuando vas a la universidad, no hay necesidad de mudarte lejos de tus padres mientras terminas tus años en la universidad, y a la vez a los padres no les molesta que te quedes mientras estás estudiando. Los Estados Unidos es tan grande, que las universidades pueden quedar lejos de la casa de tus padres, hasta en diferentes estados, así que los hijos tienen que irse a vivir solos e independizarse mientras estudian, a una más temprana edad.

Otra diferencia es más cultural. Las familias se mantienen cerca y se reúnen a menudo. Muchas veces con música, salsa con alto volumen y comida. Y las familias hispanas tienden a ser poco mas "cálidas", pero eso puede ser solo perspectiva cultural. Muchos abrazos, muchos besos, y la gente habla con más alto volumen. Las casas también son mucho más pequeñas en Puerto Rico, y no hay tanta abundancia de recursos en la isla como lo hay en los Estados Unidos. Aquí las casas son más grandes, los recursos, y oportunidades de trabajo existen en abundancia, y fácil de accesar. Pienso que esto también afecta como las familias se comportan. Con menos recursos, las familias dependen mas los unos del otro, así que hay mas cercanía entre los familiares.

Pero en general, existe el mismo amor y lealtad familiar, solo que en formas diferentes debido a las diferencias culturales y de los idiomas. Parece que no importa donde estas en el mundo, la familia es una institución muy importante en la vida de los individuos.

Translation of the Sample Student Response

I currently live in Michigan in the United States but I was born and lived almost all of my life in Puerto Rico, so I have been able to observe many differences between Puerto Rico and the United States in how families behave. In Puerto Rico, children stay with their families much later than the custom in the United States. I think this has to do with the geographic size. Puerto Rico is a very small island, so when you go to college, there is no need to move far away from your parents while you finish your years in college, and at the same time parents don't mind if you stay while you're studying. The United States is so large that universities can be far from parents' homes, even in different states, so children have to go live alone and become independent while studying at an earlier age.

Another difference is more cultural. Families stay close and gather often. Many times with music, loud salsa, and food. And Hispanic families tend to be a little more "warm," but that may be just cultural perspective. Many hugs, many kisses, and people speak louder. Houses are also much smaller in Puerto Rico, and there is not as much abundance of resources on the island as there is in the United States. Here houses are bigger, resources, and job opportunities exist abundantly and are easy to access. I think this also affects how families behave. With fewer resources, families depend more on each other, so there is more closeness among relatives.

But in general, the same family love and loyalty exists, only in different forms due to cultural and language differences. It seems that no matter where you are in the world, family is a very important institution in people's lives.

Evaluation

This response has a clear introductory paragraph, effective use of transitional elements, and demonstrated an understanding of the topic. This student based their response off of their experience living in Puerto Rico and now in Michigan. Remember, your response can be based on your experience, if you studied a particular Spanish speaking region, you could use your knowledge to improve your score. This response fulfilled the requirements, was well-composed, and showed knowledge of the culture. It would likely have earned a high score.

HOW TO SCORE PRACTICE TEST 2

Section I: Multiple Choice

Note: this score conversion chart should only be used as an estimate.

Part A: _____ × 1.154 = _____
Number Correct
(out of 30)

Part B: _____ × 1.154 = _____
Number Correct
(out of 35)

Sum = _____
Weighted
Section I Score
(Do not round)

Section II: Free Response

Question 1: _____ × 3.750 = _____
(out of 5)   (Do not round)

Question 2: _____ × 3.750 = _____
(out of 5)   (Do not round)

Question 3: _____ × 3.750 = _____
(out of 5)   (Do not round)

Question 4: _____ × 3.750 = _____
(out of 5)   (Do not round)

_____
Weighted
Section II Score
(Do not round)

AP Score Conversion Chart Spanish Language & Culture	
Composite Score Range	AP Score
107–150	5
90–106	4
73–89	3
56–72	2
0–55	1

Composite Score

_____ + _____ = _____
Weighted   Weighted   Composite Score
Section I Score   Section II Score (Round to nearest
                                    whole number)

The Princeton Review®

Completely darken bubbles with a No. 2 pencil. If you make a mistake, be sure to erase mark completely. Erase all stray marks.

1. YOUR NAME:
(Print)
Last   First   M.I.

SIGNATURE: _____   DATE: ___/___/___

HOME ADDRESS: _____
(Print)   Number and Street

_____
City   State   Zip Code

PHONE NO. : _____
(Print)

IMPORTANT: Please fill in these boxes exactly as shown on the back cover of your test book.

2. TEST FORM

3. TEST CODE

4. REGISTRATION NUMBER

5. YOUR NAME

First 4 letters of last name | | | | FIRST INIT | MID INIT

6. DATE OF BIRTH

| Month | Day | | Year | |

JAN, FEB, MAR, APR, MAY, JUN, JUL, AUG, SEP, OCT, NOV, DEC

The **Princeton Review®**

© TPR Education IP Holdings, LLC
FORM NO. 00001-PR

Section 1

Start with number 1 for each new section.
If a section has fewer questions than answer spaces, leave the extra answer spaces blank.

1. A B C D
2. A B C D
3. A B C D
4. A B C D
5. A B C D
6. A B C D
7. A B C D
8. A B C D
9. A B C D
10. A B C D
11. A B C D
12. A B C D
13. A B C D
14. A B C D
15. A B C D
16. A B C D
17. A B C D
18. A B C D
19. A B C D
20. A B C D

21. A B C D
22. A B C D
23. A B C D
24. A B C D
25. A B C D
26. A B C D
27. A B C D
28. A B C D
29. A B C D
30. A B C D
31. A B C D
32. A B C D
33. A B C D
34. A B C D
35. A B C D
36. A B C D
37. A B C D
38. A B C D
39. A B C D
40. A B C D

41. A B C D
42. A B C D
43. A B C D
44. A B C D
45. A B C D
46. A B C D
47. A B C D
48. A B C D
49. A B C D
50. A B C D
51. A B C D
52. A B C D
53. A B C D
54. A B C D
55. A B C D
56. A B C D
57. A B C D
58. A B C D
59. A B C D
60. A B C D

61. A B C D
62. A B C D
63. A B C D
64. A B C D
65. A B C D

Completely darken bubbles with a No. 2 pencil. If you make a mistake, be sure to erase mark completely. Erase all stray marks.

1. YOUR NAME: _____
(Print)   Last   First   M.I.

SIGNATURE: _____   **DATE:** ___ / ___ / ___

HOME ADDRESS: _____
(Print)   Number and Street

_____
          City   State   Zip Code

PHONE NO. : _____
(Print)

IMPORTANT: Please fill in these boxes exactly as shown on the back cover of your test book.

2. TEST FORM

3. TEST CODE   ## 4. REGISTRATION NUMBER

	A										
0	A	0	0	0	0	0	0	0	0	0	0
1	B	1	1	1	1	1	1	1	1	1	1
2	C	2	2	2	2	2	2	2	2	2	2
3	D	3	3	3	3	3	3	3	3	3	3
4	E	4	4	4	4	4	4	4	4	4	4
5	F	5	5	5	5	5	5	5	5	5	5
6	G	6	6	6	6	6	6	6	6	6	6
7		7	7	7	7	7	7	7	7	7	7
8		8	8	8	8	8	8	8	8	8	8
9		9	9	9	9	9	9	9	9	9	9

6. DATE OF BIRTH

Month	Day		Year	
○ JAN				
○ FEB				
○ MAR	0	0	0	0
○ APR	1	1	1	1
○ MAY	2	2	2	2
○ JUN	3	3	3	3
○ JUL		4	4	4
○ AUG		5	5	5
○ SEP		6	6	6
○ OCT		7	7	7
○ NOV		8	8	8
○ DEC		9	9	9

The **Princeton Review®**

© TPR Education IP Holdings, LLC
FORM NO. 00001-PR

5. YOUR NAME

First 4 letters of last name				FIRST INIT	MID INIT
A	A	A	A	A	A
B	B	B	B	B	B
C	C	C	C	C	C
D	D	D	D	D	D
E	E	E	E	E	E
F	F	F	F	F	F
G	G	G	G	G	G
H	H	H	H	H	H
I	I	I	I	I	I
J	J	J	J	J	J
K	K	K	K	K	K
L	L	L	L	L	L
M	M	M	M	M	M
N	N	N	N	N	N
O	O	O	O	O	O
P	P	P	P	P	P
Q	Q	Q	Q	Q	Q
R	R	R	R	R	R
S	S	S	S	S	S
T	T	T	T	T	T
U	U	U	U	U	U
V	V	V	V	V	V
W	W	W	W	W	W
X	X	X	X	X	X
Y	Y	Y	Y	Y	Y
Z	Z	Z	Z	Z	Z

Section 1

Start with number 1 for each new section.
If a section has fewer questions than answer spaces, leave the extra answer spaces blank.

1. A B C D
2. A B C D
3. A B C D
4. A B C D
5. A B C D
6. A B C D
7. A B C D
8. A B C D
9. A B C D
10. A B C D
11. A B C D
12. A B C D
13. A B C D
14. A B C D
15. A B C D
16. A B C D
17. A B C D
18. A B C D
19. A B C D
20. A B C D

21. A B C D
22. A B C D
23. A B C D
24. A B C D
25. A B C D
26. A B C D
27. A B C D
28. A B C D
29. A B C D
30. A B C D
31. A B C D
32. A B C D
33. A B C D
34. A B C D
35. A B C D
36. A B C D
37. A B C D
38. A B C D
39. A B C D
40. A B C D

41. A B C D
42. A B C D
43. A B C D
44. A B C D
45. A B C D
46. A B C D
47. A B C D
48. A B C D
49. A B C D
50. A B C D
51. A B C D
52. A B C D
53. A B C D
54. A B C D
55. A B C D
56. A B C D
57. A B C D
58. A B C D
59. A B C D
60. A B C D

61. A B C D
62. A B C D
63. A B C D
64. A B C D
65. A B C D